ESSENTIAL READINGS IN ECONOMICS

ESSENTIAL READINGS IN ECONOMICS

Edited by

Saul Estrin
London Business School

and

Alan Marin
London School of Economics

Selection, editorial matter and Introduction © Saul Estrin and Alan Marin 1995

For individual chapters, please see the Acknowledgements.

All rights reserved. No reproduction, copy or transmission of this publication may be made without written permission.

No paragraph of this publication may be reproduced, copied or transmitted save with written permission or in accordance with the provisions of the Copyright, Designs and Patents Act 1988, or under the terms of any licence permitting limited copying issued by the Copyright Licensing Agency, 90 Tottenham Court Road, London W1P 9HE.

Any person who does any unauthorised act in relation to this publication may be liable to criminal prosecution and civil claims for damages.

First published 1995 by
MACMILLAN PRESS LTD
Houndmills, Basingstoke, Hampshire RG21 2XS
and London
Companies and representatives
throughout the world

ISBN 0-333-59451-7 hardcover
ISBN 0-333-59452-5 paperback

A catalogue record for this book is available
from the British Library.

10 9 8 7 6 5 4 3 2 1
04 03 02 01 00 99 98 97 96 95

Typeset in 10/12 pt by EXPO Holdings, Malaysia

Printed and bound in Great Britain by
Mackays of Chatham PLC, Chatham, Kent

Contents

Acknowledgements ix

Introduction 1
S. Estrin and A. Marin

PART I THEORY OF CONSUMER DEMAND

1 The Law of Consumer's Demand 19
   J. R. Hicks

PART II THEORY OF THE FIRM AND SUPPLY

2 The Nature of the Firm 37
   R. H. Coase

3 The Concept of Monopoly and the Measurement of
   Monopoly Power 55
   A. Lerner

4 Monopoly and Resource Allocation 77
   A. C. Harberger

5 Strategic Competition among the Few – Some Recent
   Developments in the Economics of Industry 91
   J. Vickers

PART III GENERAL EQUILIBRIUM AND WELFARE

6 The Anatomy of Market Failure 129
   F. Bator

7 Diagrammatic Exposition of a Theory of
   Public Expenditure   159
   P. A. Samuelson

PART IV ECONOMICS OF UNCERTAINTY AND INFORMATION

8 The Market for 'Lemons': Quality Uncertainty and
   the Market Mechanism   175
   G. Akerlof

PART V INFLATION AND UNEMPLOYMENT

9 How Important is it to Defeat Inflation? The Evidence   191
   R. Bootle

10 The Role of Monetary Policy   215
   M. Friedman

11 Inflation and Unemployment   232
   J. Tobin

PART VI THE NATURE OF UNEMPLOYMENT

12 Unemployment Policy   257
   R. E. Lucas, Jr.

13 On Theories of Unemployment   264
   R. M. Solow

14 Efficiency Wage Models of Unemployment   280
   J. Yellen

PART VII THE BUSINESS CYCLE

15 The State of Long-Term Expectation   293
   J. M. Keynes

16 Understanding Business Cycles   306
   R. E. Lucas, Jr.

17 Real Business Cycles: A New Keynesian Perspective   328
   N. G. Mankiw

PART VIII CONTROL OF MACROECONOMIC FLUCTUATIONS

18 A Monetary and Fiscal Framework for Economic Stability   345
    M. Friedman

19 Rational Expectations and the Theory of Economic Policy   366
    T. J. Sargent and N. Wallace

20 The Monetarist Controversy, or, Should we Forsake
    Stabilization Policies?   383
    F. Modigliani

Index   409

Acknowledgements

The editors and publishers wish to thank the following for permission to use copyright material:

American Economic Association and the authors, for A. C. Harberger, 'Monopoly and Resource Allocation', *American Economic Review* (1954), pp. 77–87; M. Friedman, The Role of Monetary Policy', *American Economic Review*, 58 (1) (March 1968), pp. 1–17, and M. Friedman, 'A Monetary and Fiscal Framework for Economic Stability', *American Economic Review*, 38 (3) (June 1948), pp. 245–64; J. Tobin, 'Inflation and Unemployment', *American Economic Review*, 62 (March 1972), pp. 1–18; R. E. Lucas, Jr., 'Unemployment Policy', *American Economic Review*, 68 (2) (May 1978), pp. 353–7; R. M. Solow, 'On Theories of Unemployment', *American Economic Review*, 70 (1) (March 1980), pp. 1–11; J. Yellen, 'Efficiency Wage Models of Unemployment', *American Economic Review*, Papers and Proceedings, 74 (2) (May 1984), pp. 200–5; F. Modigliani, 'The Monetarist Controversy...', *American Economic Review*, 67 (2) (March 1977), pp. 1–17; N. G. Mankiw, 'Real Business Cycles: A New Keynesian Perspective', *Journal of Economic Perspectives*, 3 (3) (Summer 1989), pp. 79–89.

Blackwell Publishers, for R. H. Coase, 'The Nature of the Firm', *Economica*, 1937, pp. 386–405.

Elsevier Science B. V., for T. J. Sargent and N. Wallace, 'Rational Expectations and the Theory of Economic Policy', *Journal Of Monetary Economics* (July 1976), pp. 199–214; and R. E. Lucas, Jr., 'Understanding Business Cycles' in K. Brunner and A. Meltzer (eds), *Stabilization of the Domestic International Economy*, Vol. 5, Carnegie–Rochester Series on Public Policy (1977), pp. 7–29.

Macmillan Ltd, Cambridge University Press and RES, for J. M. Keynes, *The General Theory of Employment, Interest and Money*, Chap. 12 (1936), pp. 147–64.

The MIT Press, for F. Bator, 'The Anatomy of Market Failure', *Quarterly Journal of Economics* (1958), pp. 351–79; and G. Akerlof, 'The Market for "Lemons": Quality Uncertainty and the Market Mechanism', *Quarterly Journal of Economics* (1970), pp. 488–500.

Oxford University Press, for J. R. Hicks, *Value and Capital*, Chap. 2, 2nd edn (1946; 1st edn 1939), pp. 26–41; and John Vickers, 'Strategic Competition Among the Few: Some Recent Developments in the Economics of Industry', *Oxford Review of Economic Policy*, 1, 3 (1985), pp. 39–62.

Review of Economic Studies Ltd, for A. Lerner, 'The Concept of Monopoly and the Measurement of Monopoly Power', *Review of Economic Studies* (1934) 2, pp. 157–75.

The Royal Bank of Scotland plc, for R. Bootle, 'How Important is it to Defeat Inflation? The Evidence', *The Three Banks' Review* (Dec. 1981), pp. 23–47.

Paul A. Samuelson, for 'Diagrammatic Exposition of a Theory of Public Expenditure', *Review of Economics and Statistics*, 21 (May 1955), pp. 350–6.

Every effort has been made to trace all the copyright-holders, but if any have been inadvertently overlooked the publishers will be pleased to make the necessary arrangement at the first opportunity.

Introduction

S. ESTRIN and A. MARIN

Introduction

The purpose of this book of readings is to make available in a single volume some of the seminal papers in the areas of microeconomics and macroeconomics which comprise the subject matter of intermediate courses in economic principles. In cases when the original material has been deemed too technically demanding, alternative papers by leading economists have been chosen on the basis of clarity of exposition as much as originality of contribution. A few minor changes of a purely cosmetic nature have been made, such as standardization of diagram numbering and correction of obvious misprints. These do not affect the original tone of the articles. We also include a few important papers which indicate how contemporary researchers have developed or applied the principles outlined in the other readings, as an appetizer to students who are thinking of pursuing their study of economics further and as examples of the direction in which the subject is being extended beyond areas covered in mainstream intermediate textbooks.

The book is not, however, intended as a substitute for textbooks in microeconomics or macroeconomics. It has been written on the premise that students' understanding of the subject will be enormously enhanced if they are given access to some of the seminal papers which lay out problems or methods for the first time. Intellectual advances in economics often come from debates that have been long forgotten, but which offer context, depth and clarity to contemporary study. The vigour and resonance of these arguments have been muffled in the homogenizing dullness of many textbooks. Students may also be surprised to discover that many of the best economists are also excellent writers, often better able to express their arguments than those who later sought to purvey their concepts to a wider audience.

We faced a number of constraints in attempting to develop this set of essential readings. The most obvious was one of choice. Economists have been publishing in scholarly journals and books for more than two hundred years, and the range of potential outlets for research has been continuously expanding. For example, the American Economic Association publishes a quarterly journal, the *Journal of Economic Literature*, devoted largely to listing new books, papers and abstracts. The listing of new *titles* in scholarly journals alone exceeds sixty pages each quarter. We have tried in this volume to select the papers which delineate or develop the concepts which students would learn in intermediate textbooks on the principles of economics.

A consequence of this selection strategy is that a number of the papers selected are relatively old. In microeconomics, much of the subject matter of intermediate textbooks was laid out by the end of the 1950s. There have been numerous extensions to the subject since then, but many of these are very technical in nature, and would be difficult for students at this level. The problem is less acute in macroeconomics because, although technical developments have been at least as sophisticated, they have frequently involved a deeper understanding of given subject matter – unemployment, inflation, cycles or growth – rather than opening up entirely new areas. Hence one can find entirely contemporary expositions of, for example, theories of unemployment, while little has been written about basic mainstream consumer theory since the 1950s.

The rising technical content of most current economics research puts the bulk of the most recent papers beyond the reach of typical undergraduates. There is, however, a trade-off between comprehensibility to students and giving a reasonable feel to students about the development of the subject. Our approach has been to lean in the direction of a lower technical level for material which would form the subject matter of textbooks in intermediate macro- and microeconomics, but to indicate more recent development in most subjects by also including some material of a more demanding nature.

Essential readings in microeconomics

The readings have been categorized into eight parts, the first four of which concern microeconomics while the second four deal with macroeconomics. However, the dividing line is not always clearcut. Material on general equilibrium deals with the operation of the economy as a whole, rather than elements within it. Conversely, much recent theorizing in contemporary macroeconomics stems from models of monopolistic competition, and current work on the inflation–unemployment trade-off starts with careful analysis of the labour market. Indeed it is because the operation of the labour market is included in the second half of the book that the first half does not cover factor markets explicitly.

The theory of demand

The development of the theory of consumer choice from its utilitarian roots in the 1870s was the basis of the evolution of neo-classical from classical economic theory. There were, however, fundamental problems with cardinal utility theory as the conceptual basis of consumer choice. Pareto introduced the ordinal utility approach, and much of demand theory as we know it was one of the areas of economics laid out in Sir John Hicks's seminal book, *Value and Capital*. We reproduce the second chapter of the book as our first reading, as much for its clarity of exposition as for the additional insights that it contained.

Theory of the firm and supply

Economists have devoted considerable effort to analyzing the determination of prices and the operation of the market system. They have until recently devoted far less attention to the behaviour of individual firms. The basic assumption has been that firms are defined by a technology (often of a form which generates U-shaped long- and short-run average cost curves) and an objective: to maximize profits. Models of this sort are unable to address questions such as why some firms are more successful than others, why some firms permit costs to rise above minimum attainable levels for their output, or even why firms exist at all. It is to this last fundamental question that the second reading, Coase's seminal 1937 *Economica* paper, is addressed. It has been the precursor of an enormous contemporary literature on the relationship between 'principals' who, for example, own firms, and their 'agents' (in this case managers who run them).

A second standard textbook argument, which is made particularly well in the original form, is by Abba Lerner, who pins down the concept of monopoly power and for the first time indicates ways to measure it. The paper introduces the price–cost margin which is now widely referred to as the 'Lerner index' of monopoly power. This is our second paper on the supply side.

Once economics had invented a way to measure monopoly power numerically, it was only a matter of time before someone attempted to calculate it. The first paper on the subject was by Harberger, who sought to measure the welfare losses associated with monopoly power in the USA in the 1950s. He found that: 'Elimination of resource misallocation in American manufacturing in the late twenties would bring with it an improvement in consumer welfare of just a little more than a tenth of 1 per cent. In present values, this welfare gain would amount to about $2.00

per capita'. There has been much controversy about this finding since, and Cowling and Waterson, in their 1976 *Economica* paper, found a loss closer to 6 per cent of gross domestic product (GDP) for the UK. But the Harberger paper represents a seminal application of microeconomics theory with enormous policy implications. The empirical work is within the grasp of current students, and indicates how abstract theoretical concepts can be given numerical meaning.

The final paper in this part is concerned with oligopoly theory. Students will be aware that this area is particularly complicated because firms' evaluation of their marginal revenues depends on knowing or guessing about the behaviour of the other suppliers in the industry. Hence profit-maximizing behaviour (when marginal revenue equals marginal cost) cannot be defined until we have some idea of how firms evaluate the possible choices of their rivals. Developments in the area of industrial economics, and especially oligopoly theory, have been among the most sophisticated and technically demanding in microeconomics. As a result, many of the findings are only hinted at in textbooks. However, Vickers has written a lucid and comprehensive review which introduces the main issues and guides the reader carefully through recent developments. Key issues treated include use of the prisoner's dilemma game to illustrate the instability of a cartel, and of sequential game theory to analyze the role of credibility and punishment when considering the entry of new firms into an oligopolistic market.

General equilibrium and welfare

Welfare economics starts from the two fundamental welfare theorems, which establish

(a) the Pareto efficiency of the competitive general equilibrium of a free market system, and
(b) that the market can attain any Pareto efficient allocation with appropriate lump sum redistribution.

The implications of Pareto efficiency for resource allocation are summarized exhaustively by Francis Bator in the first reading of this part. The conditions for competitive markets to attain a Pareto efficient allocation – Welfare Theorem 1 – are rather restrictive; and the existence of competitive markets for all producers may be impossible. Failures include nonconvexities in technologies – for example, widespread economies of scale – or large (perverse) income effects, market imperfections, spill-over effects (externalities) and public goods. These failures provide the justification for government intervention in the economy, and are summarized in the Bator reading. It is worth adding that the role of the government in solving the allocative failures of the market is viewed much less favourably now than when Bator was writing in the 1950s. The work of Buchanan, among others, has led to the realization that the government is an economic agent like everyone else, with its own objectives (for example, to maximize votes). This means that its intervention in the economy to correct market failures will not necessarily be as principled and objective as Bator's paper suggests will be needed to achieve Pareto efficiency.

Bator introduces two market failures that have particular contemporary relevance: externalities and public goods. Externalities occur with goods which produce spill-over effects on economic agents other than their suppliers or purchasers. Externalities arise because certain goods are not priced – for example, the air we breathe or the river through our town – and hence consumers (and producers) either underconsume (or produce) or overconsume (or produce) depending on whether the externality is positive (e.g., education) or negative (e.g., pollution). In general there are three forms of solution. The first is to regulate the spill-overs: for example, setting quotas for the extent of air or water pollution in a region. The second is to tax negative externalities, and subsidize positive ones. The third was proposed by Ronald Coase and is known as the Coase Theorem, which states that externalities will be solved by the affected parties getting together to create social institutions or other arrangements whereby the externality is internalized. Efficiency can therefore be resolved without recourse to taxes, subsidies or direct government regulation. Subsequent writers have pointed out the limits of the Coase Theorem, and that many types of externality cannot be efficiently solved by negotiations. For example, much pollution is a 'public bad' in the sense of the next reading: that is, if one person breathes in smoke it does not affect the amount of smoke his neighbour breathes in, and neither can one of them negotiate with a nearby factory without affecting the amount of the pollution suffered by the other.

The paper by Paul Samuelson outlines diagrammatically the analysis of public goods: that is, goods from which consumers cannot be excluded from the benefits. The market will not provide adequate supplies of such goods because every consumer would benefit from their provision anyway, regardless of whether or not they pay, so no one would ever offer to pay (the free rider problem). Classic examples of public goods are national defence or lighthouses. A moment's thought will convince students that it is not obvious how to analyze the demand for such goods; conventional market demand curves are clearly not applicable. Samuelson provides the answer: vertical summation of individual demand curves.

The economics of uncertainty and information

Consumer and producer theory in intermediate texts tends to assume that the world is certain, and that there is no risk. In fact, many interesting microeconomic phenomena arise because the future is uncertain and, perhaps more significantly, because knowledge about the future or about the behaviour of others is not distributed equally among economic agents. The exciting and relatively recent paper by Akerlof analyzes some examples of asymmetries in information. He considers the case when one side of a transaction knows more about the product on offer than the other. His initial example is that of second-hand cars, which can be good or bad ('lemons'). He points out that bad cars tend to drive out good ones as a consequence of the asymmetry in information. This is because consumers are willing to pay only the expected value of the car, while at the price suppliers of good cars will not bring them to market. This paper was one of the first in the fast-growing literature on the economics of information. This literature has led to insights and concepts that are far removed from those of the standard textbook competitive model: for example, an equilibrium may not exist, or if it exists it may be inherently unstable.

Essential readings in macroeconomics

Although both the macroeconomic and the microeconomic readings are divided into parts, the interrelationships are probably stronger between Parts 5–8; there is a series of themes running through this macroeconomics half. This is because in macroeconomics the links between explanation, prediction and policy prescriptions are closer to the surface. This may help to explain why the macroeconomics literature often reverts to the same topics and themes, if at a greater depth of rigour and sophistication, as time goes on. Even the genuine innovations (such as the concept and implications of rational expectations in Parts 7 and 8), often largely fit into existing differences of approach, rather than just building on a commonly agreed foundation.

One way of viewing the debate in macroeconomics in the past 55 years is to see it as an extension and reaction to the 'Keynesian Revolution' following the publication of J. M. Keynes's *The General Theory of Employment, Interest and Money* in 1936. The exposition of the Keynesian approach, and analyses of policy options, has centred on the *IS-LM* version of the model, though some economists insisted that this static model missed many of Keynes's insights, including his analysis of the volatility and possible unpredictability of investment in Chapter 12 of *The General Theory* (see Chapter 15 below).

In the thirty years between 1945 and 1975 the most well known of the critics of the Keynesian approach and its policy prescriptions was Milton Friedman. His attack on Keynesian activist macroeconomic policies to control the fluctuations of employment and output (Chapter 18) began what is sometimes called the 'Monetarist Counter-revolution', and he and others who attacked major aspects of Keynesianism were, and are, known as 'Monetarists'. Similarly the newer criticisms of the Keynesian approach (Chapter 19) are sometimes called the 'New Monetarism'. In retrospect, the name 'Monetarism' is misleading. It seemed for a while in the 1960s and early 1970s that the debates centred around the use of monetary *versus* fiscal policy; and the theoretical aspects are often (wrongly) traced back to Friedman's attempted rehabilitation of his version of the 'Quantity Theory of Money'; while he based his later, widely quoted, attack on the Keynesian policy approach in terms of monetary policy (Chapter 10).

There were some Keynesians who did tend to downplay the influence of money (e.g., by concentrating on the simple multiplier or 45° diagram) but most did pay attention to money (e.g., in the *IS-LM* diagram).

The 'Monetarist' attack in terms of monetary *versus* fiscal policy was also important because for many years it contributed to misleading some of the profession into confusing (a) a constant velocity of circulation as a constant *number* with (b) 'constant velocity' as a stable *function* of other variables, such as interest rates. The confusion still appears in some textbooks. In fact, the proposition that money can change income but that fiscal policy cannot, only holds under assertion (a). Assertion (b), for example, is consistent with an upward sloping *LM* curve, where clearly both monetary and fiscal policy can affect income.

Although Friedman himself was quite clear in his theoretical articles on the distinction between a constant numerical velocity and a stable demand for money function, one contribution to confusion was his attribution to Keynesians in general of a belief in *either* the liquidity trap, *or* a view that interest rates were only determined by the demand and supply for money. Neither belief is true of Keynesians who accept an upward sloping *LM*. The confusion was then increased by a claim a few years later that only monetary policy could affect income. Some of those who had absorbed the message in the theoretical article, thought (wrongly) that the claim that only money mattered was consistent with his view that he only posited a stable demand for money function, and not a constant numerical velocity of circulation.

However, it is now widely agreed that the basic issues and themes are not primarily those of money and its role. Instead, the themes that run through macroeconomics in the period covered by the readings here, and that crop up in various guises in the macroeconomics literature, primarily concern fundamental differences of approach.

One basic difference between the variants of Keynesianism on the one hand, and those of Monetarism on the other, involves a macroeconomic application of microeconomics. This disagreement is over the extent to which a modern economy can be correctly described as the textbook, perfectly competitive, model writ large. Friedman, and other more recent critics of Keynesian approaches, usually analyze macroeconomic issues on the basis of a view of the economy that assumes (either explicitly or implicitly) that prices adjust quickly and smoothly enough for a market clearing equilibrium (i.e., one where demands equals supply) to be always the relevant concept for macroeconomic analysis and policy prescriptions.

Conversely, Keynesians of both the earlier and the 'neo-Keynesian' approaches assume that for some reason or other there are some important sectors of the economy where the simple competitive market paradigm is not applicable. The most obvious candidate for a market where such rigidities may be crucial is the labour market.

This dispute over the flexibility of wages and the clearing of the labour market obviously has implications for the causes of unemployment and of economic fluctuations. It is also important in determining whether activist macroeconomic policies are needed to control the fluctuations in the course of what is conventionally called the 'business cycle' (Chapters 15–17). Keynesians tend to feel that there are situations in which there can be a nontransient excess supply of labour, and that types of unemployment can sensibly be called involuntary. Their opponents tend to think that this distinction is unhelpful and may be misleading (Chapters 12–14).

A closely related issue to the cause of unemployment, its fluctuations and its control is the reason for variations in inflation. Although Keynes himself pointed out that inflation would result if planned aggregate expenditure were above the level corresponding to full employment, there was no explanation of *how much* inflation would ensue. Moreover, for a long time many Keynesian textbooks and models actually treated prices, as well as wages, as rigid under 'normal' circumstances: that is, they assumed (a) that levels of output below that corresponding to full employment are the norm, and (b) that price changes do not occur under such circumstances. The latter was the assumption implicit in the standard use of the *IS-LM* model as the primary mode of explanation, with no endogenous shifts in the *LM* curve due to price changes. Later there was a return to the use of the aggregate supply–demand model which did allow for changes in the price level. The aggregate supply–demand analysis, however, still only dealt with discrete changes in the price level, rather than explaining on-going inflation or its level.

This lacuna in the Keynesian analysis was filled by the Phillips Curve, named after its originator Professor Phillips. For a while the Phillips

Curve, with its prediction of a trade-off between inflation and unemployment, became the focus of policy advice. It was most often simply assumed that both unemployment and inflation were undesirable (although see Chapter 9 on inflation as well as the chapters on unemployment) and that, on the basis of Phillips Curve, a choice had to be made of the relative sacrifice between them.

The widespread acceptance of the Phillips Curve trade-off was shattered by a combination of the apparent breakdown of the empirical relationship (many countries experienced *both* higher unemployment *and* higher inflation in the early 1970s) together with (slightly earlier) attacks on its theoretical basis. There were several articles which argued that the Phillips Curve trade-off was only a short-run relationship, and that in a longer run there was only one rate of unemployment compatible with steady inflation rather than with accelerating prices. The new version has various names in the literature. These include: 'the vertical Phillips Curve', the 'Friedman–Phelps' relationship, the 'Natural Rate Hypothesis', and the 'expectations augmented Phillips Curve'. Because the article by Friedman has probably been the most influential, it is the one reprinted here (Chapter 10).

Although most economists accept the natural rate hypothesis, a few did not even at the time (Chapter 11), and more unease has been felt as a result of the experience in the 1980s, especially in EC countries. Unemployment rose, and yet inflation seemed to come down slowly, rather than accelerate downwards into falling prices as would be predicted by the vertical Phillips Curve. There were also attacks on the 'naturalness' of the 'natural rate of unemployment' (Chapter 11). Friedman's own article, and its development in the rational expectations literature of the New Monetarists, clearly had implications for the desirability of counter-cyclical policy. These analyses also assumed market clearing, and thus linked into what we described above as one of the themes of debate, namely the fundamental disagreement among macroeconomists about the appropriate description of markets.

One (related) result of the realization that many of the disputes over policy could be linked to disagreements over the applicability of the standard microeconomic perfectly competitive paradigm, was that it led to an attack by the Monetarists on the absence of microeconomic foundations for Keynesian macroeconomics. Various responses have been offered by Keynesians. Some are not featured here, as they tend to involve more sophisticated mathematical techniques, especially those which link up with notions of imperfect competition in product markets. Others try to explain labour market behaviour which leads to Keynesian types of result as a result of microeconomic behaviour which is rational, yet differs in important ways from the perfectly competitive assumptions. Some focus on bargaining, either between employers and unions, or between employers and individuals who have skills which are specific to the firm and which are costly to the firm to replace. Some consider aspects of 'fairness', as well as the need to motivate workers who might be able to vary their efforts at work. Examples can be found in Chapters 13 and 14.

Another theme that runs implicitly through much of the macroeconomic policy debates of the past fifty years, yet has sometimes not been explicitly recognized, is how to react to uncertainty. It is easy to draw diagrams on paper or to write down equations. When applied to reality, the precise numerical relationships are at best known with wide margins of error and it may not be very well known for sure whether one variable affects another at all. Often there will be uncertainty about how *long* it takes for one variable to have its effects. For example, in any particular economy at any particular time there will be uncertainty as to how much ultimate effect a 1 per cent rise in interests rates would have on spending and how much of the ultimate effect would occur within, say, 6 months. (For other examples, and their implications for policy, see the recent textbooks by one of the editors of this volume, Marin, 1992.)

In the face of uncertainty, different economists react differently in their policy prescriptions. Many Keynesians assume that governments have enough knowledge to undertake sensible policy interventions. Keynes himself (for example, in Chapter 15) at times stressed the lack of reliable knowledge of the future, and the way it led to rather arbitrary behaviour. At other times his policy proposals implied that governments do know enough to intervene (and the problem is anyway less acute when considering a long-lasting unemployment equilibrium rather than cyclical swings in macroeconomic activity). Most Keynesians have assumed sufficient knowledge for active government macroeconomic policy-making to be advisable (Chapter 20), although some have advocated a degree of caution in the face of uncertainty about the impacts of policy.

The important attack on activist policy, and the advocacy in Chapter 18 of simple, constant rules for monetary and fiscal policies was based on the government's lack of knowledge about the quantitative impact of policy and its timing. More recently, the New Monetarists have taken a diametrically opposite view on this assumption of ignorance (Chapters 16 and 19). The use of rational expectations implies that although there is irreducible ignorance about specific stochastic 'shocks' to the economy, individuals and governments do have very thorough knowledge concerning everything else, including the statistical pattern (i.e., distribution in the probability sense) of random shocks.

Thus whereas the earlier Monetarism opposed activist monetary and fiscal policies because they could make things worse due to mistakes, the later Monetarism opposed activist policies because they could not have any effect on output and employment (Chapter 19). The essence of the argument is linked to Friedman's augmentation of the simple Phillips Curve, in which unemployment affects inflation, by an allowance for expected price inflation. If the new relationship is turned around, then unemployment can be related to the gap between actual inflation and expected inflation. If people have full information about government policies and about the structure of the economy, then consistent government policy cannot drive a wedge between actual and expected inflation. Hence it cannot affect unemployment.

Partly as a result of the disagreements over whether wages and prices are flexible enough for markets to clear reasonably quickly and smoothly, or whether they are unresponsive enough for an equilibrium with continuing excess supply (at least of labour) to be an accurate description of the economy at times, another theme in the literature is that of long- versus short-run analysis. In macroeconomics the terms 'long run' and 'short run' are used less rigorously than in microeconomics. Generally writers use the term long run to mean enough time for wages and/or prices to change so as to eliminate any excess supply: that is, for markets to clear at the 'full employment' level (the older phrase) or the 'natural rate' (the newer phrase). In the Friedman version of the latter, the long run means that expectations have adapted fully to reality, so that actual and expected inflation are equal. Because of their stress on rigidities, Keynesians tend to argue that the relevant analysis for policy is the short run. It was Keynes himself who coined the phrase 'in the long-run we are all dead'. Conversely, opponents of the Keynesian views tend to concentrate on long-run analysis, and to argue that to be overly concerned about very short-run behaviour leads to serious mistakes because it overlooks the vital longer-run repercussions (e.g. Chapter 10).

We should end this overview by noting that although often individual economists' macroeconomic analyses may tend to make it tempting to classify them into being adherents of one school of thought or another, nevertheless most are open enough for such pigeonholing to be less than 100 per cent accurate.

Inflation and unemployment

This part starts with an article which questions whether inflation is necessarily very bad. Not all economists would agree with Bootle – there is for example, a widely referred-to article by Fischer and Modigliani (1978). Because it is usually taken for granted, without argument, that inflation is extremely undesirable, we have chosen a reading which presents the alternative view.

The next reading is Friedman's seminal attack on the notion that there is a choice to be made between inflation and unemployment. Friedman's article also links into many of the other themes that we have mentioned, such as the alleged arbitrariness and irrationality of Keynesian views of the functioning of the labour market. The first part is linked to an argument that was still widely viewed as important in 1967: that is, the use of monetary versus fiscal policy. Although politically this argument may still matter, most professional economists now recognize that in general both monetary and fiscal policy can affect income (see also Chapter 20).

The final article in this part is a deep defence by Tobin against the Friedman views. It denies that all markets work smoothly enough for the level of unemployment that would 'naturally' result to be a simple, optimal state where demand for labour automatically matches the supply. It is also an example of the less common Keynesian view that although Keynes himself, and most subsequent Keynesian writing, worked with equilibrium models, the real and correct insights are best seen when one recognizes that markets in an economy may normally be in disequilibrium, and that any aggregate level of economic activity will correspond to some markets being in excess supply while others are simultaneously in excess demand. His argument also concerns the themes we stressed earlier and the problems of the following sections.

Tobin's attack on the desirability of the 'natural rate' of unemployment refers not only to the Friedman article in the preceding chapter, but also to other versions by other economists (mentioned in passing above), such as that by Phelps. Some of these view unemployment as reflecting workers' choices between accepting any particular job offer and rejecting the offer in order to continue searching for a better job, as contrasted to the more traditional explanations of non-Keynesian unemployment, which centred on workers' choices between taking a job and more 'leisure' (defining this term broadly to include unpaid work in the home, etc.).

The nature of unemployment and labour markets

The next part contains a series of articles on behaviour in labour markets, and its implications for unemployment. They partially deal with the issue of whether unemployment can be 'involuntary'. This issue may appear to be no more than a terminological dispute, but it is closely linked to views on the nature of business cycles and whether macroeconomic policy should be used to expand demand at times of high unemployment. Lucas (in Chapter 12) forcefully expresses the anti-Keynesian argument, combining it with a view that considers business cycle stabilization as central to policies concerning unemployment. The contributions by Solow and by Yellen (Chapters 13 and 14) explore alternative assumptions of microeconomic motivation and/or constraints which would justify the notion that unemployment may be involuntary in a meaningful sense. A related issue which is implied by these alternative assumptions, especially in the formulations summarized by Yellen, is that even the 'natural rate' of unemployment (i.e., the long-run level of unemployment) may not correspond to 'full employment' viewed as an absence of excess supply in the labour market (in this respect these chapters reach one of the same conclusions as Tobin's, although in a different framework). Some of Solow's comments relate to ideas in the following two sections.

The results mentioned by Yellen near the beginning of Chapter 14 may puzzle some readers. One way of seeing these results is by the following derivation, where notation is the same as in Chapter 14, plus: Π = profit, P = the price level for the representative firm and for the economy as a whole, W is the money wage, so that $w = W/P$ is the real wage. Then (ignoring the cost of capital, since capital is fixed in the short run):

$$\Pi = PQ - WN = P.F\,(e\,[w]\,N) - WN = P.F\,(e\,[W/P]\,N) - WN$$

The firm chooses W, N to maximize profits (assume perfect competition so that the firm cannot affect P).

The first-order conditions are:
From:

$$\frac{\partial \Pi}{\partial N} = 0 \quad \text{then} \quad P \cdot \frac{\partial F}{\partial (eN)} \cdot \frac{\partial (eN)}{\partial N} = W$$

Therefore:

$$\frac{\partial F}{\partial (eN)} = \frac{W}{Pe} = \frac{w}{e} \tag{I.1}$$

From:

$$\frac{\partial \Pi}{\partial W} = 0, \quad \text{then} \quad P \cdot \frac{\partial F}{\partial (eN)} \cdot \frac{\partial (eN)}{\partial e} \cdot \frac{\partial e}{\partial (W/P)} \cdot \frac{\partial (W/P)}{\partial W} = N$$

Therefore:

$$\frac{\partial F}{\partial (eN)} \cdot \frac{\partial e}{\partial w} = 1 \tag{I.2}$$

Combining (I.1) and (I.2):

$$\frac{w}{e} \cdot \frac{\partial e}{\partial w} = 1 \tag{I.3}$$

(I.3) is the elasticity condition referred to in the reading.
(I.1) can be written as:

$$e \cdot \frac{\partial F}{\partial (eN)} = w$$

which is the marginal productivity condition.

The business cycle

Some of the explanations of the business cycle have already been introduced in previous parts. The reading by Keynes stresses the volatility of investment which, magnified by the multiplier, can lead to fluctuations in planned expenditure. The article by Lucas is an attempt by one of the leading New Monetarists to explain business cycles within a framework of flexible prices and market clearing. The problem faced by Lucas is that this framework, plus his assumption of rational expectations (see the next part also) implies that employment and output should always be at 'the natural rate', except for random shocks. Systematic swings over time in output and/or employment would seem to be ruled out.

One contentious part of Lucas's answer to the problem is to posit a highly elastic supply curve of labour. Since the consensus is that the supply curve of labour is very inelastic, Lucas uses a theory he developed nearly a decade earlier (in a paper with Leonard Rapping), that there is a difference between the labour supply responses to wage changes which are thought to be temporary from those expected to be permanent. The response to the former is predicted to be much greater than to the latter, as it leads to re-timing in favour of working more when wages are temporarily high and planning to take more leisure when wages fall back. (Some of the arguments by Solow, in Chapter 13, are critiques of this position.) A similar result follows from a temporary rise in interest rates; it then pays workers to work more now, and save the extra earnings. These ideas recur in the next reading.

A set of more recent attempts to deal with the problem faced by Lucas are the 'real business cycle' theories. These theories explain business cycles (within a framework of flexible prices, market clearing and rational expectations) as due to unforeseen changes in supply (e.g., due to technical change), whose effects are then spread out by their impacts on variables such as investment, which themselves affect future output. Unfortunately the articles we have seen by proponents of real business cycles are too technically demanding for inclusion here, but the article by Mankiw criticizing the theories should be accessible. The reference to the 'Solow residual' in the Mankiw article is to Solow's 1956 Growth Model and its developments: essentially, that the part of changes in output which are not due to changes in factor inputs (e.g., to changes in employment) is attributed to technological changes.

One other point that Mankiw makes may not be immediately obvious. In the real business cycle approach, because of changes in technology (and possibly of changes in the capital stock), it is the demand for labour curve which shifts over the cycle. Thus, with a constant short-run supply of labour curve, observed movements in employment and real wages represent movements *along a given labour supply* curve. Hence higher employment would be associated with higher real wages. Thus these theories can deal with the problem that there is some evidence suggesting that real wages may increase in booms (Keynes's original model in *The General Theory*, with rigid money wages and flexible prices, similar to the Aggregate Demand–Aggregate Supply treatment in some textbooks, implies that real wages are higher in slumps as prices fall then. Some New Keynesian approaches imply that real wages do not change over the business cycle). However, because even if real wages do vary procyclically they do not vary very much, a relatively flat supply curve of labour is needed; this was dealt with in our comments on the previous reading and in Mankiw's article.

Control of macroeconomic fluctuations

These articles look at the question of whether governments should attempt to control the level of macroeconomic activity. This is sometimes called the 'rules versus discretion' debate. In Chapter 18 Friedman sets out the case for steady 'rules', in which the government does not attempt to react to the perceived current state of the economy. Although the terminology of 'rules' and 'discretion' has become standard, it is not, strictly speaking, exactly correct. The terminology used in the next reading is more exact. The crucial distinction is between constant values for money and fiscal variables and 'feedback', where policy responds to the current state of the economy either in a way that is laid down in advance (a 'feedback rule') or by allowing the government some choice as to how it responds ('discretionary feedback').

As indicated earlier, although the policy prescriptions of the Friedman article and of that by Sargent and Wallace are similar, the justifications are very different. The latter is based on combining the natural rate hypothesis, including market clearing and flexible prices, with the assumption of rational expectations. The approach, and the resulting proposition, are sometimes called New Monetarism, New Classical Economics, the impotence of macro-policy, or the Lucas–Sargent–Wallace proposition. Although the article reprinted here is apparently slightly more mathematical than most of the other readings, it has a very lucid verbal commentary, and the mathematics are primarily a manipulation of symbols. (The essence of the argument was outlined above.)

Chapter 20 by Modigliani deals not only with both the earlier and new Monetarism attacks on the desirability of any stabilization policy at all, but also with the debate on the use of monetary *versus* fiscal policy to which we have already referred. (A small section of this article on specific econometric estimates has been omitted.)

Conclusions

These readings were meant to supplement and extend the understanding students could obtain from conventional intermediate textbooks. They are also intended to fuel an interest in economics as a research subject. We hope that students will be motivated by these readings to take their studies in economics further, and increasingly to refer to original papers in scholarly journals as the basis for their studies.

References

Fischer, S. and F. Modigliani (1978), 'Towards an Understanding of the Real Effects and Costs of Inflation'. *Weltwirtschaftliches Archiv* pp. 810–833.

Marin, A. (1992), *Macroeconomic Policy* (Routledge).

PART I

THEORY OF CONSUMER DEMAND

CHAPTER 1

The Law of Consumer's Demand*

J. R. HICKS

1. We have now, from the conditions of equilibrium and the basic assumption of regularity, set out in the preceding chapter, to deduce laws of market conduct – to find out what can be said about the way the consumer will react when prices change. Discussion of equilibrium conditions is always a means to an end; we seek information about the conditions governing quantities bought at given prices in order that we may use them to discover how the quantities bought will be changed when prices change.

This stage of our investigation corresponds to the stage in Marshall's theory where he deduces the downward slope of the demand curve from the law of diminishing marginal utility. The particular way in which Marshall carries out that deduction is worth noting. He assumes that the marginal utility of *money* is constant.[1] Therefore, the ratio between the marginal utility of a commodity and its price is a constant ratio. If the price falls, the marginal utility must be reduced too. But, by the law of diminishing marginal utility, this implies an increase in the amount demanded. A fall in price therefore increases the amount demanded. This is the argument we have to reconsider.

What is meant by the marginal utility of money being constant? Making our translation, it would appear to mean that changes in the consumer's supply of money (that is, with respect to the problem in hand, his income) will not affect the marginal rate of substitution between money and any particular commodity X. (For the marginal rate of substitution equals the ratio of the marginal utilities of X and money.) Therefore, if his income increases, and the price of X remains constant, the price of X will still equal the marginal rate of substitution, without any change in the

---
* Chapter 2 in *Value and Capital* (1939), pp. 26–41.

amount of X bought. The demand for X is therefore independent of income. His demand for any commodity is independent of his income.

It will appear in what follows that this is actually what the constancy of the marginal utility of money did mean for Marshall; not that he really supposed that people's demands for commodities do not depend upon their incomes, but that in his theory of demand and price he generally neglected the income side. We shall find that he had quite good reasons for doing so, that the constancy of the marginal utility of money is in fact an ingenious simplification, which is quite harmless for most of the applications Marshall gave it himself. But it is not harmless for all applications; it is not always a good thing to be vague about the effects of changes in income on demand. There are distinct advantages to be gained from having a theory of value in which the relations of demand, price, and income are all made quite clear.

2. Let us now revert to the indifference diagram, and begin by investigating the effects of changes in income. We shall go on to investigate the effects of price-changes later, but price-changes will be easier to deal with if we examine the effects of income-changes first. Let us therefore continue to suppose, as in the last chapter, that the prices of X and Y are given, but now suppose the consumer's income to vary.

We have seen before that if his income is OL (measured in terms of X) or OM (measured in terms of Y), the point of equilibrium will be at P, where LM touches an indifference curve (Figure 1.1).

If now his income increases, LM will move to the right, but the new line $L'M'$ will still be parallel to LM, so long as the prices of X and Y are unchanged. (For, then, $OM'/OL' = OM/OL$, the unchanged price-ratio.) The new point of equilibrium will be at P', where $L'M'$ touches an indifference curve.

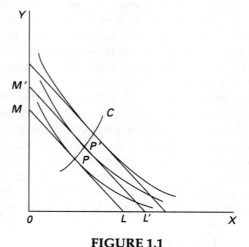

FIGURE 1.1

As income continues to increase, $L'M'$ continues to move to the right, and the point P' traces out a curve, which we may call the *income-consumption curve*.[2] It shows the way in which consumption varies, when income increases and prices remain unchanged. Through any point P on the diagram an income-consumption curve could be drawn; thus there will be an income-consumption curve corresponding to each possible system of prices.

What can be said about the form of the income-consumption curve? Mere experience in drawing diagrams is enough to convince one that it will ordinarily slope upwards and to the right; but that is not enough to show that it will necessarily behave in this way. In fact, there is only one necessary restriction on its shape. An income-consumption curve cannot intersect any particular indifference curve more than once. (For if it did so, that would mean that the indifference curve had two parallel tangents – which is impossible, if the indifference curves are always convex to the origin.) Consequently, while there is most 'room' for the income-consumption curves to slope upwards and to the right, it is also possible for them to creep round to the left or downwards (PC_1 or PC_2 in Figure 1.2) without ever cutting an indifference curve more than once.

And clearly that is as it should be. Curves such as PC_1 do occur. They are found whenever the commodity X is an 'inferior' good, largely consumed at low levels of income, but replaced, or partially replaced, by goods of higher quality when income rises. Margarine is obviously a case in point; its inferiority is well attested by statistical investigation.[3] But it can hardly be doubted that there are a great many others. Most of the poorer qualities of goods offered for sale are probably, in our sense, inferior goods.[4]

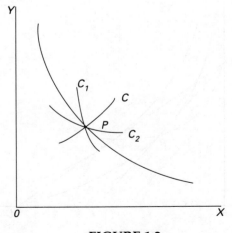

FIGURE 1.2

22 The Law of Consumer's Demand

Although the diagrammatic apparatus we have just been using is only valid for the case of two goods (X and Y), it is evident that a similar argument must hold however many are the goods among which income is being distributed. If income increases, and the increased income is spent, then there must be increased consumption in some directions, perhaps most directions or even all; but it is perfectly possible that there will be a limited number of goods whose consumption will be actually diminished. This is a very negative result and obviously needs no further elaboration.

3. Let us now pass on to consider the effects of a change in price. Here again we begin with the case of two goods. Income is now to be taken as fixed, and the price of Y as fixed; but the price of X is variable. The possibilities of consumption now open are represented in Figure 1.3 by straight lines joining M (OM is income measured in terms of Y, and is therefore fixed) to points on OX which vary as the price of X varies. Each price of X will determine a line LM (OL increasing as the price falls); and the point of equilibrium corresponding to each price will be given by the point at which the line LM touches an indifference curve. The curve MPQ joining these points may be called a *price-consumption curve*. It shows the way in which consumption varies, when the price of X varies and other things remain equal.

Starting off from a particular position of LM, we have thus two sets of straight lines, and corresponding points of contact. We have the lines parallel to LM, whose points of contact trace out the income-consumption

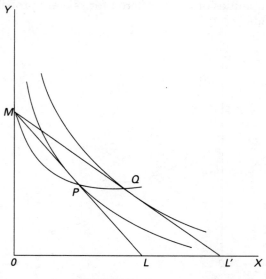

FIGURE 1.3

curve. We have the lines passing through M, whose points of contact trace out the price-consumption curve. Any particular indifference curve must be touched by one line from each of these sets. Take an indifference curve I_2, which is higher than the indifference curve I_1, touched by LM. The curve I_2 is touched by a line parallel to LM at P', by a line through M at Q. Now it is at once obvious from the diagram (it follows from the convexity of the indifference curve) that Q must lie to the right of P'. This property must hold for all indifference curves which are higher than the original curve; and it therefore follows that as we go up on to higher indifference curves the price-consumption curve through P must always lie to the right of the income-consumption curve through P (Figure 1.4).

This proposition, which looks like a mere piece of geometry, turns out to have much economic significance, and to be indeed quite fundamental to a large part of the theory of value. Let us try to see its implications.

When the price of X falls, the consumer moves along the price-consumption curve from P to Q. We now see that this movement from P to Q is equivalent to a movement from P to P' along the income-consumption curve, and a movement from P' to Q along an indifference curve. We shall find it very instructive to think of the effect of price on demand as falling into these two separate parts.

A fall in the price of a commodity does actually affect the demand for that commodity in two different ways. On the one hand, it makes the consumer better off, it raises his 'real income', and its effect along this channel is similar to that of an increase in income. On the other hand, it

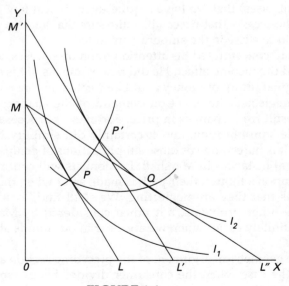

FIGURE 1.4

changes relative prices; and therefore, apart from the change in real income, there will be a tendency to substitute the commodity whose price has fallen for other commodities. The total effect on demand is the sum of these two tendencies.

The relative importance of these tendencies can be further shown to depend upon the proportions in which the consumer was dividing his expenditure between this commodity (X) and other goods. For the extent to which he is made better off by a fall in the price of X will depend upon the amount of X which he was initially buying; if that amount was large relatively to his income, he will be made much better off, and the first effect (the Income Effect, we may call it) will be very important; but if the amount was small, the gain is small, and the income effect is likely to be swamped by the Substitution Effect.

It is this last point which is the justification of Marshall's 'constant marginal utility'. It will be observed that our two effects stand on a different footing as regards the certainty of their operation. It follows from the principle of diminishing marginal rate of substitution that the substitution effect is absolutely certain – it must always work in favour of an increase in the demand for a commodity when the price of that commodity falls. But the income effect is not so reliable; ordinarily it will work the same way, but it will work in the opposite way in the case of inferior goods. It is therefore a consideration of great importance that this unreliable income effect will be of relatively little importance in all those cases where the commodity in question plays a fairly small part in the consumer's budget; for it is only in these cases (fortunately, they are most important cases) that we have a quite unequivocal law of demand. It is only in these cases that we can be quite sure that a fall in price will necessarily lead to a rise in the amount demanded.

Marshall concentrated his attention upon these cases; and therefore he neglected the income effect. He did this by means of his assumption that the marginal utility of money could be treated as constant, which meant that he neglected the effect on demand of the changes in real income which result from changes in price. For many purposes this was a quite justifiable simplification, and it certainly did simplify his theory enormously. It is indeed one of those simplifications of genius, of which there are several instances in Marshall. Economists will continue to use these simplifications, though their path is made safer when they know exactly what it is that they are neglecting. We shall find, as we proceed, that there are other problems, not much considered by Marshall, that are made definitely easier when we are clear in our minds about the income effect.

4. The geometrical argument of the preceding section appears to apply only to the case when the consumer divides his expenditure between two commodities and no more; but it is not actually as limited as that.

For suppose we regard X and Y, not as bread and potatoes, or tea and margarine (physical commodities in that sense), but as bread (some physical commodity) for one, and general purchasing power (Marshall's 'money') for the other. The choice of the consumer is a choice between spending his money on bread or keeping it available for expenditure on other things. If he decides not to spend it on bread, he will subsequently convert it into some other form by buying some other commodity or commodities with it. But even if Y were potatoes, it might still be converted into other forms, some of the potatoes being roast, some being boiled. These possibilities do not prevent us from drawing up a determinate indifference system for bread and potatoes. Similarly, so long as the terms on which money can be converted into other commodities are given, there is no reason why we should not draw up a determinate indifference system between any commodity X and money (that is to say, purchasing power in general). The distribution of purchasing power among other commodities is exactly similar to the distribution of a commodity among various uses, which may take place even if there is only one other commodity in a physical sense.

This principle is of quite general application.[5] A collection of physical things can always be treated as if they were divisible into units of a single commodity so long as their relative prices can be assumed to be unchanged, in the particular problem in hand. So long as the prices of other consumption goods are assumed to be given, they can be lumped together into one commodity 'money' or 'purchasing power in general'. Similarly, in other applications, if changes in relative wages are to be neglected, it is quite legitimate to assume all labour homogeneous. There will be other applications still to notice as we go on.[6]

For the present, we shall only use this principle to assure ourselves that the classification of the effects of price on demand into income effects and substitution effects, and the law that the substitution effect, at least, always tends to increase demand when price falls, are valid, however the consumer is spending his income.

5. In all our discussions so far, we have been concerned with the behaviour of a single individual. But economics is not, in the end, much interested in the behaviour of single individuals. Its concern is with the behaviour of groups. A study of individual demand is only a means to the study of market demand. Fortunately, with our present methods we can make the transition very easily.

Market demand has almost exactly the same properties as individual demand. This can be seen at once if we reflect that it is the actual change in the amount demanded (brought about by a small change in price) which we can divide into two parts, due respectively to the income effect and the substitution effect. The change in the demand of a group is the sum of changes in individual demands; it is therefore also divisible into two parts, one corresponding to the sum of the individual income effects, the other to the sum of the individual substitution effects. Similar propositions to those which held about the individual effects hold about the group effects.

1. Since all the individual substitution effects go in favour of increased consumption of the commodity whose price has fallen, the group substitution effect must do so also.
2. Individual income effects are not quite reliable in direction; therefore group income effects cannot be quite reliable either. A good may, of course, be inferior for some members of a group, and not be inferior for the group as a whole; the negative income effects of this section being offset by positive income effects from the rest of the group.
3. The group income effect will usually be negligible if the group as a whole spends a small proportion of its total income upon the commodity in question.

6. We are therefore in a position to sum up about the law of demand. The demand curve for a commodity must slope downwards, more being consumed when the price falls, in all cases when the commodity is not an inferior good. Even if it is an inferior good, so that the income effect is negative, the demand curve will still behave in an orthodox manner so long as the proportion of income spent upon the commodity is small, so that the income effect is small. Even if neither of these conditions is satisfied, so that the commodity is an inferior good which plays an important part in the budgets of its consumers, it still does not necessarily follow that a fall in price will diminish the amount demanded. For even a large negative income effect may be outweighed by a large substitution effect.

It is apparent what very stringent conditions need to be fulfilled before there can be any exception to the law of demand. Consumers are only likely to spend a large proportion of their incomes upon what is for them an inferior good if their standard of living is very low. The famous Giffen case, quoted by Marshall,[7] exactly fits these requirements. At a low level of income, consumers may satisfy the greater part of their need for food by one staple foodstuff (bread in the Giffen case), which will be replaced by a more varied diet if income rises. If the price of this staple falls, they have a quite considerable surplus available for expenditure, and they may spend this surplus upon more interesting foods, which then take the place of the staple, and reduce the demand for it. In such a case as this, the negative income effect may be strong enough to outweigh the substitution effect. But it is evident how rare such cases must be.

Thus, as we might expect, the simple law of demand – the downward slope of the demand curve – turns out to be almost infallible in its working. Exceptions to it are rare and unimportant. It is not in this direction that our present technique has anything new to offer.

7. But as soon as we pass beyond this standard case, we do begin to get some effective clarification.

So far we have assumed the consumer's income to be fixed in terms of money. What happens if this is not so, if he comes to the market not only as a buyer but also as a seller? Suppose he comes with a fixed stock of some commodity X, of which he is prepared to hold back some for his own consumption, if price-conditions are favourable to that course of action.

It is clear that so long as the price of X remains fixed, our previous arguments are unaffected. We may suppose, if we like, that he exchanges his whole stock into money at the fixed price, when he will find himself in exactly the same position as our consumer whose income was fixed in terms of money. He can then buy back some of his X if he wants to.

But what happens if the price of X varies? The substitution effect will be the same as before. A fall in the price of X will encourage substitution of X for other goods; this must favour increased demand for X, that is to say, diminished supply. But the income effect will not be the same as before. A fall in the price of X will make a *seller* of X worse off; this will diminish his demand (increase his supply) unless X is for him an inferior good.

The significant difference between the position of the seller and that of the buyer thus comes out at once. In the case of the buyer income effect and substitution effect work in the same direction – save in the exceptional case of inferior goods. In the case of the seller, they only work in the same direction in that exceptional case. Ordinarily they work in opposite directions.

The position is made more awkward by the fact that sellers' income effects can much more rarely be neglected. Sellers usually derive large parts of their incomes from some particular thing which they sell. We shall therefore expect to find many cases in which the income effect is just as powerful as the substitution effect, or is dominant. We must conclude that a fall in the price of X may either diminish its supply or increase it.

The practical importance of such a supply curve is no doubt most evident in the case of the factors of production. Thus a fall in wages may sometimes make the wage-earner work less hard, sometimes harder; for, on the one hand, reduced piece-rates make the effort needed for a marginal unit of output seem less worth while, or would do so, if income were unchanged; but on the other, his income is reduced, and the urge to work harder in order to make up for the loss in income may counterbalance the first tendency.[8]

Such a supply curve will appear, however, whenever there is a possibility of reservation demand; that is to say, whenever the seller

28 The Law of Consumer's Demand

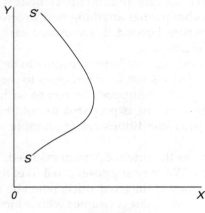

FIGURE 1.5

would prefer, other things being equal, to give up less, rather than more. The supply of agricultural products from not too specialized farms is thus another good example. Any such supply curve, drawn on a price–quantity diagram, is likely to turn back on itself at some point. We cannot be at all confident that it will be upward-sloping (Figure 1.5).

That there existed this asymmetry between supply and demand has long been familiar; it should perhaps be reckoned as one of the discoveries of Walras.[9] But so long as the reason for the asymmetry was not made clear, it was rather too easy to forget its existence. To have cleared up this matter may be regarded as the first-fruits of our new technique. It is itself a good thing to have cleared up, and, we shall find as we go on, it opens the way to some very convenient analytical methods.

Note: Consumer's Surplus

The doctrine of Consumer's Surplus has caused more trouble and controversy than anything else in book iii of Marshall's *Principles*; the results we have just reached throw some light upon it; consequently, although it lies off the main track of our present inquiry, it may usefully be examined here.

Consumer's surplus is the one instance in this field where Marshall was, perhaps, just a shade too ingenious; but he was very ingenious, and we must be careful not to fall into the most common error of writers on this matter, which is to fail to give him the credit for the ingenuity he showed. We are dealing with one of those deceptive doctrines which appear to be a good deal simpler than they are. It can easily be stated in a way which is altogether fallacious; and it is easy to overlook the fact that

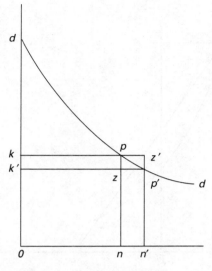

FIGURE 1.6

Marshall did go to some considerable trouble in order not to state it in a fallacious way.

It is thus useful to begin by contrasting Marshall's arguments with that of the original inventor of consumer's surplus – Dupuit. Dupuit, writing in 1844, gave a version that has none of Marshall's refinement.[10]

He held straightforwardly that 'l'économie politique doit prendre pour mesure de l'utilité d'un objet le sacrifice maximum que chaque consommateur serait disposé à faire pour se le procurer' (p. 40), and therefore that the 'utility' secured by being able to purchase On units of a commodity at the price pn is given by the area dpk on the price–quantity demand diagram (p. 63). This without any qualification. Marshall uses the same diagram (Figure 1.6) and arrives at the same result; but he makes the significant qualification that the marginal utility of money must be supposed constant.[11]

The force of this can be readily shown on the indifference diagram, measuring, as before, the commodity X along one axis and money on the other (Figure 1.7). If the consumer's income is OM, and the price of X is indicated by the slope of ML, which touches an indifference curve at P, ON will be the amount of X purchased, and PF the amount of money paid for it. Now P is on a higher indifference curve than M, and what is wanted is a money measure of this gain in 'utility'. Like Dupuit, Marshall takes 'the excess of the price which (the consumer) would be willing to pay rather than go without the thing, over that which he actually does pay'.[12] The price he actually does pay is measured on our

30 The Law of Consumer's Demand

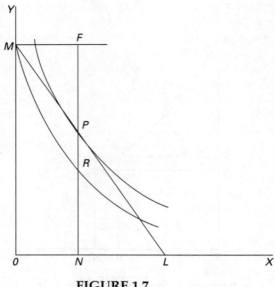

FIGURE 1.7

diagram by *PF*, the price he would be willing to pay by *RF*, where *R* lies on the same indifference curve as *M* (so that if he bought *ON* and paid *RF* for it, he would be no better off by making the transaction). Consumer's surplus is therefore the length of the line *RP*.

RP is a perfectly general representation of consumer's surplus, independent of any assumption about the marginal utility of money. But it is not necessarily equal to the area under the demand curve in Marshall's diagram, unless the marginal utility of money is constant. This can be seen as follows. If the marginal utility of money is constant, the slope of the indifference curve at *R* must be the same as the slope of the indifference curve at *P*, that is to say, the same as the slope of the line *MP*. A slight movement to the right along the indifference curve *MR* will therefore increase *RF* by the same amount as a slight movement along *MP* will increase *PF*. But the increment in *PF* is the additional amount paid for a small increment in the amount purchased at the price given by *MP*, an amount measured by the area *pnn'z'* in Figure 1.6. The length *RF* is built up out of a series of such increments, and must therefore be represented on Figure 1.6 by the area built up out of increments such as *pnn'z'*. This is nothing else than *dpnO*

RP will therefore be represented on Figure 1.6 by *dpl* – Marshall's consumer's surplus.

This is valid so long as the marginal utility of money is constant – so long as income effects can be neglected. But how legitimate is it in this case to follow Marshall in neglecting income effects? This is not a case in which they can be very safely ignored. Marshall neglects the difference between the slope of the indifference curve at P and the slope of the indifference curve at R. It is true that this difference is likely to be less important, the less important in the consumer's budget is the commodity we are considering. But the difference may still be important, even if the proportion of income spent upon the commodity is small; it will still be important, if RP itself is large, if the consumer's surplus is large, so that the loss of the opportunity of buying the commodity is equivalent to a large loss of income.

This is the weakness which remains even in Marshall's version of the consumer's surplus theory; but there is really no reason why it should be allowed to remain. We must remember that the notion of consumer's surplus is not wanted for its own sake; it is wanted as a means of demonstrating a very important proposition, which was supposed to depend upon it. However, in fact that proposition can be demonstrated without begging any questions at all.

As we have seen, the best way of looking at consumer's surplus is to regard it as a means of expressing, in terms of money income, the gain which accrues to the consumer as a result of a fall in price. Or better, it is the *compensating variation* in income, whose loss would just offset the fall in price, and leave the consumer no better off than before. Now it can be shown that this compensating variation cannot be less than a certain minimum amount, and will ordinarily be greater than that amount. This is all that is needed.

Suppose the price of oranges is $2d$. each; and at this price a person buys 6 oranges. Now suppose that the price falls to $1d$., and at the lower price he buys 10 oranges. What is the compensating variation in income? We cannot say exactly, but we can say that it cannot be less than $6d$. For suppose again that, at the same time as the price of oranges fell, his income had been reduced by $6d$. Then, in the new circumstances, he can, if he chooses, buy the same amount of oranges as before, and the same amounts of all other commodities; what had previously been his most preferred position is still open to him; so he cannot be worse off. But with the change in relative prices, it is probable that he will be able to substitute some quantity of oranges for some quantities of other things, and so make himself better off. But if he can lose $6d$. and still remain better off, $6d$. must be less than the compensating variation; he would have to lose more than $6d$. in order to be just as well off as before.[13]

This is all that is necessary in order to establish the important consequences in the theory of taxation which follow from the consumer's surplus principle. It shows, for example, why (apart from distributional effects) a tax on commodities lays a greater burden on consumers than an income tax. If the price of oranges falls from $2d$. to $1d$. as the result of a reduction in taxation, then (assuming constant costs) the reduction in tax receipts from our particular consumer is 6*d*. If this is taken from him by an income tax, he is still left better off, and the government no worse off.

Other deductions which have been drawn from the consumer's surplus principle can presumably be tested out in a similar way.[14]

Notes

1. This, of course, abolishes any distinction between the diminishing marginal utility of a commodity and the diminishing marginal rate of substitution of that commodity for money. Consequently, it explains why Marshall was satisfied with diminishing marginal utility.
2. In 'A Reconsideration of the Theory of Value' I called this the expenditure curve. It was clearly a bad name.
3. Cf. Allen and Bowley, *Family Expenditure*, pp. 36, 41.
4. It is a curious illustration of the muddle into which the theory of value was liable to fall, so long as the principle of diminishing marginal utility was not wholly abandoned, that that principle can easily be interpreted in a way which would exclude inferior goods from any place in economics. This interpretation was actually put forward by Pareto at one period in the development of his ideas (*Manuale di economia politica*, pp. 502–3; but cf. the later French edition, pp. 573–4). Instead of relying solely upon the *true* principle of diminishing marginal rate of substitution (that the rate will diminish when X is substituted for Y along an indifference curve), he put forward also what we may now justly regard as a false principle – that the marginal rate of substitution of X for Y will diminish when the supply of Y is reduced without any increase in the supply of X. If this were always true, it would exclude the possibility of X being an inferior good. Therefore this principle of Pareto's cannot be always satisfied.
5. It is, in fact, a consequence of the principle ... that the marginal marginal rate of substitution must diminish, for substitutions in any direction.
6. Beyond this, it does not seem necessary to worry about the definition of a 'commodity'. What collections of things we regard as composing a commodity must be allowed to vary with the problem in hand.
7. *Principles*, p. 132.
8. Robbins, 'Elasticity of Demand for Income in Terms of Effort' (*Economica*, 1930, p. 123).
9. Walras, *Eléments d'économie politique pure* (first published 1874), leçons 5–7.
10. Dupuit's work appeared in the *Annales des Ponts et Chaussées*, and was thus very inaccessible until M. de Bernardis' elegant reprint entitled *De l'utilité et de sa mesure* (Turin, 1933) from which I quote.
11. Marshall, *Principles*, p. 842.
12. Ibid., p. 124.
13. The compensating variation can thus be proved to be greater than the area $kpzk'$ on Fig.1.6. Can it also be proved to be less than the area $kz'p'k'$? At first sight, one might think so; but in fact it is not possible to give an equally rigorous proof on this side. This comes out clearly if we use the indifference diagram (Fig. 1.7). The line exhibiting opportunities of purchase, when the

price of oranges falls by 1*d*., and income is reduced by 10*d*., no longer passes through the original point of equilibrium *P*. Thus we have no reliable information about the indifference curve it touches. We are left to infer from our earlier argument that the compensating variation will be less than the larger rectangle, so long as the marginal utility of money can be taken as constant.

14. In an article which appeared after I had written the above ('The General Welfare in relation to Problems of Taxation and of Railway and Utility Rates', *Econometrica*, July 1938) Professor Hotelling gives a substantially similar argument and applies it to broader problems of economic welfare. It would be interesting to submit all the fundamental part of Professor Pigou's book to this sort of criticism; my impression is that most of it would come out pretty well.

PART II

THEORY OF THE FIRM AND SUPPLY

CHAPTER 2

*The Nature of the Firm**

R. H. COASE

Economic theory has suffered in the past from a failure to state clearly its assumptions. Economists in building up a theory have often omitted to examine the foundations on which it was erected. This examination is, however, essential not only to prevent the misunderstanding and needless controversy which arise from a lack of knowledge of the assumptions on which a theory is based, but also because of the extreme importance for economics of good judgement in choosing between rival sets of assumptions. For instance, it is suggested that the use of the word "firm" in economics may be different from the use of the term by the "plain man."[1] Since there is apparently a trend in economic theory towards starting analysis with the individual firm and not with the industry,[2] it is all the more necessary not only that a clear definition of the word "firm" should be given but that its difference from a firm in the "real world," if it exists, should be made clear. Mrs. Robinson has said that "the two questions to be asked of a set of assumptions in economics are: Are they tractable? and: Do they correspond with the real world?"[3] Though, as Mrs. Robinson points out, "more often one set will be manageable and the other realistic," yet there may well be branches of theory where assumptions may be both manageable and realistic. It is hoped to show in the following paper that a definition of a firm may be obtained which is not only realistic in that it corresponds to what is meant by a firm in the real world, but is tractable by two of the most powerful instruments of economic analysis developed by Marshall, the idea of the margin and that of substitution, together giving the idea of substitution at the margin.[4] Our definition must, of course, "relate to formal relations which are capable of being conceived exactly."[5]

Economica, New Series, Vol. IV (1937), pp. 386–405. Reprinted, by the courtesy of the publisher and the author, without change from the original text.

I

It is convenient if, in searching for a definition of a firm, we first consider the economic system as it is normally treated by the economist. Let us consider the description of the economic system given by Sir Arthur Salter.[6] "The normal economic system works itself. For its current operation it is under no central control, it needs no central survey. Over the whole range of human activity and human need, supply is adjusted to demand, and production to consumption, by a process that is automatic, elastic and responsive." An economist thinks of the economic system as being co-ordinated by the price mechanism and society becomes not an organisation but an organism.[7] The economic system "works itself." This does not mean that there is no planning by individuals. These exercise foresight and choose between alternatives. This is necessarily so if there is to be order in the system. But this theory assumes that the direction of resources is dependent directly on the price mechanism. Indeed, it is often considered to be an objection to economic planning that it merely tries to do what is already done by the price mechanism.[8] Sir Arthur Salter's description, however, gives a very incomplete picture of our economic system. Within a firm, the description does not fit at all. For instance, in economic theory we find that the allocation of factors of production between different uses is determined by the price mechanism. The price of factor A becomes higher in X than in Y. As a result, A moves from Y to X until the difference between the prices in X and Y, except in so far as it compensates for other differential advantages, disappears. Yet in the real world, we find that there are many areas where this does not apply. If a workman moves from department Y to department X, he does not go because of a change in relative prices, but because he is ordered to do so. Those who object to economic planning on the grounds that the problem is solved by price movements can be answered by pointing out that there is planning within our economic system which is quite different from the individual planning mentioned above and which is akin to what is normally called economic planning. The example given above is typical of a large sphere in our modern economic system. Of course, this fact has not been ignored by economists. Marshall introduces organisation as a fourth factor of production; J. B. Clark gives the co-ordinating function to the entrepreneur; Professor Knight introduces managers who co-ordinate. As D. H. Robertson points out, we find "islands of conscious power in this ocean of unconscious co-operation like lumps of butter coagulating in a pail of buttermilk."[9] But in view of the fact that it is usually argued that co-ordination will be done by the price mechanism, why is such organisation necessary? Why are there these "islands of conscious power"? Outside the firm, price movements direct production, which is co-ordinated through a series of exchange transactions on the market. Within a firm, these market transactions are eliminated and in place of the complicated market structure with exchange transactions is substituted the entrepreneur-co-ordinator, who directs production.[10] It is clear that these are alternative methods of co-ordinating production. Yet, having regard to the fact that if production is regulated by price movements, production could be carried on without any organisation at all, well might we ask, why is there any organisation?

Of course, the degree to which the price mechanism is superseded varies greatly. In a department store, the allocation of the different sections to the various locations in the building may be done by the controlling authority or it may be the result of competitive price bidding for space. In the Lancashire cotton industry, a weaver can rent power and shop-room and can obtain looms and yarn on credit.[11] This co-ordination of the various factors of production is, however, normally carried out without the intervention of the price mechanism. As is evident, the amount of "vertical" integration, involving as it does the supersession of the price mechanism, varies greatly from industry to industry and from firm to firm.

It can, I think, be assumed that the distinguishing mark of the firm is the supersession of the price mechanism. It is, of course, as Professor Robbins points out, "related to an outside network of relative prices and costs,"[12] but it is important to discover the exact nature of this relationship. This distinction between the allocation of resources in a firm and the allocation in the economic system has been very vividly described by Mr. Maurice Dobb when discussing Adam Smith's conception of the capitalist: "It began to be seen that there was something more important than the relations inside each factory or unit captained by an undertaker; there were the relations of the undertaker with the rest of the economic world outside his immediate sphere ... the undertaker busies himself with the division of labour inside each firm and he plans and organizes consciously," but "he is related to the much larger economic specialisation, of which he himself is merely one specialised unit. Here, he plays his part as a single cell in a larger organism, mainly unconscious of the wider role he fills".[13]

In view of the fact that while economists treat the price mechanism as a co-ordinating instrument, they also admit the co-ordinating function of the "entrepreneur," it is surely important to enquire why co-ordination is the work of the price mechanism in one case and of the entrepreneur in another. The purpose of this paper is to bridge what appears to be a gap in economic theory between the assumption (made for some purposes) that resources are allocated by means of the price mechanism and the assumption (made for other purposes) that this allocation is dependent on the entrepreneur–co-ordinator. We have to explain the basis on which, in practice, this choice between alternatives is effected.[14]

II

Our task is to attempt to discover why a firm emerges at all in a specialised exchange economy. The price mechanism (considered purely from the side of the direction of resources) might be superseded if the relationship which replaced it was desired for its own sake. This would be the case, for example, if some people preferred to work under the direction of some other person. Such individuals would accept less in order to work under someone, and firms would arise naturally from this. But it would appear that this cannot be a very important reason, for it would rather seem that the opposite tendency is operating if one judges from the stress normally laid on the advantage of "being one's own master."[15] Of course, if the desire was not to be controlled but to control, to exercise power over others, then people might be willing to give up something in order to direct others; that is, they would be willing to pay others more than they could get under the price mechanism in order to be able to direct them. But this implies that those who direct pay in order to be able to do this and are not paid to direct, which is clearly not true in the majority of cases.[16] Firms might also exist if purchasers preferred commodities which are produced by firms to those not so produced; but even in spheres where one would expect such preferences (if they exist) to be of negligible importance, firms are to be found in the real world.[17] Therefore there must be other elements involved.

The main reason why it is profitable to establish a firm would seem to be that there is a cost of using the price mechanism. The most obvious cost of "organising" production through the price mechanism is that of discovering what the relevant prices are.[18] This cost may be reduced but it will not be eliminated by the emergence of specialists who will sell this information. The costs of negotiating and concluding a separate contract for each exchange transaction which takes place on a market must also be taken into account.[19] Again, in certain markets, e.g., produce exchanges, a technique is devised for minimising these contract costs; but they are not eliminated. It is true that contracts are not eliminated when there is a firm but they are greatly reduced. A factor of production (or the owner thereof) does not have to make a series of contracts with the factors with whom he is co-operating within the firm, as would be necessary, of course, if this co-operation were as a direct result of the working of the price mechanism. For this series of contracts is substituted one. At this stage, it is important to note that character of the contract into which a factor enters that is employed within a firm. The contract is one whereby the factor, for a certain remuneration (which may be fixed or fluctuating), agrees to obey the directions of an entrepreneur *within certain limits*.[20] The essence of the contract is that it should only state the limits to the powers of the entrepreneur. Within these limits, he can therefore direct the other factors of production.

There are, however, other disadvantages – or costs – of using the price mechanism. It may be desired to make a long-term contract for the supply of some article or service. This may be due to the fact that if one contract is made for a longer period, instead of several shorter ones, then certain costs of making each contract will be avoided. Or, owing to the risk attitude of the people concerned, they may prefer to make a long- rather than a short-term contract. Now, owing to the difficulty of forecasting the longer the period of the contract is for the supply of the commodity or service, the less possible, and indeed, the less desirable it is for the person purchasing to specify what the other contracting party is expected to do. It may well be a matter of indifference to the person supplying the service or commodity which of several courses of action is taken, but not to the purchaser of that service or commodity. But the purchaser will not know which of these several courses he will want the supplier to take. Therefore, the service which is being provided is expressed in general terms, the exact details being left until a later date. All that is stated in the contract is the limits to what the persons supplying the commodity or service is expected to do. The details of what the supplier is expected to do are not stated in the contract but are decided later by the purchaser. When the direction of resources (within the limits of the contract) becomes dependent on the buyer in this way, that relationship which I term a "firm" may be obtained.[21] A firm is likely therefore to emerge in those cases where a very short-term contract would be unsatisfactory. It is obviously of more importance in the case of services – labour – than it is in the case of the buying of commodities. In the case of commodities, the main items can be stated in advance and the details which will be decided later will be of minor significance.

We may sum up this section of the argument by saying that the operation of a market costs something and by forming an organisation and allowing some authority (an "entrepreneur") to direct the resources, certain marketing costs are saved. The entrepreneur has to carry out his function at less cost, taking into account the fact that he may get factors of production at a lower price than the market transactions which he supersedes, because it is always possible to revert to the open market if he fails to do this.

The question of uncertainty is one which is often considered to be very relevant to the study of the equilibrium of the firm. It seems improbable that a firm would emerge without the existence of uncertainty. But those, for instance, Professor Knight, who make the *mode of payment* the distinguishing mark of the firm – fixed incomes being guaranteed to some of those engaged in production by a person who takes the residual, and fluctuating, income – would appear to be introducing a point which is irrelevant to the problem we are considering. One entrepreneur may sell his services to another for a certain sum of money, while the payment to his employees may be mainly or wholly a share in profits.[22] The significant question would appear to be why the allocation of resources is not done directly by the price mechanism.

Another factor that should be noted is that exchange transactions on a market and the same transactions organised within a firm are often treated differently by Governments or other bodies with regulatory powers. If we consider the operation of a sales tax, it is clear that it is a tax on market transactions and not on the same transactions organised within the firm. Now since these are alternative methods of "organisation" – by the price mechanism or by the entrepreneur – such a regulation would bring into existence firms which otherwise would have no *raison d'être*. It would furnish a reason for the emergence of a firm in a specialised exchange economy. Of course, to the extent that firms already exist, such a measure as a sales tax would merely tend to make them larger than they would otherwise be. Similarly, quota schemes, and methods of price control which imply that there is rationing, and which do not apply to firms producing such products for themselves, by allowing advantages to those who organise within the firm and not through the market, necessarily encourage the growth of firms. But it is difficult to believe that it is measures such as have been mentioned in this paragraph which have brought firms into existence. Such measures would, however, tend to have this is result if they did not exist for other reasons.

These, then, are the reasons why organisations such as firms exist in a specialised exchange economy in which it is generally assumed that the distribution of resources is "organised" by the price mechanism. A firm, therefore, consists of the system of relationships which comes into existence when the direction of resources is dependent on an entrepreneur.

The approach which has just been sketched would appear to offer an advantage in that it is possible to give a scientific meaning to what is meant by saying that a firm gets larger or smaller. A firm becomes larger as additional transactions (which could be exchange transactions coordinated through the price mechanism) are organised by the entrepreneur and becomes smaller as he abandons the organisation of such transactions. The question which arises is whether it is possible to study the forces which determine the size of the firm. Why does the entrepreneur not organise one less transaction or one more? It is interesting to note that Professor Knight considers that:

> the relation between efficiency and size is one of the most serious problems of theory, being, in contrast with the relation for a plant, largely a matter of personality and historical accident rather than of intelligent general principles. But the question is peculiarly vital because the possibility of monopoly gain offers

a powerful incentive to continuous and unlimited expansion of the firm, which force must be offset by some equally powerful one making for decreased efficiency (in the production of money income) with growth in size, if even boundary competition is to exist.[23]

Professor Knight would appear to consider that it is impossible to treat scientifically the determinants of the size of the firm. On the basis of the concept of the firm developed above, the task will now be attempted.

It was suggested that the introduction of the firm was due primarily to the existence of marketing costs. A pertinent question to ask would appear to be (quite apart from the monopoly considerations raised by Professor Knight), why, if by organising one can eliminate certain costs and in fact reduce the cost of production, are there any market transactions at all?[24] Why is not all production carried on by one big firm? There would appear to be certain possible explanations.

First, as a firm gets larger, there may be decreasing returns to the entrepreneur function, that is, the costs of organising additional transactions within the firm may rise.[25] Naturally, a point must be reached where the costs of organising an extra transaction within the firm are equal to the costs involved in carrying out the transaction in the open market, or, to the costs of organising by another entrepreneur. Secondly, it may be that as the transactions which are organised increase, the entrepreneur fails to place the factors of production in the uses where their value is greatest that is, fails to make the best use of the factors of production. Again, a point must be reached where the loss through the waste of resources is equal to the marketing costs of the exchange transaction in the open market or to the loss if the transaction was organized by another entrepreneur. Finally, the supply price of one or more of the factors of production may rise, because the "other advantages" of a small firm are greater than those of a large firm.[26] Of course, the actual point where the expansion of the firm ceases might be determined by a combination of the factors mentioned above. The first two reasons given most probably correspond to the economists' phrase of "diminishing returns to management."[27]

The point has been made in the previous paragraph that a firm will tend to expand until the costs of organising an extra transaction within the firm become equal to the costs of carrying out the same transaction by means of an exchange on the open market or the costs of organising in another firm. But if the firm stops its expansion at a point below the costs of marketing in the open market and at a point equal to the costs of organising in another firm, in most cases (excluding the case of "combination"[28]), this will imply that there is a market transaction between these two producers, each of whom could organise it at less than the actual marketing costs. How is the paradox to be resolved? If we consider an example the reason for this will become clear. Suppose A is buying a product from B and that both A and B could organise this marketing transaction at less than its present cost. B, we can assume, is not organising one process or stage of production, but several. If A therefore wishes to avoid a market transaction, he will have to take over all the processes of production controlled by B. Unless A takes over all the processes of production, a market transaction will still remain, although it is a different product that is bought. But we have previously assumed that as each producer expands he becomes less efficient; the additional costs of organising extra transactions increase. It is probable that A's cost of organising the transactions previously organized by B will be greater than B's cost of doing the same thing. A therefore will take over the whole of B's organisation only if his cost of organising B's work is not greater than B's cost by an amount equal to the costs of carrying out an exchange transaction on the open market. But once it becomes economical to have a market transaction, it also pays to divide production in such a way that the cost of organising an extra transaction in each firm is the same.

Up to now it has been assumed that the exchange transactions which take place through the price mechanism are homogeneous. In fact, nothing could be more diverse than the actual transactions which take place in our modern world. This would seem to imply that the costs of carrying out exchange transactions through the price mechanism will vary considerably as will also the costs of organising these transactions within the firm. It seems therefore possible that quite apart from the question of diminishing returns the costs of organising certain transactions within the firm may be greater than the costs of carrying out the exchange transactions in the open market. This would necessarily imply that there were exchange transactions carried out through the price mechanism, but would it mean that there would have to be more than one firm? Clearly not, for all those areas in the economic system where the direction of resources were not dependent directly on the price mechanism could be organised within one firm. The factors which were discussed earlier would seem to be the important ones, though it is difficult to say whether "diminishing returns to management" or the rising supply price of factors is likely to be the more important.

Other things being equal, therefore, a firm will tend to be larger:

(a) the less the costs of organising and the slower these costs rise with an increase in the transactions organised.
(b) the less likely the entrepreneur is to make mistakes and the smaller the increase in mistakes with an increase in the transactions organised.
(c) the greater the lowering (or the less the rise) in the supply price of factors of production to firms of larger size.

Apart from variations in the supply price of factors of production to firms of different sizes, it would appear that the costs of organising and the losses through mistakes will increase with an increase in the spatial distribution of the transaction organised, in the dissimilarity of the transactions, and in the probability of changes in the relevant prices.[29] As more transactions are organised by an entrepreneur, it would appear that the transactions would tend to be either different in kind or in different places. This furnishes an additional reason why efficiency will tend to decrease as the firm gets larger. Inventions which tend to bring factors of production nearer together, by lessening spatial distribution, tend to increase the size of the firm.[30] Changes like the telephone and the telegraph which tend to reduce the cost of organising spatially will tend to increase the size of the firm. All changes which improve managerial technique will tend to increase the size of the firm.[31,32]

It should be noted that the definition of a firm which was given above can be used to give more precise meanings to the terms "combination" and "integration."[33] There is a combination when transactions which were previous organised by two or more entrepreneurs become organised by one. This becomes integration when it involves the organisation of transactions which were previously carried out between the entrepreneurs on a market. A firm can expand in either or both of these two ways. The whole of the "structure of competitive industry" becomes tractable by the ordinary technique of economic analysis.

III

The problem which has been investigated in the previous section has not been entirely neglected by economists and it is now necessary to consider why the reasons given above for the emergence of a firm in a specialised exchange economy are to be preferred to the other explanations which have been offered.

It is sometimes said that the reason for the existence of a firm is to be found in the division of labour. This is the view of Professor Usher, a view which has been adopted and expanded by Mr. Maurice Dobb. The firm becomes "the result of an increasing complexity of the division of labour... The growth of this economic differentiation creates the need for some integrating force without which differentiation would collapse into chaos; and it is as the integrating force in a differentiated economy that industrial forms are chiefly significant."[34] The answer to this argument is an obvious one. The "integrating force in a differentiated economy" already exists in the form of the price mechanism. It is perhaps the main achievement of economic science that it has shown that there is no reason to suppose that specialisation must lead to chaos.³⁵ The reason given by Mr. Maurice Dobb is therefore inadmissible. What has to be explained is why one integrating force (the entrepreneur) should be substituted for another integrating force (the price mechanism).

The most interesting reasons (and probably the most widely accepted) which have been given to explain this fact are those to be found in Professor Knight's *Risk Uncertainty and Profit*. His views will be examined in some detail.

Professor Knight starts with a system in which there is no uncertainty:

> acting as individuals under absolute freedom but without collusion men are supposed to have organized economic life with the primary and secondary division of labour, the use of capital etc., developed to the point familiar in present-day America. The principal fact which calls for the exercise of the imagination is the internal organization of the productive groups or establishments. With uncertainty entirely absent, every individual being in possession of perfect knowledge of the situation, there would be no occasion for anything of the nature of responsible management or control of productive activity. Even marketing transactions in any realistic sense would not be found. The flow of raw materials and productive services to the consumer would be entirely automatic.³⁶

Professor Knight says that we can imagine this adjustment as being "the result of a long process of experimentation worked out by trial-and-error methods alone," while it is not necessary "to imagine every worker doing exactly the right thing at the right time in a sort of 'pre-established harmony' with the work of others. There might be managers, superintendents, etc., for the purpose of co-ordinating the activities of individuals," though these managers would be performing a purely routine function, "without responsibility of any sort."³⁷

Professor Knight then continues:

> With the introduction of uncertainty – the fact of ignorance and the necessity of acting upon opinion rather than knowledge – into this Eden-like situation, its character is entirely changed... With uncertainty present doing things, the actual execution of activity, becomes in a real sense a secondary part of life; the primary problem or function is deciding what to do and how to do it.³⁸

This fact of uncertainty brings about the two most important characteristics of social organisation.

> In the first place goods are produced for a market, on the basis of entirely impersonal prediction of wants, not for the satisfaction of the wants of the producers themselves. The producer takes the responsibility of forecasting the consumers' wants. In the second place, the work of forecasting and at the same time a large part of the technological direction and control of production are

still further concentrated upon a very narrow class of the producers, and we meet with a new economic functionary, the entrepreneur... When uncertainty is present and the task of deciding what to do and how to do it takes the ascendancy over that of execution the internal organisation of the productive groups is no longer a matter of indifference or a mechanical detail. Centralisation of this deciding and controlling function is imperative, a process of 'cephalisation' is inevitable.[39]

The most fundamental change is:

the system under which the confident and venturesome assume the risk or insure the doubtful and timid by guaranteeing to the latter a specified income in return for an assignment of the actual results... With human nature as we know it it would be impracticable or very unusual for one man to guarantee to another a definite result of the latter's actions without being given power to direct his work. And on the other hand the second party would not place himself under the direction of the first without such a guarantee... The result of this manifold specialisation of function is the enterprise and wage system of industry. Its existence in the world is the direct result of the fact of uncertainty.[40]

These quotations give the essence of Professor Knight's theory. The fact of uncertainty means that people have to forecast future wants. Therefore, you get a special class springing up who direct the activities of others to whom they give guaranteed wages. It acts because good judgement is generally associated with confidence in one's judgement.[41]

Professor Knight would appear to leave himself open to criticism on several grounds. First of all, as he himself points out, the fact that certain people have better judgement or better knowledge does not mean that they can only get an income from it by themselves actively taking part in production. They can sell advice or knowledge. Every business buys the services of a host of advisers. We can imagine a system where all advice or knowledge was bought as required. Again, it is possible to get a reward from better knowledge or judgement not by actively taking part in production but by making contracts with people who are producing. A merchant buying for future delivery represents an example of this. But this merely illustrates the point that it is quite possible to give a guaranteed reward providing that certain acts are performed without directing the performance of those acts. Professor Knight says that "with human nature as we know it it would be impracticable or very unusual for one man to guarantee to another a definite result of the latter's actions without being given power to direct his work." This is surely incorrect. A large proportion of jobs are done to contract, that is, the contractor is guaranteed a certain sum providing he performs certain acts. But this does not involve any direction. It does mean, however, that the system of relative prices has been changed and that there will be a new arrangement of the factors of production.[42] The fact that Professor Knight mentions that the "second party would not place himself under the direction of the first without such a guarantee" is irrelevant to the problem we are considering. Finally, it seems important to notice that even in the case of an economic system where there is no uncertainty Professor Knight considers that there would be co-ordinators, though they would perform only routine function. He immediately adds that they would be "without responsibility of any sort," which raises the question by whom are they paid and why? It seems that nowhere does Professor Knight give a reason why the price mechanism should be superseded.

IV

It would seem important to examine one further point and that is to consider the relevance of this discussion to the general question of the "cost-curve of the firm."

It has sometimes been assumed that a firm is limited in size under perfect competition if its cost curve slopes upward,[43] while under imperfect competition, it is limited in size because it will not pay to produce more than the output at which marginal cost is equal to marginal revenue.[44] But it is clear that a firm may produce more than one product and, therefore, there appears to be no *prima facie* reason why this upward slope of the cost curve in the case of perfect competition or the fact that marginal cost will not always be below marginal revenue in the case of imperfect competition should limit the size of the firm.[45] Mrs. Robinson[46] makes the simplifying assumption that only one product is being produced. But it is clearly important to investigate how the number of products produced by a firm is determined, while no theory which assumes that only one product is in fact produced can have very great practical significance.

It might be replied that under perfect competition, since everything that is produced can be sold at the prevailing price, there is no need for any other product to be produced. But this argument ignores the fact that there may be a point where it is less costly to organise the exchange transactions of a new product than to organise further exchange transactions of a new product. This point can be illustrated in the following way. Imagine, following von Thunen, that there is a town, the consuming centre, and that industries are located around this central point in rings. These conditions are illustrated in Figure 2.1 in which A, B, and C represent different industries.

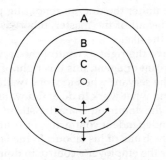

FIGURE 2.1

Imagine an entrepreneur who starts controlling exchange transactions from x. Now as he extends his activities in the same product (*B*), the cost of organising increases until at some point it becomes equal to that of a dissimilar product which is nearer. As the firm expands, it will therefore from this point include more than one product (*A* and *C*). This treatment of the problem is obviously incomplete,[47] but it is necessary to show that merely proving that the cost curve turns upwards does not give a limitation to the size of the firm. So far we have only considered the case of perfect competition: the case of imperfect competition would appear to be obvious.

To determine the size of the firm, we have to consider the marketing costs (that is, the costs of using the price mechanism), and the costs of organising of different entrepreneurs and then we can determine how many products will be produced by each firm and how much of each it will produce. It would, therefore, appear that Mr. Shove[49] in his article on "Imperfect Competition" was asking questions which Mrs. Robinson's cost curve apparatus cannot answer. The factors mentioned above would seem to be the relevant ones.

V

Only one task now remains; and that is, to see whether the concept of a firm which has been developed fits in with that existing in the real world. We can best approach the question of what constitutes a firm in practice by considering the legal relationship normally called that of "master and servant" or "employer and employee."[49] The essential of this relationship have been given as follows:

(1) the servant must be under the duty of rendering personal services to the master or the others on behalf of the master, otherwise the contract is a contract for sale of goods or the like.

(2) The master must have the right to control the servant's work, either personally or by another servant or agent. It is this right of control or interference, of being entitled to tell the servant when to work (within the hours of service) and when not to work, and what work to do and how to do it (within the terms of such service) which is the dominant characteristic in this relation and marks off the servant from an independent contractor, or from one employed merely to give to his employer the fruits of his labour. In the latter case, the contractor or performer is not under the employer's control in doing the work or effecting the service; he has to shape and manage his work so as to give the result he has contracted to effect.[50]

We thus see that it is the fact of direction which is the essence of the legal concept of "employer and employee," just as it was in the economic concept which was developed above. It is interesting to note that Professor Batt says further:

That which distinguishes an agent from a servant is not the absence or presence of a fixed wage or the payment only of commission on business done, but rather the freedom with which an agent may carry out his employment.[51]

We can therefore conclude that the definition we have given is one which approximates closely to the firm as it is considered in the real world.

Our definition is, therefore, realistic. Is it manageable? This ought to be clear. When we are considering how large a firm will be the principle of marginalism works smoothly. The question always is, will it pay to bring an extra exchange transaction under the organising authority? At the margin, the costs of organising within the firm will be equal either to the costs of organising in another firm or to the costs involved in leaving the transaction to be "organised" by the price mechanism. Business men will be constantly experimenting, controlling more or less, and in this way, equilibrium will be maintained. This gives the position of equilibrium for static analysis. But it is clear that the dynamic factors are also of considerable importance, and an investigation of the effect changes have on the cost of organising within the firm and on marketing costs generally will enable one to explain why firms get larger and smaller. We thus have a theory of moving equilibrium. The above analysis would also appear to have clarified the relationship between initiative or enterprise and management. Initiative means forecasting and operates through the price mechanism by the making of new contracts. Management proper merely reacts to price changes, rearranging the factors of production under its control. That the business man normally combines both functions is an obvious result of the marketing costs which were discussed above. Finally, this analysis enables us to state more exactly what is meant by the "marginal product" of the enterpreneur. But an elaboration of this point would take us far from our comparatively simple task of definition and clarification.

Notes

1. Joan Robinson, *Economics is a Serious Subject*, p. 12.
2. See N. Kaldor "The Equilibrium of the Firm," *The Economic Journal*, March 1934.
3. Robinson, *op. cit.*, p. 6.
4. J. M. Keynes, *Essays in Biography*, pp. 223–224.
5. L. Robbins, *Nature and Significance of Economic Science*, p. 63.
6. This description is quoted with approval by D. H. Robertson, *Control of Industry*, p. 85, and by Professor Arnold Plant, "Trends in Business Administration," *Economica*, February 1932. It appears in *Allied Shipping Control*. pp. 16–17.
7. See F. A. Hayek, "The Trend of Economic Thinking," *Economica*, May 1933.
8. See F. A. Hayek, *op. cit.*
9. Robertson, *op. cit.*, p. 85.
10. In the rest of this paper I shall use the term entrepreneur to refer to the person or persons who, in a competitive system, take the place of the price mechanism in the direction of resources.
11. *Survey of Textile Industries*, p. 26.
12. Robbins, *op. cit.*, p. 71.
13. *Capitalist Enterprise and Social Progress*, p. 20. Cf., also, Henderson. *Supply and Demand*, pp. 3–5.
14. It is easy to see when the State takes over the direction of an industry that, in planning it, it is doing something which was previously done by the price mechanism. What is usually not realised is that any businessman in organising the relations between his departments is also doing something which could be organised through the price mechanism. There is therefore point in Mr. Durbin's answer to those who emphasize the problems involved in economic planning that the same problems have to be solved by businessmen in the competitive system. (See "Economic Calculus in a Planned Economy," *The Economic Journal*, December 1936.) The important difference between these two cases is that economic planning is imposed on industry while firms arise voluntarily because they represent a more efficient method of organising production. In a competitive system, there is an "optimum" amount of planning!
15. Cf. Harry Dawes, "Labour Mobility in the Steel Industry," *The Economic Journal*, March 1954, who instances "the trek to retail shopkeeping and insurance work by the better paid of skilled men due to the desire (often the main aim in life of a worker) to be independent" (p. 86).
16. None the less, this is not altogether fanciful. Some small shopkeepers are said to earn less than their assistants.

17. G. F. Shove, "The Imperfection of the Market: a Further Note," *The Economic Journal*, March 1933, p. 116, note 1, points out that such preferences may exist, although the example he gives is almost the reverse of the instance given in the text.
18. According to N. Kaldor, "A Classificatory Note of the Determinateness of Equilibrium," *The Review of Economic Studies*, February 1934, it is one of the assumptions of static theory that "All the relevant prices are known to all individuals." But this is clearly not true of the real world.
19. This influence was noted by Professor Usher when discussing the development of capitalism. He says: "The successive buying and selling of partly finished products were sheer waste of energy." (*Introduction to the Industrial History of England*, p. 13). But he does not develop the idea nor consider why it is that buying and selling operations still exist.
20. It would be possible for no limits to the powers of the entrepreneur to be fixed. This would be voluntary slavery. According to Professor Batt, *The Law of Master and Servant*, p. 18, such a contract would be void and unenforceable.
21. Of course, it is not possible to draw a hard and fast line which determines whether there is a firm or not. There may be more or less direction. It is similar to the legal question of whether there is the relationship of master and servant or principal and agent. See the discussion of this problem below.
22. The views of Professor Knight are examined below in more detail.
23. *Risk, Uncertainty and Profit*, Preface to the Re-issue, London School of Economics Series of Reprints, No. 16, 1933.
24. There are certain marketing costs which could only be eliminated by the abolition of 'consumers' choice' and these are the costs of retailing. It is conceivable that these costs might be so high that people would be willing to accept rations because the extra product obtained was worth the loss of their choice.
25. This argument assumes that exchange transactions on a market can be considered as homogeneous; which is clearly untrue in fact. This complication is taken into account below.
26. For a discussion of the variation of the supply price of factors of production to firms of varying size, see E. A. G. Robinson, *The Structure of Competitive Industry*. It is sometimes said that the supply price of organising ability increases as the size of the firm increases because men prefer to be the heads of small independent business rather than the heads of departments in a large business. See Jones, *The Trust Problem*, p. 531, and Macgregor, *Industrial Combination*, p. 63. This is a common argument of those who advocate Rationalisation. It is said that larger units would be more efficient, but owing to the individualistic spirit of the smaller entrepreneurs, they prefer to remain independent, apparently in spite of the higher income which their increased efficiency under Rationalisation makes possible.
27. This discussion is, of course, brief and incomplete. For a more thorough discussion of this particular problem, see N. Kaldor, "The Equilibrium of the Firm," *The Economic Journal*, March 1934, and E. A. G. Robinson, "The Problem of Management and the Size of the Firm," *The Economic Journal*, June 1934.
28. A definition of this term is given below.

29. This aspect of the problem is emphasised by N. Kaldor, *op. cit.* Its importance in this connection had been previously noted by E. A. G. Robinson. *The Structure of Competitive Industry*, pp. 83–106. This assumes that an increase in the probability of price movements increases the costs of organising within a firm more than it increases the cost of carrying out an exchange transaction on the market – which is probable.
30. This would appear to be the importance of the treatment of the technical unit by E. A. G. Robinson, *op. cit.*, pp. 27–33. The larger the technical unit, the greater the concentration of factors and therefore the firm is likely to be larger.
31. It should be noted that most inventions will change both the costs of organising and the costs of using the price mechanism. In such cases, whether the invention tends to make firms larger or smaller will depend on the relative effect on these two sets of costs. For instance, if the telephone reduces the costs of using the price mechanism more than it reduces the costs of organising, then it will have the effect of reducing the size of the firm.
32. An illustration of these dynamic forces is furnished by Maurice Dobb, *Russian Economic Development*, p. 68. "With the passing of bonded labour the factory as an establishment where work was organised under the whip of the overseer, lost its *raison d'être* until this was restored to it with the introduction of power machinery after 1846." It seems important to realise that the passage from the domestic system to the factory system is not a mere historical accident, but is conditioned by economic forces. This is shown by the fact that it is possible to move from the factory system to the domestic system, as in the Russian example, as well as vice versa. It is the essence of serfdom that the price mechanism is not allowed to operate. Therefore, there has to be direction from some organiser. When, however, serfdom passed, the price mechanism was allowed to operate. It was not until machinery drew workers into one locality that it paid to supersede the price mechanism and the firm again emerged.
33. This is often called "vertical integration," combination being termed "lateral integration."
34. Usher, *op. cit.*, p. 10. Professor Usher's views are to be found in his *Introduction to the Industrial History of England*, pp. 1–18.
35. Cf. J. B. Clark, *Distribution of Wealth*, p. 19, who speaks of the theory of exchange as being the "theory of the organisation of industrial society."
36. *Risk, Uncertainty and Profit*, p. 267.
37. *Op. cit.*, pp. 267–268.
38. *Op. cit.*, p. 268.
39. *Op. cit.*, pp. 268–295.
40. *Op. cit.*, pp. 269–270.
41. *Op. cit.*, p. 270.
42. This shows that it is possible to have a private enterprise system without the existence of firms. Though, in practice, the two functions of enterprise, which actually influences the system of relative prices by forecasting wants and acting in accordance with such forecasts, and management, which accepts the system of relative prices as being given, are normally carried out by the

same persons, yet it seems important to keep them separate in theory. This point is further discussed below.
43. See Kaldor, *op. cit.*, and Robinson, *The Problem of Management and the Size of the Firm*.
44. Mr. Robinson calls this the Imperfect Competition solution for the survival of the small firm.
45. Mr. Robinson's conclusion, *op. cit.*, p. 249, note I, would appear to be definitely wrong. He is followed by Horace J. White, Jr., "Monopolistic and Perfect Competition," *The American Economic Review*, December 1936, p. 645, note 27. Mr. White states, "It is obvious that the size of the firm is limited in conditions of monopolistic competition."
46. *Economics of Imperfect Competition*.
47. As has been shown above, location is only one of the factors influencing the cost of organising.
48. C. F. Shove, "The Imperfection of the Market," *The Economic Journal*, March 1933, p. 115. In connection with an increase in demand in the suburbs and the effect on the price charged by suppliers. Mr. Shove asks . . . "why do not the old firms open branches in the suburbs?" If the argument in the text is correct, this is a question which Mrs. Robinson's apparatus cannot answer.
49. The legal concept of "employer and employee" and the economic concept of a firm are not identical, in that the firm may imply control over another person's property as well as over their labour. But the identity of these two concepts is sufficiently close for an examination of the legal concept to be of value in appraising the worth of the economic concept.
50. Batt, *The Law of Master and Servant*, p. 6.
51. *Op. cit.*, p. 7.

CHAPTER 3

The Concept of Monopoly and the Measurement of Monopoly Power*[1]

A. LERNER

I

Monopoly, says the dictionary, is the exclusive right of a person, corporation or state to sell a particular commodity. Economic science, investigating the economic aspects of this legal right, found that they all resolved themselves into the implications of the power of the monopolist – as distinguished from a seller in a competitive market – arbitrarily to decide the price of the commodity, leaving it to the buyers to decide how much they will buy at that price, or, alternatively, to decide the quantity he will sell, by so fixing the price as to induce buyers to purchase just this quantity. Technically this is expressed by saying that the monopolist is confronted with a falling demand curve for his product or that the elasticity of demand for his product is less than infinity, while the seller in a purely[2] competitive market has a horizontal demand curve or the elasticity of demand for his product is equal to infinity.

The monopolist is normally assumed to tend to fix the price at the level at which he makes the greatest profit or "monopoly revenue." This monopoly revenue constitutes a levy upon the consumers that the monopolist is able to appropriate for himself purely in virtue of his restrictive powers *qua* monopolist, and it is the consumers' objection to paying this levy that lies at the base of popular feeling against the monopolist.

The Review of Economic Studies (1934), pp. 157–75.

In addition to this it is claimed that monopoly is harmful in a more objective sense. A levy which involves a mere transference from buyer to monopolist cannot be said to be harmful from a social point of view unless it can be shown that the monopolist is less deserving of the levy than the people who have to pay it; either because he is in general a less deserving kind of person, or because the transference will increase the evils of inequality of incomes. But the levy is not a mere transference. The method of raising it, namely, by increasing the price of the monopolised commodity, causes buyers to divert their expenditure to other, less satisfactory purchases. This constitutes a loss to the consumer which is not balanced by any gain reaped by the monopolist, so that there is a net social loss.

The nature of the loss here loosely expressed seems to have defied attempts *at more exact* exposition, the difficulties encountered on these attempts having even induced some to declare that this commonsense view of a social loss is an illusion, while more careful sceptics prefer to say that nothing "scientific" can be said about it. The account given above clearly will not do as a general and accurate description of the nature of the social loss. Where a consumer spends as much as before on the monopolised commodity when the price is raised, he cannot be said to divert expenditure to other and less satisfactory channels, and where he spends more[3] upon the commodity than at the lower competitive price it might even be argued that there is a net social gain in so far as the consumer is induced to spend more on the commodity which is more urgently needed and less on other commodities! There seems little to choose between this argument and the counter-argument, that as long as the elasticity is greater than zero some consumer (or unit of consumption) is induced to change the direction of his expenditure so that he suffers the uncompensated inconvenience which constitutes the net social loss. Does this mean that if a man's demand is completely inelastic (so that the increased price brings no diminution in the amount of the monopolised commodity consumed and the whole of the levy is sacrificed ultimately in the form of other commodities) the expenditure of the income, as diminished by the amount of the levy, is not interfered with by the existence of the monopoly? – i.e., that if he had paid the levy in cash and prices were not affected he would have reduced his consumption of other commodities in the same way? Or is it more reasonable to suppose that a rise in a particular price will always tend to diminish purchases of the dearer commodity, where a cash levy (prices remaining unchanged) would diminish all expenditures in the same proportion so that if the same amount of the monopolised commodity is bought at the higher price, a cash diminution in income of the size of the levy would have *increased* the demand for that commodity? The problems do not seem to be amenable to treatment on these lines.[4]

The commonsense attitude is, however, not easily balked. Another attempt was made to deal with the problem by Marshall, by means of the apparatus of consumers' surplus. If it is assumed that the marginal utility of money is unchanged, or that the change is so small that it may legitimately be neglected, it can be shown that the money value of the consumers' surplus lost is greater than the monopoly revenue gained, so that we have a theoretical measure of the net social loss due to the monopoly. There are, of course, many important weaknesses in this treatment, and some ways of applying it are completely wrong. The marginal utility of money can be considered unchanged only if we are considering a small change in the price of only one commodity. This makes it impossible to add the consumers' surplus obtained by an individual from different goods. Quite wrong is any attempt to speak of the consumers' surplus of a community and to derive it from the communal demand curve. And there are other traps to be avoided in this connection which are quite well known. But the exclusive preoccupation of teachers of economics with putting their pupils on their guard against these insufficiencies and dangers has tended to make them deny the problem with which the concept of consumers' surplus was intended to deal – the net social loss and its nature. It is not intended here to deny or even to belittle the dangers and confusions attendant on the use of the concept of consumers' surplus, but it does seem that some light can be thrown on the problem by its use.

From the consumers' surplus approach there has emerged a clarification of the rent element in monopoly revenue. It is only in the case of constant or decreasing average cost that the amount of monopoly revenue is necessarily less than the loss of consumers' surplus. The monopoly revenue will be greater if the average cost curve rises steeply enough. This gave the impression that the monopolistic restriction brought about a net social gain so that the competitive output was too great and it would be beneficial to tax industries which were "subject to diminishing returns." In correcting this view it was shown that against the monopoly revenue was to be reckoned not only the loss of consumers' surplus, but also the reduction in rents as compared with those receivable under competition. If the reductions of rent [are] not allowed for, the diminution of costs of the marginal units, as output is restricted, is attributed to all the *infra*-marginal costs where there has been no reduction in social costs, but only a transference of income from the receivers of rent. In the accompanying Figure 3.1 *AR* is the average revenue or demand curve (which, to avoid the quarrels over consumers' surplus, we can consider as the sum of number of identical demand curves of similar individuals), *MR* is the marginal revenue curve, *AC* is average costs, and *MC* is marginal costs. *P'* will be the competitive point where output is *OM'* and price is *M'P'*, and *P*, which is perpendicularly

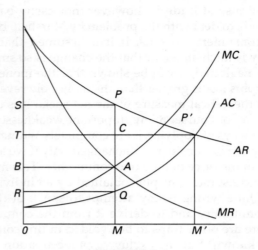

FIGURE 3.1

above A, where MR and MC cut, will be the monopoly point where output is OM and price is MP. Consumers' surplus lost is equal to $SPP'T$, while monopoly revenue is $SPQR$, which may be greater. But against this must be reckoned the loss in rents, $RQP'T$, so that there is a net social loss of PQP'.

One is tempted to divide the monopoly revenue $SPQR$ into two parts, $SPCT$ and $RQCT$, and to say that the former is the monopoly revenue extracted from consumers while the latter is the monopoly revenue extracted from receivers of rent or producers' surplus. It is exactly parallel to the extraction of monopoly revenue from the receivers of consumers' surplus, but is obtained in virtue of the monopolist being confronted with a rising supply curve instead of with a falling demand curve. It is a gain obtained by a "single" buyer instead of a gain obtained by a "single" seller. The appropriate parallel name for it would be *Monopsony Revenue*.[5] This dichotomy of the monopoly revenue is based on a comparison of the monopoly position with the competitive position.[6] PC is the rise in price and QC is the fall in average cost, so that these quantities multiplied by the monopolistic output give the monopoly revenue and the monopsony revenue respectively.

It will, however, not do to compare the monopoly position with the competitive position for the purpose of making the dichotomy, for by this procedure it is made to depend upon the shape of the curves for outputs between the monopolistic output OM and the competitive output OM', which may be a long way from it. It does not seem reasonable that the degree of monopsony or monopoly at output OM should be dependent upon what happens to demand or cost curves in the vicinity of output *OM'*. And apart from this the taking of the competitive output and price as a base from which everything is to be measured leads to more concrete inconsistencies. Thus we may attempt to find the amount of monopoly revenue (in the more exact sense, that is, not including monopsony revenue) by considering what it would be if the average cost were constant at the competitive level so that there was no monopsony. *AC* and *MC* would then coincide with *TP'*, and the monopoly revenue would not be *SPCT* but some other larger amount, for the output could not be *OM* but some other amount. If we reverse this process, assuming that the demand curve and the *MR* curve are horizontal, we again find that the monopsony revenue is not *RQCT* but some other larger amount, and the output is not *OM* but, again, some other amount.[7]

The direct comparison of monopolistic with competitive equilibrium further assumes that cost conditions are the same and that demand conditions are the same. Neither of these is likely, and the combination of both is much less likely.

A more reasonable procedure for the allocation of the gains as between monopoly and monopsony revenue is to take as a basis not the price which would obtain if there were neither monopoly nor monopsony, but instead of that the actual conditions of the monopoly–monopsony equilibrium. With the given demand curve pure[8] monopoly output could only be *OM* if the horizontal *AC* curve were coincident with *AB*, in which case the monopoly revenue would be equal to *SPAB*. With the given *AC* curve the pure monopsony output could only be *OM* if the horizontal demand curve is coincident with *AB*, in which case the monopsony revenue would be equal to *RQAB*, and *RQAB* and *SPAB* do add up to the monopoly–monopsony revenue *SPQR*.

From this it appears that the monopoly revenue per unit of output, *AP*, is the excess of price over marginal cost, so that the mark of the absence of monopoly is the equality of price or *average* receipts to *marginal* cost, and the mark of the absence of monopsony is the equality of *average* cost to *marginal* receipts.[9]

The test more usually accepted is the equality of average costs to price or average receipts. It is this equation which is regularly given as the definition of "competitive" position,[10] and a suggestion like the one here given is likely to meet with a lecture on the impropriety of comparing averages with marginal values. It would seem, however, that the orthodox point of view is not only based upon too great a readiness to consider perfect competition as the ideal type of economic phenomena towards which all things tend, but are deterred more or less only by "frictions" (for in perfect competition all these equations become identical), but is in some measure induced by the habit of using straight lines in diagrams dealing with monopoly, and thus missing the problem. For in this case, *AB* of Figure 3.1 would coincide with *P'T*, and the two dichotomies of the monopoly-cum-monopsony revenue are identical.

The point at issue is not merely a verbal one of definition – a quibble as to what it is better to call the "competitive" position. The importance of the competitive position lies in its implications of being a position which in some way or another is better than other positions. It is the position in which the "Invisible Hand" has exerted its beneficial influences to the utmost. It has become the symbol for the social optimum. Its importance for us here is in giving us a basis against which we can compare the effect of monopoly in order to see the social loss, if any, that the existence of a monopoly brings about. Is the social optimum that position at which prices are equal to average cost, or that at which price equals marginal cost and average cost equals marginal revenue?

The social optimum relative to any distribution of resources (or income) between different individuals (and we cannot here go into the problems connected with optimum distribution) will be reached only if the resources which are to be devoted to satisfying the wants of each individual are so allocated between the different things he wants, that his total satisfaction would not be increased by any transference of resources from the provision of any one of the things he gets to any other thing he wants. This would show itself in the impossibility of any individual being put in a preferred position without putting another individual in a worse position. We may adopt this as our criterion or test of the achievement of the relative optimum. If in any set of circumstances it is possible to move one individual into a preferred position without moving another individual into a worse position (i.e. such that the original position is preferred to it by the individual affected), we may say that the relative optimum is not reached; but if such a movement is impossible, we may say that the relative optimum has been attained. The conditions which must be satisfied if the optimum is attained can be formulated quite simply.

Any change in the position of any individual means a change in the quantity of goods (and services) he consumes. For any such a change to take place it is necessary that there shall be either (a) a *similar* change in the total quantity of goods produced or (b) an *opposite* change in the total quantity of goods consumed by others, or (c) some combination of (a) and (b). In the case of (a), consumption by other people need not be interfered with by the change, the whole change in the consumption by one individual being covered by changes in production. In the case of (b), there need be no change in production, any increase in the consumption of particular goods by one individual being provided by decreases in their consumption by others, and any decreases in the consumption of other goods by one individual being covered by increases in their consumption by others. In case (c) both kinds of compensating movements

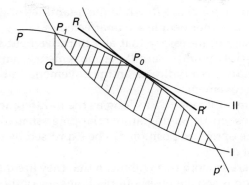

FIGURE 3.2

take place, but these can be separated and dealt with as cases of (a) and (b) so that no special treatment is necessary.

If a change in the consumption of various goods by one individual which improves his position is compensated solely by a movement of type (a), consumption by all other individuals need not be affected. This means that the effect of the movement from the previous position was to make one individual better off without making any other individual worse off. The previous position could not, therefore, have been an optimum position. One condition, then, of the optimum position is that any change in the quantity of goods consumed by any individual which improves his position cannot be compensated by a movement of type (a).

This is illustrated in Figure 3.2.[11] PP' is a section of the displacement cost curve (or productive indifference curve) of the whole community. I and II are consumption indifference curves of one individual. The indifference curves are superimposed upon the displacement cost curve, so that the point on the indifference map which represents the quantities of the commodities X (measured horizontally) and Y (measured vertically), consumed by the individual in the initial position, coincides with the point on the communal displacement cost curve which represents the total amount of the commodities (X and Y) produced in the whole community in the initial position. If P_1 is this position, a movement from P_1 to any point above I represents a movement favourable to one individual. Compensating movements of type (a) from P_1 are, however, limited to points below PP'. The shaded area in the diagram represents positions to which movements from P_1 are favourable to one individual and can be compensated by movements of type (a). Thus a movement from P_1 to P_0 represents a diminution in the production of Y by an amount P_1Q and an increase in the production of X by an amount QP_0,[12] accompanied by a similar change in one individual's consumption which moves him on to the higher indifference curve II; while the quantities of goods remaining to be consumed by other people are unaffected.

It is, of course, not necessary that any improvement should go up to the highest possible point – here P_0. A movement from P_1 to any other point in the shaded area indicates an improvement, but leaves room for still further improvement.

Such a movement is possible as long as the indifference curve cuts the displacement cost curve, giving an overlapping (shaded) area. Our first condition for the optimum position can be expressed by saying that these curves must not cut.

If the curves are smooth this will mean that they are tangential as at P_0, but our condition is satisfied without the tangency of the curves, if either (or both) of the curves changes directions suddenly at the point where the curves meet or that it forms an angle. What is necessary is merely that the curves shall meet at P_0 without cutting. This condition must be fulfilled for every individual in the community.

The movement of one individual to a preferred position may, however, be covered by opposite changes in the consumption of others. This, too, can be examined in the same diagram. Let I and II represent the same indifference curves as before, but let PP' represent now not the displacement cost curve, but the indifference curve of any other individual, turned through 180° around the common point which shows the combinations of goods consumed by the individual. If the indifference curves cut, as they do in our diagram if P_1 is the common point, there is an overlapping area, shaded in the diagram, showing the possibility of improving the position of one without worsening the position of the other. A movement from P_1 to P_0 improves the position of *one* individual and leaves the other at another point on the same indifference curve PP', and, therefore, not worse off. Movements from P_1 to any intermediate point in the shaded area would make both individuals better off. In order to satisfy the condition of the optimum it is therefore again necessary that there should be no gap between the curves, i.e. that they should not cut. If they are smooth, it means that they are tangential, and that the slopes of the indifference curves of both individuals were parallel in the initial position, since the turning of curve through 180° does not change any slopes.

The diagrammatical treatment restricts one to the consideration of only two commodities. This does not matter for the present purpose, since the relationships described have to obtain for every pair of all the commodities in the economy. This is because the failure of the conditions to be satisfied for *any* pair of commodities shows a possibility for improvement which is incompatible with an optimum position.

If both of these conditions are satisfied, as between each individual's indifference curves and the communal displacement costs curve on the one hand, and as between each individual's indifference curves and every other individual's (inverted) indifference curves, on the other hand, it is impossible to improve the position of any individual without worsening the position of some other individual. The optimum position, relative to the distribution of income between individuals, is attained.

Can we make any use of such a complicated set of conditions? If it were necessary to investigate separately the slopes of the indifference curves of all individuals for all pairs of commodities in order to discover whether the conditions are satisfied, it would be most profitable to discontinue this analysis at once. But there is no need for all this. We need merely assume that some of the indifference curves are smooth at the positions representing the amounts consumed by the individuals, and that each individual, in buying goods for his own consumption, considers the price as given. Under these conditions the relative prices of each pair of goods in the market will accurately reflect the slopes of the indifference curves where these are smooth; and for those cases where an indifference curve forms an angle, the ratio between the prices will give a line (RR' in Figure 3.2) of such slope that the indifference curve will lie wholly *above* it, meeting it but not cutting it if it is superimposed on the consumption point P_0. The mere existence of a free market in consumption goods thus satisfies the second of our two conditions.

The first condition is satisfied if the price ratio on the market, represented by the slope of the line RR', is such that the displacement curve lies wholly *below* it, meeting it at the production–consumption point P_0, but not cutting it. If the displacement cost curve is smooth and, therefore, tangential to RR', this will mean that the price ratio is proportional to the marginal displacement costs, which condition is satisfied if *price is equal to marginal cost*.

From this analysis we see that the optimum is reached when the price reflects the alternatives given up at the margin, whether this alternative is considered in physical terms of some other commodity or whether we go direct to the satisfactions that the physical alternatives represent. The loss involved in monopoly can be seen in the divergence between price and this marginal cost. The loss involved in monopsony is of exactly the same nature, and a parallel analysis is rendered unnecessary if we translate the rising supply curve that is seen by the monopsonist into a falling demand curve by considering the purchase of A for B as the sale of B for A. This loss is avoided only if price to the consumer (AR) is equal to marginal cost (MC), and if the wages of labour (AC) are equal to its marginal product ($=MR$). If we prefer we may put the latter statement in the form of demand. The price of leisure demanded by [a] labourer (AR) (which is his wage) must be equal to the marginal cost of his leisure (MC) (which is equal to the marginal product of the labour withdrawn).

II

In considering the degree of monopoly in a particular field one's first inclination seems to be to hark back to the etymological meaning of the word and to see how close the situation is to the conditions which accompany a "single seller." On this line one would say that there is complete monopoly if there is actually only one seller, and that the monopoly element diminishes as the number of sellers increases. One could construct some kind of index of the degree of monopoly, such as the inverse of the number of sellers, which would give values ranging from unity in the case of this kind of "complete" monopoly to zero in the case of an infinite number of sellers.

The most obvious of the many reasons why this will not do is that there may be a very high degree of monopoly (in any sense other than that of the formula for such an index), even where there are many sellers, if one or two sellers control a sufficiently large proportion of the total supply. For this reason one turns instead to discover how great a proportion of the total supply is controlled by one or a few individuals or organisations. The same information may also be sought more indirectly by inquiries into the size of firms.

This procedure, however, is still quite inappropriate for measuring the degree of monopoly if we are interested in its economic and social implications of control over price and social loss as discussed in the first part of this paper. This is seen most clearly when we observe that control by a single firm of 100 per cent of the supply of a commodity for which the demand is infinitely elastic (which will always be the case if there is some equally satisfactory substitute available at a constant price) is absolutely unimportant and has no economic significance, while a "partial" monopoly of a commodity for which the demand is inelastic may be able to raise price by reducing output and is clearly a much more effective case of monopoly.

The statistical method of measuring monopoly, besides missing the main issue in this way, encounters enormous practical difficulties in which investigators can hardly hope to avoid getting entangled. The problems of allowing for changes in taste and technique, in transport and in business organisation, of dealing with firms making many products and of discovering the degree to which different firms compete with one another or mitigate the competition by Gentlemen's Agreements, trade conventions, business alliances, and so on, are just a few worth mentioning, but there is one that interests us particularly here, and that is the relatively simple one of defining the commodity.

A man may have a considerable degree of monopolistic power although he is in control of only a very small part of the supply of a commodity if he is afforded some protection from the competition of the rest of the supply by the cost of transporting other supplies to his market. Under these conditions the price of the commodity will be different in different places. The best way of dealing with this is to declare that objects having the same physical characteristics are not the same goods if they are at different places. Location is an essential and distinguishing characteristic of economic goods, and the only relationship between the prices of similar goods in different places is that which results from the possibilities of transforming the one good into the other by transporting it from the one place to the other.

And location is not the only variant of this kind, but rather the simplest species of a large genus, and is useful for a simplified exposition of the problems involved. Every specialised gradation of every particular quality of every "commodity" may be treated as "distance," and the cost of changing the quality to a particular grade as the cost of "transport." Some of these problems are dealt with by Hotelling in his article, "Stability in Competition," *Economic Journal*, 1929, p. 41, where he gives examples ranging from the sweetness of cider to the service of churches.

To these variants must be added also all fictitious variations, such as are successfully imposed upon the minds of buyers by skilful advertising, as well as the tendencies of customers to buy from one seller rather than from another by sheer force of habit. Here the "distance" is the fictitious difference in quality or the goodwill of the customer, while the "transport costs" are the costs involved in overcoming the "goodwill" whether by reducing price or by counter-advertisement.

This splitting up of the conception of a commodity of course multiplies the number of commodities indefinitely, and seems to create monopolies in the most unexpected places. Carried to its logical extreme, every firm now becomes a monopoly, since it is impossible for more than one unit of product to be in the same place. But even without going to such extremes it becomes impossible to apply the simple measures of monopoly that we are criticising. Further difficulties are yet to arise.

While the idea of considering the same things at different places as different goods seems to have spread considerably, the full revolutionary implications of this step forward in the picturing of the equilibrial forces do not seem to have been quite realised.

In calling the same thing at different places different commodities, we have rejected the criterion of physical similarity as a basis for the recognition or classification of commodities and have put in its place the principle of substitutability at the margin.

If the same thing at a different place is not the same commodity it is only because the difference in its location prevents it from being substituted for, or used in the same way as, the same thing here. But this principle can be applied in the converse form too. With substitutability as the principle it is no longer necessary for different units of the same commodity to have the same physical characteristics as long as they are substitutable at the margin for the purpose that the buyer wants them.

This means that if one pound of coal gives me the same heating power as four pounds of wood, that both of these items cost the same on the market, and I am indifferent as to which I have, then one pound of coal and four pounds of wood represent the same number of units of the same commodity. It means, further, that if I am indifferent as to whether I have one hundredweight of coal every week during the winter, or an overcoat to keep me warm, then a winter's coal and an overcoat are equal quantities of the same commodity. Further still, if I am indifferent as to whether I have a wireless set for £10 or whether I have the satisfaction of saving ten Chinese children from starvation, the wireless set in London is the same quantity of the same commodity as £10 worth of rice in China; while if I get the same satisfaction from a £100 motor-car here and now as I could from a Mediterranean cruise next year, which costs £100 plus the accumulated interest on the money, then the motor-car here and now and the Mediterranean cruise next year are equal quantities of the same commodity. Physical qualities, spatial and temporal position are irrelevant now that we have the ultimate criterion of substitutability at the margin. If any quantity or complex of goods and services can be substituted at the margin for any other quantity of goods and services (and therefore have the same market value), then they are both equal quantities of the same commodity. It would perhaps be best to give terminological recognition to such a break with traditional usage by speaking of "units of accommodation" instead of units of commodities.

If this way of looking at things seems paradoxical, it is only because we have not yet completely freed ourselves from the crudely materialistic conception of goods with which the Physiocrats and Adam Smith were the first to wrestle. The inadequacy of a purely physical criterion of commodities is obvious when we consider the enormous physical difference which we neglect if they do not affect the qualities in which we are interested (that is which affect our satisfaction), of which we are often completely unconscious, but which are of so much importance to Mr. Sherlock Holmes. Physically there are no two similar articles even apart from location. If two objects are considered to be items of the same good, it is only because they are "good for" the same purpose – always, ultimately, the satisfaction of a want. It is futile to say that the motor-car and the Mediterranean cruise satisfy different wants until we are able to define "similar" wants otherwise than as wants that are satisfied by physically similar objects. There is no *qualitative* criterion of wants. Wants can only be considered as similar when the person who feels them displays equal concern for their satisfaction and thus shows them to be equal in *quantity*. To follow any other course is to sacrifice the logic of the science to the irrelevant convenience of the shopkeeper.

It may be objected that this concept of commodity is so abstract and elusive as to be unusable. That is perfectly correct. But therein lies a great part of its advantages. It cannot be used like the more material conception to drown the theory in irrelevant statistics. It puts an end to attempts, here, to find a measure of monopoly in terms of the proportion of the supply of a commodity under single control and clears the way to a better understanding.

Another line of approach that suggests itself is to compare the amount of monopoly revenue with the total receipts, and to take this ratio as a measure of the degree of monopoly power. Allowance is thus made for the size of the industry or the firm. We will obtain values ranging from 0 in the case of perfect competition to 1 where the whole of receipts is monopoly revenue, and at first glance all seems well.

This procedure will, however, not do, for what we want in the measure of monopoly is not the amount of tribute individuals can obtain for themselves from the rest of the community, by being in an advantageous monopolistic position, but the divergence of the system from the social optimum that is reached in perfect competition. From this point of view the monopolist gains are not to be distinguished from rents of scarce property that he owns, or any other source of individual income. The independence of the monopolist gain from the social loss can perhaps most clearly be brought out by a consideration of how far they can vary independently. The limiting case is seen where the demand curve for the product of a monopolist coincides over considerable range with his average cost curve. Here the monopoly revenue is zero wherever the monopolist produces within this range, yet he has control over price, and the social loss will be different according to what output the monopolist decides to produce. It clearly will not do to say that the degree of monopoly power in such a case is zero.

If the average cost curve is horizontal such a divergence cannot occur. The firm can only change output while keeping monopoly revenue zero if the demand curve is also horizontal, and that means perfect competition in either case and no social loss. But in such a case we are comparing not merely monopoly revenue with total receipts, which is the same as the ratio between average receipts minus costs and average receipts (and which is also seen in the ratio between average costs and average receipts), but also *marginal costs* with *average receipts,* and it is in divergence between these, as we have seen above, that the essence of monopoly is to be found.

In such cases (where the cost curve is horizontal) the ratio of monopoly revenue to total receipts coincides exactly with the ratio of the divergence of price from marginal cost to price, and it is this latter formula that I wish to put forward as the measure of monopoly power. If P = price and C = marginal cost, then the index of the degree of monopoly power is

$$\frac{P-C}{P}.$$

It will be observed that this formula looks like the inverse of the formula for the elasticity of demand. It differs from it only in that the item marginal cost replaces the item marginal receipts. In equilibrium as normally conceived marginal costs coincide with marginal receipts so that our formula becomes identical with the inverse of the elasticity of demand. It will be best to consider this as a special case.

In this special case we can find the degree of monopoly power via the elasticity of demand. The determination of this elasticity of demand is not to be confused with that of Pigou and Schultz in finding the elasticity of demand (as part of the demand function) for a materially (physically) defined commodity on a market. What we want here is the elasticity of demand for the product of a particular firm. This is much easier to obtain, for it is only when he knows the shape of the demand curve for his product that any entrepreneur can obtain his maximum profit; and he is, therefore, always appplying himself energetically to obtaining as accurate an estimate as possible of this elasticity. This does not mean that the entrepreneur will be able to fill in the elasticity of demand on a questionnaire form. He will rarely know what the term means. But his unfamiliarity with the technical jargon of economists must not be held to show an ignorance of so primary a principle for intelligent business management as the urgency of knowing the effect of price changes on sales. His behaviour in running the business for maximum profit will enable any student to deduce the (estimated) elasticity of demand from the firm's cost curve and the selling price. From the average cost curve the marginal cost curve can be derived. The marginal cost is equal to the marginal receipt, output being adjusted so as to make them equal if profit is maximised. The elasticity of demand is equal to the price divided by the difference between price and marginal cost – it is the inverse of our formula for the measurement of the degree of monopoly power.

In finding the degree of monopoly in this special case "via the elasticity of demand" we found that the easiest way of finding the elasticity of demand was via the degree of monopoly. We may, therefore, leave out the elasticity of demand altogether and just keep to our formula all the time. In the special case both come to the same thing, but we must use the new formula and not the inverse of the elasticity of demand whenever we consider cases where the maximum monopoly revenue is not obtained in practice.

This may be accidental, as when the monopolist does not know the shape of his demand curve and his estimate of the elasticity of demand at the actual output is erroneous; or it may be intentional. The price and output may intentionally be fixed in a manner which does not give the maximum monopoly revenue:

(a) when the monopolist is not working on purely business principles, but for social, philanthropic or conventional reasons sells *below* this price commodities which it is considered socially desirable to cheapen – as when a public authority supplies cheap transport facilities – or sells *above* this price commodities which are considered socially harmful – as may be done by a State liquor monopoly;

(b) when the monopolist is working on purely business principles, but keeps the price and his profits lower than they might be so as to avoid political opposition or the entry of new competitors. The second could, perhaps, better be considered as a case where the demand is more elastic in the long period, taking into account the contingent competition, than in the short period, and where the monopolist takes a long period view.

In all such cases our formula is not equal to the inverse of the elasticity of demand; but wherever there appears a divergence between the two it is our formula and not the inverse of the elasticity of demand which gives the measure of what we want. In the first cases – where the monopolist's estimate of the elasticity of demand is erroneous – the consumers will in every way be in exactly the same position as if the elasticity were what the monopolist thinks it is. If he over-estimates the elasticity of demand he will sell a larger amount at a lower price. If he thinks the elasticity is infinite – i.e. that if he produced less he would not be able to get a better price – he will make price equal to marginal cost, and the effect on consumers will be the same as if there were perfect competition.[13] The unused monopoly power will be there, but being unknown and unused it is, economically, as if it were not there. For practical purposes we must read monopoly power not as *potential* monopoly, but as monopoly *in force*.

If the monopolist underestimates the elasticity of demand he will sell a smaller quantity and at a higher price than at the point of maximum monopoly revenue. The only influence between this and the previous case is that the monopolist's error brings a loss to consumers instead of a gain. The monopolist himself, of course, loses by the error in either case. The consumer here has to pay a higher price or else do without. It is again just as if the elasticity of demand were what the monopolist thinks it is. This may sound as if the monopoly *in force* is here greater than the *potential* monopoly power, but the inverse of the elasticity of demand at the maximum revenue point does not really give the potential monopoly power. It gives just that degree of monopoly power which it is necessary to put into force in order to obtain the maximum revenue and which is in force where the maximum revenue is being obtained. The monopolist always has power in excess of this; but as the employment of it can only bring him a loss, he normally does not use it intentionally. If he chooses to use it he can, of course, for the exercise of this power consists of diminishing the amount he produces. Potential monopoly power is only used to its maximum when the monopolist stops all production. What our formula gives is the degree of monopoly power in force.

The same arguments apply to cases where the maximum monopoly revenue is not obtained for social, philanthropic or conventional reasons or for the purpose of avoiding political opposition or contingent competition. In the last case, our procedure saves us all further investigation into the complications involved in considering the length of the period upon which the demand curve is based. The appropriate costs to be reckoned are those of the present, or rather of the immediate future, so as to enable us to measure temporary monopolies. The degree of monopoly over a long period is perhaps best expressed in an average of the short-period monopolies over the period.

The primary unit to which our measure of monopoly applies is the firm in the very shortest period. In order to get a measure of monopoly over an industry we have to follow the same procedure and find an average of monopoly of the separate firms included in the industry. The "industry" is to be considered as a group of firms, chosen for the purpose of the special investigation. It is quite unnecessary, for this purpose, to say anything at all about the "commodity" which the "industry" produces, nor is there any need to be able to draw demand or supply curves for the industry. All the difficulties of definition of "commodity" or "industry" are completely avoided.

More strictly a simple average of the degrees of monopoly in firms may be used to indicate the degree of monopoly in an industry only in the very limited sense of the degree of monopoly *at that stage*. It is not a measure of the degree to which the application of the resources of the community to the production of the products of the "industry" diverges from the social optimum. That depends upon two other sets of conditions in addition to this *local* element of monopoly.

The first of these is the degree of monopoly in the firms (or "industries") producing the raw materials for all the previous stages in the production of the products. The restriction of production in any stage has its effects in all the succeeding stages. The final degree of reduction of product will depend upon the degree of monopoly in all the preceding stages. These have to be aggregated so as to give the tendency to divergence from the social optimum in the weak series of the production stages of the product; this phenomenon may be called the transitiveness of monopoly.

Theoretically, this can be done quite simply. What we want is the divergence between the price of the product and its marginal *social* cost. If in all the previous stages price is equal to marginal cost, the marginal cost to the firm is also the marginal social cost. If in any stage there is a divergence, price being above marginal cost, that divergence is a gap in the social cost. The social cost can then be calculated by multiplying the price by a factor for each stage in production, each factor being the ratio of the marginal cost to the price in the corresponding stage. Thus, if there are five stages and in each stage the degree of monopoly is $\frac{1}{5}$, marginal cost over price in each stage is $\frac{4}{5}$, the social cost is $(\frac{4}{5})^5$, of the price of the final product, and by our formula the "social" degree of monopoly is $1 - (\frac{4}{5})^5$.

Practical difficulties that arise in attempts to measure the "social" degree of monopoly, or different products may be attacked by any of the tricks of the trade of mathematical statistics. It may be necessary to assume average degrees of monopoly in separate stages and to calculate "social" degree of monopoly by the number of stages, and so on; but it is not intended here to discuss anything but the simplest theoretical implications.

The second set of complicating considerations arise when we ask the even more ambitious question: What is the (social) degree of monopoly in the society as a whole? From this general point of view the conditions for that optimum distribution of resources between different commodities that we designate the absence of monopoly are satisfied if prices are all *proportional* to social marginal cost. If the "social" degree of monopoly is the same for *all* final products (including leisure) there is no monopolistic alteration from the optimum at all. The absolute height of "social" degrees of monopoly becomes completely unimportant.

This is because if the "social" degree of monopoly is the same for all products it *must* be equal to zero in real terms. For from the social point of view the marginal cost of any product is always some other product. If the "social" degree of monopoly for product A is positive, this means that the price of A is greater than the price of some other product B which is the alternative foregone. The price of B cannot then be greater than the price of A. If both degrees of monopoly are equal they must both be zero.

What is important is the deviations between the degrees of monopoly; and it is this which must be measured in order to answer our question. A suitable measure for this is the standard deviation of the "social" degrees of monopoly of all final products in the society.

Another complication arises in the growingly important cases where it is found to be profitable to extend or maintain the amount sold, not by reducing price but by expenditure on advertising, salesmanship, gifts, coupons and beautiful wrapping – all of which can be subsumed under the headings of "marketing costs." In such cases what becomes of the elasticity of demand?

In the recent cost controversy, "marketing costs" were eagerly seized upon in attempts at a conciliation between decreasing costs and competitive equilibrium.[14] Such arguments may be described with some justification as contriving to exhibit decreasing costs at peace with competitive equilibrium by the device of leaving out of account the marketing element in the costs which is increasing so rapidly that *total costs* are not decreasing at all; the contradiction being hidden by a separation of "productive" from "marketing" costs.

This solution of the problem cannot, however, be dismissed as mere word-jugglery. It does show the actual working of the forces involved and it is only the terminology that is unfortunate. What we have here is not perfect competition but *monopolistic* or *imperfect* competition. Chamberlin and Robinson have developed a more satisfactory line of attack on these problems, but how are we to find the falling demand curve which will entitle us to put these cases into this category and enable us to deal with them in the same way?

In order to obtain this it is essential to separate productive from marketing costs. The marketing costs involved in selling a given quantity of product must be subtracted from the gross receipts, just as if they were all direct or indirect reductions in price, leaving a definite total and average net receipts. For each quantity produced different prices may be charged and different marketing costs incurred. For each output some combination of prices charged and marketing costs incurred will leave a maximum average (and total) residue after subtracting the average (or total) marketing costs, and this maximum is the relevant Average Net Receipts for that output. The locus of such points will be the Average Net Receipts curve for the firm, and this is the "demand curve" which we need. This average net receipts curve and the corresponding marginal net receipts curve have to be used in conjunction with the 'productive' cost curves which we may call "net" cost curves.

If the average net receipts curve is negatively inclined, one proceeds just as in the simple analysis of imperfect competition where there are no selling costs. The firm equates its marginal net cost to its marginal net receipts, and the degree of monopoly is equal to average net receipts over average net receipts minus marginal net costs, and the divergence of the position from the social optimum is illustrated by the fact that production is not carried on at the minimum average cost, but the firm produces less than this optimum output, stopping at a point where the average net cost curve is tangential to the average net receipts curve. The social loss, if any, due to the expenditure of resources on advertising is *not* taken into account in the measurement of monopoly. The measure will be the same whether the marketing costs are large or small, and whether they are given to the consumer in forms corresponding to cash, or whether they have important influences on his tastes for good or for bad. The social effects of different kinds of advertising constitute a quite separate problem.

If the average net receipts curve is horizontal where the marginal net costs curve cuts it, there is no monopoly. The existence of marketing costs is quite another matter.

But there is no reason why the average net receipts curve should not slope upwards! It may well be that a larger quantity can be sold at a higher price at the same or a smaller *average* cost of marketing, and there is no ground for considering such a combination of circumstances as in any way exceptional. We must apply the same analysis here and not be deterred if the results at first appear a little strange.

If the firm with a rising average net revenue curve has a constant cost curve, or can acquire more of the product from other firms without affecting its marketing possibilities, we have another form of the paradox of the incompatibility of equilibrium, with a horizontal demand curve and a falling average cost curve below it. The marginal revenue and the marginal cost curves cannot meet until the conditions are changed. Either the receipts curves must begin to fall or the cost curves must rise.

The interesting case – the one which can remain in equilibrium in these conditions – is the case where the average costs of the firm rise after a time as output increases, and where it cannot obtain more from other firms at the same price, either because the other firms' costs rise or because to do this would interfere with the reputation of the firm and upset its marketing possibilities.

This is shown in Figure 3.3, where the firm is in equilibrium producing an output *OM*.

Average net receipts (*ANR*) are equal to average net costs (*ANC*), and marginal net receipts (*MNR*) are equal to marginal net costs (*MNC*). The degree of monopoly is here *negative* since marginal cost is greater than average receipts. This may appear surprising, but it merely means that the divergence from the social optimum is in the direction opposite to that usually brought about by monopolies. Instead of the firm producing *less* than it should, it is producing *more*; the same kind of social harm is done, and it is reflected in the same way by the excess of the average cost over the minimum.

In finding an average degree of monopoly in an "industry," positive and negative monopolies may cancel out in whole or in part. Does this harm our apparatus?

I do not think it does this at all. It rather brings out the true nature of our measure as an index of *divergence* from an optimum. In any group of firms taken together to make an "industry," divergences may, and should, be expected to some extent to cancel out. For we are now considering the application of resources to this "industry" as against the rest of the economy. If of two firms within the "industry," one is producing too much and the other too little from the point of view of the economy as a whole; the industry may not be producing either too much or too little. The maladjustment becomes a local affair which we must neglect in this larger consideration.

When our "industry" becomes the whole society, there cannot be too much or too little resources used, and as we have seen above, all the individual positive and negative monopolies must cancel out. This does

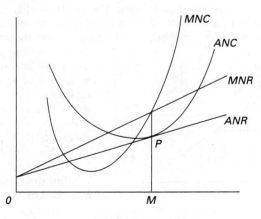

FIGURE 3.3

not mean that society as a whole must always be in an optimum position, nor does it take any meaning away from the concept. It only means that the larger the fraction of the whole society one wishes to examine, the less legitimate is it to use particular analysis. In applying the particular mechanism to the whole economy we get the appropriate *reductio ad absurdum*. What is relevant for general analysis is not the *sum* of individual degrees of monopoly but their *deviations*. The standard deviations as suggested above may perhaps be used one day to give an estimate of the divergence of society from the social optimum of production relative to a given distribution of income.

Notes

1. The great advances made in the subject of this article since the major part of it was written – particularly in the work of Mr. Chamberlin and Mrs. Robinson – have rendered many parts of it out of date. In preparing it for publication, while cutting out some of these parts, I have been so much under the influence of this recent work that I cannot say how much of what is here published is really my own. – A. P. LERNER.
2. "Pure" competition is different from "perfect" competition. The former implies perfection of competition only in respect of the complete absence of monopoly and abstracts from other aspects of perfection in competition. This useful distinction is suggested by Chamberlin. See his *Theory of Monopolistic Competition* , p. 6.
3. Where as much or more is spent on a commodity when the price is raised the elasticity of demand is equal to or less than unity. This may appear incompatible with the condition of monopolistic equilibrium that elasticity of demand shall be greater than unity (as long as marginal cost is positive). There is, however, no incompatibility, for the two elasticities of demand are different things. The elasticity that has to be greater than unity for monopolistic equilibrium is the elasticity at the *point* on the demand curve corresponding to the position of monopolistic equilibrium. The elasticity that is equal to or less than unity when the amount spent on the commodity remains unchanged or increases as the price is raised, is the elasticity over the *arc* of the demand curve from the point of competitive equilibrium to the point of monopolistic equilibrium. The arc elasticity in this sense will normally be less than the point elasticity, as will appear from the diagram. If tT is the demand curve (here drawn a straight line), P' the point of competitive equilibrium, and P the point of monopolistic equilibrium, then the

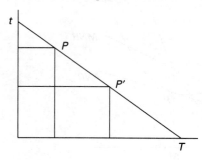

point elasticity at the monopoly equilibrium will be $\dfrac{PT}{Pt}$ while the *arc* elasticity will be $\dfrac{P'T}{Pt}$ which is smaller. The arc elasticity must be smaller unless the demand curve is so concave (upwards) that it shows a constant or increasing point elasticity as price is lowered. The point elasticity at the competitive position will, of course be $\dfrac{P'T}{P't}$. For the explanation of this definition of "arc elasticity," see my note on "The Diagrammatical Representation of Elasticity of Demand," in No. 1 of the *Review*.

4. In the last few months Dr. J. R. Hicks and Mr. R. G. D. Allen have been making investigations on these lines and have demonstrated by means of the indifference curve apparatus that, with continuous indifference curves, an absolutely inelastic demand curve must be accompanied by a negatively sloping expenditure curve. This means that a change in income (prices remain unchanged) would bring about a change *in inverse direction* of the amount of the commodity bought. They have not been interested, however, in the problems dealt with in this article.

5. Joan Robinson, in *The Economics of Imperfect Competition*, introduces the word Monopsony, but does not speak of Monopsony Revenue.

6. By monopoly position is meant a position in which the demand curve does not appear horizontal to all the firms in the industry. The simplest case of this is when there is only one firm which coincides with the whole industry, and that is what is shown in Fig. 3.1 at the monopoly position P. Monopoly is essentially a property of *firms* and by a monopolistic industry is meant nothing more than an industry in which *firms* have downward-sloping demand curves. And, of course, only a firm is interested in maximizing monopoly revenue. If the demand curve for the whole industry is horizontal, the industry is in a competitive condition, but that is only because in this case every firm in the industry must also have a horizontal demand curve – even if there is only one firm.

7. In Fig. 3.1, where both AR and AC are concave upwards, the output under monopoly without monopsony would be less than OM, and the output under monopsony without monopoly would be greater than OM. The outputs are given by the abscissae of the points where TP' is cut by MR and MC respectively. If AR and AC are convex, the outputs would move in the opposite direction. If they are straight lines, or if the convexity of one is just offset by the concavity of the other, the output will be the same as when the monopoly and monopsony are found in combination. If the elimination of monopsony changes the output in one direction, the elimination of monopoly would change output in the other direction, and *vice versa*.

8. By *pure monopoly* is meant a case where one is confronted with a falling demand curve for the commodity one sells, but with a horizontal supply curve for the factors one has to buy for the production of the commodity; so that one sells as a monopolist but buys in a perfect market. Similarly, *pure monopsony* stands for perfect competition in the market where one sells, but

monopsony stands for perfect competition in the market where one sells, but monopsony in the market where one buys – being confronted with a horizontal demand curve but a rising supply curve. *Pure monopoly* is monopoly free from all elements of monopsony. *Pure monopsony* is monopsony free from all elements of monopoly. *Pure competition* stands for freedom from all elements of both monopoly and monopsony. The *purity* of monopoly or of monopsony has nothing to do with the *degree* of monopoly or monopsony.

9. *Marginal* cost and *marginal* receipts are, of course, always equal to each other in any equilibrium, whether monopolistic or monopsonistic, or both or neither. It is, therefore, possible to express the same relationships in terms of the equality of price or average receipts to marginal receipts and the equality of average costs to marginal costs. But this procedure rules out conditions of disequilibrium together with monopoly or monopsony, so that to affirm this would be merely to say in other words that the demand or supply curve is horizontal, so that by definition there is no monopoly or monopsony. The relationships given in the text are not the merely mathematical relationships between an average and its corresponding marginal curve, but between real conditions of costs on the one hand and of receipts on the other. It will be seen below that these relationships will not always coincide with the tautologous alternatives suggested in this footnote.

10. Even Mrs. Robinson defines "competitive output" and "competitive price" as that output or price at which $AC = AR$ or price (*op. cit.*, p. 160), although she demonstrates most clearly in other parts of the book how this condition ($AC = AR$) is also reached in monopolistic or imperfectly competitive equilibrium.

11. I am indebted to Mr. V. Edelberg for the suggestion of the application of the indifference curve apparatus to the problem in this manner.

12. It is not necessary that all or any of the identical units of factors set free from the production of Y should used in the production of X. They, or a part of them, may go to the production of a third commodity Z, as substitutes for other factors which are released to produce the additional X; and there may be any number of such steps. This, of course, does not mean that every commodity is a *direct* displacement cost for every other commodity at the margin (in the sense that factors can move directly from one to the other without economic loss), as would be the case if each factor had the same marginal productivity in all uses – universal substitutability of factors at the margin. It only means that there is some path, however indirect, whereby a diminution in the production of one commodity permits an increase in the production of any other commodity, leaving the quantity of the rest of the commodities unaffected. That is what is meant by drawing a displacement cost curve for any two commodities.

13. Mrs. Robinson has pointed out to me that the delusion that elasticity is infinite would persist only if MC happened to equal price already. This is the easiest case for the correction of a mistaken estimate in the process of adjustment to it. The same possibility exists with any estimated elasticity of demand as long as the marginal cost and the estimated marginal receipts do not coincide and so preclude any adjustments.

CHAPTER 4

Monopoly and Resource Allocation*[1]

A. C. HARBERGER

One of the first things we learn when we begin to study price theory is that the main effects of monopoly are to misallocate resources, to reduce aggregate welfare, and to redistribute income in favor of monopolists. In the light of this fact, it is a little curious that our empirical efforts at studying monopoly have so largely concentrated on other things. We have studied particular industries and have come up with a formidable list of monopolistic practices: identical pricing, price leadership, market sharing, patent suppression, basing points, and so on. And we have also studied the whole economy, using the concentration of production in the hands of small number of firms as the measure of monopoly. On this basis we obtained the impression that some 20 or 30 per cent of our economy is effectively monopolized.

In this paper I propose to look at the American economy, and in particular at American manufacturing industry, and try to get some quantitative notion of the allocative and welfare effects of monopoly. It should be clear from the outset that this is not the kind of job one can do with great precision. The best we can hope for is to get a feeling for the general orders of magnitude that are involved.

I take it as an operating hypothesis that, in the long run, resources can be allocated among our manufacturing industries in such a way as to yield roughly constant returns. That is, long-run average costs are close to constant in the relevant range, for both the firm and the industry. This hypothesis gives us the wedge we need to get something from the data. For as is well known, the malallocative effects of monopoly stem from the difference between marginal cost and price, and marginal

---

American Economic Review (1954), pp. 77–87.

Monopoly and Resource Allocation

costs are at first glance terribly difficult to pin down empirically for a wide range of firms and industries. But once we are ready to proceed on the basis of constant average costs, we can utilize the fact that under such circumstances marginal and average costs are the same, and we can easily get some ideas of average costs.

But that does not solve all the problems, for cost and profit to the economist are not the same things as cost and profit to the accountant, and the accountants make our data. To move into this question, I should like to conjure up an idealized picture of an economy in equilibrium. In this picture all firms are operating on their long-run cost curves, the cost curves are so defined as to yield each firm an equal return on its invested capital, and markets are cleared. I think it is fair to say that this is a picture of optimal resource allocation. Now, we never see this idyllic picture in the real world, but if long-run costs are in fact close to constant and markets are cleared, we can pick out the places where resources are misallocated by looking at the rates of return on capital. Those industries which are returning higher than average rates have too few resources; and those yielding lower than average rates have too many resources. To get an idea of how big a shift of resources it would take to equalize profit rates in all industries, we have to know something about the elasticities of demand for the goods in question. In Figure 4.1, I illustrate a hypothetical case. The industry in question is earning 20 per cent on a capital of 10 million dollars, while the average return to capital is only 10 per cent. We therefore build a 10 per cent return into the cost curve, which leaves the industry with 1 million in excess profits. If the elasticity of demand for the industry's product is unity, it will take a shift of 1 million in resources in order to expand supply enough to wipe out the excess profits.

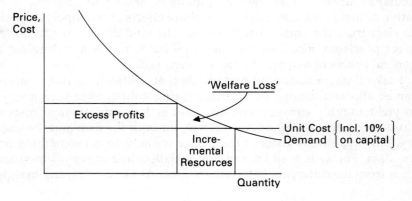

FIGURE 4.1

The above argument gives a general picture of what I have done empirically. The first empirical job was to find a period which met two conditions. First, it had to be reasonably close to a long-run equilibrium period; that is, no violent shifts in demand or economic structure were to be in process. And second, it had to be a period for which accounting values of capital could be supposed to be pretty close to actual values. In particular, because of the disastrous effect of inflation and deflation on book values of capital, it had to be a period of fairly stable prices, which in turn had been preceded by a period of stable prices. It seemed to me that the late twenties came as close as one could hope to meeting both these requirements.

The late twenties had an additional advantage for me – because my choice of this period enabled me to use Professor Ralph C. Epstein's excellent study, *Industrial Profits in the United States* (National Bureau of Economic Research, 1934), as a source of data. Professor Epstein there gives, for the years 1924–28, the rates of total profit to total capital for seventy-three manufacturing industries, with total capital defined as book capital plus bonded indebtedness and total profit defined as book profit plus interest on the indebtedness. To get rid of factors producing short-period variations in these rates of return, I average the rates, for each industry, for the five-year period. The results are given in column 1 of Table 4.1. The differences among these profit rates, as between industries, give a broad indication of the extent of resource malallocation in American manufacturing in the late twenties.

Column 2 presents the amount by which the profits in each industry diverged from what that industry would have obtained if it had gotten the average rate of profit for all manufacturing industry. In column 3, these excesses and shortages of profit are expressed as a per cent of sales in the industry. By analogy with Figure 4.1, you can see that this column really tells by what percentage prices in each industry were "too high" or "too low" when compared with those that would generate an optimal resource allocation.

Now suppose we ask how much reallocation of resources it would take to eliminate the observed divergences in profit rates. This depends, as you can see in Figure 4.1, on the demand elasticities confronting the industries in question. How high are these elasticities? It seems to me that one need only look at the list of industries in Table 4.1 in order to get the feeling that the elasticities in question are probably quite low. The presumption of low elasticity is further strengthened by the fact that what we envisage is not the substitution of one industry's product against all other products, but rather the substitution of one great aggregate of products (those yielding high rates of return) for another aggregate (those yielding low rates of return). In the light of these

TABLE 4.1

Industry	(1) Rate of profit on capital (1924–28)	(2) Amount by which profits diverged from 'average' (Millions)	(3) Column (2) as per cent of sales	(4) Welfare cost of divergence in column (2) (Millions)
Bakery products	17.5%	$17	5.3%	$.452
Flour	11.9	1	0.4	.002
Confectionery	17.0	7	6.1	.215
Package foods	17.9	7	3.3	.116
Dairying	11.8	3	0.7	.010
Canned goods	12.4	1	0.6	.003
Meat packing	4.4	−69	−1.7	.596
Beverages	5.8	−2	−4.0	.080
Tobacco	14.1	27	0.3	.373
Miscellaneous foods	8.1	−13	−2.4	.164
Cotton spinning	10.0	−0	0	0
Cotton converting	8.0	−1	−0.6	.008
Cotton weaving	4.7	−15	−5.5	.415
Weaving woolens	2.6	−16	−9.5	.762
Silk weaving	7.9	−3	−2.3	.035
Carpets	9.8	−1	−1.3	.006
Men's clothing	11.4	1	0.5	.002
Knit goods	12.9	3	1.9	.028
Miscellaneous clothing	13.1	1	1.1	.006
Miscellaneous textiles	9.2	−2	−0.9	.008
Boots and shoes	15.8	9	3.8	.172
Miscellaneous leather products	7.7	−3	−2.1	.032
Rubber	7.6	−23	−2.5	.283
Lumber manufacturing	7.8	−6	−3.9	.118
Planing mills	13.1	1	3.2	.016
Millwork	7.3	−1	−2.9	.014
Furniture	13.4	2	2.2	.022
Miscellaneous lumber	12.9	4	1.7	.034
Blank paper	6.6	−17	−6.2	.524
Cardboard boxes	13.6	2	3.1	.031
Stationery	7.5	−2	−3.0	.030
Miscellaneous paper	9.3	−1	−1.1	.005
Newspapers	20.1	37	8.5	1.570
Books and music	14.6	2	4.3	.042

TABLE 4.1—continued

Industry	(1) Rate of profit on capital (1924–28)	(2) Amount by which profits diverged from 'average' ($ Millions)	(3) Column (2) as per cent of sales	(4) Welfare cost of divergence in column (2) ($ Millions)
Miscellaneous printing and publishing	18.6	1	5.6	.028
Crude chemicals	10.2	–0	0	0
Paints	14.6	5	3.3	.082
Petroleum refining	8.4	–114	–3.6	2.032
Proprietary preparations	20.9	25	11.7	1.460
Toilet preparations	30.4	3	15.0	.225
Cleaning preparations	20.8	15	5.5	.413
Miscellaneous chemicals	15.6	45	8.8	.197
Ceramics	10.8	1	1.0	.005
Glass	13.5	4	2.6	.052
Portland cement	14.3	10	8.4	.420
Miscellaneous clay and stone	17.6	14	8.0	.560
Castings and forgings	5.6	–234	–7.7	8.994
Sheet metal	10.5	0	0	0
Wire and nails	11.6	1	1.2	.006
Heating machinery	13.3	3	1.6	.024
Electrical machinery	15.7	48	5.3	1.281
Textile machinery	13.6	3	6.1	.092
Printing machinery	9.7	–0	0	0
Road machinery	17.3	10	6.8	.374
Engines	13.7	2	5.9	.059
Mining machinery	11.0	1	0.7	.004
Factory machinery	11.7	33	3.0	.045
Office machinery	16.1	7	5.6	.194
Railway equipment	6.0	–24	–9.6	1.148
Motor vehicles	18.5	161	4.4	3.878
Firearms	12.9	1	2.0	.010
Hardware	12.8	8	2.3	.092
Tools	11.6	1	1.1	.006
Bolts and nuts	15.4	1	3.1	.016
Miscellaneous machinery	12.6	3	2.2	.032
Nonferrous metals	11.9	15	1.4	.106

TABLE 4.1—continued

Industry	(1) Rate of profit on capital (1924–28)	(2) Amount by which profits diverged from 'average' ($ Millions)	(3) Column (2) as per cent of sales	(4) Welfare cost of divergence in column (2) ($ Millions)
Jewelry	10.6	0	0	0
Miscellaneous metals	12.5	14	2.0	0.140
Scientific instruments	21.2	20	11.6	1.163
Toys	15.0	1	3.2	0.016
Pianos	9.9	–0	0	0
Miscellaneous special manufacturing	12.0	4	1.4	0.027
Job printing	13.8	4	2.2	0.044

Col. (1) – from Ralph C. Epstein, *Industrial Profits in the United States* (N.B.E.R., 1934), Tables 43D through 53D. Entries in column (1) are the arithmetic means of the annual entries in the source tables.
Col. (2) – divergences in the profit rates given in column (1) from their mean (10.4) are here applied to the 1928 volume of capital in each industry. Total capital is the sum of book capital (Epstein, Appendix Table 6C) plus bonded debt (Epstein, Appendix Table 6D).
Col. (3) – 1928 figures were used for sales (Epstein, Appendix Table 6A).
Col. (4) – measures the amount by which consumer "welfare" fell short of the level it would have attained if resources had been so allocated as to give each industry an equal return on capital. It assumes that the elasticity of demand for the products of each industry is unity and approximates the area designated as "welfare loss" in Figure. 4.1.

considerations, I think an elasticity of unity is about as high as one can reasonably allow for, though a somewhat higher elasticity would not seriously affect the general tenor of my results.

Returning again to Figure 4.1, we can see that once the assumption of unit elasticity is made the amount of excess profit measures the amount of resources that must be called into an industry in order to bring its profit rate into line. When I say resources here I mean the services of labour and capital plus the materials bought by the industry from other industries. In many ways it seems preferable to define resources as simply the services of labor and capital. This could be done by applying to the value added in the industry the percentage of excess profits to sales. The trouble here is that adding to the output of industry X calls resources not only into that industry but also into the industries that supply it. And by the time we take all the increments in value added of all these supplying industries that would be generated by the initial increase in output of industry X, we come pretty close to the incremental value of sales in industry X. Of course, the movement to an optimal resource allocation entails some industries expanding their output, like X, and others, say Y, contracting their output. If we really traced through the increments to value added which are required in their supplying industries, say Z, we would often find that there was some cancellation of the required changes in the output of Z. Hence by using sales rather than value added as our measure of resource transfer, we rather overstate the necessary movement.

Keeping this in mind, let us return to the data. If we add up all the pluses and all the minuses in column 2, we find that to obtain equilibrium we would have to transfer about 550 million dollars in resources from low-profit to high-profit industries. But this is not the end. Those of you who are familiar with Epstein's study are aware that it is based on a sample of 2,046 corporations, which account for some 45 per cent of the sales and capital in manufacturing industry. Pending a discussion of possible biases in the sample a little later, we can proceed to blow up our 550 million figure to cover total manufacturing. The result is 1.2 billion. Hence we tentatively conclude that the misallocations of resources which existed in United States manufacturing in the period 1924–28 could have been eliminated by a net transfer of roughly 4 per cent of the resources in manufacturing industry, or $1\frac{1}{2}$ per cent of the total resources of the economy.

Now let us suppose that somehow we effected these desired resource transfers. By how much would people be better off? This general question was answered in 1938 for an analogous problem by Harold Hotelling.[2] His general formula would be strictly applicable here if all our industries were producing products for direct consumption. The question thus arises, how to treat industries producing intermediate products. If we neglect them altogether, we would be overlooking the fact that their resource shifts and price changes do ultimately change the prices and amounts of consumer goods. If, on the other hand, we pretend that these intermediate industries face the consumer directly and thus directly affect consumer welfare, we neglect the fact that some of the resource shifts in the intermediate sector will have opposing influences on the prices and quantities of consumer goods. Obviously, this second possibility is the safer of the two, in the sense that it can only overestimate, not underestimate, the improvement in welfare that will take place. We can therefore follow this course in applying the Hotelling formula to our data. The results are shown in column 4 of Table 4.1. This gives, opposite each industry, the amount by which consumer welfare would increase if that industry either acquired or divested itself of the appropriate amount of resources. The total improvement in consumer welfare which might come from our sample of firms thus turns out to be about 26.5 million dollars. Blowing up this figure to cover the whole economy, we get what we really want: an estimate of by how much consumer welfare would have improved if resources had been optimally allocated throughout American manufacturing in the late twenties. The answer is 59 million dollars – less than one-tenth of 1 per cent of the national income. Translated into today's national income and today's prices, this comes out to 225 million dollars, or less than $1.50 for every man, woman, and child in the United States.

Before drawing any lessons from this, I should like to spend a little time evaluating the estimate. First let us look at the basic assumption that long-run costs are constant. My belief is that this is a good assumption, but that if it is wrong, costs in all probability tend to be increasing rather than decreasing in American industry. And the presence of increasing costs would result in a lowering of both our estimates. Less resources would have to be transferred in order to equalize profit rates, and the increase in consumer welfare resulting from the transfer would be correspondingly less.

On the other hand, flaws in the data probably operate to make our estimate of the welfare loss too low. Take for example the question of patents and good will. To the extent that these items are assigned a value on the books of a corporation, monopoly profits are capitalized, and the profit rate which we have used is an understatement of the actual profit rate on real capital. Fortunately for us, Professor Epstein has gone into this question in his study. He finds that excluding intangibles from the capital figures makes a significant difference in the earning rates of only eight of the seventy-three industries. I have accordingly recomputed my figures for these eight industries.[3] As a result, the estimated amount of resource transfer goes up from about $1\frac{1}{2}$ per cent to about $1\frac{3}{4}$ per cent of the national total. And the welfare loss due to resource misallocations gets raised to about 81 million dollars, just over a tenth of 1 per cent of the national income.

There is also another problem arising out of the data. Epstein's sample of firms had an average profit rate of 10.4 per cent during the period I investigated, while in manufacturing as a whole the rate of return was 8 per cent. The reason for this divergence seems to be an overweighting of high-profit industries in Epstein's sample. It can be shown, however, that a correct weighting procedure would raise our estimate of the welfare cost of equalizing profit rates in all industries by no more than 10 million dollars.[4]

Finally, there is a problem associated with the aggregation of manufacturing into seventy-three industries. My analysis assumes high substitutability among the products produced by different firms within any industry and relatively low substitutablitiy among the products of different industries. Yet Epstein's industrial classification undoubtedly lumps together in particular industries products which are only remote substitutes and which are produced by quite distinct groups of firms. In short, Epstein's industries are in some instances aggregates of subindustries, and for our purposes it would have been appropriate to deal with the subindustries directly. It can be shown that the use of aggregates in such cases biases our estimate of the welfare loss downward, but experiments with hypothetical examples reveal that the probable extent of the bias is small.[5]

Thus we come to our final conclusion. Elimination of resource misallocations in American manufacturing in the late twenties would bring with it an improvement in consumer welfare of just a little more than a tenth of a per cent. In present values, this welfare gain would amount to about $2.00 per capita.

Now we can stop to ask what resource misallocations we have measured. We actually have included in the measurement not only monopoly misallocations but also misallocations coming out of the dynamics of economic growth and development and all the other elements which would cause divergent profit rates to persist for some time even in an effectively competitive economy. I know of no way to get at the precise share of the total welfare loss that is due to monopoly, but I do think I have a reasonable way of pinning our estimate down just a little more tightly. My argument here is based on two props. First of all, I think it only reasonable to roughly identify monopoly power with high rates of profit. And secondly, I think it quite implausible that more than a third of our manufacturing profits should be monopoly profits; that is, profits which are above and beyond the normal return to capital and are obtained by exercise of monopoly power. I doubt that this second premise needs any special defense. After all, we know that capital is a highly productive resource. On the first premise, identifying monopoly power with high profits, I think we need only run down the list of high-profit industries to verify its plausibility. Cosmetics are at the top, with a 30 per cent return on capital. They are followed by scientific instruments, drugs, soaps, newspapers, automobiles, cereals, road machinery, bakery products, tobacco, and so on. But even apart from the fact that it makes sense in terms of other evidence to consider these industries monopolistic, there is a still stronger reason for making this assumption. For given the elasticity of demand for an industry's product, the welfare loss associated with that product increases as the square of its greater-than-normal profits. Thus, granted that we are prepared to say that no more than a third of manufacturing profits were monopoly profits, we get the biggest welfare effect by distributing this monopoly profit first to the highest profit industries, then to the next highest, and so on. When this is done, we come to the conclusion that monopoly misallocations entail a welfare loss of no more than a thirteenth of a per cent of the national income. Or, in the present values, no more than about $1.40 per capita.

Before going on, I should like to mention a couple of other possible ways in which this estimate might fail to reflect the actual cost of monopoly misallocations to the American consumer. First, there is the possibility that book capital might be overstated, not because of patents and good will, but as a result of mergers and acquisitions. In testing possibility I had recourse to Professor J. Fred Weston's recent study of mergers. He found that mergers and acquisitions accounted for only a quarter of the growth of seventy-odd corporations in the last half-century (*The Role of Mergers in the Growth of Large Firms*, pp. 100–102). Even a quite substantial overstatement of the portion of their capital involved in the mergers would thus not seriously affect the profit rates. And furthermore, much of the merger growth that Weston found came in the very early years of the century; so that no one can reasonably expect that most of the assets which may have been overvalued in these early mergers were off the books by the period that I investigated.

The second possibility concerns advertising expenditures. These are included as cost in accounting data, but it may be appropriate for our present purpose to include part of them as a sort of quasi-monopoly profit. I was unable to make any systematic adjustment of my data to account for this possibility, but I did make a cursory examination of some recent data on advertising expenditures. They suggest that advertising costs are well under 2 per cent of sales for all of the industries in Table 4.1. Adjustment of our results to allow for a maximal distorting effect of advertising expenditures would accordingly make only a slight difference, perhaps raising our estimate of the welfare cost of monopoly in present values to $1.50 per capita, but not significantly higher.[6]

I should like now to review what has been done. In reaching our estimate of the welfare loss due to monopoly misallocations of resources we have assumed constant rather than increasing costs in manufacturing industry and have assumed elasticities of demand which are too high, I believe. On both counts we therefore tend to overstate the loss. Furthermore, we have treated intermediate products in such a way as to overstate the loss. Finally, we have attributed to monopoly an implausibly large share – $33\frac{1}{3}$ per cent – of manufacturing profits, and have possible welfare loss consistent with the idea that monopolies tend to make high profits. In short, we have labored at each stage to get a big estimate of the welfare loss, and we have come out in the end with less than a tenth of a per cent of the national income.

I must confess that I was amazed at this result. I never really tried to quantify my notions of what monopoly misallocations amounted to, and I doubt that many other people have. Still, it seems to me that our literature of the last twenty or so years reflects a general belief that monopoly distortions to our resources structure are much greater than they seem in fact to be.

Let me therefore state the beliefs to which the foregoing analysis has led me. First of all, I do not want to minimize the effects of monopoly. A tenth of a per cent of the national income is still over 300 million dollars, so we dare not pooh-pooh the efforts of those – economists and others – who have dedicated themselves to reducing the losses due to monopoly. But it seems to me that the monopoly problem does take on a rather different perspective in the light of present study. Our economy emphatically does not seem to be monopoly capitalism in big red letters. We can neglect monopoly elements and still gain an early understanding of how our economic process works and how our resources are allocated. When we are interested in the big picture of our manufacturing economy, we need not apologize for treating it as competitive, for in fact it is awfully close to being so. On the other hand, when we are interested in the doings of particular industries, it may often be wise to take monopoly elements into account. Even though monopoly elements in cosmetics are a drop in the bucket in the big picture of American manufacturing, they still mean a lot when we are studying the behavior of this particular industry.

Finally I should like to point out that I have discussed only the welfare effects of resource misallocations due to monopoly. I have not analyzed the redistributions of income that arise when monopoly is present. I originally planned to discuss this redistribution aspect as well, but finally decided against it. All I want to say here is that monopoly does not seem to affect aggregate welfare very seriously through its effect on resource allocation. What it does through its effect on income distribution I leave to my more metaphysically inclined colleagues to decide. I am impelled to add a final note in order to forestall misunderstandings arising out of matters of definition. Resource misallocations may clearly arise from causes other than those considered here: tariffs, excise taxes, subsidies, trade-union practices, and the devices of agricultural policy are some obvious examples. Some of these sources of misallocation will be discussed in a forthcoming paper. Suffice it to say here that the present paper is not concerned with them.

Notes

1. I am indebted to my colleagues D. Gale Johnson, H. Gregg Lewis, and George S. Tolley for stimulating discussions and comments during the preparation of this paper. They are, of course, not responsible for errors that may remain.
2. Harold Hotelling, "The General Welfare in Relation to Problems of Taxation and of Railway and Utility Rates," *Econometrica*, July, 1938, pp. 242–269. The applicability of Hotelling's proof to the present problem can be seen by

referring to p. 252 ff. He there indicates that he hypothecates a transformation locus which is a hyperplane. This is given us by our assumption of constant costs. He then inquires what will be the loss in moving from a point Q on the hyperplane, at which the marginal conditions of competitive equilibrium are met, to a point Q' at which these conditions of competitive equilibrium are not met. At Q' a nonoptimal set of prices P' prevails. These are, in our example, actual prices, while the equilibrium price-vector P is given costs, defined to included normal profits. Hotelling's expression of the welfare loss in shifting from Q to Q' is $\frac{1}{2}\Sigma dp_i dq_i$, where p_i and q_i are the price and quantity of the i-the commodity. We obtain this by defining our units so that the cost of each commodity is $1.00. The equilibrium quantity of each commodity under the assumption of unit elasticities is then equal to the value of sales of that commodity. If we call r_i the percentage divergence of actual price from cost, we may write the total welfare loss due to monopoly as $\frac{1}{2}\Sigma r_i^2 q_i$ if the elasticities of demand are unity, and as $\frac{1}{2}\Sigma r_i^2 q_i k_i$, if the elasticities of demand are k_i. In column 4 of Table 4.1, I attribute to each commodity a welfare loss equal to $\frac{1}{2} r_i^2 q_i$. This measure of the welfare loss due to monopoly abstracts from distributional considerations. Essentially it assumes that the marginal utility of money is the same for all individuals. Alternatively, it may be viewed as measuring the welfare gain which would occur if resources were shifted from producing Q' to producing Q, and at the same time the necessary fiscal adjustments were made to keep everybody's money income the same.

3. Following is a breakdown of the eight industries in question.

Industry	Adjusted profit rate*	Adjusted rate of excess profit	Adjusted amount of excess profits (millions)	Adjusted welfare loss (millions)
Confectionery	21.1	10.7	11	0.530
Tobacco	19.0	8.6	66	2.225
Men's clothing	14.9	4.5	5	0.068
Stationery	8.8	–	–	–
Newspaper publishing	27.9	17.5	67	5.148
Proprietary preparations	27.8	17.4	42	4.121
Toilet preparations	50.8	40.4	6	1.400
Printing machinery	12.9	2.5	2	0.064
			199	13.556
Less previous amount of excess profit or welfare loss			−100	−3.845
Net adjustment			99	9.711

* R. C. Epstein, *op. cit.*, p. 530.

4. Epstein's results in samples from small corporations (not included in his main sample) indicate that their earning rates tend to be quite close, industry by industry, to the earning rates of the large corporations in the main sample. This suggests that the average rate of profit in the main sample (10.4 per cent) was higher than the average for all industry (8 per cent) because high-profit industries were overweighted in the sample rather than because the sampled firms tended to be the high-profit firms within each industry. The overweighting of high-profit industries affects our estimate of the welfare cost of resource misallocations in two ways. First, quite obviously, it tends to overstate the cost by pretending that the high-profit industries account for a larger share of the aggregate product of the economy than they actually do. Second, and perhaps not so obviously, it tends to understate the cost by overstating the average rate of profit in all manufacturing, and hence overstating the amount of profit which is "built in" to the cost curves in the present analysis. The estimated adjustment of 10 million dollars presented in the text corrects only for this second effect of overweighting and is obtained by imputing as the normal return to capital in the Epstein sample only 8 per cent rather than 10.4 per cent and recomputing the welfare costs of resource misallocations by the method followed in Table 4.1. It takes no account of the first effect of overweighting, mentioned above, and thus results in an overstatement of the actual amount of welfare costs.

5. The extent of the bias is proportional to the difference between the average of the squares of a set of numbers and the square of the average, the numbers in question being the rates of excess profit in the subindustries. Consider an industry composed of three subindustries, each of equal weight. Assume, for extreme example, that the rates of excess profit (excess profit expressed as a per cent of sales) are 10 per cent, 20 per cent, and 30 per cent in the three subindustries. The average rate of excess profit of the aggregate industry would then be 20 per cent, and, by our procedure, the estimate of the welfare loss due to that industry would be 2 per cent of its sales. If we had been able to deal with the hypothetical industry data directly, we would have estimated the welfare loss associated with them at $2\frac{1}{3}$ per cent of the aggregate sales.

6. I was unable similarly to take account of selling costs other than advertising expenditures, even though some of such costs may be the price paid by firms to enhance market control or monopoly position. In principle, clearly, some share of selling costs should be taken into account, and it is a limitation of the present study that no adjustment for such costs was possible. Scrutinizing Table 4.1, however, I should suggest that such selling costs are important in only a few of the industries listed, and that an allowance for them would almost certainly not alter the general order of magnitude of the estimates here presented. It should be pointed out, also, that the general conclusions reached in this paper are not closely dependent on the precise data used. Suppose, for example, that we had observed the following situation: industries accounting for half the output of American manufacturing were charging prices which yielded them a 10 per cent "monopoly profit" on sales, while the remainder of industries earned a constant rate of profit on capital (here called normal profit) but no more. If we were, in this situation, to reallocate resources so as to equalize profit rates in all industries, the prices of competitive products

would rise and those of monopolistic products would fall. If demand for the product of each sector were assumed to be of unit elasticity, we would estimate the gain in welfare incident upon the reallocation of resource at 0.125 per cent of total industrial sales. This would be just about a tenth of a per cent of the national income if the ratio of manufacturing sales to national income approximated is 1924–28 figure. The estimated welfare gain is obtained as follows: Under our elasticity assumption, prices would rise by 5 per cent in the competitive sector and fall by 5 per cent in the monopolistic sector, and quantities would change inversely by an equal percentage. Taking 100 as the aggregate sales of manufacturing, the change in output in each sector will be 2.5, and taking 1 as the index of initial prices in each sector, the change in price in each sector will be .05. According to the Hotelling formula, the welfare gain coming from each sector will be $\frac{1}{2}$ (2.5) (.05), and when these gains are added together the aggregate gain turns out to be .125.

CHAPTER 5

*Strategic Competition among the Few – Some Recent Developments in the Economics of Industry**

J. VICKERS

I Introduction

The title of this article is intended as a signal of two things. First, we are concerned with industries where several – but not many – firms are actually or potentially in competition with each other. Thus our topic is competition among the few,[1] or oligopoly, rather than the polar extremes of textbook perfect competition and pure monopoly. Secondly, we are interested in the strategic nature of competition between firms, where the meaning of 'strategic' can be explained as follows:

> If the essence of a game of strategy is the dependence of each person's proper choice of action on what he expects the other to do, it may be useful to define a 'strategic move' as follows: A strategic move is one that influences the other person's choice, in a manner favourable to one's self, by affecting the other person's expectations of how one's self will behave. Schelling (1960, p. 150)

The definition is taken from Thomas Schelling's classic book The *Strategy of Conflict*, which has inspired much recent work on strategic

---

*Oxford Review of Economic Policy, Vol. 1, No. 3 (1985), pp. 99–62.

moves such as threats, promises and commitments in the economics of industry. This work is sometimes described as 'The New Industrial Economics', but we shall steer clear of the controversial business of applying that label.

The recent work on strategic competition among the few can be compared with the older traditions in industrial economics associated with Harvard and Chicago. The structure–conduct–performance paradigm pioneered by Edward Mason at Harvard in 1930s was developed by Joe Bain and others in the 1950s and 1960s. This approach regards market *structure* (the number and sizes of firms in the industry, entry barriers, etc.) as determining the *conduct* of firms (their policies regarding price, advertising, capacity, innovation, etc.), which in turn determines the *performance* of the industry (its allocative efficiency and technological progress, for example). Of course proponents of this view would not claim that causality flows in one direction only – from structure to conduct to performance – but they do emphasise relationships involving that causal flow (see Scherer (1980) pp. 4–5). The recent work on strategic competition has explored many of the aspects of industry structure and conduct that were recognised as being important by economists in the Harvard tradition. A prime example is the theory of entry barriers and entry deterrence, which will be described below. But there are important differences between the approaches that should be noted. The apparently general applicability of the structure–conduct–performance paradigm caused attention to be focused on features shared by different industries, rather than upon the idiosyncracies of particular industries. More recently, however, there has been some tendency to study industries on a case by case basis (see Schmalensee (1982) and Spence (1981)). A second difference is that much recent work has been concerned with the determinants of market structure, rather than with the dependence of conduct and performance *upon* structure. One concern has been to show how the fundamentals of consumer preferences and technological relationships, together with the behaviour of firms, determine market structure endogenously.

The "Chicago tradition" has been to view industrial economics "through the lens of price theory".[2] This approach places much greater faith in the operation of market forces than does the Harvard approach, and is correspondingly less convinced of the need or desirability of government intervention to do something about apparent "market power." To the contrary, government policy is seen as being one of the main causes of restrictions upon free competition – for example, legal barriers to entry into certain markets. These views are closely linked with the emphasis of the "Austrian School" upon dynamic competition by innovation and the threat of new entry. Such topics as these have also been addressed in the recent work that is reported below, but the conclusions reached –

especially regarding government policy – have often differed markedly from those of the Chicago school.

The lens of *game theory* has been used to study the economics of strategic competition. Game theory provides a framework for analysing situations in which there is interdependence between agents in the sense that the decisions of one agent affect the other agents. It is not necessary to use game theory to study pure monopoly (where there is only one decision-maker) or perfect competition (where each individual is too small to have any appreciable effect upon others), but game theory is most appropriate to the study of competition among the few. The next section contains a very brief outline of some basic notions in games theory, and introduces some illustrative examples that are developed in the subsequent discussion.

Section III discusses strategic competition between existing firms, and section IV is concerned with strategic competition between existing firms and potential rivals. These two issues are closely related, but it is helpful as a first step to address them separately. Section III has three main themes: the dynamic nature of strategic competition between firms, the dependence of market structure on the fundamental conditions of consumer preferences and technology, and the role of strategic commitment. The first theme is illustrated in part 1 of the section, which is about collusion between firms. Using the perspective of repeated games, it is shown how firms may be able effectively to collude noncooperatively, i.e., in the absence of explicit cartel arrangements. This demonstrates that it would be fallacious to argue that such collusion would inevitably be undermined by each firm's incentive to undercut its rivals. The theme of the endogeneity of market structure is developed in parts 2 and 3, which are concerned with R&D competition and product differentiation, respectively. The final part discusses strategic commitment of R&D as an illustration of how the decisions of a firm are made partly with a view to influencing the behaviour of its rivals int he industry. Each firm attempts to gain a position of strategic advantage over its rivals, and to avoid being put at a disadvantage by its rivals' efforts. It is hoped that these examples convey some of the flavour of main theories of strategic competition between existing firms. They do not constitute an exhaustive survey.

Section IV is concerned with the effect of potential competition upon firms already in a market. The seminal work of Bain (1956) on barriers to new competition has recently been subject to intensive reappraisal. Baumol (1982) and others have proposed a controversial theory of 'contestable markets', in which there are no barriers to new competition. Other authors, more in the spirit of Bain, have shown in a rigorous fashion how an existing firm in a market might be able to deter entry into the market by strategic investment in capacity, R&D advertising, brand proliferation, or predatory pricing, for example. These developments are reviewed below.

Section V draws some broad implications for policy. ... The first broad implication is that market structure and conduct are determined jointly by the fundamental conditions of consumer preferences and technological relationships. This contrasts with the view that market structure is somehow given, and that it determines conduct in the industry. Rather, industry structure may be as much a symptom of underlying factors as a root cause of undesirable conduct and performance. A related implication is the importance of potential competition. The threat of new entry can be a potent influence upon the behaviour of existing firms; on the other hand that threat may be thwarted by strategic moves by existing firms. A third broad implication is that competition among the few does not necessarily produce socially desirable results – a point well illustrated by R&D competition. It follows that there is an important role for public policy to influence the outcome of strategic competition among the few. As a final point, recent work in industrial economics should not be seen as delivering generally applicable policy prescriptions. On the contrary, it has served to highlight the heterogeneous nature of industries while providing useful tools and valuable perspectives for the study of particular cases.

II Interdependent Decision-making

When there are only a few firms in an industry, they are *interdependent* in the following sense. The behaviour of any one firm has an appreciable effect upon the other firms, and the best plan of action for one firm to adopt depends upon the plans of action chosen by the other firms. Each firm is trying to second-guess the others – the behaviour of one firm depends upon what it expects the other firms to do, and they in turn are making their decisions on the basis of their expectations of what their rivals (including the first firm) will do. The situation is rather like that found in games like poker, bridge, or the children's game involving scissors, paper and rocks. Indeed, the framework for studying situations of interdependence decision is called the *theory of games*. This theory was developed by von Neumann and Morgenstern and has been refined and employed in numerous applications.

This section has two purposes. The first is informally to describe some basic notions of game theory, which will be useful for the economic analysis to follow. The second is to introduce two illustrations of games – concerning cooperation between firms and predatory pricing – which will be developed in the subsequent sections.

(1) *Some elements of game theory*

A situation of interdependent decision-making, as described in the paragraphs above, is called a game. The participants in the game are the *players*. In our case the firms in the industry are the players. Each player pursues some objective: each player is intent upon maximising his *payoff*. The payoff that a player receives measures how well he achieves his objective. We shall suppose for the most part that the payoff of a firm is its profit (or, in dynamic contexts, the discounted value of its profit stream). Thus we are assuming that firms are intent upon maximising their profits. The payoffs of the players depend upon the decisions that they make. In general, the payoff of player 1 depends not only on his decision, but also upon the decisions made by the other players. This is precisely the element of interdependence that game theory attempts to study.

Each player chooses a *strategy*. A strategy is a plan of action, or a complete contingency plan, which specifies what the player will do in any of the circumstances in which he might find himself. A strategy is therefore quite different from a *move*. A move is the action that a player makes on a particular occasion, whereas his strategy specifies for the whole range of possible circumstances what move he would make in each particular circumstance. The distinction is rather like the difference in chess between Karpov's game plan (his strategy) and his move pawn-to-king-four.

To summarise so far: the description of a game includes:

(i)   the set of *players*:
(ii) the set of *strategies* available to each player from which each player chooses one: and
(iii) each player's *payoff*, which depends on the strategies chosen by the various players.

It is sometimes necessary to describe a game in more detail. A fuller description would include:

(iv) the *move order* in the game – i.e. who moves when; and
(v)   the *information* conditions in the game.

By (v) is meant the knowledge that each player has at every stage concerning (a) the prior moves made by the various players, and (b) the motivations of, and strategies available to, the other players in the game.

One way to categorise games is according to the degree of harmony or disharmony between the interests of players. At one extreme is the pure *coordination* game, in which all players have the same objective. At the other extreme is the game of pure *conflict*, in which there are two players with completely opposed interests – what is good for one is bad for the other. Usually, however, there is a mixture of conflict and coordination of interests. Such *mixed motive* games will be our main concern.

It was stated above that in most games the best strategy for one player to choose depends upon what the other players choose. Hence the importance of expectations about the others' choices. But sometimes a player has a strategy that is best irrespective of what the others do. This is called a *dominant* strategy, and the other, inferior strategies are called *dominated* strategies. The first example in the next subsection is one in which each player has a dominant strategy.

It is easy to deduce what will happen in games with dominant strategies – each player simply chooses his dominant strategy. But in general it is hard to work out what will happen, because the best strategy for each player depends upon what the others do. A situation in which each player is choosing the best strategy available to him, given the strategies chosen by other players, is called a *Nash equilibrium*. Nash equilibrium corresponds to the idea of self-fulfilled expectations. If each player expected the others to play their part in the equilibrium, then it would be rational for him to do likewise. If the same is true for all players, then all have their expectations fulfilled at equilibrium. Similarly, Nash equilibrium corresponds to the idea of a tacit, self-supporting agreement. If the players were somehow to agree to a plan of Nash equilibrium behaviour, then none would have an incentive to depart from the agreement. No external mechanism would be required to enforce the agreement. However, any agreement that is not a Nash equilibrium would require a means of enforcement.

The concept is named after John Nash, an economist who made some fundamental advances in game theory in the 1950s. The concept is in fact a development of that introduced in the 1830s by Cournot, a French mathematician, who examined the output decisions of the two firms in a duopoly. He defined equilibrium as a position in which each firm is producing his optimal output level, given the output level chosen by the other firm.

(2) Two illustrations

Following the rather general outline of game theory above, we now consider two illustrative examples. They are concerned with

(i) the problems of collusion; and
(ii) predatory pricing.

Both examples will be developed in later sections of this paper.

(i) The problem of collusion Figure 5.1 represents a very simple game[3] in which the players are two firms, A and B. Each firm has a choice between two alternatives – a high output strategy or a low output strategy. The numbers in the boxes give the payoffs of the players, which can be thought of as the firms' profits. The convention is that firm A's payoff is written in the bottom left-hand corner of a box, and B's payoff appears in the top right-hand corner.

In the example, the best thing that can happen for a firm is for it to produce high output while its rival produces low output. The low output level of its rival means that price is not driven down too much, and so a good profit margin is earned. The worst thing that can happen is to produce low output while the rival produces high output. Then price is fairly low – due to the rival's high output – and revenues are barely sufficient to cover total costs. If both firms produce high output, then price is low but profits are positive. It is better for both to restrain output, and thereby to raise price. We shall refer to this as the collusive outcome.

What will happen in this game? In fact it is a dominant strategy for each firm to choose a high output level. This is the best strategy for firm A whether firm B produces a high level of output or a low one. Similarly for firm B. Thus the "noncooperative" outcome is for each firm to get a

| | FIRM B's OUTPUT LEVEL ||
	HIGH	LOW
FIRM A's OUTPUT LEVEL — HIGH	1 / 1	3 / 0
FIRM A's OUTPUT LEVEL — LOW	0 / 3	2 / 2

FIGURE 5.1

payoff of 1. However, if the firms had somehow been able to attain the collusive outcome (i.e., both produce low levels of output), then both would have received a superior payoff of 2. The problem of collusion is for the firms to achieve this superior outcome notwithstanding the seemingly compelling argument that high output levels will be chosen. In section III it will be seen how this problem can be resolved when a game such as that depicted in Figure 5.1 is repeated. After all, in reality firms are in competition on a long-term basis; they are not engaged in a "one-shot" game like the one just considered. When account is taken of this fact, collusion can be sustained by threats of retaliation against non-cooperative behaviour.

(ii) Predatory pricing Figure 5.2 represents a simple game[4] in which predatory pricing is possible. Note that the method of representation differs from that in Figure 5.1. Here we have made the order of moves explicit. The players are two firms – a potential entrant is contemplating entry into a market currently dominated by an incumbent firm. The potential entrant chooses between going IN to the market, or remaining OUT of it.

If entry occurs, the incumbent can either FIGHT entry, which is costly to both firms, or he can ACQUIESCE so as to arrive at some peaceful coexistence, which is more profitable. The best thing for the incumbent is for entry not to take place. In that event, the potential entrant does better than if its entry were fought, but not as well as if its entry were met with acquiescence.

What will happen in the game? In fact there are two Nash equilibria:

(a) Potential entrant chooses IN, and incumbent chooses to ACQUIESCE in the event of entry, and

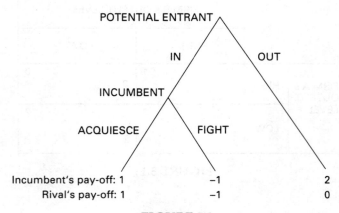

FIGURE 5.2

(b) Potential entrant chooses OUT, and incumbent chooses to FIGHT in the event of entry.

In each case, each player gets his maximum payoff given the strategy chosen by the other player. But equilibrium (b) is implausible, because it is clear that, faced with the fact of entry, the incumbent would find it profitable to ACQUIESCE, rather than to FIGHT entry. Relying on this fact, the potential entrant would choose IN, and we would get equilibrium (a). In other words, the incumbent's threat to FIGHT is not *credible* – it is an empty threat that would not be believed. The concept of Nash equilibrium has been refined to rule out these peculiar equilibria involving incredible threats. The concept of *perfect equilibrium*, developed by Selten (1965; 1975), requires that the strategies chosen by the players be a Nash equilibrium, not only in the game as a whole, but also in every subgame of the game. In Figure 5.2 there is a subgame beginning at the node alongside the word "incumbent". Perfect equilibrium rules out the undesirable equilibrium (b), leaving only the intuitively reasonable equilibrium (a): entry occurs and is met with acquiescence.

The game in Figure 5.2 is sufficiently simple for it to be possible to work out what will happen without bothering with the jargon above. But in more sophisticated – and realistic – examples this is not so. The two examples above were intended to illustrate how game theory is used to analyse strategic competition among the few, and to prepare some of the ground for the discussion to follow.

III Strategic competition between existing firms

The aim of this section is to describe some recent developments in the analysis of strategic competition between existing firms. The next section considers competition between existing firms and potential rivals. Neither section is intended to be anything like a survey. Rather, the intention is to try to convey the flavour of some recent developments, by way of illustrative examples.

The present section has four parts. The first continues the discussion of collusion from the previous section. It is shown that, using the perspective of repeated games, it may be possible for firms effectively to collude in the absence of explicit agreement to do so, even though each is exclusively concerned to maximise its own profits. The second and third parts of this section both develop the theme of the "endogeneity" of market structure by showing the importance of the fundamentals of consumer preferences and technological relationships. The model of R&D competition by Dasgupta and Stiglitz (1980) is the main subject of part 2, and part 3 discusses recent work on product differentiation, notably that of Shaked and Sutton (1983). Strategic commitment is the topic in the final part of this section, which contains an account of Brander and Spencer's (1983) model in which firms choose their levels of R&D activity partly with a view of influencing their rivals' behaviour.

(1) *Non-cooperative collusion*

The paradoxical title of this subsection indicates that we are asking whether collusive outcomes can be sustained by non-cooperative behaviour, i.e. in the absence of explicit, enforceable agreements between firms. In the simple illustration of Figure 5.1 above this was not possible, but that illustration had evident shortcomings. In particular, it represented a "one-shot" game, whereas in reality firms are commonly in competition with their rivals on a longer term basis. That is to say, they are in a repeated game. Is non-cooperative collusion possible in a repeated game?

The answer to this question depends upon at least four things:

(i) whether the game is repeated indefinitely, or only a finite number of times;
(ii) whether the players in the game are fully informed as to the objectives of, and opportunities available to, their rivals;
(iii) whether the players know the prior moves made by their rivals – so that "cheating" can be detected; and
(iv) how much weight the players attach to the future in their calculations.

The particular circumstances of an industry determine what it is appropriate to assume in relation to (i) – (iv). Rather than look at particular industries, our approach here will be to explore the consequences of the various assumptions that could be made. Initially, we shall do this by developing the illustrative example shown in Figure 5.1.

Suppose for the moment that the game is repeated a finite number of times, and that there is complete and perfect information. Firms are assumed to maximise the (possibly discounted) sum of their profits in the game as a whole. Unfortunately (for the firms) the collusive low output outcome cannot be sustained. Suppose that the game is repeated 137 times. At the last round, it is clear from previous argument (see p. 97) that it is a dominant strategy for both firms to produce high output. This fact implies that neither firm has any incentive to cooperate by producing low output at the 136th repetition, since it is clear to all what will happen at the last round. And the same is true at the 135th repetition. The argument proceeds, by backwards induction, to the conclusion that there is never any collusion – both firms produce high output at every stage of the game. Since there is nothing special about the number 137, the same conclusion holds for any finite number of repetitions of the game.

As well as being unhappy (for the firms), this result is rather unsatisfactory. First, our intuition suggests that some collusion would occur, at least early on in the game, despite the fact that the number of repetitions is finite. Secondly, the experimental evidence (see Axelrod, 1984) accords with this intuition. How can this intuition, supported by experimental evidence, be squared with apparently compelling game theoretical logic?

Before answering this question, let us consider the *infinitely* repeated version of the game depicted in Figure 5.1. Suppose that firms discount the future at rate w, where w is a number between zero and one. That is, firms attach weight w to what happens next period, weight w^2 to what happens the period after that, and so on. The closer w is to zero, the less weight they attach to the future relative to the present, i.e., the more short-sighted they are.

Provided that w is not too small, it is now possible for non-cooperative collusion to occur. Suppose that firm B plays the *trigger strategy*, which is to choose low output in period 1 and in any subsequent period provided that firm A has never produced high output, but to produce high output forever more once firm A ever produces high output.[5] The idea is that firm B cooperates with A unless and until A "defects", in which case B is triggered into perpetual non-cooperation. What is A's best response to this trigger strategy by B? If A were also to adopt the trigger strategy, then there would always be collusion – each firm would always choose low output and receive 2 in each period. The discounted value of this profit flow is

$$2 + 2w + 2w^2 + \ldots = 2/(1-w).$$

In fact A gets this payoff with any strategy in which he is not the first to defect. If, however, A chooses a strategy in which he defects at any stage, then he gets a payoff of 3 in the first period of defection (because B chooses low output), and a payoff of no more than 1 in every subsequent period (because B has been triggered into perpetual non-cooperation). So his payoff is at most

$$3 + w + w^2 + w^3 + \ldots = 3 + w/(1-w).$$

Comparing the two payoffs, we see that it is better not to defect so long as

$$w \geq 1/2$$

This precise answer depends of course upon the particular numbers chosen for the illustration. But the general point is clear. Provided that the firms give enough weight to the future, then non-cooperative collusion can be sustained, for example by trigger strategies. The collusion is non-cooperative in the sense that the firms are not acting in concert; each is independently doing the best it can given the strategy adopted by the other firm. In other words, the trigger strategies constitute a Nash equilibrium, or a self-enforcing agreement. Trigger strategies are not the only way to sustain the collusive outcome non-cooperatively. Another leading strategy is tit-for-tat, according to which a player chooses in the current period what the other player chose in the previous period.

Now let us return to the question of how collusion might occur non-cooperatively, even in the finitely repeated game. Recall that we found a tension between intuition and experimental evidence on one hand, and game theoretic logic on the other. Intuition said that collusion could happen – at least in the earlier rounds – but game theory apparently said that it could not. An important and elegant resolution of this paradox has been provided by Kreps *et al.* (1982). They relax the assumption of complete information, and suppose instead that one player has a small amount of doubt in his mind as to the motivation of the other player. Suppose, for example, that A is not absolutely certain that B's pay-offs are as described above (i.e., the discounted sum of the pay-offs in Figure 5.1). Suppose that A attaches some tiny probability p to B preferring – or being committed – to playing the trigger strategy.[6] It turns out that even if p is very small indeed, the players will effectively collude until some point towards the end of the game. This occurs because it is not worth A detecting in view of the risk that the non-collusive outcome will obtain for the rest of the game, and because B wishes to maintain his reputation for possibly preferring, or being committed to, the trigger strategy. Thus the analysis also yields a satisfying account of how reputation can operate to maintain effective collusion, at least for a substantial part of the time. What is remarkable about the result is that a small degree of doubt about the motivation of one of the players can yield much effective collusion. Once the strict assumption of complete information is slightly relaxed, the outcome of the game changes radically.[7]

So far in the discussion of collusion we have focused on the simple example in Figure 5.1, in which two firms have a choice between a high or low output level. But there may be several firms in an industry, and in fact firms have a much broader choice. If output is their decision variable, they can choose from a wide range of possible output levels. Or it may be that their decision variable is price, not to mention other aspects of company behaviour such as investment, advertising and R&D. Be that as it may, more or less the same analysis can be applied straightforwardly in the more complex settings. In those settings new possibilities arise. For example, Abreu (1984) has investigated the most effective credible strategies for 'punishing' deviations from collusive behaviour. The more effective the punishment, the greater is the deterrent effect, and the greater is the degree of collusion than can be sustained. In an infinitely repeated game where firms choose output levels, the most effective credible punishment strategy consists of a stick and a carrot – the carrot is the attraction of collusion, and the stick is a swift episode of high output levels and a correspondingly low price level. If any firm deviates from collusive behaviour, there would immediately occur one unpleasant period of punishment (the stick), followed by a return to collusion (the carrot). This punishment strategy is credible because it would be entirely rational for the other firms to punish the defector in the way described. In the model no firm actually chooses to defect, because the credible threat of punishment acts as a sufficient deterrent.

We have not yet faced up to the problem of detecting defection from a collusive arrangement. Implicitly we have been supposing that firms can observe one another's behaviour, but this assumption of perfect information may be unjustified. It is perhaps more reasonable to suppose that the firms in a collusive arrangement can observe the price prevailing in their market, but not the output levels chosen by the individual firms that are party to the arrangement. If the demand curve facing the industry is not known for certain, then one firm cannot infer exactly what the others have done. Suppose that a low price is observed in some period. That might be because demand for the product of the industry is low; or it might be because some firm has defected from the collusive arrangement by producing a high level of output. There is the problem of inferring which is the true cause.

This question has been examined by Green and Porter (1984). They consider equilibrium strategies in which firms collude so long as price remains above some critical level P, but they revert to an episode of more aggressive, non-cooperative behaviour if price ever falls below P, before restoring collusive behaviour T periods after the initial price drop.[8] The (credible) threat of the episode of non-cooperative behaviour is sufficient to deter defection from the collusive outcome, but occasionally there is an episode of non-cooperation when demand is especially low. This theory offers an interesting interpretation of the pattern of prices in an industry characterised by occasional, temporary falls in price. One view is to regard the falls in price as collapses in cartel discipline, but the account given by Green and Porter suggests the alternative view that they *help ensure* cartel discipline.

There are numerous other devices that might be used by firms to facilitate non-cooperative collusion by oligopolists. Salop (1985) has explored *facilitating practices* such as most-favoured-nation (MFN) clauses and meeting-competition-clauses (MCCs) that are commonly observed in sales contracts. An MFN clause is one that promises the buyer that the seller will not supply another buyer at a lower price. (If the commodity in question is an input for the buyer's business, then the buyer would not face the risk that another buyer would gain a competitive advantage over him by obtaining the input more cheaply). Several common pricing conventions – for example, posting list prices – have effects similar to an MFN clause. An MCC says that the seller will match the price of any seller supplying at a lower price. The effect of practices of this sort is to alter the incentives of the firms in the oligopoly in such a way that price reductions are less attractive. In addition, they tend to make it easier for one firm to monitor the behaviour of others. Thus they facilitate oligopolistic collusion. In similar vein Klemperer (1984) has shown how switching costs can promote collusive behaviour.[9] Switching costs are present when it is costly for a consumer to switch from his current supplier to a different supplier (even though extante suppliers are on a par). Examples are accountants, and airlines that offer frequently flyer discounts. Sometimes switching costs occur naturally (as with accountants), but sometimes they occur because of the deliberate actions of firms (as with airline discounts), although the motivation for those actions is not necessarily to facilitate collusion.

We conclude this discussion of non-cooperative collusion by mentioning some problems for public policy that will be developed in section V. We have seen that effective collusion does not necessarily require explicit agreements between firms. Antitrust policy generally declares explicit agreements to be unlawful, but it is not clear how it can or should be directed against tacit, non-cooperative collusion. One difficulty is to identify the actions of firms that are unlawful. After all, each firm is independently pursuing its legitimate business interests. Nevertheless we saw that in some contexts the process of collusion might be facilitated by certain practices – for example price clauses in sales contracts. The question arises of whether these facilitating practices are a suitable target for antitrust policy.

(2) *Market structure and cost reducing innovation*

One of the themes emphasised in the introduction was the endogeneity of market structure. Rather than take market structure as given, we wish to understand how the basic conditions of consumer preferences, technology, and so on determine market structure and the conduct of firms. To make the point very crudely, we wish to see how the basic conditions jointly determine structure, conduct and performance, whereas the traditional S–C–P paradigm is more concerned with the causal flow from structure to conduct to performance.

Below we set out the model of market structure and cost-reducing innovation due to Dasgupta and Stiglitz (1980).[10] It is very much a 'bare bones', stylised model, and deliberately so. It shows with great clarity that relationships and correlations – such as those between market structure and R&D efforts – do not necessarily imply causality, and that other explanations are available. This affects how we interpret empirical correlations between market structure and innovation.

The model brings out another, quite separate point. The message of much economic theory concerning the production decisions of firms is that the free market generates results that are broadly desirable from the social point of view, especially if the market is competitive. It is well known, however, that this happy conclusion breaks down in a wide range of circumstances. Technological competition is a leading case in point. After presenting the Dasgupta–Stiglitz model, we shall discuss why this is so.

The model The unit costs of a firm are assumed to depend on its R&D efforts. Let $c(x)$ be the unit production cost of a firm that spends x on R&D. As x increases, c falls. There are n identical firms in the industry producing the same product. We will see shortly how n is determined. If total industry output is Q, price is $P(Q)$, where P falls as Q rises. The profits of a firm with output q and R&D expenditure x can be written

$$\pi = [P(Q) - c(x)]q - x$$

The term in square brackets is the profit margin. When multiplied by q this gives gross profit, from which R&D expenditure x is deducted. If all firms produce the same level of output q then total industry output Q is equal to nq.

Each firm chooses its output q and its R&D expenditure x to maximise its profits π. Each firm assumes that its own decisions about x and q do not affect the decision of other firms about their output and R&D. In other words, we are interested in the Nash equilibrium of the game.

As to the determination of n, the number of firms, there are two leading possibilities. One is that n is given exogenously – there happen to be n firms and that's that. But this assumption seems to be rather arbitrary. At least it calls for some justification. Another possibility is that n is determined endogenously, by *free entry* into the industry. If there is free entry, then firms will continue to come into the industry until it would be unprofitable for the next firm to do so. As an approximation, we may say that entry occurs up to the point where profits are zero. The free entry condition is not the only way that n could be determined endogenously. Alternatively one could suppose that barriers to entry do exist, and these could be modelled explicitly. However, we shall assume free entry in this illustration, because it suffices to make the points at hand.

Let us remind ourselves of the variables of interest. Our index of market *structure* is n, the number of firms. As n falls, the industry becomes more concentrated. The *conduct* of firms includes their decisions on output q and R&D expenditure x. The *performance* of the industry is measured by such things as profits π, the price-cost margin $(P-c)/P$, and innovative advance (i.e. the rate of cost reduction).

It remains to say more about consumer *preferences* and *technological* relationships. Consumer preferences determine demand conditions for the output of the industry, i.e. the relationship between P and Q. To be specific, let the (inverse) demand curve have the form

$$P(Q) = \sigma Q^{-\epsilon} \quad ; \quad \sigma, \epsilon > 0$$

This specification turns out to be particularly convenient. The size of the market is measured by σ and the sensitivity of price to output is measured by ϵ. The price elasticity of demand is $1/\epsilon$. As to technological conditions, the relationship between unit costs and R&D expenditure is given the form

$$c(x) = \beta x^{-\alpha} \quad ; \quad \alpha, \beta > 0$$

Here β measures the level of costs, and α measures the sensitivity of units costs to R&D expenditure. When α is large, unit costs fall more rapidly with R&D efforts. Thus, "innovative opportunities" are greater.

The four parameters α, β, ϵ and σ are the basic conditions of demand and technology. Together they determine the structure, conduct and performance variables in the model. It turns out that α and ϵ (the elasticities of cost reduction and of demand) are especially important. A number of interesting results holds at the (free entry) equilibrium in the model.

The number of firms is given by

$$n = \epsilon (1 + \alpha)/\alpha$$

Thus an industry is more concentrated (n is smaller) when innovation opportunities (α) are greater. Industries with less elastic demand (that is, lower $1/\epsilon$, or higher ϵ) are less concentrated. The size of the market (σ) does not affect n. If the market is larger, the level of R&D per firm is greater, and units costs are correspondingly lower.

The price-cost margin at equilibrium is

$$\frac{P-c}{P} = \frac{\epsilon}{n}$$

Thus the price–cost margin is negatively related to the elasticity of demand $(1/\epsilon)$ and positively related to the level of concentration $(1/n)$. However, care is necessary in interpreting this familiar relationship, because n is determined endogenously, within the model, rather than being fixed. Indeed, by combining the last two equations we obtain

$$\frac{P-c}{P} = \frac{\alpha}{1+\alpha}$$

The price–cost margin is seen to depend on the basic parameter α. This margin is greater in industries where innovative opportunities are greater. This is because firms' R&D expenditures – which have to be covered by the price–cost margin – are higher in these industries. In fact research intensity, as measured by the ratio of R&D expenditure to sales revenue is

$$\frac{nx}{PQ} = \frac{\alpha}{1+\alpha}$$

which is the same price-cost margin. Recall that industries with greater innovative opportunities also tend to be more concentrated. *Thus there tends to be a positive relationship between concentration, the price–cost margin, and research intensity, but there is no causal relationship between these variables*: they are all determined by the underlying parameters of technology and demand.

The equilibrium outcome described above can be compared with the socially optimal research and production plan. In the Dasgupta–Stiglitz (1980) model, costs are not reduced as much as is socially optimal, and price is too high. At the same time, total R&D expenditure is likely to be too great, because there is excessive duplication between the research efforts of different firms.

Spence (1984) examines cost reducing innovation in a richer model. He focuses on the classic appropriability problem in R&D. The problem has two parts: (i) the incentive of a firm to do R&D depends on the degree to which it appropriates the benefits of its R&D; if there are "spillovers", so that one firm benefits from the R&D of another, then incentives are reduced; (ii) on the other hand, knowledge is optimally diffused among firms if it is priced at the marginal cost of its dissemination (which is often close to zero). The problem, then, is that incentives for innovation require inefficient diffusion of knowledge. Spence shows that the market may perform poorly irrespective of concentration and the extent of spillovers, but potential performance improves when spillovers are high. R&D *subsidies* improve market performance substantially. They drive a wedge between the price received by a supplier of R&D output and the price paid by its buyers. A possible solution to the problem of excessive duplication of R&D efforts is to encourage cooperative R&D. However, there is the danger that this facilitates anticompetitive behaviour, such as collusion in product markets or entry deterrence. For a discussion of policy towards R&D intensive sectors, see Ordover and Willig (1985).

This subsection has described only a tiny fraction of the work that has been done on the relationships between market structure and innovation. It has concentrated on cost-reducing innovation, where the costs of a firm depend smoothly upon its (and possibly its rivals') R&D efforts. Product innovations has not been discussed, and nor have R&D contests such as patent races. On these important matters see the extensive surveys by Kamien and Schwartz (1982), and Stoneman (1983).

(3) *Product differentiation and market structure*

The study of product differentiation has been central to industrial economics ever since its inception. The 'spatial' representation of product differentiation, first used in Hotelling's 1929 *Economic Journal* article, has been the basic framework for much work on the topic. In Hotelling's representation, sellers are positioned at points along a line, along which consumers are distributed. One can think of the line as, for example, a stretch of beach (with the sellers being ice-cream vendors) or as a representation of the sweetness/dryness of cider (with very sweet cider at one end and very dry cider at the other). Consumers prefer to patronise sellers positioned close to them (because they save on 'travel costs'), and are therefore prepared to pay some price-premium to obtain their favoured variety. The framework can be extended in many directions – to several dimensions, circles rather than lines, and so on. Several interesting questions can be posed within this framework. For example, will there be a tendency for sellers to differentiate their products as much as possible, or will they tend to agglomerate at a point? How does the nature of price competition between firms depend on their locations? Can an incumbent monopolist deter entry into his market by introducing a proliferation of brands at different locations? And so on.

Rather than discuss any of these questions in the Hotelling tradition, I shall focus instead upon recent work on *vertical* product differentiation, and its bearing on the issue of the determination of market structure. Products are said to be 'vertically differentiated' when they differ in respect of *quality*. If two vertically differentiated products were offered to consumers at the same price, one of the two products would be preferred by all – i.e., the one with higher quality. (This is, of course, *not* the case in Hotelling's framework, where there is 'horizontal' product differentiation. In that case, if two goods were offered at the same price, some consumers would prefer one of them, and other consumers would prefer the other – a consumer would prefer the product closer to him in product space). Since quality differences are manifest features of many markets, it is clearly important to study vertical product differentiation.

Shaked and Sutton (1983) have examined the determination of market structure in markets with vertically differentiated products (see also Shaked and Sutton (1982)). Their major result concerning market structure is that there may be an upper limit to the number of firms that can co-exist at equilibrium irrespective of the size of the market. In that case, a certain degree of market concentration is inevitable. (By 'equilibrium' is meant Nash equilibrium in prices given quality levels).

A market in which this property holds is called a *natural oligopoly*. This result contrasts with the property of horizontally differentiated markets that there is no limit to the number of firms that can coexist at equilibrium if the market is large enough.

Whether or not a market is a natural oligopoly depends in a subtle way upon the interaction between consumer preferences and the technology of product improvement. Let $c(u)$ be the unit variable cost of supplying a product with quality level u. We would expect c to increase with u, but what matters is how rapidly c increases with u. If unit variable costs rise 'sufficiently slowly' as quality increases, then the market is a natural oligopoly – there is a limit to the number of firms that can coexist at equilibrium, no matter how big the market is. More generally, this result holds if it is the case that all consumers would have the same ranking of products if all products were offered at their respective unit variable costs. If this property does not hold, it is possible for a new firm to attract custom by entering with a quality level intermediate between two existing quality levels and selling at a price close to unit variable cost. It follows that there is no limit to the number of firms that can exist as the market grows. However, when the property does hold, a firm adopting such a policy would not necessarily gain any custom, because consumers would be prepared to pay the extra for the higher quality product already on the market, for example.

The details of Shaked and Sutton's analysis are complex and subtle; the account above does not do justice to them. The central point to emerge is that market structure depends critically upon the technology of product improvement and upon consumers' preferences – in particular their willingness to pay for quality improvements.

Shaked and Sutton observe that the condition that the cost of quality improvement does not rise rapidly in relation to consumers' willingness to pay for it, is most likely to be met in industries where product quality depends more on fixed costs (e.g., R&D) than on unit variable costs.

110 *Strategic Competition among the few*

Expenditure on quality improvement and the number and sizes of firms in the market therefore jointly depend upon consumer preferences and upon technological relationships. Thus we have seen in this section – as in the last – that market structure is not the exogenously given determinant of firms' conduct. Rather, conduct and structure are jointly determined by the fundamental of preferences and technology.

(4) *Strategic commitment with R&D*

Strategic moves are an important feature of competition between existing firms. Recall that a strategic move is one designed to induce another player to make a choice more favourable to the strategic mover than would otherwise have happened. The purpose of this subsection is to examine strategic commitment in the particular contexts of R&D competition, following Brander and Spencer (1983).

Consider an industry containing two firms, each of which is to decide on its level of cost-reducing R&D expenditure. Whereas in subsection (2) it was assumed that firms chose their R&D and output levels simultaneously, we shall now suppose that R&D decisions are made before output decisions are made. This is realistic inasmuch as R&D expenditure [is] irreversible and long–term in nature, whereas output decisions are more readily changed. Since the firms' output decisions now depend partly upon their R&D decisions, a *strategic motive* is added to the efficiency motive for research expenditures. In particular, firm 1 would like to curb the output of firm 2, because market price is then higher. By reducing its own costs through research expenditure, firm 1 credibly threatens to produce greater output. This has the desired effect of discouraging firm 2 from producing such high output. High R&D expenditure is thus a strategic move that works by influencing the output decision of the other firm. Owing to the attractiveness of this move, firms tend to overinvest in R&D, in the sense that the output that they eventually supply is produced inefficiently: too much R&D, and too little of the other factors of production, are employed. This strategic source of inefficiency is quite separate from those mentioned earlier in this section.

In more precise terms, the problem is analysed as a two-stage game. Levels of R&D are chosen at stage one, and output levels are chosen at stage two. Being interested only in threats that are credible, we characterise the perfect equilibrium of the game. The easiest way to do this is first to calculate the equilibrium outputs at stage two as a function of the R&D levels chosen at stage one. Having found the dependency of outputs upon R&D, it is then possible to find equilibrium in the choice of R&D levels at stage one. In fact the analysis does not depend on the strategic variable being R&D. Exactly the same applies to any fixed factor of production that reduces costs – such as capital. However, the analysis is sensitive to the assumptions that are made about stage two of the game. We assumed that the firms achieved equilibrium in output levels, in which case there is excessive R&D. But if equilibrium is in prices, the opposite result can hold: each firm underinvests in R&D to induce the other to charge a higher price. The intuitive explanation is that by investing less in R&D, a firm causes its equilibrium price to be slightly higher. This in turn causes the rival's equilibrium price to be slightly higher, which is beneficial to the first firm. This sort of sensitivity of results to assumptions that appear equally plausible bedevils theorists of market structure.

Strategic commitment with R&D is but one illustration of the strategic nature of competition between existing firms. Other instruments of commitment include advertising, the introduction of new brands, and patenting. These themes are taken up again when strategic commitment to deter new entry is examined.

IV Potential competition and strategic entry deterrence

The threat to existing firms posed by potential competitors has long been recognised as an important influence upon market structure and conduct. The force of this threat depends on the extent to which there are *barriers to entry* into the market. In his classic analysis, Bain (1956, p. 3) defines barriers to entry as

> the advantages of establishment sellers in an industry over potential entrant sellers, those advantages being reflected in the extent to which established sellers can persistently raise their prices above a competitive level without attracting new firms to enter the industry.

He identified three sources of barriers to new competition:

(i) Product Differentiation: customer loyalty to existing products puts new entrants at a disadvantage.
(ii) Absolute Cost Advantages: incumbent firms might enjoy absolute cost advantages, due perhaps to exclusive access to superior technologies, or to accumulated experience.
(iii) Economies of Scale: if the minimum efficient scale of production for a firm is large in relation to total demand in the market, then a new entrant faces a dilemma – entry at small scale involves high production costs, but entry at efficient scale would expand industry supply so that price would fall.

Bain's analysis has been subject to recent critical scrutiny (see, for example, von Weizsäcker (1980)) and at the same time attempts have been made to develop his insights in a rigorous, detailed fashion. As to the causes of barriers to entry, an important distinction, due to Salop (1979), is between *innocent* and *strategic* barriers to entry. An innocent barrier to entry is the incidental result of the short-run profit-maximising behaviour of existing firms. A strategic barrier to entry is constructed by design, with the intent of deterring new entrants into the market. The erection of a strategic barrier to entry involves the sacrifice of short-run profits with a view to the longer-run gains of deterring entry. Strategic entry deterrence is the subject of section IV.2. The next section, however, is about the controversial theory of contestable markets, in which there are no barriers to new competition and the threat of entry is at its most potent.

(1) *The theory of contestable markets*

The idea that potential competition affects the conduct of existing firms is by no means novel, but it has recently been examined in its purest form in the theory of contestable markets, developed by Baumol, Panzar and Willig (1982) and their colleagues. Much of their work concerns the economics of multi-product industries, but here we shall concentrate on their analysis of *new entry* into the markets. (Although there are important relationships between the topics of entry and multi-product firms, most of the main ideas concerning the former can be discussed with reference to single-product industries). Important claims have been made on behalf of contestability theory. Baumol (1982, p. 1) in his Presidential address to the American Economic Association claims that the theory

> enables us to look at industry structure and behaviour in a way that is novel in some respects, that it provides a unifying analytical structure to the subject area, and that it offers useful insights for empirical work and for the formulation of policy.

A contestable market is one into which there is ultra-free entry (to use Shepherd's (1984) phrase). All firms – actual and potential – have access to the same technology and hence they enjoy the same cost function. Furthermore, and most importantly, exit from a contestable market is absolutely costless, in the sense that an entrant incurs no *sunk costs* (i.e. irrecoverable expenditures). Thus a contestable market is vulnerable to *hit-and-run entry*:

> Even a very transient profit opportunity need not to be neglected by a potential entrant, for he can go in, and, before prices change, collect his gains and then depart without cost, should the climate grow hostile. (Baumol (1982) p. 4)

Contestability is not inconsistent with the existence of economics of scale. Even it there are fixed costs of production, a market can be contestable provide that there are no sunk costs.

The following conditions hold at equilibrium in a contestable market.

(i) Profits are zero. If they were positive, then new firms would be attracted to enter. If they were negative, then some existing firms would exit from the market.
(ii) Production is efficient. Otherwise a new firm would enter the market, attracted by the prospect of producing efficiently, undercutting the existing inefficient firms, and making a profit.
(iii) Price P is at least as great as marginal cost MC. Otherwise a new firm would be able to make more profits than some existing firm by entering on a slightly smaller scale.
(iv) When there are two or more firms in the market, P cannot exceed MC. Together with (iii) this implies that $P = MC$. This condition is desirable from the point of view of welfare (ignoring 'second best problems'), because it implies that production occurs up to the point where the marginal cost of output equals its marginal benefit as measured by price. (When just one firm is in the market, this condition might not hold: see Baumol (1982, p. 5)).
(v) There is no cross-subsidisation between products. Otherwise there would again be a profit opportunity for a new firm. This follows from (iii).
(vi) The number and configuration of firms is always such as to produce the industry's output at minimum total cost.

Properties (i) to (vi) are highly desirable, according to the canons of traditional welfare economics.[11] The final property is of particular interest. It is another instance of the idea that market structure is endogeneously determined by the basic conditions of demand and technology, rather than being given exogeneously.

The theory has been subject to critical review – see, for example, Shepherd (1984). It is most implausible that real-world markets (or at any rate a significant number of them) fit the assumptions of the theory of contestable markets, even approximately. In particular, the theory depends on the twin assumptions:

(a) that there are no sunk costs; and
(b) that an entrant can come into a market, and set up on full scale, before the existing firm(s) respond by changing price.

Both these assumptions are dubious in respect of real-world markets. Assumption (b) is the *opposite* of the natural assumption to make, since price can be generally altered more rapidly than a new firm can establish itself in a market.

Against these criticisms, it might be said that, although real-world markets do not exactly fit the assumptions of the theory, a significant number of them approximately do so, or could be made to do so by appropriate policy measures. It is unclear how this response could meet the objection to assumption (b), and in any event there is a further difficulty. It is that if the assumptions of contestability theory are changed slightly (for example by supposing that sunk costs are positive but small), the predictions of the theory can alter radically. For instance, even tiny sunk costs can substantially reduce – or even eliminate – the force of the threat of entry upon existing firms. This *lack of robustness* is a major reason to doubt the applicability of the theory to practical problems.

That being said, the theory of contestable markets is a timely reminder that the threat of new entry can be potent force that shapes market structure and the conduct of existing firms. It underlines the importance of measures to liberalise markets by reducing barriers to entry and exit, where it is possible to do so.[12] However, the theory is not built on sufficiently strong foundations to justify the confidence that is sometimes placed in the 'invisible hand' results derived from it. For example, it would be a grave error to suppose that there is no need to regulate private natural monopolists, on the grounds that the threat of entry compels them to behave benignly.

(2) *Strategic entry deterrence*

In a contestable market, the only way to deter the entry of new firms is to meet the needs of consumers with maximum efficiency. This is far from being true in other, perhaps more plausible, contexts. The purpose of this subsection is to describe some of the devices that existing firms might use to deter entry in a strategic fashion. That is to say, we are interested in strategic moves designed to benefit existing firms by inducing potential rivals to choose not to enter their markets. Salop (1979) gives an account of early work on this topic. See also Salop (ed.) (1981).

For the sake of simplicity, we shall focus on the case where one incumbent firm is seeking to deter the entry of one potential rival.[13] The entry decision of the rival depends upon his beliefs as to the likely profitability of being in the market. Entry will occur if and only if the expected profits exceed the expected costs of entry. How can the incumbent influence those beliefs in such a way as to deter entry?

We shall address this question in two steps. First, we shall suppose that each firm is fully informed about the behaviour, opportunities and motivation of the other. In that case, the game between firms is one of complete and perfect information. Secondly, we shall relax these assumptions

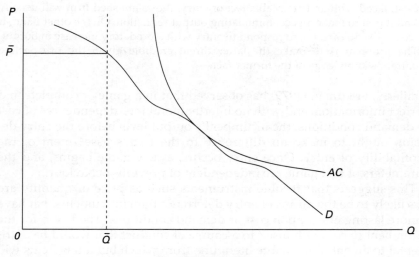

FIGURE 5.3

about the information available to the firms, and examine the roles of signalling and reputation in entry deterrence.

An instructive place to start is with the Bain–Sylos model of entry deterrence.[14] According to the Bain–Sylos postulate, the rival assumes that the output of the incumbent after entry would be the same as his output before entry. Given this postulate, it follows that the incumbent can influence the rival's assessment of post-entry profitability by varying his own pre-entry output. Figure 5.3 shows the 'limit output', and corresponding 'limit price' sufficient to deter entry. The demand curve for the industry is D, which is drawn relative to the vertical axis at 0. The AC curve is the average cost curve of the rival. It is drawn relative to the vertical axis given by the dashed line at output level $\bar{Q}$ because the D curve relative to that axis is the residual demand faced by the rival.

The limit output and limit price are $\bar{Q}$ and $\bar{P}$, respectively. If output is less than $\bar{Q}$, the AC curve is shifted left, and a portion of it would lie below the demand curve, in which case the rival could enter profitably. An output level greater than or equal to $\bar{Q}$ suffices to deter entry. The incumbent may choose to deter or to accommodate entry, depending on the profitability to him of each course of action.

The above analysis is instructive, but not altogether convincing. The difficulty lies with the postulate that the rival expects the incumbent not to change his output level in the event. Dixit (1980, p. 97) questions the postulate on two counts:

First, faced with an irrevocable fact of entry, the established firm will usually find it best to make an accommodating output reduction. On the other hand, it would like to threaten to respond to entry with a predatory increase in output. The problem is to make the latter threat credible given the prospective entrant's knowledge of the former fact.

Similarly, Friedman (1979) has observed that in a game of complete and perfect information, and with no intertemporal interdependences of cost or demand conditions, the incumbent's output level before the entry decision ought to make no difference to the rival's assessment of the profitability of entry. Once entry occurs, a new game begins, and the parameters of that game are independent of previous behaviour.

This suggests that flexible instruments such as price or quantity are less likely to be the means of entry deterrence than instruments that have a more lasting effect upon cost or demand conditions. The key is for the incumbent to *commit* himself to a course of conduct that would be detrimental to an entrant. A large literature, from which but a few items will be mentioned,[15] has explored this theme. Figure 5.4 below sketches a simple schema.

First, the incumbent chooses the level of some strategic variable K. Numerous interpretations can be given to K, but for the moment regard it as the incumbent's capacity level. If the rival chooses not to enter, he gets zero, and the incumbent gets $I^0(K)$, as shown at the foot of the right-hand branch. Note that the incumbent's payoff depends on K even if entry does not occur. If entry does take place, a duopoly exists. Without examining the details of the duopolists' interactions, let us assume that the upshot of the 'market game' between them is that the incumbent gets $I^e(K)$ and the rival gets $R^E(K)$ in the event of entry. The schema is broad enough to allow for the rival also to choose some strategic variable, after

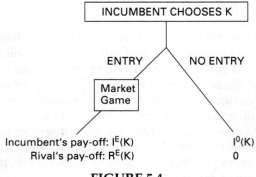

FIGURE 5.4

the incumbent's choice of K. This would be included in the black box of the market game.

The incumbent's choice of K deters entry if $R^E(K) < 0$. It may be that entry is deterred even by the level of K that would have been chosen by a pure monopolist facing no threat of entry. The entry is said to be blockaded. Or it may be that the incumbent does better to permit entry than to deter it. But here our concern is with the remaining case, in which strategic entry deterrence is optimal for the incumbent.

What are the likely instruments of entry deterrence? It is useful to distinguish between those that affect costs (the incumbent's and/or the rival's) and those that affect demand. As to the former, Dixit (1980) showed how the incumbent's choice of *capacity* could deter entry, but in Dixit's model, excess (in the sense of idle) capacity is not observed.[16] More generally, K can be interpreted as the incumbent's level of *capital input*. Strategic entry deterrence commonly implies over-capitalisation, in the sense that the output eventually produced by the imcumbent could have been produced more efficiently with a lower level of capital, and a correspondingly higher level of variable factors of production (see Spence, 1977). The same holds when K is interpreted as the incumbent's cost-reducing R&D expenditure. (Note the parallel with section III (4) above). In all these examples, the incumbent's commitment of high K promises that he will supply a high output level, or charge a low price, in the market game. The choice of K is therefore unattractive to the rival, not because of its direct effects, but because of its indirect influence upon the outcome of the market game.

In criticism of the Bain–Sylos analysis, it was stated above that the incumbent's pre-entry output would not affect the rival's entry decision if there were no intertemporal interdependences of cost or demand. But such interdependences do hold if the *experience curve* effect operates – i.e. if a firm's cost level is a declining function of its cumulative output. In that case it is possible for the incumbent's choice of output to deter entry strategically: see Spence (1981) and Fudenberg and Tirole (1983).

As well as the incumbent lowering his own costs, there may be ways for him to *raise the rival's cost*: see Salop and Scheffman (1983). For example, by setting high wage rates in the industry, the incumbent increases his own costs and those of an entrant. The direct effect of this upon the incumbent is unfavourable, but if the indirect effect is to deter the rival's entry, then the ploy may well be beneficial to him in overall terms.

Another way in which entry might be deterred is for the incumbent to deny the rival access to technology that would allow him to compete. Gilbert and Newbery (1982) examine *pre-emptive patenting* – the acquisition of a patent by an incumbent firm with the purpose of denying the patent, and hence an entry opportunity, to a potential rival. An important factor here is that the incumbent's incentive to win the patent is likely to exceed the rival's incentive, even if the patent is for a technology inferior to that already enjoyed by the incumbent. This is because the incumbent's monopoly persists if he denies entry to the rival, whereas competition, which is less profitable than monopoly, occurs in the event of entry. This result has an important bearing on the question of the persistence of monopoly, for the advantage of the incumbent arises from his *strategic position*; intrinsically the incumbent may be no different from the rival. The result also offers an explanation of the phenomenon of sleeping (i.e., unused) patents, because the pre-emption result does not depend upon the patent being for a technology that is superior to the incumbent's existing technology.

Turning from the cost side to the demand side, there are further ways in which an incumbent firm can make the prospect of entry unattractive for a rival firm. In some circumstances, strategic advertising deters entry, although in Schmalensee's (1983) exploration of advertising and entry deterrence, it emerged that low advertising was the way to deter entry. The reason was that high advertising would cause the incumbent to have a higher price in the market game. For the rival, the favourable latter effect outweighed the disadvantage of high advertising, and made entry more attractive. *Brand proliferation* – the introduction of numerous new products – can also serve to deter entry (see Schmalensee (1978)). To use the locational analogy common in the analysis of product differentiation, brand proliferation fills up product space in such a way that there are no remaining slots or niches for profitable entry.

Product differentiation was one of Bain's three sources of barriers to entry (see p. 113 above). Although advertising is often regarded as a measure of product differentiation, Bain did not see it as the heart of the problem. Schmalensee (1982) shows how buyers' uncertainty about the quality of new brands can give established (or pioneering) brands an advantage in a differentiated market. The new brand would have to be priced substantially below the existing brand to induce consumers to experiment with it; part of the cost of the experiment is the loss of surplus currently being enjoyed on the existing brand. This is again an example where the incumbent has strategic advantage solely because of already being in the market.

To summarise so far, there are numerous ways in which an incumbent firm can influence cost and/or demand conditions by strategic investments in such a way as to discourage entry into his market. Bulow *et al.* (1985b) and Fudenberg and Tirole (1984) have examined in general terms various types of entry deterrence. Returning to the schema on p. 116 above, we can ask whether over- or underinvestment in the strategic variable K deters entry. The answer depends of course upon the specification of the market game. In some instances (such as excess capacity deterring entry), the incumbent deters entry by being 'large'. Fudenberg and Tirole call this the Top Dog Effect. In other instances, the incumbent deters entry by being 'small', and thereby promises an aggressive response in the event of entry. This is the Lean and Hungry Look. It may be better for the incumbent to accommodate, rather than deter entry. Then he will act strategically to influence the nature of entry, either by being 'large' (a Top Dog) or 'small' (the Puppy Dog Ploy). The aim of all these strategic moves is to cause the rival to choose to act more favourably for the incumbent than he would otherwise do.

So far we have supposed that firms are fully informed about each other's opportunities and motivation, but we now turn to the second step in the analysis of strategic entry deterrence by relaxing this assumption. Milgrom and Roberts (1982b) have shown how limit pricing may be used to deter entry when the potential entrant is uncertain as to the cost level of the incumbent firm. The rival's expectations concerning that cost level – and hence his entry decision – are influenced by the price charged by the incumbent before the entry decision is made. Therefore the pre-entry price can act as a signal of the incumbent's efficiency. An incumbent with low costs would like to signal that fact, because the potential rival would then be more reluctant to enter his market. By the same token, an inefficient incumbent would like to masquerade as a low-cost firm in order to make entry less likely. This incentive to signal in an uncertain environment means that the incumbent's pricing may be used as an instrument of entry deterrence. Note that consumers benefit from this kind of limit pricing insofar as it lowers price. Other interesting issues arise when there is uncertainty about demand as well as the incumbent's cost level. Then a low pre-entry price might signal either low demand or low costs: see Matthews and Mirman (1983).

Milgrom and Roberts (1982a) and Kreps and Wilson (1982) have explored another context in which uncertainty about the incumbent plays a role in entry deterrence, namely in connection with *predatory pricing*. They examine a game due to Selten (1978) in which an incumbent firm – a chain store – is threatened by entry in each of a number of towns. More precisely, they look at a game in which the predatory pricing game in Figure 5.2 is repeated a finite number of times. Intuitively, one would expect that the incumbent would fight entry if challenged in town early in the sequence, in order to deter later entrants. However, this is not so if the entrants have complete information about the opportunities and motivation of the incumbent, because in that case he would never fight entry. This is because it is common knowledge that he would not fight in the last town; and so he would not fight in the last but one; and so on. But if the assumption of complete information is very slightly relaxed – so that there is a possibility that the incumbent is somehow committed to fighting – then even an uncommitted incumbent would (rationally) fight entry in early towns to keep up the *reputation* of possibly being a committed fighter. This reputation effect is very powerful, in the sense that a very small amount of imperfect information can make it rational to fight in a large number of towns. There is an exact parallel between this and the work of Kreps *et al.* (1982) on the repeated Prisoners' Dilemma described in section III (1).

(3)   *Potential competition: concluding remarks*

To summarise, potential competition affects the behaviour of existing firms insofar as it impels them to behave in such a way that entry is an unattractive prospect. In a contestable market, where entry is ultrafree, entry is unattractive only when existing firms, singly and in combination, meet consumers' demands with maximum efficiency. In other, perhaps more realistic circumstances, this need not be so. Incumbent firms may choose to act strategically to deter entry. Since the key to strategic commitment is some degree of irreversibility, price is perhaps less likely to be the instrument of strategic entry deterrence than non-price instruments such as capacity, R&D or brand proliferation (although price was regarded as the instrument in conventional theory of entry deterrence). However, when firms are uncertain about each other and their environment, richer possibilities exist, and firms' behaviour may be chosen partly with a view to the signals conveyed to rivals. The theory of industrial organisation has made important advances in understanding these matters.

V   Conclusions and policy implications

...The purpose of this paper has been to explain some recent developments in industrial economics so as to give a background for the consideration of policy. In this concluding section, some of the main themes of the foregoing discussion are highlighted, and it is suggested how they bear on policy questions.

A major theme is the *endogeneity of market structure* (see e.g. Section III (2) and III (3) above). Recent theory has examined the dependence of market structure and conduct upon the basic parameters of technology and demand, whereas previously much emphasis was placed upon the causal flow from structure to conduct and performance. If structure is regarded as a symptom of underlying forces, rather than as the root cause of (say) undesirable forms of conduct, then the perspective on policy alters.

A related theme is the role of *potential competition*. If conditions of entry into an industry are free and easy, then, even thought there may be only a few firms actually in the industry, they may be compelled to perform well, in terms of productive, dynamic and allocative efficiency, due to the threat of entry. It is for this reason that policies designed to liberalise entry are on the whole desirable. The results of the liberalisation of the US airline markets, and of the market for terminal equipment in telecommunications, are examples in point. As a theoretical proposition it is not always the case that liberalisation is desirable, but there must be a strong – though rebuttable – presumption in favour of that claim.

There are numerous ways in which incumbent firms can seek to thwart the threat of entry – for example by predatory practices. Unless these practices are somehow checked, the danger is that other measures of liberalisation will not be effective. If threats of predatory behaviour deter entry, then liberalisation has not properly taken place.[17] In any event, it would be a serious mistake to suppose that measures of liberalisation are always sufficient to ensure good industry performance. In a contestable market (see section IV (1) above) that is indeed the case, but the assumptions of the theory of contestable markets are both strict and sensitive to small variations. The implications of that theory for policy are therefore doubtful, save insofar as the theory underlines the point that entry conditions are important. In some industries (including natural monopolies) no amount of liberalisation will ensure good industry performance. There is then a case for regulation – either in the form of control of public enterprise, or as regulation of private enterprise.[18]

Another broad theme is that strategic competition among the few can produce results that are not socially desirable. For example, it was shown in section III (1) that effective collusion between firms can occur even when there is no opportunity for them to make enforceable agreements. In Section III (4) it was shown how a firm might over-invest in R&D or capital equipment (and therefore produce its output inefficiently) in an attempt to gain strategic advantage relative to its competitors. Section IV (2) on strategic entry deterrence contained numerous examples of entry deterring devices that are costly to society both directly and because they thwart competition.

The classic example of market failure is perhaps that of R&D competition (see section III (2)), which has been a major topic in recent industrial economics. The free market allocates resources inefficiently to R&D for several reasons, including appropriability problems (the innovator requires reward, but static efficiency requires free access to his results) and duplication of research. These considerations are the justification for government policies such as patent protection, subsidies for R&D, and measures to promote collaborative R&D (e.g. joint ventures). By its industrial policies, government can influence conditions in the game between firms – their payoffs, strategies, and so on – and thereby influence its outcome. Moreover, one government may be engaged in a game with others, in which each is choosing industrial and commercial policies to further its objectives. Many of the tools and concepts recently employed in industrial economics – such as commitments, threats and collusion – are being applied to the study of government policy using this game perspective.

Recent developments in the theory of industrial organisation have added considerably to our understanding of the workings of competition between the few. Although the perspective gained should and will influence the making and the implementation of competition policy and industrial policy, the new theory has not delivered generally applicable policy guidelines, and it is unlikely that it will do so in future. It would be wrong to blame theory for this shortcoming, for the reason is that industries are intrinsically different from one another, and the prospect of generally applicable guidelines is therefore unlikely. However, recent developments in industrial economics are providing most illuminating perspectives on the nature of industrial conflict.

Appreciation of the strategic nature of competition among the few underlines this point. The successful strategist (say a threatener or a promiser) is he who arranges things in such a way that the other parties think it sufficiently likely that the threat or promise will be carried out. Whether and how this can be done depends on the particular circumstances at hand, and is largely a matter of tactics and opportunism. The economists recently studying strategic competitions among the few have been investigating phenomena well-known to others: an eminent businessman, who had just been told of recent developments in the economics of industry exclaimed: I feel like the character in Molière who learns that all the while he has been speaking prose.

Notes

1. This phrase is borrowed (i.e. stolen) from the title of Fellner's (1949) book on oligopoly. For an excellent recent survey of the economics of industry, see Waterson (1984).
2. This phrase is due to Aaron Director – see Williamson (1979, p. 919).
3. The game is a version of the well-known Prisoners' Dilemma Game.
4. Dixit's excellent (1982) survey contains an account of this game.
5. See Friedman (1971).
6. In fact Kreps *et al*. (1982) suppose that the small probability is attached to B playing the tit-for-tat strategy, which had emerged as a successful strategy in experiments – see Axelrod (1984).
7. The same point emerges in the work on predatory pricing by the authors of Kreps *et al*. (1982) reported on p. 102.
8. Abreu *et al*. (1984) have shown that in Green and Porter's (1984) model, the most effective way to police the cartel is to have a severe reversionary episode lasting one period. The parallel with Abreu (1984) is clear.

9. By contrast, von Weizsäcker (1984) has constructed a model in which higher switching costs cause there to be more competition. See Klemperer (1984) for a discussion.
10. See also Dasgupta (1985) for a review of the theory of technological competition.
11. Another property is that in multiproduct natural monopoly industries, 'Ramsey prices' obtain at equilibrium for the product set of the industry in question: see Baumol et al. (1982). Ramsey prices maximise social welfare subject to the constraint that the firms earn a given profit level.
12. Most economists would agree with the proposition that on the whole it is desirable for entry to be as free as possible. This statement is qualified because in some circumstances it is possible that free entry would damage welfare: see e.g. von Weizsäcker (1980).
13. The case where several incumbents seek non-cooperatively to deter entry has been studied by Gilbert and Vives (1985).
14. See Bain (1956) and Sylos-Labini (1962).
15. A fuller survey, and an extensive bibliography, are provided by Geroski and Jacquemin (1984).
16. Bulow et al. (1985a) show that idle capacity is possible when Dixit's assumptions on demand are relaxed.
17. For a brief account of the economics of predatory practises, see Vickers (1985) and the references therein.
18. The natural monopoly problem in general, and electricity and telecommunications in particular, are discussed in Vickers and Yarrow (1985).

References

Abreu, D. (1984), "Infinitely repeated games with discounting: a general theory", unpublished paper, Princeton University.
Abreu, D., D. Pearce and E. Stacchetti (1984), "Optimal cartel equilibrium with imperfect monitoring", Harvard Institute of Economic Research Discussion Paper 1090.
Axelrod, R. (1984), *The Evolution of Cooperation* (New York: Basic Books).
Bain, J. (1956), *Barriers to new competition* (Cambridge, MA: Harvard University Press).
Baumol, W. (1982), "Contestable Markets: an uprising in the theory of industry structure", *American Economic Review*, 72, 1–15.
Baumol, W., J. Panzar and R. Willig (1982), *Contestable markets and the theory of industry structure* (San Diego CA: Harcourt Brace Jovanovich).
Brander, J. and B. Spencer (1983), "Strategic commitment with R&D: the symmetric case", *Bell Journal of Economics*, 14, 225–235.
Bulow, J., J. Geanakopolos and P. Klemperer (1985a), "Holding idle capacity to deter entry", *Economic Journal*, 95, 178–82.
Bulow, J., J. Geanakopolos and P. Klemperer (1985b), "Multimarket oligopoly", *Journal of Political Economy*, 93, 488–511.
Dasgupta, P. (1985), "The theory of technological competition", in F. Mattewson and J. Stiglitz (ed.), *New developments in the analysis of market structure* (Boston, MA: MIT Press).

Dasgupta, P. and J. Stiglitz (1980), "Industrial structure and the nature of innovative activity", *Economic Journal*, 90, 266–93.

Dixit, A. (1980), "The role of investment in entry deterrence", *Economic Journal*, 90, 95–106.

Dixit, A. (1982), "Recent developments in oligopoly theory", *American Economic Review Papers and Proceedings*, 72, 12–17.

Fellner, W. (1949), *Competition among the few* (New York: Knopf).

Friedman, J. (1971), "A non-cooperative equilibrium for supergames", *Review of Economic Studies*, 28, 1–12.

Friedman, J. (1977), *Oligopoly and the theory of games* (Amsterdam: North-Holland).

Friedman, J. (1979), "On entry preventing behaviour and limit price models of entry", in Brams *et al.* (eds.), *Applied Game Theory* (Vienna: Physica-Verlag).

Fudenberg, D. and J. Tirole (1983), "Learning by doing and market performance", *Bell Journal of Economics*, 14, 522–30.

Fudenberg, D. and J. Tirole (1984), "The fat-cat effect, the puppy-dog ploy, and the lean and hungry look", *American Economic Review Papers and Proceedings*, 74, 361–6.

Geroski, P. and A. Jacquemin (1984), "Dominant firms and their alleged decline", *International Journal of Industrial Organization*, 2, 1–27.

Gilbert, R. and D. Newbery (1982), "Pre-emptive patenting and the persistence of monopoly", *American Economic Review*, 72, 514–26.

Gilbert, R. and X. Vives (1985), "Non-cooperative entry deterrence and the free rider problem", mimeo, University of Pennsylvania.

Green, E. and R. Porter (1984), "Non-cooperative collusion under imperfect price information", *Econometrica*, 52, 87–100.

Kamien, M. and N. Schwartz (1982). *Market structure and innovation* (Cambridge: Cambridge University Press).

Klemperer, P. (1984), "Collusion via switching costs", Stanford University Graduate School of Business Discussion Paper no. 786.

Kreps D., P. Milgrom, J. Roberts and R. Wilson (1982), "Rational cooperation in a finitely repeated prisoners' dilemma game", *Journal of Economic Theory*, 27, 245–52.

Kreps, D. and R. Wilson (1982), "Reputation and imperfect information", *Journal of Economic Theory*, 27, 253–79.

Matthews, S. and L. Mirman (1983), "Equilibrium limit pricing: the effects of private information and stochastic demand", *Econometrica*, 51, 981–96.

Milgrom, R. and J. Roberts (1982b), "Limit pricing and entry under incomplete information: An equilibrium analysis", *Econometrica*, 50, 443–59.

Milgrom, R. and J. Roberts (1982a), "Predation, reputation and entry deterrence", *Journal of Economic Theory*, 27, 280–312.

Ordover, J. and R. Willig (1985), "Antitrust for high-technology industries: assessing research joint ventures and mergers", Woodrow Wilson School Discussion Paper no. 87.

Salop, S. (1979), "Strategic entry deterrence", *American Economic Review Papers and Proceedings*, 69, 335–8.

Salop, S. (ed.) (1981), *Strategy, predation and antitrust analysis* (Washington DC: F.T.C.).

Salop, S. (1985), "Practices that facilitate Oligopoly Coordination", in F. Mathewson and J. Stiglitz (eds) *New developments in the analysis of market structure* (Boston MA: MIT Press).

Salop, S. and D. Scheffman, (1983), "Raising rivals' costs", *American Economic Review Papers and Proceedings*, 73, 267–71.

Schelling, T. (1960), *The strategy of conflict* (Cambridge MA: Harvard University Press).

Scherer, F. (1980), *Industrial Market Structure and Economic Performance* (2nd ed., Chicago: Rand-McNally).

Schmalensee, R. (1978), "Entry deterrence in the ready to eat breakfast cereal industry", *Bell Journal of Economics*, 9, 305–27.

Schmalensee, R. (1982), "Product Differentiation Advantages of Pioneering Brands", *American Economic Review*, 82, 349–65.

Schmalensee, R. (1983), "Advertising and Entry Deterrance: an Exploratory Model", *Journal of Political Economy*, 90, 636–53.

Selten, R. (1965), "Spieltheoretische Behandlung eines Oligopolmodells mit Nachfragetragheit", *Zeitschrift fur die gesamte Staatswissenschaft*, 121, 301–24 and 667–89.

Selten, R. (1975), "Re-examination of the Perfectness Concept for Equlibrium Points in Extensive Games", *International Journal of Game Theory*, 4, 25–55.

Selten, R. (1978), "The Chain Store Paradox", *Theory and Decision*, 9, 127–59.

Shaked, A. and J. Sutton (1982), "Relaxing Price Competition through Product Differentiation", *Review of Economic Studies*, 49, 3–14.

Shaked, A. and J. Sutton (1983), "Natural Oligopolies", *Econometrica*, 51, 1469–84.

Shepherd, W. (1984), "'Contestability' vs Competition", *American Economic Review*, 74, 572–87.

Spence, M. (1977), "Entry, capacity, investment and oligopolistic pricing", *Bell Journal of Economics*, 8, 534–44.

Spence, M. (1981), "The learning curve and competition", *Bell Journal of Economics*, 12, 49–70.

Spence, M. (1984), "Cost Reduction, Competition, and Industry Performance", *Econometrica*, 52, 101–21.

Stoneman, P. (1983), The *Economic Analysis of Technological Change* (Oxford: Oxford University Press).

Sylos-Labini, P. (1962), *Oligopoly and Technical Progress* (Cambridge, MA: Harvard University Press).

Vickers, J. (1985), "The Economics of Predatory Practices", *Fiscal Studies*, 6(3), 24–36.

Vickers, J. and G. Yarrow (1985), *Privatization and the Natural Monopolies* (London: Public Policy Centre).

von Weizsäcker, C. (1980), "A Welfare Analysis of Barriers to Entry", *Bell Journal of Economics*, 11, 399–420.

von Weizsäcker, C. (1984), "The costs of substitution", *Econometrica*, 52, 1085–116.

Waterson, M. (1984), *Economic Theory of the Industry* (Cambridge: Cambridge University Press).

Williamson, O. (1979), "Symposium on Antitrust Law and Economics: Symposium Introduction", *University of Pennsylvania Law Review*, 127, 918–24.

PART III

GENERAL EQUILIBRIUM AND WELFARE

The Anatomy of Market Failure*

F. BATOR

What is it we mean by "market failure"? Typically, at least in allocation theory, we mean the failure of a more or less idealized system of price-market institutions to sustain "desirable" activities or to estop "undesirable" activites.[1] The desirability of an activity, in turn, is evaluated relative to the solution values of some explicit or implied maximum-welfare problem.

It is the central theorem of modern welfare economics that under certain strong assumptions about technology, tastes and producers' motivations, the equilibrium conditions which characterize a system of competitive markets will exactly correspond to the requirements of Paretian efficiency.[2] Further, if competitively imputed incomes are continuously redistributed in costless lump-sum fashion so as to achieve the income-distribution implied by a social welfare function then the competitive market solution will correspond to the one electronically calculated Pareto-efficient solution which maximizes subject only to tastes, technology and initial endowments, that particular welfare function.[3]

Many things in the real world violate such correspondence: imperfect information, inertia and resistance to change, the infeasibility of costless lump-sum taxes, businessmen's desire for a "quiet life," uncertainty and inconsistent expectations, the vagaries of aggregate demand, etc. With most of these I am not here concerned: they have to do with the efficiency of "real life" market institutions operated by "real life" people in a nonstationary world of uncertainty, miscalculation, etc.

---

*Quarterly Journal of Economics (1958), pp. 351–79.

What follows is an attempt, rather, to explore and order those phenomena which cause even errorless profit- and preference-maximizing calculation in a stationary context of perfect (though limited) information and foresight to fail to sustain Pareto-efficient allocation. I am concerned, in other words, with the decentralizing efficiency of that regime of signals, rules and built-in sanctions which defines a price-market system.[4]

Specifically, Section I sets out the necessary conditions for efficiency of decentralized price-profit calculations both in a "laissez-faire" and in a "socialist" setting of Lange–Lerner civil servants. Section II is a brief digression on an often discussed mode of failure in these conditions: neoclassical external economies. It is concluded that the modern formulation of the doctrine, in terms of "direct interaction," begs more questions than it answers; further, that the usual emphasis on "divorce of scarcity from effective ownership" is misplaced. Section III, then, suggests a comprehensive ordering of types of market failure, with generalized indivisibility, public goods, and, last and least, nonappropriability as the villains of the piece. Section IV consists of some comments on the Meade and Scitovsky classifications of external economies; on the analytical link between indivisibility and public goods; on the significance of "exclusion"; on organizational arrangements designed to offset externality; and on blends of the various types of market failure. Section V concludes with some cautionary notes on the relevance of market-efficiency for choice of institutions.

I   The conditions of market efficiency

The central theorem of modern welfare economics, the so-called *duality theorem*, asserts a correspondence between Pareto efficiency and market performance. Its analytical essence lies in the remarkable fact that with all-round convexity, independence of tastes, etc., the technocratically formulated, institutionally neutral, Paretian maximum-of-welfare problem has embedded within it a set of constants: "duals," Lagrangean multipliers, shadow-prices, which have all the analytical characteristics of prices, wages, rents, interest rates.[5] Correspondence between Pareto-efficiency and market performance implies, at the least, that decentralized decisions in response to these "prices" by atomistic profit- and satisfaction-maximizers sustain just that constellation of inputs, outputs and commodity-distribution that the maximum of the specified social welfare function calls for. It implies, in other words, that decentralized market calculations correctly account for all "economic" costs and benefits to which the relevant W-function is sensitive.[6]

Duality can fail in many ways. Specifically, and in a statical and 'laissez-faire' context:[7]

(1) Duality will fail unless the Pareto-efficient (a) input–output points (production) and (b) associated commodity distribution points (exchange) which associate with the maximum of the welfare function in hand are characterized by a complete set of marginal-rate-of-substitution (MRS) equalities (or limiting inequalities) which, in turn, yield a set of price-like constants. Where no such constants exist, reference will be to *failure of existence*.[8]

(2) Should such an associated set of Lagrangean parameters exist, duality would nevertheless fail, specifically in production, unless the bliss configuration of inputs and outputs, evaluated in terms of these price parameters, will yield: (a) a local profit-maximum position for each producer, rather than, as possible, a profit minimum; (b) non-negative profits for all producers from whom production is required; (c) maximum profits-in-the-large for each producer. Failure on counts (a) and (c) will be labeled *failure by signal*, that on count (b) *failure by incentive*.[9]

(3) Even if all efficient production configurations, or the one which maximizes a particular welfare-function, coincide with points of maximum and non-negative producers' profits, market mediation may fail in production. If prices are determined by market forces, they will not correspond to a Paretian maximum unless self-policing perfect competition obtains in all markets. Self-policing competition requires "very many" producers in every market.[10] If, then, for whatever reason, some markets are saturated by a few firms of "efficient" scale, the full welfare-maximum solution of inputs, outputs *and prices* will not be sustained. There will be *failure by structure*.

(4) Finally, even if all above is satisfied, market performance could still fail, and fail in a statical sense, due to arbitrary legal and organizational "imperfections," or feasibility limitations on "keeping book," such as leave some inputs or outputs "hidden," or preclude their explicit allocation or capture by market processes (e.g., the restriction, unless I go into baseball, on the sale of the capitalized value of my lifetime services). Failure is *by enforcement*.

All the above are germane to duality in its usual sense, to the statical Pareto-efficiency of laissez-faire markets with genuine profit- and satisfaction-seekers.[11] Conditions (1), (2) and (4) are relevant, also, to the decentralizing efficiency of a Lange–Lerner type organizational scheme. In its "capitalist" version, with profit-motivated operation of privately-owned means of production where it is simply an anti-monopoly device to assure parametric take-prices-as-given behavior, conditions (1), (2) and (4) are all necessary for efficiency. Of course condition (3), self-policing competition, no longer matters.

In its true socialist version, a Lange–Lerner system can afford to "fail" also "by incentive," (2b). Socialist civil servants, under injunction to maximize profit (in the small) in terms of fixed centrally-quoted prices, care or should care not at all about absolute profitability. By assumption the scheme can dispense with the built-in incentive of positive profit: the lure of bureaucratic advancement, the image of Siberia, or the old school tie presumably substitute for the urge to get rich. But if prices and the injunction to maximize profit are to be used to decentralize, condition (1): existence, and (2a) and (2c): correct and unambiguous signals, remain crucial.[12] So does condition (4) the solution of quantities and prices need not be profitable and self-enforcing, but it does have to be enforceable. If the nectar in apple blossoms is scarce and carries a positive shadow price, it must be possible to make every beekeeper pay for his charges' meals.

It warrants repetition that this has to do with whether a decentralized price-market game will or will not *sustain* a Pareto-efficient configuration. The word sustain is critical. There exists a host of further considerations which bear on dynamical questions of adjustment, of "how the system gets there." (E.g. will some "natural" price-market type computational routine of price–quantity responses with a meaningful institutional counterpart tend to track the solution?) These are not here at issue. We shall be concerned only with the prior problem of whether a price-market system which finds itself at the maximum-welfare point will or will not tend to remain there.[13]

The relevant literature is rich but confusing. It abounds in mutually reinforcing and overlapping descriptions and explanations of market failure: external economies, indivisibility, nonappropriability, direct interaction, public goods, atmosphere, etc. In a sense, our problem is simply to sort out the relations among these. In doing so, it is appropriate and useful to begin with a brief review of the neoclassical doctrine of external economies and of its modern formulation in terms of "direct interaction."

II Neoclassical external economies: a digression

By way of some history

Marshall, as has often been pointed out, proposed the external economy argument to explain, without resort to dynamics, the phenomenon of a negatively sloped ("forward falling") long-run industry supply curve in terms consistent with a horizontal or rising marginal cost curve (MC) in the "representative" firm. The device permits – in logic, if not in fact –

long-run competitive equilibrium of many firms within an industry, each producing at its profit-maximum price-equal-to-a-rising-MC position, without foreclosing the possibility of a falling supply price with rising industry output.[14]

The mechanism is simple. It is postulated that an expansion in the output of the industry as a whole brings into play economies which cause a downward shift of the cost curves of all the component firms. These economies, however, are not subject to exploitation by any one of the myriad of tiny atomized firms. Their own MC curves, at $p = MC$, rise both before and after the shift, due, presumably, to internal diseconomies associated with the entrepreneurial function which defines the firm. Even the modern formulation is not entirely without ambiguity – institutional ambiguity is intrinsic to the device of parametrization: how many firms does it take for the demand curve of each to be perfectly horizontal? – but it does provide a means for "saving" the competitive model, of ducking the monopoly problem.

Marshall, and also Professor Pigou, "preferred," as it were, the other horn of what they perhaps saw as a dilemma. The external economy device, while saving competition, implies a flaw in the efficacy of the "invisible hand" in guiding production.[15] "Price equal to MC" is saved, but wrong. Market forces, they argued, will not give enough output by industries enjoying external economies and will cause industries with rising supply curves to overexpand. Hence the Marshall–Pigou prescription: to harmonize private production decisions with public welfare, tax the latter set of industries and subsidize the former.

It took the better part of thirty years, and the cumulative powers of Allyn Young, and Messrs. Robertson, Knight, Sraffa, and Viner, to unravel the threads of truth and error which run through the Marshall–Pigou argument.[16] The crucial distinction, which provides the key to it all, is between what Viner labeled technological external economies, on the one hand, and pecuniary external economies on the other. The latter, if dominant, cause the long-run supply curve of an industry, say A, to decline because the price of an input, B, falls in response to an increase in A's demand for it. The technological variety, on the other hand, though also a reversible function of industry output, consists in organizational or other improvements in efficiency which do not show up in input prices.[17]

As regards pecuniary external economies, Robertson and Sraffa made it clear that in a sense both the Marshall–Pigou conclusions were wrong. For one thing, no subsidy is called for. The implied gains in efficiency are adequately signaled by the input price, and profit-maximizing output levels by the A-firms are socially efficient. Second, monopoly troubles may be with us, via, as it were, the back door. For what causes the price of B to drop in response to increased demand? We are back where we started: a declining long-run supply curve.

In the end, then, if *internal* technological economies of scale are ruled out, we are left with only *technological* external economies. All pecuniary external economies must be due to technological economies somewhere in the system.[18] It is true – and this is what remains of the original Marshall–Pigou proposition – that technological externalities are not correctly accounted for by prices, that they violate the efficiency of decentralized market calculation.

The modern formulation[19]

In its modern version, the notion of external economies – external economies proper, that is: Viner's technological variety – belongs to a more general doctrine of "direct interaction." Such interaction, whether it involves producer–producer, consumer–consumer, producer–consumer, or employer–employee relations, consists in interdependences that are external to the price system, hence unaccounted for by market valuations. Analytically, it implies the nonindependence of various preference and production functions. Its effect is to cause divergence between private and social cost-benefit calculation.

That this is so, is easily demonstrated by means of a simplified variant of a production model suggested by J. E. Meade.[20] Assume a world of all-round perfect competition where a single purchasable and inelastically supplied input, labor ($\bar{L}$), is used to produce two homogeneous and divisible goods, apples (A) and honey (H), at nonincreasing returns to scale. But while the output of A is dependent only on L_A: $A = A(L_A)$, honey production is sensitive also to the level of apple output: $H = H(L_H, A(L_A))$. (Professor Meade makes pleasurable the thought of apple blossoms making for honey abundance.)[21]

By solving the usual constrained maximum problem for the production-possibility curve, it can be shown that Paretian production efficiency implies

$$p_H \frac{\partial H}{\partial L_H} = w \qquad (6.1)$$

$$p_A \frac{dA}{dL_A} + p_H \frac{\partial H}{\partial A} \frac{dA}{dL_A} = w \qquad (6.2)$$

where p_H, p_A, and w represent the prices, respectively, of honey, apples and labor.[22] Equation (6.1) is familiar enough and consistent with profit maximizing. Each competitive honey producer will do for profit what he must for efficiency: hire labor until the value of its social as well as private marginal product equals the wage rate. Not so the apple producers; unless $\frac{\partial H}{\partial A} = 0$ – unless the cross effect of apples on honey is zero – their profit-maximizing production decisions will be nonefficient. Specifically, if apples have a positive external effect on honey output, market-determined L_A will be less than is socially desirable.[23]

A different way to see this is to examine the relations of private to social marginal cost. The marginal money cost of apples to the competitive apple producer is $\frac{w}{dA/dL_A}$; that of honey to the beekeeper, $\frac{w}{\partial H/\partial L_H}$.

It is the ratio of the two: $\frac{\partial H/\partial L_H}{dA/dL_A}$ that competitive market-mediation brings into equality with the equilibrating configuration of relative prices. Markets will be efficient if, and only if, this private marginal cost ratio reflects the true marginal cost to society of an extra apple in terms of forgone honey: the marginal rate of transformation between H and A.

What is MRT in the model? Differentiating (totally) the two production functions and dividing the value of one derivative into the other, we get, in absolute (cost) terms:

$$MRT \equiv \left|\frac{dH}{dA}\right| = \frac{\partial H/\partial L_H}{dA/dL_A} - \frac{\partial H}{\partial A}$$

If, then, $\frac{\partial H}{\partial A} > 0$, the true marginal *social* cost of an "extra" apple, in terms of honey forgone, is less than the market-indicated private cost. It is less precisely by the amount of positive "feedback" on honey output due the "extra" apple.

By combining (6.1) and (6.2), eliminating w, and dividing through by p_H and, $\frac{dA}{dL_A}$ we get the condition for Pareto efficiency in terms of private MC's:

$$\frac{\partial H/\partial L_H}{dA/dL_A} = \frac{P_A}{P_H} + \frac{\partial H}{\partial A}$$

Clearly, price equal to private marginal cost will not do. Further, if prices are market-determined, they will diverge from true, *social* marginal cost.

Any number of variations on the model suggest themselves. As Meade pointed out, interactions can be mutual and need not be associated with the outputs. Even in the above case, it is perhaps more suggestive to think of L_A as producing some social value-product both in the A industry and the H industry. In the most general formulation, one can simply think of each production function as containing all the other variables of the system, some perhaps with zero weight. Moreover, by introducing two or more nonproduced inputs one can, as Meade does, work out the consequences for income distribution and input proportions.[24]

Some queries

The modern formulation of the doctrine of external economies, in terms of direct interaction, is not only internally consistent: it also yields insight. Yet one may well retain about it some dissatisfaction. There is no doubt that the Robertson–Sraffa–Viner distinction between the technological and the pecuniary sort gets to the nub of what is the matter with the original Marshallian analysis. It cuts right through the confusion which led Marshall and Pigou to conclude that the price mechanism is faulty in situations where in truth it is at its best: in allocating inputs in less than infinitely elastic supply between alternative productive uses. It also facilitates unambiguous formulation of the more difficult "falling supply price" case. But in a sense it only begs the fundamental question: what is it that gives rise to "direct interaction," to short circuit, as it were, of the signaling system?

Most modern writers have let matters rest with the Ellis–Fellner type explanation: "the divorce of scarcity from effective ownership."[25] Does nonappropriability then explain all direct interaction? In a sense it does, yet by directing attention to institutional and feasibility considerations which make it impracticable for "real life" market-institutions to mimic a price–profit–preference computation, it diverts attention from some deeper issues. Surely the word "ownership" serves to illuminate but poorly the phenomenon of a temperance leaguer's reaction to a hard-drinking neighbor's (sound insulated and solitary) Saturday night, or the reason why a price system, if efficient, will not permit full "compensation," in an age of electronic scramblers, for an advertisement-less radio program, or for the "services" of a bridge.[26]

It may be argued, of course, that at least the two latter examples are out of order, that radio programs and bridges do not involve "direct," i.e., non-price, interaction. But is this really so? Does not the introduction of a new program directly affect my and your consumption possibilities, in ways other than by a change in relative prices? Does not a bridge, or a road, have a direct effect on the production possibilities of neighboring producers, in precisely the sense in which apples affect the possibilities of beekeepers?[27]

True, perhaps bridges and roads are unfair: they violate the neoclassical assumption of perfect divisibility and nonincreasing returns to scale. But they surely do involve non-price interaction. In fact, lumpiness and increasing returns are perhaps the most important causes of such interaction. Are they to be denied status as externalities? More generally, are we to exclude from the class of externalities any direct interaction not due to difficulties with "effective ownership," any failures other than "by enforcement"?

It would be, of course, perfectly legitimate to do so – tastes are various. But I think it more natural and useful to broaden rather than restrict, to let "externality" denote any situation where some Paretian costs and benefits remain *external* to decentralized cost–revenue calculations in terms of prices.[28] If, however, we do so, then clearly nonappropriability[29] will not do as a complete explanation. Its concern with the inability of decentralized markets to sustain the solution-prices and quantities called for by a price–profit–preference type calculation, as computed by a team of mathematicians working with IBM machines, tends to mask the possibility that such machine-calculated solution q's may well be nonefficient.[30] It explains failure "by enforcement," but leaves hidden the empirically more important phenomena which cause failure by "nonexistence," "signal," and "incentive." Section III is designed to bring these deeper causes of generalized externality into the foreground.

III Statical externalities: an ordering

If nonappropriability is, by itself, too flimsy a base for a doctrine of generalized (statical) externality, what broader foundation is there? Section I's hierarchy of possible modes of market failure suggests a fivefold classification. If, however, one looks for an organizing principle not to modes of failure but to causes, there appear to be three polar types: (1) Ownership Externalities, (2) Technical Externalities,[31] and (3) Public Good Externalities. These are not mutually exclusive: most externality phenomena are in fact blends. Yet there emerges a sufficient three-cornered clustering to warrant consolidation.[32]

Type (1): Ownership Externalities

Imagine a world which exhibits generalized technological and taste convexity, where the electronically calculated solution of a Paretian maximum-of-welfare problem yields not only a unique set of inputs, outputs and commodity-distribution, but where initial endowments plus lump-sum transfers render income distribution optimal in terms of the community's social welfare function. Assume, further, that everything that matters is divisible, conventionally rationable, and either available in inelastic total supply,[33] or producible at constant returns to scale; also that tastes are sensitive only to own-consumption. We know, then, from the duality theorem, that the bliss-point implies a unique[34] set of prices, wages and rents, such as would cause atomistic profit- and preference-maximizers to do exactly what is necessary for bliss. In particular, all required production points give maximum and non-negative producer's profits.

This is an Adam Smith dream world. Yet it is possible that due to more or less arbitrary and accidental circumstances of institutions, laws, customs or feasibility, competitive markets would not be Pareto-efficient. Take, for instance, the Meade example of apples and honey. Apple blossoms are "produced" at constant returns to scale and are (we assumed) an ordinary, private, exhaustible good: the more nectar for one bee, the less for another. It is easy to show that if apple blossoms have a positive effect on honey production (and abstracting from possible satiation and redundancy) a maximum-of-welfare solution, or any Pareto-efficient solution, will associate with apple blossoms a positive Lagrangean shadow-price.[35] If, then, apple producers are unable to protect their equity in apple-nectar and markets do not impute to apple blossoms their correct shadow value, profit-maximizing decisions will fail correctly to allocate resources (e.g. L) at the margin. There will be failure "by enforcement."

This is what I would call an *ownership* externality. It is essentially Meade's "unpaid factor" case. Nonappropriation, divorce of scarcity from effective *ownership*, is *the* binding consideration. Certain "goods" or "bads" with determinate non-zero shadow-values are simply not attributed. It is irrelevant here whether this is because the lake where people fish happens to be in the public domain, or because "keeping book" on who produces, and who gets what, may be impossible, clumsy, or costly in terms of resources.[36] For whatever legal or feasibility reasons, certain variables which have positive or negative shadow value are not "assigned" axes. The beekeeper thinks only in terms of labor, the orchard-owner only in terms of apples.

The important point is that the difficulties reside in institutional arrangements, the feasibility of keeping tab, etc. The scarcities at issue are rationable and finely divisible and there are no difficulties with "total conditions": at the bliss-configuration every activity would pay for itself. Apple nectar has a positive shadow price, which would, if only payment were enforceable, cause nectar production in precisely the right amount and even distribution would be correctly rationed. The difficulty is due exclusively to the difficulty of keeping accounts on the nectar-take of Capulet bees as against Montague bees.[37]

Many of the few examples of interproducer external economies of the reversible technological variety are of this type: "shared deposits" of fish, water, etc.[38] Much more important, so are certain irreversible dynamical examples associated with investment. For instance, many of Pigou's first category of externalities: those that arise in connection with owner–tenant relationships where durable investments are involved, have a primarily organizational quality.[39] Perhaps the most important instance is the training of nonslave labor to skills – as distinct from education in a broader sense (which partakes more of Type (3)). In the end, however, and in particular if restricted to reversible statical cases, it is not easy to think of many significant "ownership externalities" pure and simple. Yet it turns out that only this type of externality is really due to nonappropriability.

Type (2): Technical Externalities

Assume, again, that all goods and services are rationable, exhaustible, scarcities, that individual ordinal indifference maps are convex and sensitive only to own-consumption and that there exist no ownership "defects" of Type (1). If, then, the technology exhibits indivisibility or smooth increasing returns to scale in the relevant range of output, these give rise to a second and much more important type of market failure: "technical externality."[40]

The essential analytical consequence of indivisibility,[41] whether in inputs, outputs or processes, as well as of smooth increasing returns to scale, is to render the set of feasible points in production (input–output space) nonconvex. A connecting straight line between some pairs of feasible points will pass outside the feasible set. Nonconvexity, in turn, has a devastating effect on duality.[42]

In situations of pure "technical externality" there does, of course, still exist a maximal production possibility frontier (FF); and with a Samuelson-type social indifference map (SS) – i.e., a map "corrected" for income distribution which provides a ranking for the community as a whole of all conceivable output combinations[43] – it is possible, in concept, to define a bliss-point(s).[44] Also, where indivisibility is exhibited by outputs, and only outputs, or, stronger, where smoothly increasing returns to scale are the only variety of nonconvexity – isoquants for one, are properly convex – the locus of efficient output combinations can be defined in terms of conditions on marginal-rates-of-input-substitution.[45] Moreover, bliss could possibly occur at a point where SS is internally tangent to FF, perhaps to a convex FF. But even in the least "pathological," most neoclassically well-behaved case, where there exists a meaningfully defined set of shadow prices associated with the bliss-point, genuinely profit-seeking competitive producers, responding to that set of prices, would fail to sustain optimal production. At best, even if at the bliss-configuration all *MC*'s are rising, some producers would have to make continuing losses, hence would go out of business: market calculations would necessarily fail "by incentive." If, in turn, prices are not centrally quoted but permitted to set themselves monopoly behavior will result. There will be failure "by structure."

Further, bliss may require production at levels of output where losses are not only positive, but at a constrained maximum:[46] $p = MC$ may be correct, though MC at that point is falling. If so, the embedded Lagrangean constants may still retain meaning as marginal rates of transformation, but they will fail to sustain efficient production even by Lange–Lerner civil servants who care only about margins and not about absolute totals. There will be failure "by signal": producers under injunction to maximize profit (in the small) will not remain where they ought to be.

If, moreover, we drop the assumption of smooth increasing returns to scale and permit indivisibilities such as give scallop-like effects and kinks in cost curves and in the production-possibility curve, things get even more complicated. Bliss could require production at points of positive but locally minimum profit, where MC exceeds AC but is falling. Worse, even if bliss should occur at points where production functions are locally convex and MC (greater than AC) is rising, prequoted prices may still not sustain the solution unless production functions are in fact convex throughout. Though positive and at a local maximum, profits may not be at their maximum-maximorum: other hills with higher peaks may induce producers with vision at a distance to rush away from bliss. Alternatively, if prices are not administered, competition may not be self-policing and markets could fail "by structure."[47]

On the other hand, given our assumptions, the Paretian contract locus of maximal (ordinal) utility combinations which is associated with any one particular output point is defined, as in the trouble-free neoclassical model, by the usual subjective, taste-determined, marginal-rate-of-substitution equalities (or, at corners, inequalities). These *MRS* equalities, in turn, imply a set of shadow-prices which, if centrally quoted, would efficiently ration among consumers the associated (fixed) totals of goods. In the sphere of exchange, then, a decentralized price system works without flaw.

In what sense do these Type (2) situations exhibit "externality"? In the (generalized) sense that some social costs and benefits remain external to decentralized profitability calculations. With Type (1) externalities, though it is not feasible to police the bliss value of all quantities and prices, there exists embedded in the solution a set of prices whose use for purposes of decentralized signaling would sustain, if only appropriation or exclusion were feasible, both itself and the maximum welfare configuration of inputs, outputs, and distribution. This is not the case here. In Type (1) situations, at the bliss point there is complete correspondence between social and private pay-off, both at the margin and in totals.[48] Profits are at their maxima and non-negative throughout. Here there is no such correspondence: there may well be divergence, either at the margin: bliss profits may be at a "minimum," or in *totals*. The private totals in terms of which producers in an (idealized) market calculate – total revenue minus total cost – will not reliably signal the social costs and benefits implied by the relevant social indifference curves.[49] Hence at the set of prices which would correctly ration the bliss point bill of goods, that bill of goods may not be produced by profit seekers, or even by Lange–Lerner civil servants.[50]

A point to note, in all this, is that in relation to "technical externalities" the nonappropriability notion, as generally conceived, tends to miss the point. Strictly speaking, it is, of course, true that price mediation, if efficient, cannot be counted on to "appropriate" the full social benefits of activities showing increasing returns to scale or other types of indivisibility to those engaged in them. But the existence of such "uncompensated services" has in this case nothing whatever to do with "divorce of scarcity from ownership," with feasibility limitations on "exclusion." It is entirely feasible to own a bridge and profitably ration crossings; indeed, a private owner would do so. The point is, rather, that such profitable rationing, such "compensation" for services rendered, would inefficiently misallocate the "output" of bridge crossings. If in terms of scarce resource inputs the marginal cost of an additional crossing is zero, any positive toll will, in general, have the usual monopolistic effect: the resulting output configuration will not be efficient.[51]

This, incidentally, is where most pecuniary external economies lead: a supplier is required to produce in a range of declining AC due to internal technological economies of scale and hence cannot make "ends meet" at the socially correct price. The crucial associated difficulty at the level of social organization is monopoly.

Can we leave matters at that? Not quite. There is a third kind of externality, recently emphasized by Professor Samuelson, caused by so-called "public goods."

Type (3): Public Good Externalities

In some recent writings on public expenditure theory, Samuelson has reintroduced the notion of the collective or public good. The defining quality of a pure public good is that "each individual's consumption of such a good leads to no subtractions from any other individual's consumption of that good...",[52] hence, "it differs from a private consumption good in that each man's consumption of it, X_2^1 and X_2^2 respectively, is related to the total X_2 by a condition of *equality* rather than of summation. Thus, by definition, $X_2^1 = X_2$ and $X_2^2 = X_2$."[53]

As Samuelson has shown, the form of the marginal rate of substitution conditions which define the Pareto-efficient utility possibility frontier in a world where such public goods exist, or at least where there are outputs with important "public" qualities, renders any kind of price-market routine virtually useless for the computation of output-mix and of distribution, hence, also, for organizational decentralization. Where some restraints in the maximum problem take the form: total production of X *equals* consumption by Crusoe of X *equals* consumption of X by Friday. Pareto efficiency requires that the marginal rate of transformation in production between X and Y equal not the (equalized) MRS of each separate consumer, but rather the algebraic *sum* of such MRS's. This holds, of course, in what in other respects is a conventionally neoclassical world: preference and production functions are of well-behaved curvature, all is convex.

If, then, at the bliss point, with Y as numeraire, P_x is equated to the marginal cost of X in production (as is required to get optimal production), and X is offered for the sale at that p_x preference-maximizing consumers adjusting their purchases so as to equate their individual MRS's to p_x will necessarily under-use X. Moreover, a pricing game will not induce consumers truthfully to reveal their preferences. It pays each consumer to understate his desire for X relative to Y, since his enjoyment of X is a function only of total X, rather than as is true of a pure private good, just of that fraction of X he pays for.

The two Samuelson articles[54] explore both the analytics and the general implications of "public goods." Here the notion is of relevance because much externality is due precisely to the "public" qualities of a great many activities. For example, the externality associated with the generation of ideas, knowledge, etc., is due in good part to the public character of these "commodities." Many interconsumer externalities are of this sort: my party is my neighbor's disturbance, your nice garden is any passerby's nice view, my children's education is your children's good company, my Strategic Air Command is your Strategic Air Command, etc. The same consumption item enters, positively or negatively, both our preference functions. The consumptions involved are intrinsically and essentially joint.

This kind of externality is distinct from either of the other two pure types. Here technological nonconvexities need in no way be involved. In fact the $MRT = \Sigma MRS$ condition is certain to hold true precisely where production takes place at constant or nonincreasing returns, and hence where the production possibility set is necessarily convex. Further, there are no decentralized organizational rearrangements, no private bookkeeping devices, which would, if only feasibility were not at issue, eliminate the difficulty. It is the central implication of the Samuelson model that where public good phenomena are present, there does not exist a set of prices associated with the (perfectly definable) bliss-point, which would sustain the bliss configuration. The set of prices which would induce profit-seeking competitors to produce the optimal bill of goods would be necessarily inefficient in allocating that bill of goods. Moreover, even abstracting from production, no single set of relative prices will efficiently ration any fixed bill of goods so as to place the system on its contract locus, except in the singular case where at that output and income-distribution MRS's of every individual are identically the same (or zero for all but one). There is failure "by existence."

IV Comments

Type (1). In a sense, Type (1) is not symmetrical with the other two categories. One can think of some nontrivial instances where the institutional element does appear to be "binding": skill-training of people, for example. But even there, it could be argued that the crucial elements are durability, uncertainty, and the fact that slavery as a mode of organization is itself in the nature of a public good which enters people's preference functions, or the implicit social welfare function, inseparably from the narrowly "economic" variables. In those instances, in turn, where bookkeeping feasibility appears to be the cause of the trouble, the question arises why bookkeeping is less feasible than where it is in fact being done. In the end, it may be that much of what appears to partake of Type (1) is really a compound of Types (2) and (3), with dynamical durability and uncertainty elements thrown in. At any rate, a deeper analysis of this category may cause it substantially to shrink.

Nonproduced scarcities. One particular instance where what appears like Type (1) is really Type (2) warrants special mention. Public ownership of nonproduced resources, e.g., the lakes and mountains of national parks, may make it appear that externality is due to statutory barriers to private ownership and commercial rental. But this is missing the point. Take, for instance, a community which has available a single source of fresh water of fixed capacity. Assume that the bliss solution gives out a positive ration-price per gallon such as would make sale of the water commercially profitable. Yet a laissez-faire system would fail, "by structure," to sustain bliss. A private owner of the single indivisible well, if given his head, would take advantage of the tilt in the demand curve. The real cause of externality is not the arbitrary rapaciousness of public authority but the indivisibility of the source of supply. This case, by the way, is akin to where indivisibility or increasing returns to scale within a range allow profitable scope for one or a few efficient producers, but for no more. At the bliss price all will do the right thing, but if prices are not administered, oligopoly or monopoly will result. A capitalist Lange–Lerner system with private ownership but administered prices would work fine, but laissez-faire markets would fail.

Meade's "atmosphere." The relation of any tri-cornered ordering to Meade's polar categories is of interest.[55] His first category, "unpaid factors," is identical to my Type (1). But his second, labeled "atmosphere," is a rather curious composite. Meade's qualitative characterization of "atmosphere" (e.g., of afforestation-induced rainfall), comes very close to the public good notion.[56] He links this, however, as necessarily bound up with increasing returns to scale in production to society at large, hence a J. B. Clark-like overexhaustion, adding-up problem.[57]

If, following Meade, one abstracts from shared water-table phenomena (let rain-caused water input be rigidly proportional to area) then Farmer Jones' rain is Farmer Smith's rain and we have my Type (3). But nothing in this situation requires that either farmer's full production function (with an axis for rain) need show increasing returns to scale. It may be that returns to additional bundles of non-rain inputs, with given constant rainfall, diminish sharply, and that it takes proportional increases of land, labor *and rain* to get a proportional effect on output. If so, Meade's overexhaustion problem will not arise. But all would not be well: the public good quality of rainfall would cause an independent difficulty, one that Meade, if I understand him correctly, does not take into account, i.e., that rain ought to be "produced" by timber growers until its MC is equal to the sum of all the affected farmers, MRS's for rain as an input, whatever may be the curvature of the latter's production functions.[58]

On the other hand, Meade's formal mathematical treatment of "atmosphere," is distinct from his verbal characterization and his example, suggests that it is a nonappropriable, and therefore unpaid factor which gives rise to increasing returns to scale to society though not to the individual producer. At least this is all he needs for the effect he is looking for: a self-policing though nonoptimal competitive situation, where, because the full production functions (i.e., with an axis for rain) are of greater than first degree, the correction of externality via subsidies to promote the creation of favorable atmosphere requires net additions to society's fiscal burden. If this is the crucial consequence of "atmosphere," then it need have no "public" quality. All this would happen even though Smith and Jones were "competing" for the water from the shared water-table under their subsoil, just like bees competing for nectar.

Scitovsky's "two concepts,"[59] Professor Scitovsky, in turn, in his suggestive 1954 article, distinguishes between the statical direct interactions of equilibrium theory and the kinds of pecuniary external economies emphasized in the economic development literature. He classifies the former as consumer–consumer, producer–consumer, and producer–producer interactions, labels the last as external economies and asserts that they are rare and, on the whole, unimportant.

While Scitovsky does not raise the question of what gives rise to such producer–producer interactions, both his examples, and his conclusion that they are of little significance, suggest that he is thinking primarily of Type (1), nonappropriability. But this is to ignore public goods – surely a more important cause of interaction. Moreover, by taking full account of these, Scitovsky's "fifth and important case, which, however, does not quite fit into ... [his] ... classification ..., where society provides social services through communal action and makes these available free of charge to all persons and firms," can be made nicely to fall into place.[60]

Samuelson on Types (2) and (3). While the public good model helps to sort out the phenomena Meade lumped under "atmosphere," Samuelson himself emphasizes the analytical bond between indivisibility and public good situations. In both an explicit "summing in" is required of "all direct and indirect utilities and costs in all social decisions."[61] In Type (2) situations it is the intramarginal consumer's and producer's surpluses associated with various all or nothing decisions "in-the-lump" that have to be properly (interpersonally) weighted and summed, while in Type (3) it is only utilities and costs at the margin that require adding. But, and this is the crucial shared quality of the two categories, both make it necessary to sum utilities over many people.[62]

Exclusion. One more comment may be warranted on the significance, in a public good type situation of nonappropriability. "Exclusion" is almost never impossible. A recluse can build a wall around his garden, Jones can keep his educated children away from those of Smith, etc. But if thereby some people (e.g., the recluse) are made happier and some (e.g., the passer-by) less happy, any decision about whether to "exclude" or not implies an algebraic summing of the somehow-weighted utilites of the people involved. And if the wall requires scarce resources, the final utility sum must be matched against the cost of the wall. When Type (3) blends with indivisibility in production, as it does in the case of the wall, or in the case of a lighthouse, the comparison has to be made between intramarginal totals. Where no lumpiness is involved (e.g., the decibels at which I play my radio) only *MRS* and perhaps *MC* calculations are called for. But the really crucial decision may well be about how much perfectly feasible appropriation and exclusion is desirable.

Arrangements to offset. It is of interest to speculate what, if any, organizational rearrangements could offset the three categories of externality and avoid the need for centrally calculated tax-subsidy schemes.[63] In concept, Type (1) can be offset by rearrangements of ownership and by "proper" bookkeeping, such as need not violate the structural requirements of decentralized competition. Further, no resort to nonmarket tests would be required.[64]

Types (2) and (3) are not so amenable to correction consistent with decentralized institutions. The easiest possible case occurs where increasing returns obtain on the level of single producers' good plants, much of whose production can be absorbed by a single user firm. Here vertical integration takes care of the problem. Not every process inside a well-run firm is expected to cover its cost in terms of the correct set of internal accounting (shadow) prices. Total profits are the only criterion, and it may pay a firm to build a private bridge between its two installations on opposite sides of a river yet charge a zero accounting price for its use by the various decentralized manufacturing and administrative divisions: the bridge would make accounting losses, yet total company profits will have increased. As long, then, as such integration is consistent with the many-firms requirement for competition, no extra-market tests are required.[65] The private total conditions: TR less TC, correctly account for social gain.

Where a producers'-good firm, required to produce at a stage of falling AC, sells to many customer firms and industries, an adding up of all the associated TR's and TC's at the precalculated "as if" competitive prices associated with the bliss point would again effectively "mop up" all social costs and benefits.[66] But the institutional reorganization required to get correct decentralized calculation involves horizontal and vertical integration, and the monopoly or oligopoly problem looms large indeed. The Type (3) case of a pure *producers*'s public good belongs here: only input MRS's along production functions require summing.

In the general case of a mixed procedure-consumer good (or of a pure consumer good) which is "public" or is produced under conditions of increasing returns to scale, it is impossible to avoid comparison of multi-person utility totals. Explicit administrative consideration must be given, if you like, to consumer's and producer's surpluses for which no market-institution tests exist short of that provided by a perfectly discriminating monopolist. But to invoke perfect discrimination is to beg the question. It implies knowledge of all preference functions, while as Samuelson has emphasized,[67] the crucial game-theoretical quality of the situation is that consumers will not correctly reveal their preferences; it will pay them to "cheat".

Blends. Examination is needed of various blends of Types (2) and (3), such as Sidgwick's lighthouse;[68] or, for that matter, and as suggested by Samuelson, of blends of public and private goods even where all production functions are fully convex. There are many puzzling cases. Do bridge crossings differ in kind from radio programs? Both involve indivisibility and, where variable cost is zero for the bridge, zero MC's. The correct price for an extra stroller, as for an extra listener, is clearly zero. Yet bridge crossings have a distinctly private quality: bridges get congested, physical capacity is finite. This is not true of a broadcast. There is no finite limit to the number of sets that can costlessly tune in.[69] Radio programs, then, have a public dimension. Yet, in a sense so do bridges. While your bridge crossing is not my bridge crossing, in fact could limit my crossings, your bridge is my bridge. What is involved here is that most things are multi-dimensional and more than one dimension may matter.

V Efficiency, markets and choice of institutions

All the above has to do with the statical efficiency of price-directed allocation in more or less idealized market situations. Relevance to choice of institutions depends, of course, on the prevalence of the phenomena which cause externality and on the importance to be attached to statical efficiency. Space precludes extensive discussion of these important issues, but a few casual comments, in the form of *dicta*, are perhaps warranted.

How important are nonappropriability, nonconvexity and public goods? I would be inclined to argue that while nonappropriability is of small import,[70] the same cannot be said of the other two. True enough, it is difficult to think of many examples of pure public goods. Most things – even battleships, and certainly open air concerts and schools (though not knowledge) – have an "if more for you then less for me" quality. But this is of little comfort. As long as activities have even a trace of publicness, price calculations are inefficient.[71] And it is surely hard to gainsay that some degree of public quality pervades much of even narrowly "economic" activity.

Lumpiness, in turn, and nonlinearity of the increasing returns sort, while in most instances a matter of degree, and, within limits of choice, are also in the nature of things. The universe is full of singularities, thresholds and nonproportionalities: speed of light, gravitational constant, the relation of circumference to area, etc. As economists we can cajole or bully engineers into designing processes and installations that save on congealed inputs and give smaller maximal service yields, especially when designing for low-income communities. But the economically perhaps arbitrary, not completely physics-imposed quality of indivisibilities associated with standard designs and ways of doing things should not blind. Nonlinearity and lumpiness are evident facts of nature.[72]

More important, at this level of discourse[73] – though perhaps it hardly need be said – is that statical market efficiency is neither sufficient nor necessary for market institutions to be the "preferred" mode of social organization. Quite apart from institutional considerations, Pareto efficiency as such may not be necessary for bliss.[74] If, e.g., people are sensitive not only to their own jobs but to other people's as well, or more generally, if such things as relative status, power, and the like, matter, the injunction to maximize output, to hug the production-possibility frontier, can hardly be assumed "neutral," and points on the utility frontier may associate with points inside the production frontier.[75] Furthermore, there is nothing preordained about welfare functions which are sensitive only to individual consumer's preferences. As a matter of fact, few people would take such preferences seriously enough to argue against any and all protection of individuals against their own mistakes (though no external effects be involved).

All this is true even when maximization is subject only to technological and resource limitations. Once we admit other side relations, which link input–output variables with "noneconomic" political and organizational values, matters become much more complicated. If markets be ends as well as means, their nonefficiency is hardly sufficient ground for rejection.[76] On the other hand, efficient markets may not do, even though Pareto-efficiency is necessary for bliss. Even with utopian lump-sum redistribution, efficiency of the "invisible hand" does not preclude preference for other efficient modes of organization, if there be any.[77]

Yet when all is said, and despite the host of crucial feasibility considerations which render choice in the real world inevitably a problem in the strategy of "second best," it is surely interesting and useful to explore the implications of Paretian efficiency. Indeed, much remains to be done. There is need, in particular, for more systematic exploration of the inadequacies of market calculation in a setting of growth.[78]

Notes

1. "Activities" broadly defined, to cover consumption as well as production.
2. I.e., to the conditions which define the attainable frontier of maximal utility combinations with given preference functions, resource endowments and technology. A community is on its Paretian frontier if it is impossible to make anyone better off (in terms of his own ordinal preference function) without making someone else worse off. Associated with the utility possibility frontier, in turn, is a production possibility frontier denoting maximal alternative output combinations. (Cf. my "Simple Analytics of Welfare Maximization," *American Economic Review*, XLVII (Mar 1957), 22–59, and references therein.)
3. In other words, given the "right" lump-sum taxes, markets will match the allocation called for by the point of tangency of the relevant W-function with the utility-possibility frontier, i.e., by the "bliss point." The W-function need not, of course, be explicit – it could be implicit in the political power-configuration which characterizes a community. On the other hand, it cannot be just any kind of function. It has to have some special characteristics which reflect a number of ethic-loaded restrictions, e.g., that individuals' preference functions are to count, and to count positively (cf., *ibid.*, and Section V below).

4. In most of what follows, I shall assume that individual preferences, though not necessarily sensitive only to own-consumption, are representable by strictly convex indifference surfaces, i.e., by an ordering (one for each individual) such that all points on a straight line connecting two equivalent points x and y are preferred to x (hence to y). But convexity is too restrictive. It excludes not only such characteristics of man's psyche as violate the "usual" regularities – these I do want to exclude – but also such physical and topographical facts as lumpy consumption-goods. Rather than attempt a specification of preferences with convex-like properties where choice must be made among discrete bundles, I dodge the problem by attributing lumpiness only to inputs (including, however, inputs that are intermediate outputs).
5. The theorem holds for the statical steady-state flow model of the Walrasian sort where the solution values are stationary time-rates; it holds, also, for dynamical systems involving capital formation (given, still, convexity throughout). For these last, the solution values are time paths of inputs, outputs, prices, etc. (A set of points is convex if, and only if, the straight lines connecting all possible pairs do not anywhere pass outside the set. The set of feasible output points bounded by a production possibility curve is convex, for instance, if the curve itself is concave-to-the-origin or a straight line. On all this, see Section V of "Simple Analytics," *ibid*).
6. Given, again, optimal lump-sum redistribution of as-imputed incomes. While I make use of the lump-sum transfer device throughout this paper to abstract from the income distribution problem and permit exclusive attention to Pareto efficiency, it is well to note that this involves a measure of sleight-of-hand. No decentralized price-market type "game" can reveal the pattern of taxes and transfers that would maximize a particular welfare function. "Central" calculation – implicit if not explicit – is unavoidable. Moreover, since distribution (hence correct redistribution) of numeraire-incomes interdependents with allocation in production and exchange, the supposedly automatic, nonpolitical character of market mediation is a myth on the strictest neoclassical assumptions. This is not to say, even on our stratospheric levels of abstraction, that markets are "useless." Where they do compute well we are saved an awful lot of calculation.
7. With optimal redistribution.
8. We could consider, instead, the configuration which associates with the initial pattern of ownership of endowment. Or we could play it safe and extend the conditions to cover each and every Pareto efficient configuration. But this would be overly strict, since many efficient situations have no relevance either to any interesting W-functions or in terms of the initial distribution of scarcities.

It may be worth noting, incidentally, that "existence," as used above, is not the same as existence in the sense of, e.g., Arrow and Debreu (in "Existence of an Equilibrium for a Competitive Economy," *Econometrica*, Vol. 22 (July 1954), pp. 265–90). They use the term to denote the complete set of conditions which defines competitive equilibrium, and this includes, in addition to all that is implied by (1) above, conditions akin to my conditions (2), and some analogous conditions on consumers.

9. This is slightly misleading: as we shall see, failure on count (c) leads both to signaling and to incentive troubles. Anyway, the labels are only for expository convenience.
10. Or at least the potentiality of very many producers, ready and able to "enter the fray" instantaneously. This may be sufficient in the constant-cost case, where the equilibrium number of firms per industry is indeterminate.
11. The mathematically minded will object that (3) and (4), at least, do not really violate "duality" in its strict mathematical sense: the dual minimum problem still yields Lagrangean constants. True, yet I think it suggestive to use 'duality' rather more loosely as a label for the general welfare theorem, particularly as this does not lead, in this context, to any ambiguity.
12. It is tempting, but wrong, to suggest that in a true Lange–Lerner world totals do not matter and only margins count. It is true that the non-negativeness of profits is immaterial. Where there is any sharing of shadow-price sets by two or more production points, however totals necessarily become a part of the signaling system and if 2(c) does not hold they may lead down the garden path.
13. More precisely, whether the point of maximum welfare is or is not a point of self-policing and "enforceable" market equilibrium, where, following common usage, equilibrium is defined to subsume both the first-order and the second-order inequalities for a maximun. A firm, for instance, is taken to be in equilibrium only at a point of maximun profit. This way of defining equilibrium does bring in issues of stability, hence some implicit dynamics. In particular, the word "sustain" is taken to imply some scanning or reconnaissance by producers and consumers at least in the neighborhood of equilibrium. But I do not think it does any harm to subsume this much stability in the equilibrium notion. The possibility of a firm in *unstable* "equilibrium," i.e., in equilibrium at a point of minimum profit, is hardly likely to be of import.

    On the other hand, correspondence between Pareto-efficiency and the equilibrium state of perfectly conpetitive markets is not sufficient to ensure market efficiency. It is the burden of "failure by structure" that markets may fail to be competitive, and of "failure by enforcement" that legal or institutional constraints may prevent competitive markets from allocating efficiently, even though there does exist a competitive equilibrium for each Pareto-efficient configuration. "Existence" in the sense of Arrow and Debreu (*op. cit.*) is necessary but not sufficient for market–efficiency in the present context.
14. This refers to a so-called Marshallian supply curve. It has nothing whatever to do with the Walrasian "maximum quantity supplied at a given price" type schedule.
15. That there are difficulties also with income distribution was by that time generally recognized.
16. The strategic articles with the exception of Young's "Pigou's *Wealth and Welfare*," this *Journal*, XXVII (1913), 672–86, as well as Ellis and Fellner's 1943 treatment, have all been reprinted in American Economic Association, *Readings in Price Theory*, ed. Stigler and Boulding. For an excellent modern discussion, see R. L. Bishop. *Economic Theory* (to appear).

17. Note, however, that there need be nothing about an organizational improvement to make it obvious in advance whether it will turn out to be technological or, through "internalization," pecuniary. Many trade-association type services which are justified by the scale of an industry could as well be provided commercially, and vice versa.
18. Pecuniary diseconomies, in contrast, need have no technological counterpart. Finite-elastic supplies of unproduced inputs are a sufficient cause. Recall, incidentally, that only narrowly statical reversible phenomena are admissible here.
19. While this section makes some slight use of elementary calculus, the reader uninterested in technicalities may avoid, without loss of continuity, all but some simple notation.
20. *Economic Journal*, LXII, Mar. 1952. Meade uses a two factor model and, while he does not explicitly solve the Paretian maximum problem, shows that market imputed rates of remuneration will not match marginal social product.
21. Both functions are assumed homogeneous of degree one. Moreover, apple blossoms (or the nectar therein) are exhaustible, rationable "private" goods: more nectar to one bee means less to another. On the need for this assumption, see Section III(3).
22. Assuming internal tangencies and all-round convexity (the last is implicit in constant returns to L: the A-effect on H reinforces convexity), as well as nonsatiation and nonredundancy ($\bar{L} = L_A + L_H$), the maximization of $p_A A + p_H H$, subject to the production functions and the supply of labor, is equivalent to finding a critical value for the Lagrangean expression, $F = p_A A(L_A) + p_H H[L_H; A(L_A)] + w(\bar{L} - L_A - L_H)$. To do so, differentiate F with respect to L_A and L_H, treating p_A, p_H and w as arbitrary constants and set the resulting first order partial derivatives equal to zero. This will give exactly (6.1) and (6.2). (Needless to say, the value weights can be varied at will, or taken as given.)
23. To see this, rewrite (6.2) to read

$$\frac{dA}{dL_A} = \frac{w}{p_A + p_H \frac{\partial H}{\partial A}}$$

and match it against the profit-maximizing rule,

$$\frac{dA}{dL_A} = \frac{w}{p_A}$$

Clearly,

$$\left(\frac{\partial H}{\partial A}\right) \lesseqgtr 0 \rightarrow$$

$$\left(\frac{dA}{dL_A}\right) \text{Private} \lesseqgtr \left(\frac{dA}{dL_A}\right) \text{Social}$$

24. The question of whether technological external economies involve shifts of each other's production functions, or mutually induced movements along such functions, is purely definitional. If one chooses so to define each producer's function as to give axes only to inputs and outputs that are purchased and sold, or at least "controlled," and the effects of everything else impinging on production (e.g., of humidity, apple blossoms, etc.) are built into the curvature of the function, then it follows that externalities will consist in shifts of some functions in response to movements along others. On the other hand, if, as in our apple–honey case, it seems useful to think of the production function for H as having an A-axis, then, clearly, induced movement along the function is a signal of externality.
25. Op. cit.
26. Moreover, in the one sense in which nonappropriability fits all cases of direct interaction, it explains none. If all it denotes is the failure of a price-market game properly to account for [or] to appropriate all relevant costs and benefits, then it is simply a synonym for market failure for generalized externality, and cannot be used to explain what causes any particular instance of such failure. I use it in a much narrower sense, to mean the inability of a producer of a good or service physically to exclude users, or to control the rationing of his produce among them. In my sense not only bridges but also, say, television programs are fully appropriable: it is always possible to use scramblers.
27. It is possible, of course, to interpret these examples as involving very large changes in price: from infinity to zero. But it does not help to do so. The shared characteristic of bridges and programs is that there is no price which will efficiently mediate both supply and demand.

    I have puzzled over ways of limiting the notion of "direct interaction" to something less than all instances where there is some interaction not adequately signaled by price. Robert Solow has suggested to me that this might be done by distinguishing situations where something is not subject to a market test at all from instances where no single price constitutes a correct test for both sides of a transaction (e.g., where the correct ration price for the services of an expensive facility is zero). I am inclined, rather, to drop the attempt to use "direct interaction" as an explanation of market failure; it is best used, if at all, as yet another synonym for such failure.
28. Recall that it is the existence of such "externality," of residue, at the blisspoint, of Pigouvian "uncompensated services" and "incidental uncharged disservices" that defines market failure. It may be objected that to generalize the externality notion in this way is to rob it of all but descriptive significance. But surely there is not much to rob; even in its strictest neoclassical formulation it begs more than it answers. In its generalized sense it at least has the virtue of suggesting the right questions.
29. As defined in n. 26 above.
30. Or that the algorism may break down for lack of a consistent set of p's.
31. I should much prefer "technological," but since this would necessarily confuse my Type (2) with Professor Viner's "technological" I fixed on "technical."
32. In effect, we end up with a five-by-three ordering of types of "failure": five "modes" vs three "causes." Its relation to Meade's categories (op. cit.) and to

Tibor Scitovsky's classification (in "Two Concepts of External Economies," *Journal of Political Economy*, LXII, April 1954) is discussed in Section IV below. I have had the benefit of reading, also, William Fellner's "Individual Investment Projects in Growing Economies," *Investment Criteria and Economic Growth* (Proceedings of a Conference, Center for International Studies, Massachusetts Institute of Technology, 1955) and an unpublished paper by Svend Laursen, "External Economies and Economic Growth."

33. The supply of such nonproduced scarcities need not, of course, remain constant. On the other hand, their ownership distribution must not be so concentrated as to preclude competitive rationing. There must exist no "indivisible" lake full of fish, etc., such as might be subject to monopolization, but thousands of lakes, all perfect substitutes.
34. Or, where there are corners, only inessentially indeterminate.
35. Set up a variant of the Apple–Honey model of Section II, introducing apple blossoms, B, explicitly. Add a production function, $B = B(L_A)$, and substitute $B(L_A)$ for $A(L_A)$ as the second input in honey production. The solution will give out a positive Lagrangean shadow price for B, and profit-maximizing producers of the joint products, A and B, will push L_A to the socially desirable margin.
36. Though on this last, see Section IV, first paragraph.
37. More generally, it could as well be due to difficulty in knowing who "produced" the "benefit" – oil wells drawing on the same pool are an example. The owner cannot protect his own; in fact, it is difficult to know what one means by "his own." Moreover, in the case of *dis*economies, at least, it may be that both the source and the recipient of the "bad" are identified: one factory producing soot and nothing but one laundry in the neighborhood, yet it is difficult to see how a price can be brought to bear on the situation. Presumably the laundry can pay for negative units of smoke.
38. Though indivisibility elements enter into some of these. Why can't somebody "own" part of a lakeful of fish?
39. When not simply due, in a world of uncertainty, to inconsistent expectations.
40. Again, this is not the same as Viner's "technological." Note, incidentally, that the above formulation unabashedly begs the question of whether smooth increasing returns to scale could or could not arise without indivisibility somewhere. The issue is entirely definitional: it is conceptually impossible to disprove either view by reference to empirical evidence. (Cf. Bator, "Simple Analytics," *loc. cit.*, fn 37 and references.)

The pioneer work on decreasing cost situations is Jules Dupuit's remarkable 1844 essay, "On the Measurement of Utility of Public Works," translated in *International Economic Papers*, No. 2, ed. A. T. Peacock *et al.* Harold Hotelling's "The General Welfare in Relation to Problems of Taxation and of Railway and Utility Rates," in the July 1938 issue of *Econometrica*, is the originating modern formulation. Cf., also references to work by R. Frisch, J. E. Mesde, W. A. Lewis and others in Nancy Ruggles' excellent survey articles on marginal cost pricing (*Review of Economic Studies*, XVII (1949–50), 29–46, and 107–26.

41. Indivisibility means lumpiness "in scale" and not the kind of indivisibility-in-time we call durability. (Durability, as such, does not violate convexity.) Lumpiness has to do with the impossibility to vary continuously, e.g., the capacity service-yield per unit time of such things as bridges.
42. The best known and perhaps most important variety of nonconvexity occurs where isoquants are properly convex, but returns to scale are increasing, hence the full set of feasible input–output points is nonconvex. In a two-input, one-output situation, slices by (vertical) planes through the origin perpendicular to the input plane will cut the production surface in such a way as to give a nonconvex boundary. A production point lying in an "increasing returns" region of a production function implies that (1) the associated average cost curve (AC) is downward sloping at that level of output; (2) the associated marginal cost curve (MC), while it may be rising, could as well be falling and will certainly lie below AC: and (3) the production possibility curve of the community may be nonconvex. On all this, see Part V of "Simple Analytics," loc. cit.
43. Cf. P. A. Samuelson, "Social Indifference Curves," this *Journal* LXX (Feb. 1956), 1–22. Such a function presumes that *numeraire*-incomes are continuously redistributed so as to maximize in utility space over the community's operative social welfare function.
44. This is saying very little, of course, except on the level of metaphysics.
45. Inequalities due to kinks and corners are as good as equalities where all is smooth.
46. Subject to the requirement that total cost for that level of output be a minimum, i.e., that each producer be on his least-cost expansion path.
47. Where sharp indivisibility gives a nonconvex production possibility curve with corners and kinks, duality may fail even if there exists a price vector in terms of which decentralized producer-calculations would sustain the bliss-point output mix. The existence of such a vector does not assure that it will coincide with the price-vector which would efficiently ration that bill of goods among consumers. The point is that there may not exist a *single* set of prices which will at the same time keep both consumers and producers from rushing away from where they ought to be. The prices which will effectively mediate production may cause consumers' calculations to go wrong and vice versa.

    It should be noted, incidentally, that none of the above takes space and distance considerations into account. For some interesting effects of plant-indivisibility where there are interplant flows and transport takes resources, see T. C. Koopmans and M. Beckmann. "Assignment Problems and the Location of Economic Activities," *Econometrica*, Vol. 25 (Jan. 1957).
48. More correctly, there would be such correspondence, if only the p's could be policed.
49. This is particularly awkward since the very nonconvexities which cause a divergence between private and social total conditions render output-mix calculations based on margins alone wholly inadequate. Even if bliss gives all local profit maxima, there may be several such open to any one producer, hence he must make total calculations in order to choose.

50. There is one qualification to be made to the above. It may be that the bliss configuration gives unique and positive profit maxima throughout, though some production functions exhibit nonconvexities at a distance. It was to exclude this case that we assumed that increasing returns or indivisibility obtain in the "relevant ranges." Should this happen, no "externality" divergence of social and private calculation will occur, at least in a statical context. But unless all is convex throughout, the existence of such a locally stable tangency cannot be taken as evidence that the point is in fact the bliss-point – a difficulty of considerable significance for dynamical efficiency.
51. Of course, if at bliss the bridge were to be used "to capacity," it is possible that the Lagrangean ration price (now positive) would make commercial operation profitable. If so, an administered price setup would efficiently mediate the demand and supply of crossings. But while a Lange–Lerner system would work fine, laissez-faire markets would fail "by structure."
52. P. A. Samuelson, *Review of Economics and Statistics*, XXXVI (Nov. 1954), p. 387.
53. P. A. Samuelson, *Review of Economics and Statistics*, XXXVII (Nov. 1955), p. 350.
54. And a third unpublished paper, which was read at the 1955 American Economic Association meetings and to a copy of which I came to have access while this paper was being written. For earlier writings on public goods, by Wicksell, Lindahl, Musgrave, Bowen and others see references in the above cited Samuelson articles.
55. Meade, *op. cit.* (This and the next section can be omitted without loss of continuity.)
56. See esp. bottom of p. 61 and top of p. 62, *op. cit.*
57. Since his argument is restricted to competitive situations, hence necessarily excludes increasing-returns-to-paid-factors such as would require production at a loss, Meade specifies constant returns to proportional variation of labor and land in wheat farming, though the full production function for wheat, including the atmosphere input "rain," exhibits increasing returns to scale. But the individual farmer does not pay for rain, hence his factor payments just match his sales revenue, by the Euler Theorem.
58. Formally, Meade denotes "atmosphere" as a situation where the production function, e.g., of farmers takes the form $X_1 = H_1(L_1,C_1)A_1(X_2)$, with L as labor, C as capital and A the atmosphere effect on X_1 of X_2. The full function exhibits increasing returns to scale but the H function alone, with A constant, is homogeneous of first degree. But why can't this be put in terms of Meade's unpaid factor type function where $X_1 = H_1(L_1,C_1,X_2)$? Example: $X_1 = L_1^a C_1^{1-a} X_2$. All this has nothing to do with whether $A = A_1 + A_2$ or rather $A = A_1 = A_2$. Unfortunately, the example itself tends to mislead. The fact that exclusion of rain-users (farmers) by producers (timber-growers) is hardly feasible, i.e., that rain is like Type 1, distracts attention from the important point that *if* rain is, as Meade tells us, a public good, then rationing it by price would be inefficient even if it were feasible. (It should be said that Meade concludes his article: "But, in fact, of course, external economies or

diseconomies may not fall into either of these precise divisions and may contain features of both of them.")

59. *Op. cit.*
60. *Ibid*, in 3, p. 144. Scitovsky, following Meade, restricts his "first concept" of external economies to phenomena consistent with competitive equilibrium. He treats indivisibilities and increasing returns to scale as belonging to his "second concept" which has to do with disequilibrium, investment decisions, and growth. It is, of course, entirely legitimate to restrict analysis to competitive situations. But the Scitovsky treatment must not be taken to imply that lumpiness is irrelevant to statical analysis of stationary solution points. If one is interested in the statical efficiency of decentralized price calculations, they are crucial. But this is carping. Scitovsky's important contribution lies in emphasizing and clarifying the point first hinted at by P. N. Rosenstein-Rodan, that in a world of disequilibrium dynamics pecuniary external economies may play an independent role – one distinct, that is, from simply being an unreliable signal of monopoly troubles (*Economic Journal*, LIII, 1943, 202–11).
61. *Ibid.*, p. 9.
62. There is one qualification to be made: if all public good and increasing returns to scale industries produce only intermediate products, all externalities may cancel out in intra-business-sector transactions. If so, only total revenues and total costs have to be summed. Incidentally, the exposition may misleadingly suggest another symmetry between Types (2) and (3). In a pure Type (3) situation, *if* there are no public producers' goods, then while prices cannot be used to ration the bliss point output-mix, they can be used efficiently to mediate production. In Type (2), on the other hand, *if* all final consumables are divisible, price calculations, while failing in production, will work in exchange. This symmetry break down, of course, as soon as one violates, as does the real world, the two "if's."
63. For illustrative derivation of the formulas for corrective taxes and subsidies in Type (1) situations, see Meade, *op. cit.*
64. The Emancipation Proclamation could constitute, of course, a substantial barrier.
65. If, however, the "break even" scale of operation of the integrated firm (i.e., where MC cuts AC from below) is much greater than if the river had not been there to span, or could be spanned by some means of a lower fixed-cost-to-variable-cost ratio, the monopoly problem may simply be "pushed forward" to consumer markets.
66. Assuming that all consumer goods are finely divisible and require no lumpy decisions by consumers.
67. Cf any of the three "Public Expenditure" articles (*supra*).
68. Sidgwick, by the way, as also Pigou, thought of a lighthouse as of Type (1). It is, of course, "inconvenient" to levy tolls on ships, but it is hardly impossible to "exclude," for instance by means of "scrambling" devices (though poor Sidgwick could hardly have known about such things). The point is, rather, that it would be inefficient to do so: the marginal cost to society of an additional ship taking directional guidance from the beacon atop the Statue of Liberty is zero, *ipso* price should be zero. In the case of lighthouse this is

twice true: because the beacon is in the nature of a public good: more for the Queen Mary means no loss for the Liberté, and because a lighthouse is virtually an all-fixed-cost, zero variable-cost facility.

69. Richard Eckaus has suggested to me that it is possible to exhaust the space to which the broadcast is limited and that this makes the situation a little more like that of a bridge. Neither of us is entirely satisfied, however.
70. Except for labor skills – and these would take us beyond the bounds of reversible statics.
71. This is not to say that there exist other feasible modes of social calculation and organization which are more efficient.
72. Their quantitative significance is, of course, very sensitive to scale, to "size" of markets. This explains the particular emphasis on the role of "social overheads" in low income countries.
73. Where recourse to strategic considerations of feasibility, crucial though they be, is quite out of order.
74. That it is never sufficient is, of course, well known. Of the infinite Pareto-efficient configurations at best only one: that which gives the "right" distribution of income in terms of the W-function that is to count, has normative prescriptive significance. Moreover, most interesting W-functions are likely to be sensitive to "noneconomic" factors, such as are, if not inconsistent, at least extraneous to Paretian considerations. Where such additional values of a political or social nature are separable from input–output values (i.e., where the two sets can be varied independently of each other) one "can" of course separate the overall W-function into a "political" and an "economic" component and maximize separately over each.
75. This is different from the usual case of consumer sensitivity to the input–output configuration of producers, e.g. factory soot or a functional but ugly plant spoiling the view. Such joint-product "bads" can be treated as inputs and treated in the usual Paretian fashion. It is a different matter that their public quality will violate duality, hence render market calculation inefficient.
76. This is too crude a formulation. It is not necessary that markets as such be an "ultimate" value. Political and social (non-output) values relating to the configuration of power, initiative, opportunity, etc., may be so much better served by some form of nonefficient market institutions than by possible alternative modes of more efficient organization as to warrant choice of the former. The analytical point, in all this, is that the outcome of a maximization process and the significance of "efficiency" are as sensitive to the choice of side-conditions as to the welfare-function and that these need be "given" to the economist in the same sense that a welfare function has to be given.
77. The above is still strictly statical. For related dynamical problems, e.g., possible conflict between one-period and intertemporal efficiency, cf., "On Capital Productivity, Input Allocation and Growth," this *Journal*, LXXI (Feb. 1957).
78. The development literature on market failure, while full of suggestive insight, is in a state of considerable confusion. Much work is needed to exhaust and elucidate the seminal ideas of Young, Rosenstein-Rodan. Nurkse and others. For important beginnings, Scitovsky (*op. cit.*), M. Fleming, "External Economies and the Doctrine of Balanced Growth," *Economic Journal*, LXV (June 1955), and Fellner (*op. cit.*)."

The view that we should not turn social historian or what not, that the logic of economizing has some prescriptive significance, rests on the belief that narrowly "economic" efficiency is important in terms of many politically relevant W-functions, and consistent with a wide variety of power and status configurations and modes of social organization. On the other hand, some may feel that the very language of Paretian welfare economics: "welfare function," "utility-frontier," in relation to choice of social institutions, is grotesque. What is at stake, of course, is not the esthetics of language on which I yield without demur, but abstraction and rigorous theorizing.

CHAPTER 7

Diagrammatic Exposition of a Theory of Public Expenditure*

P. A. SAMUELSON

In the November 1954 issue of this *Review* my paper on "The Pure Theory of Public Expenditure" presented a mathematical exposition of a public expenditure theory that goes back to Italian, Austrian, and Scandinavian writers of the last 75 years. After providing that theory with its needed logically-complete optimal conditions, I went on to demonstrate the fatal inability of any decentralized market or voting mechanism to attain or compute this optimum. The present note presents in terms of two-dimensional diagrams an essentially equivalent formulation of the theory's optimum conditions and briefly discusses some criticisms.

A polar-case model of government

Doctrinal history shows that theoretical insight often comes from considering strong or extreme cases. The grand Walrasian model of competitive general equilibrium is one such extreme polar case. We can formulate it so stringently as to leave no economic role for government. What strong polar case shall the student of public expenditure set alongside this pure private economy?

One possibility is the model of a group-mind. Such a model, which has been extensively used by nationalists and by Romantic critics of classical economics, can justify any, and every, configuration of government. So there is perhaps little that an economic theorist can usefully say about it.

Review of Economics and Statistics, Vol. 21 (May 1955), pp. 350–6.

My alternative is a slightly more sophisticated one, but still – intentionally – an extreme polar case. It is consistent with individualism, yet at the same time it explicitly introduces the vital external interdependencies that no theory of government can do without. Its basic assumption is an oversharp distinction between the following two kinds of goods:

(i) A *private* consumption good, like bread, whose total can be parcelled out among two or more persons, with one man having a loaf less if another gets a loaf more. Thus is X_1 is total bread, and X_1^1 and X_1^2 are the respective private consumptions of Man I and Man 2, we can say that the total equals the sum of the separate consumptions – or $X_1 = X_1^1 + X_1^2$.

(ii) A *public* consumption good, like an outdoor circus or national defense, which is provided for each person to enjoy or not, according to his tastes. I assume the public good can be varied in total quantity, and write X_2 for its magnitude. It differs from a private consumption good in that each man's consumption of it, X_2^1 and X_2^2 respectively, is related to the total X_2 by a condition of *equality* rather than of summation. Thus, by definition, $X_2^1 = X_2$, and $X_2^2 = X_2$.

Obviously, I am introducing a strong polar case. We could easily lighten the stringency of our assumptions. But on reflection, I think most economists will see that this is a natural antipodal case to the admittedly extreme polar case of traditional individualistic general equilibrium. The careful empiricist will recognize that many – though not all – of the realistic cases of government activity can be fruitfully analyzed as some kind of a blend of these two extreme polar cases.

Graphical depiction of tastes and technology

The first three charts summarize our assumptions about tastes and technology. Each diagram has a private good, such as bread, on its vertical axis; each has a public good on its horizontal axis. The heavy indifference curves of Figure 7.1 summarize Man 1's preferences between public and private goods. Figure 7.2's indifference curves do the same for Man 2; and the relative flatness of the contour shows that, in a sense, he has less liking for the public good.

The heavy production-possibility of opportunity-cost curve AB in Figure 7.3 relates the total productions of public and private goods in the usual familiar manner: the curve is convex from above to reflect the usual assumption of increasing relative marginal costs (or generalized diminishing returns).[1]

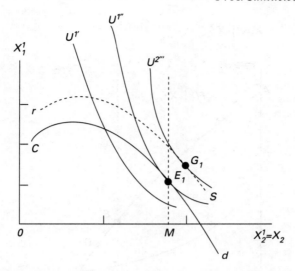

FIGURE 7.1 Indifference contours relating Man 1's consumption of public and private goods

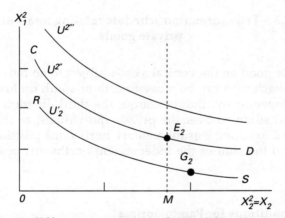

FIGURE 7.2 Indifference contours relating Man 2's consumption of public and private goods

Because of our special definition of a public good, the three diagrams are not independent. Each must be lined up with *exactly the same horizontal scale*. Because increasing a public good for society simultaneously increases it for each and every man, we must always be simultaneously at exactly the same longitude in all three figures. Moving an inch east in one diagram moves us the same amount east in all.

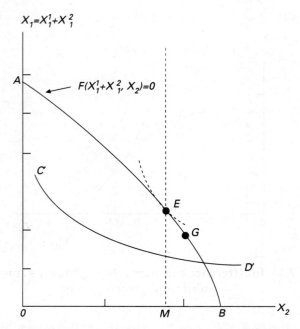

FIGURE 7.3 Transformation schedule relating totals of public and private goods

The private good on the vertical axis is subject to no new and unusual restrictions. Each man can be moved north or south on his indifference diagram independently. But, of course, the third diagram does list the total of bread summed over the private individuals; so it must have a larger vertical axis, and our momentary northward position on it must correspond to the sum of the independent northward positions of the separate individuals.

Tangency conditions for Pareto optima

What is the best or ideal state of the world for such a simple system? That is, what three vertically-aligned points corresponding to a determination of a given total of both goods and a determinate parcelling out of them among all separate individuals will be the ethically preferred final configuration?

To answer this ethical, normative question we must be given a set of norms in the form of a *social welfare function* that renders interpersonal judgements. For expository convenience, let us suppose that this will be supplied later and that we know in advance it will have the following special individualistic property: leaving each person on his same indifference level will leave social welfare unchanged; at any point, a move of each man to a higher indifference curve can be found that will increase social welfare.

Given this rather weak assurance about the forthcoming social welfare function, we can proceed to determine tangency conditions of an "efficiency" type that are at least necessary, though definitely not sufficient. We do this by setting up a preliminary maximum problem which will eventually necessarily have to be satisfied.

Holding all but one man at specified levels of indifference, how can we be sure that the remaining man reaches his highest indifference level?

Concretely, this is how we define such a tangency optimum: Set Man 2 on a specified indifference curve, say his middle one CD. Paying attention to Mother Nature's scarcity, as summarized in Figure 7.3's AB curve, and following Man 1's tastes as given by Figure 7.1's indifference curves, how high on those indifference curves can we move Man 1?

The answer is given by the tangency point E_1, and the corresponding aligned points E_2 and E.

How is this derived? Copy CD on Figure 7.3, and call it $C'D'$. The distance between $C'D'$ and AB represents the amounts of the two goods that are physically available to Man 1. So substract $C'D'$ vertically from AB and plot the algebraic result as cd in Figure 7.1. Now where on cd would Man 1 be best off? Obviously at the tangency point E_1 where cd touches (but does not cross) his highest attainable indifference contour.[2]

How many such Pareto-optimal points are there? Obviously, for each of the infinite possible initial indifference curves to put Man 2 on, we can derive a new highest attainable tangency level for Man 1. So there are an infinity of such optimal points – as many in number as there are points on the usual contract curve. All of these Pareto-optimal points have the property that from them there exists no physically-feasible movement that will make every man better off. Of course we cannot compare two different Pareto points until we are given a social welfare function. For a move from one Pareto point to another must always hurt one man while it is helping another, and an interpersonal way of comparing these changes must be supplied.

Figure 7.4 indicates these utility possibilities on an ordinal diagram. Each axis provides an indicator of the two men's respective indifference curve levels. The utility frontier of Pareto-optimal points is given by pp: the double fold infinity of "inefficient," non-Pareto-optimal points is given by the shaded area; the pp frontier passes from northwest to southeast to reflect the inevitable conflict of interests characterizing any contract locus; the curvature of the pp locus is of no particular type since we have no need to put unique cardinal numbers along the indifference

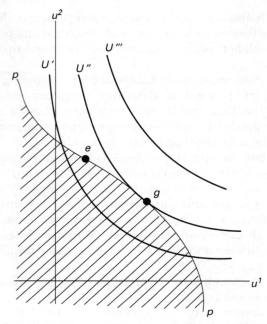

FIGURE 7.4 Utility frontier of Pareto-optimal efficiency points and its tangency to highest attainable social welfare contour

contours and can content ourselves with east–west and north–south relationships in Figure 7.4 without regard to numerical degree and to uneven stretchings of either utility axis.

The optimum of all the Pareto optima

Now we can answer the fundamental question: what is the best configuration for this society?

Use of the word "best" indicates we are in the ascientific area of "welfare economics" and must be provided with a set of norms. Economic science cannot deduce a social welfare function; what it can do is neutrally interpret any arbitrarily specified welfare function.

The heavy contours labelled U', U'', and U''' summarize all that is relevant in the provided social welfare function (they provide the needed ordinal scoring of every state of the world, involving different levels of indifference for the separate individuals).[3]

Obviously society cannot be best off inside the utility frontier. Where then on the utility frontier will the "best obtainable bliss-point" be? We will move along the utility frontier pp until we touch the highest social indifference curve: this will be at g where pp tangentially touches, without crossing, the highest obtainable social welfare level U''. In words, we can interpret this final tangency condition[4] in the following terms:

(i) The social welfare significance of a unit of any private good allocated to private individuals must at the margin be the same for each and every person.

(ii) The Pareto-optimal condition, which makes relative marginal social cost equal to the sum of all persons' marginal rates of substitution, is already assured by virtue of the fact that bliss lies on the utility frontier.[5]

Relations with earlier theories

This completes the graphical interpretation of my mathematical model. There remains the pleasant task of relating this graphical treatment to earlier work of Bowen[6] and others.

To do this, look at Figure 7.5, which gives an alternative depiction of the optimal tangency condition at a point like E. I use the private good X_1 as numeraire, measuring all values in terms of it. The MC curve is derived from the AB curve of Figure 7.3: it is nothing but the absolute slope of that production-possibility schedule plotted against varying amounts of the public good; it is therefore a marginal cost curve, with MC measured in terms of the numeraire good.

The marginal rate of substitution curves MRS^1 and MRS^2 are derived in a similar fashion from the respective indifference curves of Man 1 and Man 2: thus, MRS^1 is the absolute slope of the $u^{1''}$ indifference curve plotted against varying amounts of the public good; MRS^2 is the similar slope function derived from Man 2's indifference curve CD. (All three are 'marginal' curves, bearing the usual relationship to their respective 'total' curves.)

These schedules look like demand curves. We are accustomed to adding horizontally or laterally the separate demand curves of individuals to arrive at total market demand. But this is valid only for private goods. As Bowen rightly says, *we must in the case of public goods add different individuals' curves vertically*.

This gives us the heavy ΣMRS curve for the whole community. Where is equilibrium? It is at E, where the community MC curve intersects the community ΣMRS curve. Upon reflection the reader will realize that the equality $MC = \Sigma MRS = MRS^1 + MRS^2$ is the precise equivalent of my mathematical equation (2) and of our Pareto-type tangency condition at E_1, E_2, or E. Why? Because of the stipulated requirement that Figure 7.5's curves are to depict the absolute slopes of the curves of Figures 7.1–3.

Except for minor details of notation and assumption, Figure 7.5 is identical with the figure shown on page 31 of the first Bowen reference, and duplicated on p. 177 of the second reference. I am happy to acknowledge this priority. Indeed anyone familiar with Musgrave's valuable summary of the literature bearing on this area[7] will be struck with the similarity between this Bowen type of diagram and the Lindahl 100-per cent diagram reproduced by Musgrave.[8]

Once the economic theorist has related my graphical and mathematical analysis to the Lindahl and Bowen diagrams, he is in a position, I believe, to discern the logical advantage of the present formulation. For there is something circular and unsatisfactory about both the Bowen and Lindahl constructions: they show what the final equilibrium looks like, but by themselves they are not generally able to find the desired equilibrium. To see this, note that whereas we might know MC in Figure 7.5, we would not know the appropriate MRS schedules for *all* men until we already were familiar with the final E intersection point. (We might know MRS^2 from the specification that Man 2 is to be on the AB level;

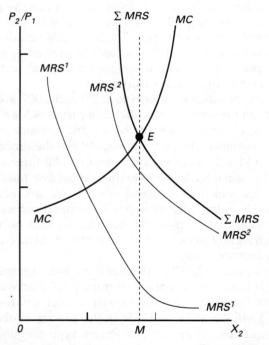

FIGURE 7.5 Intersection of public good's marginal cost schedule and the vertically-summed individual's marginal rates of substitution, as envisaged by Lindahl and Bowen

but then we wouldn't know MRS^1 until Figure 7.1's tangency had given us Man 1's highest attainable level, $u^{1'''}$.) Under conditions of general equilibrium, Figures 7.1–3 logically contain Figure 7.5 inside them, but not vice versa. Moreover, Figures 7.1–3 explicitly call attention to the fact that there is an infinite number of different diagrams of the Lindahl–Bowen type, one for each specified level of relative interpersonal well-being.[9]

Concluding reflections

I hope that the analytic model outlined here may help make a small and modest step toward understanding the complicated realities of political economy. Much remains to be done. This is not the place to discuss the wider implications and difficulties of the presented economic theory.[10] However, I should like to comment briefly on some of the questions about this theory that have been raised in this Review.[11]

(i) On the deductive side, the theory presented here is, I believe, a logically coherent one. This is true whether expressed in my original mathematical notation or in the present diagrammatic form. Admittedly, the latter widens the circle of economists who can understand and follow what is being said. The present version, with its tangencies of methodologically the same type as characterize Cournot–Marshall marginal theory and Bergson–Pigou welfare theory, should from its easily recognized equivalence with the mathematical version make clear my refusal to agree with Dr. Enke's view that my use of mathematics was limited "to notation."

(ii) In terms of the history of similar theories, I hope the present paper will make clear relationships to earlier writers. (In particular, see the above discussion relating my early diagrams and equations to the Bowen–Lindahl formulation.) I shall not bore the reader with irrelevant details of independent rediscoveries of doctrine that my ignorance of the available literature may have made necessary. Yet is it presumptuous to suggest that there does not exist in the present economic literature very much in the way of "conclusions and reasoning" that are, in Dr.Margolis' words, "familiar"? Except for the writers I have cited, and the important unpublished thoughts of Dr. Musgrave, there is much opaqueness in the literature. Much of what goes by the name of the "voluntary exchange theory of public finance" seems pure obfuscation.[12]

(iii) Far from my formulation's being, as some correspondents have thought, a revival of the voluntary exchange theory – it is in fact an attempt to demonstrate how right Wicksell was to worry about the inherent political difficulty of ever getting men to reveal their tastes so as to attain the definable optimum. This intrinsic "game theory" problem has been sufficiently stressed in my early paper so that it has not been emphasized here. I may put the point most clearly in terms of the familiar tools of modern literary economics as follows.

Government supplies products jointly to many people. In ordinary market economics, as you increase the number of sellers of a homogeneous product indefinitely, you pass from monopoly through indeterminate oligopoly and can hope to reach a determinate competitive equilibrium in the limit. It is sometimes thought that increasing the number of citizens who are jointly supplied public goods leads to a similar determinate result. This is reasoning from an incorrect analogy. A truer analogy in private economics would be the case of a bilateral-monopoly supplier of joint products whose number of joint products – meat, horn, hide, and so on – is allowed to increase without number: such a process does not lead to a determinate equilibrium of the harmonistic type praised in the literature. My simple model is able to demonstrate this point – which does have "policy implications."

(iv) I regret using "the" in the title of my earlier paper and have accordingly changed the present title. Admittedly, public expenditure and regulation proceed from considerations other than those emphasized in my models. Here are a few.

a. Taxes and expenditure aim at redistributing incomes. I am anxious to clear myself from Dr. Margolis' understandable suspicion that I am the type of liberal who would insist that all redistributions take place through tax policies and transfer expenditures: much public expenditure on education, hospitals, and so on, can be justified by the feasibility consideration that, even if these are not 100 per cent efficient in avoiding avoidable dead-weight loss, they may be better than the attainable imperfect tax alternatives.[13]

b. Paternalistic policies are voted upon themselves by a democratic people because they do not regard the results from spontaneous market action as optimal. Education and forced paces of economic development are good examples of this.

c. Governments provide or regulate services that are incapable of being produced under the strict conditions of constant returns that go to characterize optimal self-regulating atomistic competition.

d. Myriad "generalized external economy and diseconomy" situations, where private pecuniary interest can be expected to deviate from social interests, provide obvious needs for government activity.

I am sure this list of basic considerations underlying government expenditure could be extended farther, including even areas where government probably ought not to operate from almost anyone's viewpoint.

(v) This brief list can end with the most important criticism that the various commentators on my paper have put forth. They all ask: "Is it factually true that most – or any! – of the functions of government can be properly fitted into your extreme category of a public good? Can education, the courts, public defense, highway programs, police and fire protection be put into this rigid category of a "public good available to all?" In practically every one of these cases isn't there an element of variability in the benefit that can go to one citizen *at the expense* of some other citizens?"

To this criticism, I fully agree. And that is why in the present formulation I have insisted upon the polar nature of my category. However, to say that a thing is not located at the South Pole does not logically place it at the North Pole. To deny that most public functions fit into my extreme definition of a public good is not to grant that they satisfy the logically equally-extreme category of a private good. To say that your absence at a concert may contribute to my enjoyment is not to say that the elements of public services can be put into homogeneous additive packages capable of being optimally handled by the ordinary market calculus.

Indeed, I am rash enough to think that in almost every one of the legitimate functions of government that critics put forward there is to be found a blending of the extreme antipodal models. One might even venture the tentative suspicion that any function of government not possessing any trace of the defined public good (and no one of the related earlier described characteristics) ought to be carefully scrutinized to see whether it is truly a legitimate function of government.

(vi) Whether or not I have overstated the applicability of this one theoretical model to actual governmental functions, I believe I did not go far enough in claiming for it relevance to the vast area of decreasing costs that constitutes an important part of economic reality and of the welfare economics of monopolistic competition. I must leave it to future research discussions of these vital issues.

Economic theory should add what it can to our understanding of governmental activity. I join with critics in hoping that its pretentious claims will not discourage other economic approaches, other contributions from neighboring disciplines, and concrete empirical investigations.

Notes

1. Even though a public good is being compared with a private good, the indifference curves are drawn with the usual convexity to the origin. This assumption, as well as the one about diminishing returns, could be relaxed without hurting the theory. Indeed, we could recognize the possible case where one man's circus is another man's poison, by permitting indifference curves to bend forward. This would not affect the analysis but would

answer a critic's minor objection. Mathematically, we could without loss of generality set X_2^1 = any function of X_2, relaxing strict equality.

2. The reader can easily derive rs and the tangency point G_1 corresponding to an original specification of Man 2's indifference level at the lower level RS rather than at AB. He can also interchange the roles of the two men, thereby deriving the point E_2 by a tangency condition. As a third approach, he can *vertically add* Man 2's specified indifference curve to each and every indifference curve of Man 1; the resulting family of contours can be conveniently plotted on Figure 7.3, and the final optimum can be read off from the tangency of AB to that family at the point E – as shown by the short broken-line indifference curve at E. It is easy to show that any of these tangencies are, in the two-good case, equivalent to Equation (2) of my cited paper; with a single private good my Equation (1) becomes redundant.

3. These social welfare or social indifference contours are given no particular curvature. Why? Again because we are permitting any arbitrary ordinal indicator of utility to be used on the axes of Figure 7.4.

An ethical postulate ruling out all "dog-in-the-manger phenomena" will make all partial derivatives of the social welfare function $U(u^1, u^2, \ldots)$ always positive. This will assure the usual negative slopes to the U contours of Figure 7.4. However, without hurting the Pareto part of the new welfare economics, we can relax this assumption a little and let the contours bend forward. If, at every point there can be found at least one positive partial derivative, this will be sufficient to rule out satiation points and will imply the necessity of the Pareto-optimal tangency condition of the earlier diagrams.

4. This tangency condition would have to be expressed mathematically in terms of numerical indicators of utility that are not invariant under a monotonic renumbering. However, it is easy to combine this tangency with the earlier Pareto-type tangency to get the formulation (3) of my cited paper, which is independent of the choice of numerical indicators of U, u^1, or u^2.

5. A remarkable duality property of private and public goods should be noted. Private goods whose totals add – such as $X_1 = X_1^1 + X_1^2$ – lead ultimately to marginal conditions of simultaneous equality – such as $MC = MRS^1 = MRS^2$. Public goods whose totals satisfy a relation of simultaneous equality – such as $X_1 = X_2^1 = X_2^2$ – lead ultimately to marginal conditions that add – such as $MC = MRS^1 + MRS^2$.

6. Howard R. Bowen, "The Interpretation of Voting in the Allocation of Economic Resources," *Quarterly Journal of Economics*, LVIII (November 1943), 27–49. Much of this is also in Bowen's *Toward Social Economy* (New York, 1948), ch. 18.

7. Richard A. Musgrave, "The Voluntary Exchange Theory of Public Economy." *Quarterly Journal of Economics*, LIII (February 1939), pp. 213–17. This gives citations to the relevant works of Sax, De Viti de Marco, Wicksell, and Lindahl. I have greatly benefited from preliminary study of Professor Musgrave's forthcoming treatise on public finance, which I am sure will constitute a landmark in this area.

8. Musgrave, *op. cit.*, 216, which is an acknowledged adaption from Erik Lindahl, *Die Gerechtigkeit in der Besteuerung* (Lund, 1919), 89. I have not had

access to this important work. This diagram plots instead of the functions of Figure 7.5 the exact same functions after each has been divided by the *MC* function. The equilibrium intersection corresponding to *E* now shows up as the point at which all persons will together voluntarily provide 100 per cent of the full (unit? marginal?) cost of the public service. (If *MC* is not constant, some modifications in the Musgrave diagram may be required.)

9. The earlier writers from Wicksell on were well aware of this. They explicitly introduce the assumption that there is to have been a *prior* optimal interpersonal distribution of income, so what I have labelled *E* might better be labelled *G*. But the general equilibrium analyst asks: how can the appropriate distribution of income be decided on a prior basis *before* the significant problems of public consumptions have been determined? A satisfactory general analysis can resist the temptation to assume (i) the level of government expenditure must be so small as not to affect appreciably the marginal social significance of money to the different individuals; (ii) each man's indifference curves run parallel to each other in a vertical direction so that every and all indifference curves in Figure 7.1 (or in Figure 7.2) give rise to the same MRS^1 (or MRS^2) curve in Figure 7.5. The modern theorist is anxious to free his analysis from the incubus of unnecessarily restrictive partial equilibrium assumptions.

10. At the 1955 Christmas Meetings of the American Economic Association and Econometric Society, I hope to present some further developments and qualifications of this approach.

11. Stephen Enke, "More on the Misuse of Mathematics in Economics: A Rejoinder," this *Review*, XXXVII (May 1955), 131–33; Julius Margolis, "On Samuelson on the Pure Theory of Public Expenditure," this issue, 347.

12. See Gerhard Colm, "The Theory of Public Expenditure," *Annals of the American Academy of Political and Social Sciences*, CLXXXIII (January 1936), I–II, reprinted in his *Essays in Public Finance and Fiscal Policy* (New York, 1955), 27–43 for an admirable criticism of the Graziani statement. "We know that the tax tends to take away from each and all that quantity of wealth which they would each have voluntarily yielded to the state for the satisfaction of their purely collective wants" (p. 32).

13. See my "Evaluation of Real National Income," *Oxford Economic Papers*, N.S.II (January 1950), 18 ff. for analytic discussion of this important truth.

PART IV

ECONOMICS OF UNCERTAINTY AND INFORMATION

CHAPTER 8

The Market for "Lemons": Quality Uncertainty and the Market Mechanism[*1]

G. AKERLOF

Introduction

This paper relates quality and uncertainty. The existence of goods of many grades poses interesting and important problems for the theory of markets. On the one hand, the interaction of quality differences and uncertainty may explain important institutions of the labor market. On the other hand, this paper presents a struggling attempt to give structure to the statement: "Business in under-developed countries is difficult"; in particular, a structure is given for determining the economic costs of dishonesty. Additional applications of the theory include comments on the structure of money markets, on the notion of "insurability," on the liquidity of durables, and on brand-name goods.

There are many markets in which buyers use some market statistic to judge the quality of prospective purchases. In this case there is incentive for sellers to market poor quality merchandise, since the returns for good quality accrue mainly to the entire group whose statistic is affected rather than to the individual seller. As a result there tends to be a reduction in the average quality of goods and also in the size of the market. It should also be perceived that in these markets social and private returns differ, and therefore, in some cases, governmental intervention may increase the welfare of all parties. Or private institutions may arise to take advantage of the potential increases in welfare which can accrue to all parties. By nature, however, these institutions are nonatomistic, and

---

Quarterly Journal of Economics (1970), pp. 488–500.

therefore concentrations of power – with ill consequences of their own – can develop.

The automobile market is used as a finger exercise to illustrate and develop these thoughts. It should be emphasized that this market is chosen for its concreteness and ease in understanding rather than for its importance or realism.

The model with automobiles as an example

The automobiles market

The example of used cars captures the essence of the problem. From time to time one hears either mention of or surprise at the large price difference between new cars and those which have just left the showroom. The usual lunch table justification for this phenomenon is the pure joy of owning a "new" car. We offer a different explanation. Suppose (for the sake of clarity rather than reality) that there are just four kinds of cars. There are new cars and used cars. There are good cars and bad cars (which in America are known as "lemons"). A new car may be a good car or a lemon, and of course the same is true of used cars.

The individuals in this market buy a new automobile without knowing whether the car they buy will be good or a lemon. But they do know that with probability q it is a good car and with probability $(1-q)$ it is a lemon; by assumption, q is the proportion of good cars produced and $(1-q)$ is the proportion of lemons.

After owning a specific car, however, for a length of time, the car owner can form a good idea of the quality of this machine; i.e., the owner assigns a new probability to the event that his car is a lemon. This estimate is more accurate than the original estimate. An asymmetry in available information has developed: for the sellers now have more knowledge about the quality of a car than the buyers. But good cars and bad cars must still sell at the same price – since it is impossible for a buyer to tell the difference between a good car and a bad car. It is apparent that a used car cannot have the same valuation as a new car – if it did have the same valuation, it would clearly be advantageous to trade a lemon at the price of new car, and buy another new car, at a higher probability q of being good and a lower probability of being bad. Thus the owner of a good machine must be locked in. Not only is it true that he cannot receive the true value of his car, but he cannot even obtain the expected value of a new car.

Gresham's law has made a modified reappearance. For most cars traded will be the "lemons," and good cars may not be traded at all. The "bad" cars tend to drive out the good (in much the same way that bad money drives out the good). But the analogy with Gresham's law is not quite complete: bad cars drive out the good because they sell at the same price as good cars; similarly, bad money drives out good because the exchange rate is even. But the bad cars sell at the same price as good cars since it is impossible for a buyer to tell the difference between a good and a bad car; only the seller knows. In Gresham's law, however, presumably both buyer and seller can tell the difference between good and bad money. So the analogy is instructive, but not complete.

Asymmetrical information

It has been seen that the good cars may be driven out of the market by the lemons. But in a more continuous case with different grades of goods, even worse pathologies can exist. For it is quite possible to have the bad driving out the not-so-bad driving out the medium driving out the not-so-good driving out the good in such a sequence of events that no market exists at all.

One can assume that the demand for used automobiles depends most strongly upon two variables – the price of the automobile p and the average quality of used cars traded, μ, or $Q^d = D(p, \mu)$. Both the supply of used cars and also the average quality μ will depend upon the price, or $\mu = \mu(p)$ and $S = S(p)$. And in equilibrium the supply must equal the demand for the given average quality, or $S(p) = D(p, \mu(p))$. As the price falls, normally the quality will also fall. And it is quite possible that no goods will be traded at any price level.

Such an example can be derived from utility theory. Assume that there are just two groups of traders: groups one and two. Give group one a utility function

$$U_1 = M + \sum_{i=1}^{n} x_i$$

where M is the consumption of goods other than automobiles, x_i is the quality of the ith automobile, and n is the number of automobiles.

Similarly, let

$$U_2 = M + \sum_{i=1}^{n} 3/2 x_i$$

where M, x_i, and n are defined as above.

Three comments should be made about these utility functions: (1) without linear utility (say with logarithmic utility) one gets needlessly mired in algebraic complication. (2) The use of linear utility allows a focus on the effects of asymmetry of information; with a concave utility function we would have to deal jointly with the usual risk-variance effects of uncertainty and the special effects we wish to discuss here. (3) U_1 and U_2 have the odd characteristic that the addition of a second car, or indeed a kth car, adds the same amount of utility as the first. Again realism is sacrificed to avoid a diversion from the proper focus.

To continue, it is assumed (a) that both type one traders and type two traders are von Neumann–Morgenstern maximizers of expected utility; (b) that group one has N cars with uniformly distributed quality x, $0 \leq x \leq 2$, and group two has no cars; (c) that the price of "other goods" M is unity.

Denote the income (including that derived from the sale of automobiles) of all type one traders as Y_1 and the income of all type two traders as Y_2. The demand for used cars will be the sum of the demands by both groups. When one ignores indivisibilities, the demand for automobiles by type one traders will be

$$D_1 = Y_1/p \qquad \mu/p > 1$$
$$D_1 = 0 \qquad \mu/p < 1$$

And the supply of cars offered by type one traders is

$$S_2 = pN/2 \qquad p \leq 2 \qquad (8.1)$$

with average quality

$$\mu = p/2. \qquad (8.2)$$

(To derive (8.1) and (8.2), the uniform distribution of automobile quality is used.)

Similarly the demand of type two traders is

$$D_2 = Y_2/p \qquad 3\mu/2 > p$$
$$D_2 = 0 \qquad 3\mu/2 < p$$

and

$$S_2 = 0.$$

Thus total demand $D(p, \mu)$ is

$$D(p, \mu) = (Y_2 + Y_1)/p \qquad \text{if } p < \mu$$
$$D(p, \mu) = Y_2/p \qquad \text{if } \mu < p < 3\mu/2$$
$$D(p, \mu) = 0 \qquad \text{if } p > 3\mu/2.$$

However, with price p, average quality is $p/2$ and therefore at no price will any trade take place at all: in spite of the fact that *at any given price between 0 and 3* there are traders of type one who are willing to sell their automobiles at a price which traders of type two are willing to pay.

Symmetric information

The foregoing is contrasted with the case of symmetric information. Suppose that the quality of all cars is uniformly distributed, $0 \leq x \leq 2$. Then the demand curves and supply curves can be written as follows:
  Supply

$$S(p) = N \qquad\qquad p > 1$$
$$S(p) = 0 \qquad\qquad p < 1.$$

And the demand curves are

$$D(p) = (Y_2 + Y_1)/p \qquad\qquad p < 1$$
$$D(p) = (Y_2/p) \qquad\qquad 1 < p < 3/2$$
$$D(p) = 0 \qquad\qquad p > 3/2.$$

In equilibrium

$p = 1$	if $Y_2 < N$	(8.3)
$p = Y_2/N$	if $2Y_2/3 < N < Y_2$	(8.4)
$p = 3/2$	if $N < 2Y_2/3$.	(8.5)

If $N < Y_2$ there is a gain in utility over the case of asymmetrical information of $N/2$. (If $N > Y_2$, in which case the income of type two traders is insufficient to buy all N automobiles, there is a gain in utility of $Y_2/2$ units.)

Finally, it should be mentioned that in this example, if traders of groups one and two have the same probabilistic estimates about the quality of individual automobiles – though these estimates may vary from automobile to automobile – (8.3), (8.4), and (8.5) will still describe equilibrium with one slight change: p will then represent the expected price of one quality unit.

Examples and applications

Insurance

It is well-known fact that people over 65 have great difficulty in buying medical insurance. The natural question arises: why doesn't the price rise to match the risk?

Our answer is that as the price level rises the people who insure themselves will be those who are increasingly certain that they will need the insurance; for error in medical check-ups, doctors' sympathy with older patients, and so on make it much easier for the applicant to assess the risks involved than the insurance company. The result is that the average medical condition of insurance applicants deteriorates as the price level rises – with the result that no insurance sales may take place at any price.[2] This is strictly analogous to our automobiles case, where the average quality of used cars supplied fell with a corresponding fall in the price level. This agrees with the explanation in insurance textbooks:

> Generally speaking policies are not available at ages materially greater than sixty-five... The term premiums are too high for any but the most pessimistic (which is to say the least healthy) insureds to find attractive. Thus there is a severe problem of adverse selection at these ages.[3]

The statistics do not contradict this conclusion. While demands for health insurance rise with age, a 1956 national sample survey of 2,809 families with 8,898 persons shows that hospital insurance coverage drops from 63 per cent of those aged 45 to 54, to 31 per cent for those over 65. And surprisingly, this survey also finds average medical expenses for males aged 55 to 64 of $88, while males over 65 pay an average of $77.[4] While noninsured expenditure rises from $66 to $80 in these age groups, insured expenditure declines from $105 to $70. The conclusion is tempting that insurance companies are particularly wary of giving medical insurance to older people.

The principle of "adverse selection" is potentially present in all lines of insurance. The following statement appears in an insurance textbook written at the Wharton School:

> There is potential adverse selection in the fact that healthy term insurance policy holders may decide to terminate their coverage when they become older and premiums mount. This action could leave an insurer with an undue proportion of below average risks and claims might be higher than anticipated. Adverse selection 'appears (or at least is possible) whenever the individual or group insured has freedom to buy or not to buy, to choose the amount or plan of insurance, and to persist or to discontinue as a policy holder'.[5]

Group insurance, which is the most common form of medical insurance in the United States, picks out the healthy, for generally adequate health is a precondition for employment. At the same time this means that medical insurance is least available to those who need it most, for the insurance companies do their own "adverse selection."

This adds one major argument in favor of Medicare.[6] On a cost benefit basis Medicare may pay off; for it is quite possible that every individual in the market would be willing to pay the expected cost of his Medicare and buy insurance, yet no insurance company can afford to sell him a policy – for at any price it will attract too many "lemons." The welfare economics of Medicare, in this view, is *exactly* analogous to the usual classroom argument for public expenditure on roads.

The employment of minorities

The Lemons Principle also casts light on the employment of minorities. Employers may refuse to hire members of minority groups for certain types of jobs. This decision may not reflect irrationality or prejudice – but profit maximization. For race may serve as a good *statistic* for the applicant's social background, quality of schooling, and general job capabilities.

Good quality schooling could serve as a substitute for this statistic; by grading students the schooling system can give a better indicator of quality than other more superficial characteristics. As T. W. Schultz writes, "The educational establishment *discovers* and cultivates potential talent. The capabilities of children and mature students can never be known until *found* and cultivated"[7] (italics added). An untrained worker may have valuable natural talents, but these talents must be certified by "the educational establishment" before a company can afford to use them. The certifying establishment, however, must be credible; the unreliability of slum schools decreases the economic possibilities of their students.

This lack may be particularly disadvantageous to members of already disadvantaged minority groups. For an employer may make a rational decision not to hire any members of these groups in responsible positions – because it is difficult to distinguish those with good job qualifications from those with bad qualifications. This type of decision is clearly what George Stigler had in mind when he wrote, "in a regime of ignorance Enrico Fermi would have been a gardener, Von Neumann a checkout clerk at a drugstore."[8]

As a result, however, the rewards for work in slum schools tend to accrue to the group as a whole – in raising its average quality – rather than to the individual. Only insofar as information in addition to race is used is there any incentive for training.

An additional worry is that the Office of Economic Opportunity is going to use cost-benefit analysis to evaluate its programs. For many benefits may be external. The benefit from training minority groups may arise as much from raising the average quality of the group as from raising the quality of the individual trainee; and, likewise, the returns may be distributed over the whole group rather than to the individual.

The costs of dishonesty

The Lemons model can be used to make some comments on the costs of dishonesty. Consider a market in which goods are sold honestly or dishonestly; quality may be represented, or it may be misrepresented. The purchaser's problem, of course, is to identify quality. The presence of people in the market who are willing to offer inferior goods tends to drive the market out of existence – as in the case of our automobile "lemons." It is this possibility that represents the major costs of dishonesty – for dishonest dealings tend to drive honest dealings out of the market. There may be potential buyers of good quality products and there may be potential sellers of such products in the appropriate price range; however, the presence of people who wish to pawn bad wares as good wares tends to drive out the legitimate business. The cost of dishonesty, therefore, lies not only in the amount by which the purchaser is cheated; the cost also must include the loss incurred from driving legitimate business out of existence.

Dishonesty in business is a serious problem in underdeveloped countries. Our model gives a possible structure to this statement and delineates the nature of the "external" economies involved. In particular, in the model economy described, dishonesty, or the misrepresentation of the quality of automobiles, cost $1/2$ unit of utility per automobile; furthermore, it reduces the size of the used car market from N to 0. We can, consequently, directly evaluate the costs of dishonesty – at least in theory.

There is considerable evidence that quality variation is greater in underdeveloped than in developed areas. For instance, the need for quality control of exports and State Trading Corporations can be taken as one indicator. In India, for example, under the Export Quality Control and Inspection Act of 1963, "about 85 per cent of Indian exports are covered under one or the other type of quality control."[9] Indian housewives must carefully glean the rice of the local bazaar to sort out stones of the same color and shape which have been intentionally added to the rice. Any comparison of the heterogeneity of quality in the street market and the canned qualities of the American supermarket suggests that quality variation is a greater problem in the East than in the West.

In one traditional pattern of development the merchants of the pre-industrial generation turn into the first entrepreneurs of the next. The best-documented case is Japan,[10] but this also may have been the pattern for Britain and America.[11] In *our* picture the important skill of the merchant is identifying the quality of merchandise; those who can identify used cars in our example and can guarantee the quality may profit by as much as the difference between type two traders' buying price and type one traders' selling price. These people are the merchants. In production these skills are equally necessary – both to be able to identify the quality of inputs and to certify the quality of outputs. And this is one (added) reason why the merchants may logically become the first entrepreneurs.

The problem, of course, is that entrepreneurship may be a scarce resource; no development text leaves entrepreneurship unemphasized. Some treat it as central.[12] Given, then, that entrepreneurship is scarce, there are two ways in which product variations impede development. First, the pay-off to trade is great for would-be entrepreneurs, and hence they are diverted from production; second, the amount of entrepreneurial time per unit output is greater, the greater are the quality variations.

Credit markets in underdeveloped countries

(1) Credit markets in underdeveloped countries often strongly reflect the operation of the Lemons Principle. In India a major fraction of industrial enterprise is controlled by managing agencies (according to a recent survey, these "managing agencies" controlled 65.7 per cent of the net worth of public limited companies and 66 per cent of total assets).[13] Here is a historian's account of the function and genesis of the "managing agency system":

> The management of the South Asian commercial scene remained the function of merchant houses, and a type of organization peculiar to South Asia known as the Managing Agency. When a new venture was promoted (such as a manufacturing plant, a plantation, or a trading venture), the promoters would approach an established managing agency. The promoters might be Indian or British, and they might have technical or financial resources or merely a concession. In any case they would turn to the agency because of its reputation, which would encourage confidence in the venture and stimulate investment.[14]

In turn, a second major feature of the Indian industrial scene has been the dominance of these managing agencies by caste (or, more accurately, communal) groups. Thus firms can usually be classified according to communal origin.[15] In this environment, in which outside investors are likely to be bilked of their holdings, either (1) firms establish a reputation for "honest" dealing, which confers upon them a monopoly rent insofar as their services are limited in supply, or (2) the sources of finance are limited to local communal groups which can use communal – and possibly familial – ties to encourage honest dealing *within* the community. It is, in Indian economic history, extraordinarily difficult to discern whether the savings of rich landlords failed to be invested in the industrial sector (1) because of a fear to invest in ventures controlled by other communities, (2) because of inflated propensities to consume, or (3) because of low rates of return.[16] At the very least, however, it is clear that the British-owned managing agencies tended to have an equity holding whose communal origin was more heterogeneous than the Indian-controlled agency houses, and would usually include both Indian and British investors.

(2) A second example of the workings of the Lemons Principle concerns the extortionate rates which the local moneylender charges his clients. In India these high rates of interest have been the leading factor in landlessness; the so-called "Cooperative Movement" was meant to counteract this growing landlessness by setting up banks to compete with the local moneylenders.[17] While the large banks in the central cities have prime interest rates of 6, 8, and 10 per cent, the local moneylender charges 15, 25, and even 50 per cent. The answer to this seeming paradox is that credit is granted only where the granter has (1) easy means of enforcing his contract or (2) personal knowledge of the character of the borrower. The middleman who tries to arbitrage between the rates of the moneylender and the central bank is apt to attract all the "lemons" and thereby make a loss.

This interpretation can be seen in Sir Malcolm Darling's interpretation of the village moneylender's power:

> It is only fair to remember that in the Indian village the money-lender is often the one thrifty person amongst a generally thriftless people; and that his methods of business, though demoralizing under modern conditions, suit the happy-go-lucky ways of the peasant. He is always accessible, even at night; dispenses with troublesome formalities, asks no inconvenient questions, advances promptly, and if interest is paid, does not press for repayment of principal. He keeps in close personal touch with his clients, and in many villages shares their occasions of weal or woe. *With his intimate knowledge of those around him he is able, without serious risk, to finance those who would otherwise get no loan at all.* [Italics added][18]

Or look at Barbara Ward's account:

> A small shopkeeper in a Hong Kong fishing village told me: 'I give credit to anyone who anchors regularly in our bay; but if it is someone I don't know well, then I think twice about it unless I can find out all about him.'[19]

Or, a profitable sideline of cotton ginning in Iran is the loaning of money for the next season, since the ginning companies often have a line of credit from Teheran banks at the market rate of interest. But in the first years of operation large losses are expected from unpaid debts – due to poor knowledge of the local scene.[20]

Counteracting institutions

Numerous institutions arise to counteract the effects of quality uncertainty. One obvious institution is guarantees. Most consumer durables carry guarantees to ensure the buyer of some normal expected quality. One natural result of our model is that the risk is borne by the seller rather than by the buyer.

A second example of an institution which counteracts the effect of quality uncertainty is the brand-name good. Brand names not only indicate quality but also give the consumer a means of retaliation if the quality does not meet expectations. For the consumer will then curtail future purchases. Often too, new products are associated with old brand names. This ensures the prospective consumer of the quality of the product.

Chains – such as hotel chains or restaurant chains – are similar to brand names. One observation consistent with our approach is the chain restaurant. These restaurants, at least in the United States, most often appear on interurban highways. The customers are seldom local. The reason is that these well-known chains offer a better hamburger than the *average* local restaurant; at the same time, the local customer, who knows his area, can usually choose a place he prefers.

Licensing practices also reduce quality uncertainty. For instance, there is the licensing of doctors, lawyers, and barbers. Most skilled labor carries some certification indicating the attainment of certain levels of proficiency. The high school diploma, the baccalaureate degree, the Ph.D., even the Nobel Prize, to some degree, serve this function of certification. And education and labor markets themselves have their own "brand names."

Conclusion

We have been discussing economic models in which 'trust' is important. Informal unwritten guarantees are preconditions for trade and production. Where these guarantees are indefinite, business will suffer – as indicated by our generalized Gresham's law. This aspect of uncertainty has been explored by game theorists, as in the Prisoner's Dilemma, but usually it has not been incorporated in the more traditional Arrow–Debreu approach to uncertainty.[21] But the difficulty of distinguishing good quality from bad is inherent in the business world; this may indeed explain many economic institutions and may in fact be one of the more important aspects of uncertainty.

Notes

1. The author would especially like to thank Thomas Rothenberg for invaluable comments and inspiration. In addition he is indebted to Roy Radner, Albert Fishlow, Bernard Saffran, William D. Nordhaus, Giorgio La Malfa, Charles C. Holt, John Letiche, and the referee for help and suggestions. He would also like to thank the Indian Statistical Institute and the Ford Foundation for financial support.
2. Arrow's fine article, "Uncertainty and Medical Care" (*American Economic Review*, Vol. 53, 1963), does not make this point explicitly. He emphasizes "moral hazard" rather than "adverse selection." In its strict sense the presence of "moral hazard" is equally disadvantageous for both governmental and private programs; in its broader sense, which includes "adverse selection," "moral hazard" gives a decided advantage to government insurance programs.
3. O. D. Dickerson, *Health Insurance* (Homewood, Ill.: Irwin, 1959), p. 333.
4. O. W. Anderson (with J. J. Feldman), *Family Medical Costs and Insurance* (New York: McGraw-Hill, 1956).
5. H. S. Denenberg, R. D. Eilers, G. W. Hoffman, C. A. Kline, J. J. Melone, and H. W. Snider, *Risk and Insurance* (Englewood Cliffs, N.J.: Prentice Hall, 1964), p. 446.
6. The following quote, again taken from an insurance textbook, shows how far the medical insurance market is from perfect competition:
   …insurance companies must screen their applicants. Naturally it is true that many people will voluntarily seek adequate insurance on their own initiative. But in such lines as accident and health insurance, companies are likely to give a second look to persons who voluntarily seek insurance without being approached by an agent. (F. J. Angell, *Insurance, Principles and Practices*, New York: The Ronald Press, 1957, pp. 8–9.)
   This shows that insurance is *not* a commodity for sale on the open market.
7. T. W. Schultz, *The Economic Value of Education* (New York: Columbia University Press, 1964), p. 42.
8. G. J. Stigler, "Information and the Labor Market," *Journal of Political Economy*, Vol. 70 (Oct. 1962), Supplement, p. 104.
9. *The Times of India*, Nov. 10, 1967, p. 1.

10. See M. J. Levy, Jr., "Contrasting Factors in the Modernization of China and Japan," in *Economic Growth: Brazil, India, Japan*, ed. S. Kuznets *et al.* (Durham, NC: Duke University Press, 1955).
11. C. P. Kindleberger, *Economic Development* (New York: McGraw-Hill, 1958), p. 86.
12. For example, see W. Arthur Lewis, *The Theory of Economic Growth* (Homewood, Ill.: Irwin, 1955), p. 196.
13. *Report of the Committee on the Distribution of Income and Levels of Living*, Part I, Government of India, Planning Commission, Feb. 1964, p. 44.
14. H. Tinker, *South Asia: A Short History* (New York: Praeger, 1966), p. 134.
15. The existence of the following table (and also the small per cent of firms under mixed control) indicates the communalization of the control of firms.

    Source: M. M. Mehta, *Structure of Indian Industries* (Bombay: Popular Book Depot, 1955), p. 314.

Distribution of industrial control by community

	1911	1931	1951
		(number of firms)	
British	281	416	382
Parsis	15	25	19
Gujratis	3	11	17
Jews	5	9	3
Muslims	–	10	3
Bengalis	8	5	20
Marwaris	–	6	96
Mixed control	28	28	79
Total	341	510	619

   Also, for the cotton industry see H. Fukuzawa, "Cotton Mill Industry," in V. B. Singh, editor, *Economic History of India, 1857–1956* (Bombay: Allied Publishers, 1965).

16. For the mixed record of industrial profit, see D. H. Buchanan, *The Development of Capitalist Enterprise in India* (New York: Kelley, 1966, reprinted.
17. The leading authority on this is Sir Malcolm Darling, See his *Punjabi Peasant in Prosperity and Debt*. The following table may also prove instructive:

	Secured loans (per cent)	Commonest rates for – Unsecured loans (per cent)	Grain loans (per cent)
Punjab	6 to 12	12 to 24 ($18\frac{3}{4}$ commonest)	25
United Provinces	9 to 12	24 to $37\frac{1}{2}$	25 (50 in Oudh)
Bihar		$18\frac{3}{4}$	50
Orissa	12 to $18\frac{3}{4}$	25	25
Bengal	8 to 12	9 to 18 for 'respectable clients' $18\frac{3}{4}$ to $37\frac{1}{2}$ (the latter common to agriculturalists)	
Central Provinces	6 to 12	15 for proprietors 24 for occupancy tenants $37\frac{1}{2}$ for ryots with no right of transfer	25
Bombay	9 to 12	12 to 25 (18 commonest)	
Sind		36	
Madras	12	15 to 18 (in insecure tracts 24 not uncommon)	20 to 50

Source: *Punjabi Peasant in Prosperity and Debt*, 3rd ed. (Oxford University Press, 1932), p. 190.

18. Darling, *op. cit.*, p. 204.
19. B. Ward, "Cash or Credit Crops," *Economic Development and Cultural Change*, Vol. 8 (Jan. 1960), reprinted in *Peasant Society: A reader*, ed. G. Foster *et al.* (Boston: Little, Brown and Company 1967). Quote on p. 142. In the same volume, see also G. W. Skinner, "Marketing and Social Structure in Rural China," and S. W. Mintz, "Pratik: Haitian Personal Economic Relations."
20. Personal conversation with mill manager, April 1968.
21. R. Radner, "Équilibre de Marchés à Terme et au Comptant en Cas d'Incertitude," in *Cahiers d'Econometrie*, Vol. 12 (Nov. 1967), Centre National de la Recherche Scientifique, Paris.

PART V

INFLATION AND UNEMPLOYMENT

CHAPTER 9

How Important is it to Defeat Inflation? The Evidence*

R. BOOTLE[1]

I Introduction

We all know that the fundamental aim of Mrs Thatcher's Government is to defeat inflation. The importance of this aim has been reiterated time and again by Government spokesmen, and was recently reaffirmed at the Conservative Party Conference in October. Moreover, it is clear that the pursuit of this end subordinates all others, including not only the traditional policy objective of 'full' employment, but also the particularly Conservative objective of reducing taxation. The overwhelming importance accredited to this aim derives from the belief that persistent inflation has lain at the root of Britain's economic malaise, and that its defeat is a prerequisite for the achievement and maintenance of higher rates of real economic growth. Yet although the debate has raged about how best to defeat inflation, the basic premise has gone largely unchallenged.[2] Why should the defeat of inflation be so important? What is wrong with inflation anyway?

To ask this question is not to deny the costs which inflation can bring; although there have probably been occasions when inflation has brought net benefits by overcoming some blockage in the economic system, at the very least it is inefficient, and on occasions it has brought terrible injustice and even the virtual collapse of the economic and social system. Rather the purpose of asking this question is to establish perspective, for few western governments either face the danger of hyper-inflation on the

---

The Three Banks' Review (1981), pp. 23–47.

one hand, or can reasonably envisage achieving complete price stability on the other. Their choice is between having more or less inflation, within the range 0 to 30 per cent per annum, and by general consensus it is better to have less. But how much better?

This paper examines the theoretical and empirical evidence on the costs of inflation. Its objective is not to provide a definitive measure of those costs; that would in any case be thwarted by the intangible nature of so many of the elements. Instead, its aim is, by analysing the nature of the costs involved, and such estimates of these costs as can be readily made, to assess how far the *primacy* of the anti-inflation objective is justified by the evidence.

The paper begins by examining the costs of inflation in the macro sphere, and in particular the links between inflation and unemployment. It concludes that, contrary to common belief, generalised inflation does not necessarily cause macro problems, and that the source of any difficulties at this level arises from changes in *relative* values which cannot properly be ascribed to inflation as such.

Turning to the micro level, it argues that although unanticipated inflation may cause countless distortions of far-reaching consequence, when it is anticipated the problems come down to only two. The evidence that inflation is more likely to be less well anticipated the higher it is, is discussed and found to be unsatisfactory, which throws the spotlight onto the two costs of anticipated inflation. The evidence on one of these – the cost of actually changing wages and prices – suggests that it is fairly small, and whilst some existing theoretical and empirical material on the other – the welfare losses from reduced money holdings – suggests that these are highly significant, this material is shown to be based on invalid assumptions.

In the penultimate section, the association between growth rates and inflation rates across countries is briefly reviewed, and it is concluded that there is no obvious relationship between inflation and growth. Finally, there are some concluding remarks on the implications for current UK economic policy.

II Inflation and unemployment

Such costs as inflation imposes reduce economic welfare below what it would otherwise have been, and in so far as the relevant welfare items enter into the national accounts, they will lower national product as well, and may directly affect the rate at which national product grows. Analysis of the effect of inflation on unemployment is a useful, though imperfect guide to this effect on national product. It is given great weight in the following discussion largely because it is an aspect most strongly emphasised by Government ministers. Nevertheless, it should be noted that the message of this analysis also applies to the national product more generally, and not simply to the employment of labour.

Until about five years ago the policy maker's view of the connection between inflation and unemployment was dominated by the Phillips Curve – higher inflation was the cost (some would have said the cause) of lower unemployment.[3] When it was realised that the combination in many western countries of sharply increased levels of both unemployment and inflation required a reinterpretation, the Friedman–Phelps view that the Phillips relation rested on the assumption of money illusion, and that in the long run there was no relation between the two variables, was a popular choice.[4] Many people, including Government ministers, however, have gone further and have seen the explanation of increased unemployment at the time of higher inflation, not as the result of slowly adjusting expectations, or changes in the natural rate of unemployment (as Friedman and the monetarists do), but as evidence of the harm done by inflation; in short, they have come to believe that inflation *creates* unemployment, and that reducing inflation would reduce unemployment.

This view was recently aired in the House of Commons in July 1981 when Mr Leon Brittan, Chief Secretary to the Treasury, said, 'We have put at the forefront the goal of reducing inflation by responsible monetary control because by doing that we are tackling the problem that has been at the heart of our trouble. It is not a question of choosing to tackle inflation rather than unemployment. It is rather a recognition that past inflation has been the cause of present unemployment'.[5]

It is difficult to know exactly what the Government has in mind when it says that inflation creates unemployment. Of course, in a trivial sense inflation 'creates' unemployment because the attempt to reduce it by deflation creates unemployment. This amounts to saying that something is bad because when you try to stop it bad things follow, which will hardly do. There are, however, a number of ways in which inflation may legitimately be said to create unemployment, once it is posited that the inflation is uneven, that is once it is assumed that the structure of *relative values* is changed adversely by inflation.

If inflation is greater in the UK, for instance, than it is abroad, and if the exchange rate does not adjust sufficiently to correct this imbalance, domestic producers will lose price competitiveness in markets both at home and abroad, thus tending to worsen the trade balance, impair profitability, and reduce levels of output and employment. But the exchange rate is crucial; if the rate adjusted to the excess of domestic inflation over inflation abroad (net of productivity changes) there would be no problem on the score of competitiveness.

Over the twenty years to 1975, unit labour costs for manufacturing in the UK expressed in sterling increased by more than the average of our major competitors expressed in their currencies, but this did not impair competitiveness over the period as a whole since the exchange rate depreciated sufficiently to compensate. In the period since 1975, however, UK unit labour costs have increased by even more relative to our international competitors, but rather than being offset by a depreciation of the exchange rate as in the earlier period, the effect of this excess has been compounded by a substantial appreciation. This combination yielded a massive loss of competitiveness, estimated at 55 per cent to the second quarter of 1981.[6] Although the recent weakening of sterling has substantially helped, it remains a formidable problem. It would be quite wrong, however, to attribute this lack of competitiveness to inflation as such.

An examination of the implications of inflation for competitiveness which does not take account of the exchange rate effects is rather like a production of *Hamlet* without the Prince of Denmark. It is by no means obvious that getting a lower rate of increase in domestic costs will succeed in improving competitiveness for, *ceteris paribus*, this will tend to increase the exchange rate. Indeed, even countries with very low rates of increase of domestic costs have experienced very large losses of competitiveness, solely as a result of exchange rate changes. In Switzerland in 1978, for instance, the domestic inflation rate was about 1 per cent, well below the average of her competitors, but by late September the exchange rate had risen by nearly 34 per cent against a year before, placing Switzerland's trading position in danger, so much so that the Swiss authorities decided to abandon their monetary target and direct their monetary policy towards lowering the exchange rate.[7]

The question of exchange rate behaviour is especially interesting in the context of current UK policy since the Government openly looked to an appreciation of the exchange rate as one of the prime agents for lowering inflation. It is difficult for the same Government to cite loss of competitiveness as one of the evils which justify the primacy of the anti-inflation objective.[8]

This difficulty is perhaps best illustrated in an international context. Nearly all governments now attach a very high degree of importance to defeating inflation, and attempt to reconcile this pursuit with the objective of promoting employment much in the manner of Mr Brittan's statement quoted earlier. But just as monetary policy cannot work as a cure for inflation for *all* countries by raising exchange rates, so inflation cannot cause unemployment for all countries through impairing competitiveness. Competitiveness is impaired only when one country's costs rise relative to costs elsewhere; it is clearly impossible for all countries' relative costs to increase.

Perhaps the most fundamental way in which inflation may be thought to create unemployment is through increasing real personal incomes at the expense of profits and thereby shifting income from capital to labour. Such a shift would inhibit employment directly, but would also tend to have indirect effects through the discouragement of investment. For this transfer to occur during inflation, of course, wages must rise faster than prices, but if this does indeed occur during an inflation, this is not enough to conclude that inflation has *caused* the change in relative values. Clearly, shifts in relative income shares may take place without inflation, or inflation may itself be the *result* of an attempt to increase labour incomes at the expense of profits.

Certainly there is no real evidence that pressure on profits in the UK has been caused by inflation as such (although clearly *pay* inflation has been a very significant contributor). Moreover, the attempt to reduce inflation by deflation of demand has undoubtedly been largely responsible for the recent sharp twist against profits. During 1980, indeed, a year over which the inflation rate (as measured by the Retail Prices Index) was on a falling trend, real personal incomes increased by 4 per cent whilst the real rate of return in industrial and commercial companies (excluding North Sea Oil) fell to a record low of less than 3 per cent. The share of domestic income accounted for by income from employment rose from 65 per cent in the last quarter of 1979 to 68.9 per cent in the last quarter of 1980, and the share going to profits (gross of stock appreciation) fell from 14.8 per cent to 10.5 per cent.

Of course much of the Government's effort has been directed towards trying to reduce pay inflation, but short of an incomes policy, and apart from exhortation (which is a relatively new addition to its armoury), the Government can only hope to reduce pay inflation in the private sector by putting pressure on companies through high interest rates, low demand, and a high exchange rate – pressure which limits the rate at which companies can raise prices. The likely result of such pressure is that the rate of pay inflation will indeed fall, but not necessarily faster than price inflation. Once again, looking at the absolute rate of increase (of pay in this case), is misleading; the key concept is a relative value which is not certain to move in the desired direction as pressure is exerted to lower the absolute rate of increase. In the case of the UK, moreover, at least until recently, this relative value appears to have moved in the opposite direction.

There is another channel, however, through which inflation could reduce real incomes and employment by lowering investment, and which does not depend on a fall in profits, namely increased uncertainty. But again this problem is substantially one of relative values – does the high nominal interest rate at which investment funds can be borrowed accurately reflect the prospective increase in prices over the investment period? Will the rate of increase of product prices keep pace with the cost of raw materials and labour? Will the exchange rate depreciate to offset any excess of domestic inflation over inflation abroad? These are the key issues which will affect the investment decision, but it is not obvious that the uncertainty concerning the answers to these questions will increase as the inflation rate increases. (This is closely bound up with the degree to which inflation is anticipated, which is discussed in Section III and IV below.) Moreover, if the chief worry about inflation is its effects on investment, then the policy of combating it by deflation of demand again appears self-defeating, for both through its effects on profits, and by reducing pressure on productive capacity, deflation acts as a disincentive to investment.

A further sense in which inflation may be said to cause unemployment is by depressing consumption expenditures. Inflation erodes the real value of savings fixed in money terms, and since individuals like to maintain a fairly stable relationship between their incomes and their liquid assets, it may be argued, faster inflation causes individuals to reduce consumption in order to rebuild their real assets by further saving.

There seems no reason to object to this as a description of the way people may react to inflation, but even if it is accurate, it is perverse to argue from it that inflation creates unemployment, for all it accounts for is a deflation of demand through one channel which can easily by offset through another. There would be no reason for the Government to wait for inflation to fall to restimulate consumption expenditures when they could be stimulated (and with the same effect in extra inflationary pressure) by tax cuts. Moreover, it would be ridiculous to try to justify support for a policy of deflating demand to reduce inflation on the grounds that inflation caused unemployment by depressing consumption expenditures.

This analysis has identified three senses in which inflation could legitimately be said to cause unemployment – but all of them operate through changing a relative value, or by creating uncertainty about relative values. Yet there is no evidence that inflation must necessarily change relative values in the directions required by the explanation. Moreover, the policy of monetary stringency adopted by the present Government has had the direct effect of worsening all three key macro relative values.

So far, however, this discussion has dealt only with the macro aspects; inflation can also have profound implications on a micro level, most notably through its effects on the whole structure of relative prices and other values (including incomes). If these effects reduced efficiency, or reduced investment, by making economic activity less productive, they would in themselves tend to increase unemployment. To what extent inflation does have such serious effects at the micro level is discussed below.

III Anticipated and unanticipated inflation

Modern theory on the welfare costs of inflation has centred around the distinction between perfectly and imperfectly anticipated inflation. This does not imply that anyone thinks that perfectly anticipated inflation has ever occurred; indeed the conditions required for *perfectly* anticipated inflation are so stringent as to make this virtually impossible, since not only is it necessary that the actual inflation rate conforms to the 'expected' rate, in the sense of the average rate of inflation anticipated, but also that this expectation be held confidently by every member of society. Nevertheless, the analytical distinction between perfectly and imperfectly anticipated inflation is of key importance; its point is to distinguish between costs of inflation which can be expected to fall as the general level of inflation falls, and costs which can be expected to fall as the general level of inflation is better anticipated.

As long as inflation is not perfectly anticipated, it distorts the structure of relative prices (and other money values) and both income distribution and allocative signals are thereby disturbed in an essentially arbitrary fashion. Except in particular instances where such disturbances redress a prior imbalance in the structure, they are bound to impair economic efficiency, and to create unfairness. Moreover, without full anticipation, economic agents will find it difficult to distinguish genuine relative price changes from inflationary price changes, and their consequent uncertainty about the relative price structure will both cause them to make wrong decisions, and to put extra resources into shopping around in order to avoid such mistakes.

The difference which would be made by the complete anticipation of inflation is profound. Prices, incomes, all sorts of money values and contracts in money, could be fixed with the rate of inflation firmly in view, so that the structure of relative values need not be disturbed. (Of course, in order to preserve the structure of relative values, at faster rates of inflation the frequency of price and other money value changes would have to be increased. Changing prices is an expensive business and the cost of doing this more frequently may be legitimately counted as one of the losses from even perfectly anticipated inflation.[9] This is discussed in Section V below.) Indeed nearly all the major problems associated with inflation disappear once it is assumed that the inflation is perfectly anticipated.

A good example of this is shown in the analysis developed by the late Arthur Okun (1975) in which he divided the economy into what he termed auction markets and customer markets. Auction (e.g. commodities) markets are markets on which the price responds flexibly to the pressure of supply and demand; on customer markets (e.g. in the service industries) by contrast, prices are administered with a view to maintaining a relationship between supplier and customer. Although prices on customer markets might seem in a pure sense to be inefficient, in fact the economy derives great benefits from this system of price determination since it economises on shopping and information gathering, which are expensive.

Inflation threatens to undermine customer markets, argues Okun, since it requires firms to shorten the time lags between cost changes and price changes and/or to widen their margins. Moreover, the co-existence of auction and customer markets necessarily implies that relative prices are distorted by inflation, with auction prices in the vanguard of the inflationary process and customer prices lagging behind.

Yet the distinction between anticipated and unanticipated inflation is crucial. Provided that it is anticipated, there seems no reason why inflation should spell the end of customer markets. If the general rate of inflation is known, sellers should be able to raise prices in line with it, confident that others will follow suit, and customers will come to expect increases in prices in line with the general rate of inflation as part of the 'customer bargain' they strike with suppliers. Moreover, although inflation will undoubtedly present price-setters in customer markets with the choice between increasing the frequency of price changes and allowing relative prices to be distorted, even if they choose the latter, provided again that inflation is anticipated, these distortions should offset each other through time, rather than be self-reinforcing. Nor is it likely that 'customer' prices would continue to lag in the inflationary process; it is surely only continuing *surprise* about inflation which can prevent customer markets from adjusting, and thus sustain a continued distortion of the price structure between auction and customer markets.

Okun's approach has strong similarities with Hicks's distinction between flexprice and fixprice markets. The social advantages of fixed prices, argued Hicks (1974), are not only that they save on the costs of information gathering, but also that they save on the cost of disputes about what is a 'fair' price (or wage). 'Any system of prices ... is bound to work more easily if it is allowed to acquire, to some degree, the sanction of custom – if it is not, at frequent intervals, being torn up by the roots'.[10] But if the inflation is perfectly anticipated, why should the striking of a bargain or the fixing of prices become any more difficult? There probably is a sense in which any change is disputed so that Hicks's point holds, but once again it is surely uncertainty about the inflation rate which is the real bugbear.

Jaffee and Kleiman (1977) have highlighted the importance of certainty about inflation, as opposed to merely subsequently turning out to be right about inflation. In order for the costs of inflation to be only those of perfectly anticipated inflation, they argue, economic agents must *know* the prospective inflation rate. Equivalence between the mean of the distribution of their expected inflation rates and the actual inflation rate is not good enough, because unless they believe in this rate with complete confidence, they will take (expensive) action to mitigate the consequences of inflation turning out to be worse than their central expectation.

Jaffee and Kleiman argue that in order to protect themselves against inflation, economic agents will hold a higher proportion of real assets in their portfolios, thereby incurring increased transaction costs of switching from financial to real assets, and wasting the resources tied up in the assets themselves. They argue that the attempt by individuals to protect themselves in this way, and therefore these associated costs, will increase not only with the dispersion of the distribution of anticipated possible inflation rates about their mean, but also with the mean itself. Thus, if higher rates of inflation lead to higher expectations of inflation, as seems reasonable, these costs will increase with the rate of inflation.

For the costs of holding financial assets to increase with the mean expected rate of inflation, however, it must be true that the nominal yield on financial assets does not rise to reflect these expectations. Yet there are strong theoretical reasons for supposing that the nominal yield does rise to reflect inflation. It has to be admitted, of course, that in the UK, on an ex-post basis, fixed interest securities have failed to show a positive real rate of return for most of the post-war period. It is very doubtful, though, that this is because fund managers and others have been satisfied with a negative real return. More probably, this result is due to persistent underestimation of the prospective inflation rate. The current high level of real returns in the gilt-edged market supports this interpretation.

Of course, increases in nominal yields on financial assets are of no assistance to the holders of existing fixed interest stock; they quite definitely lose, just as the holders of fixed interest liabilities gain. But what is relevant to the investment decision is the *prospective* return, and provided that the prospective nominal return adjusts to compensate for inflation, then the costs incurred by holding more real assets, described by Jaffee and Kleiman, although increasing with the *dispersion* of the inflation rate, should remain invariant to its level.

Nevertheless, it must be admitted that even perfect anticipation of inflation would not be able to reduce the losses from inflation if economic agents were unable to fix and re-fix prices in accordance with anticipations. This will happen with contracts negotiated before inflation is anticipated, and when administrative arrangements preclude changes to keep up with inflation. There is no doubt that losses from this source can be substantial when an inflation begins, or when it changes pace, but beyond the immediate short run it need not present much of a problem. Contracts and administrative arrangements can be made with the prospective inflation rate firmly in view, or altered (via indexation) to keep pace with inflation. The fact that this sometimes is not done is often due, not so much to an inherent characteristic of inflation, but rather to the characteristics of the agents concerned. A frequently cited cost of inflation is, for instance, the diminution of the real value of fixed incomes such as old age pensions. Yet the solution to the problem of state pensions (and many others) is in the hands of the government, namely the automatic increase of such benefits in line with inflation. Indeed, the increase of social security benefits and tax allowances with inflation is now automatic in the UK, unless expressly over-ridden by the Government, as has recently happened.

As inflation is currently experienced in the UK, there can be no doubt that even though it is fairly well anticipated, substantial distortions arise from the varying degree to which these anticipations are reflected in setting money values. Some money values (e.g., wages) are set with an eagle eye on past, current and prospective rates of inflation, whilst others (e.g., fines) are entrapped by a web of administrative procedure, and adjust only slowly. This discrepancy must cause losses compared to the position in which inflation is zero and is expected to be zero. It is not obvious, however, that starting from the position in which we find ourselves, a sharp reduction in inflation would bring net benefits on this score. For large parts of the economy are built on the assumption of continued inflation, and if there were a substantial reduction, considerable distortions would follow.

Two notable examples of this are the housing market and the gilt-edged market. The scale on which millions of people have taken on nominal liabilities (mortgages) to acquire real assets (houses) has been heavily influenced by the experience of the last generation. Such large nominal liabilities have tended to be rapidly eroded in real value by inflation.

Similarly, the high rates of interest on most issues of Government debt (to the payment of which the Government is committed, in some instances, well into the next century) are predicated on the continuance of high inflation. High nominal interest payments represent a form of compensation to the stock holder for the gradual erosion of his capital in real terms by inflation. In effect they constitute a part-repayment of capital. For this reason, the government is able to finance the bulk of its debt servicing costs by further borrowing without necessarily increasing the real value of Government debt outstanding, and hence without increasing the 'burden' of this debt on the economy. If, for the sake of argument, inflation were to stop, the real redemption value of existing stock would no longer be diminished, but the high interest payments designed to compensate for such diminution would persist. If the Government continued to finance its interest payments by further borrowing, the real value of Government debt outstanding would increase, and when existing debts had to be refinanced, the 'burden' of debt on the system would be correspondingly greater. The only way to avoid this would be to finance debt interest payments by cutting expenditure or raising taxes. Since this Government would certainly not wish to see the ratio of National Debt to National Income rise, it would be faced with this stark choice if it succeeded in substantially reducing inflation.

The distinction between anticipated and unanticipated inflation holds clear policy implications. Provided that the costs of even perfectly anticipated inflation are not great (which is discussed below), there is a good case for trying to cope with inflation by improving the degree to which inflation is anticipated, and ensuring that all parts of the economy are allowed to adjust to it. Anticipation would probably be more easily achieved if the inflation rate were stable, but there is a suggestion that higher inflation rates are associated with greater variability of inflation. If this were true, it would follow that inflation would tend to be steadier, and hence better anticipated, the lower it was; the objective of perfectly anticipated inflation would then be coincident with the objective of no inflation.

IV The relationship between the level and variability of inflation

Assessing the ease with which an inflation rate may be anticipated is a tricky business. Depending on the circumstances of the time and the quality of information dissemination, a wide variety of inflation experience may be capable of ready anticipation. Nevertheless, the variability of inflation provides a starting point. If inflation is perfectly steady, we may be reasonably sure that it may be more readily anticipated than if it is variable, and the more variable it is, the less likely it is to be capable of ready anticipation.

At the outset, we should be clear that what matters is the *absolute* amount of variation in inflation. The variation between, say, 10 per cent and 12 per cent is comparable in its effects with the variation between, say, 1 per cent and 3 per cent, rather than between 1 per cent and 1.2 per cent.

Even so, it is far from clear that higher rates of inflation are more variable than lower rates. Moreover, the attempts to provide a theoretical backing for this proposition look decidedly lame. Friedman (1977) argued that at higher rates of inflation, governments are forced to take tough deflationary measures, with the result that there is a politically induced instability in inflation rates. This is, of course, a cause of variability which would be eliminated by accepting that the harm of inflation lies in its variability. In contrast to Friedman, however, Okun (1971) argued that although the variability of inflation depends on the determination of public policy to apply corrective measures, higher rates would tend to be more variable because public policy would be unable to resist when inflation exceeded acceptable limits.

The only other attempt I have discovered to give a theoretical rationale for a positive relationship between the level and variability of inflation comes from Logue and Willett (1976). They argued that higher rates of inflation would be more variable due to volatility of investment arising from greater variability in expected returns, which would itself be brought about by greater volatility of inflation expectations. Quite apart from the fact that it goes against the grain to accept as an explanation of a supposedly general relationship something as partial as one related to investment behaviour, even on its own terms, it seems to beg the question. Why after all should expectations of inflation be more volatile at higher rates of inflation? We cannot say because inflation is more volatile, for that is precisely what we are trying to establish.

As students of economics have come to expect, however, lack of a satisfactory theoretical rationale for such a relationship has not deterred attempts to confirm and measure it empirically. Okun (1971) examined data for most OECD countries over the period 1951 and 1968 and concluded that those with high average rates of inflation had more widely fluctuating rates from year to year. Yet when Gordon (1971) divided this period into two sub-periods, 1951–59, and 1960–68, the relationship was strong in the first sub-period but non-existent in the second.

Logue and Willett took a longer period for their study (1949–70) and a larger number of countries (41, both industrial and non-industrial). They found a strong positive relationship between the level and variability of inflation both for the period as a whole, and when divided into two sub-periods. The relationship was very weak, however, for the highly industrialised countries in the group. The authors tried to establish whether it was the level of industrialisation which was the material factor or whether this was a proxy for some other factor such as, for instance, the level of inflation. When the sample was divided into quartiles by average inflation rate, it emerged that the posited relationship between the level and variability of inflation held only at high inflation rates. For the lowest quartile, the relationship was actually negative, and the authors concluded that the range of inflation at which inflation uncertainty was at a minimum was probably 2–4 per cent.

To some minds, this result might suggest support for a policy of reducing inflation to, and maintaining it within, the range of 2–4 per cent per annum. I doubt, though, whether even Logue and Willett would go that far. Matters of high social and economic policy cannot depend on mere statistical associations, and certainly not on results as fragile as these. The fact that the authors could find only a very weak relationship for the industrialised countries is particularly important. It is ironic, moreover, that one implication of the results is that for most of the postwar period one of the most anti-inflationary of countries, Germany, could have secured greater stability by increasing its inflation rate.

Results of this kind should be treated with the greatest caution. In so far as there is any association between the level and variability of inflation, it could well be due to a common third factor, for example, the struggle between competing interest groups for income shares. The greater the intensity of this struggle, the greater may be the tendency to variability of inflation rates, due to the ebb and flow of periods of advancement, catching up, and acceptance, by the various groups. But inflation, at least in the first instance, presents an easy way of accommodating mutually incompatible income demands. It may, therefore, tend to be higher in societies where the struggle over income shares is most intense. If that were so, despite a statistical association between the level and variability of inflation, deflating demand in order to reduce the average rate of inflation might leave its variability unaffected.

A further difficulty concerns the use of statistical measures of variability as an index of uncertainty. This is particularly important with regard to Latin America, where the data are dominated by powerful inflationary and deflationary trends. These are bound to increase dispersion about the mean, and hence increase variability in a statistical sense, but variability such as this could easily be consistent with complete anticipation of inflation. It is *surprise* which is the problem, and surprise may occur when the inflation rate does *not* increase in line with trend.

Despite the theoretical and empirical problems surrounding the relationship between the level and the variability of inflation. Minford and Hilliard (1978) have made an estimate of the cost of inflation from greater uncertainty, assuming that the variability of inflation does increase with the level of inflation. The results are reproduced here in column three of Table 9.1. The size of these estimated losses is not insignificant, but the most noteworthy feature of the results is how little the losses increase as the rate of inflation increases. Indeed, the losses are little different at 30 per cent and 2 per cent.

V The costs of changing wages and prices

However well an economy may be brought to anticipate inflation in its setting of all sorts of money values, inflation could still cause large losses, since even perfectly anticipated inflation has its costs. The first of these arises from the greater frequency of money value changes required in an inflationary system in order to keep the structure of relative values unchanged through time. The sheer business of changing these values is costly – making the decisions, changing the price tags, slot machines, wage arrangements, and disseminating the information, all take time, effort and money.

TABLE 9.1 The nonmonetary costs of inflation (per cent of GDP)

Annual rate of inflation (per cent)	Costs of known inflation	Costs of uncertainty due to inflation
0	0.000	0.000
2	0.06	0.25
4	0.065	0.25
6	0.07	0.25
8	0.075	0.25
10	0.08	0.255
15	0.09	0.26
20	0.10	0.27
25	0.11	0.28
30	0.115	0.295

Source: Minford and Hilliard (1978), calculated on the basis of 1976 (Quarter 3) GDP figures (as per Minford and Hilliard).

Any estimate of this factor is bound to be a shot in the dark, although it is more directly measurable than uncertainty. In their study, Minford and Hilliard took the number of days lost due to wage disputes in proportion to total days worked as an estimate of the costs of wage negotiations, and were able to use direct data from a firm in manufacturing industry to calculate the total salary bill of all staff working full-time on implementing price increases, and the costs of new price lists.

This procedure produced results which the authors felt were an underestimate. They are reproduced here in column two of Table 9.1. Once again these estimated losses, although not insignificant, are hardly substantial and again they increase much less than proportionately with the level of inflation. The difference between a 'British' level of inflation of 10 per cent (0.08 per cent of GDP) and a 'Swiss' level of 2 per cent (0.06 per cent) is barely noticeable. In 1980 terms this amounts to roughly £40 million per annum.

VI The costs of perfectly anticipated inflation – lower real money holding

The second (and apparently only other major) source of loss from perfectly anticipated inflation is its tendency to encourage people to reduce their holdings of money balances in real terms. This may seem obscure to the non-specialist but (significantly I think) it is an aspect of inflation on which an enormous research effort has been lavished. In many studies, losses from this source constitute a large proportion of the total losses from inflation.

An approach to this question which has generated much empirical research derives from an analysis developed by Bailey (1956). If inflation is perfectly anticipated, he argued, nominal rates of interest would rise but the rate of return on money would not. Yet the nominal return on other assets is the opportunity cost of holding money, and as (anticipated) inflation increases, therefore, this opportunity cost would increase, which would provide an incentive to economise on money holdings. As a result, although the nominal amount of money held would tend to rise with the price level, it would tend not to rise by quite as much, giving a fall in real money balances as inflation increased.

The effects of this reduction in the holdings of a particular asset can be likened to the welfare loss induced by taxation; there is a loss of consumers' surplus on the reduced money holdings. Yet since money is virtually costless to produce, it is often argued, the total loss from this reduction comprises not only the consumers' surplus, but also the amount which would normally constitute the cost of production, in other words the whole of the relevant area under the demand curve. In Figure 9.1 this is represented by the area $ABCD$, as opposed to the consumers' surplus ABE. So far, so good, but actually attributing meaning to this loss, and measuring its size is a different matter.

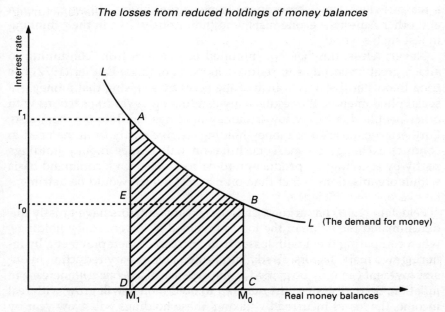

FIGURE 9.1   The losses from reduced holdings of money balances

There is no doubt that, at very high rates of inflation, the losses connected with lower real money holdings can be enormous. In the limit, money is no longer acceptable in exchange for goods and services, and the established system of production and exchange breaks down. During the German hyperinflation of 1923, for instance, shops opened for only short periods so that shopkeepers could rush out to spend their receipts before they lost almost all value. It is noteworthy, however, just how much the inflation rate had to accelerate to reach this point. During the early part of even this most terrible of inflations, production in Germany was booming, and although it is possible to dispute how much of this effort was worthwhile, there is no doubt that the system of production and exchange worked.[11] Moreover, many countries (e.g. Brazil) have more recently managed to combine very high inflation rates with high real growth rates. In the majority of industrial countries which, like the UK, have experienced more moderate rates of growth of both real output and prices, it is difficult even to recognise the ways in which lower real money holdings have brought substantial losses of welfare.

Friedman (1969) has suggested that a reduction in real money holdings involves costs by necessitating more trips to the bank, but this can be no more than a starting point. Indeed Hicks has cast aspersions on the significance of this point when noting that 'there is just one sophisticated reason why it (perfectly anticipated inflation) may be of some importance, a reason which has been brought to our attention by Milton Friedman and other American economists who (notoriously) live in their thinking in just such a world'.[12]

Nevertheless, this has not inhibited economists from continuing to attach great importance to reduced money holdings. Laidler (1977) has tried to bolster the significance of the point by stressing that money is a social phenomenon; the result of my conducting fewer transactions with other people due to my lower money holdings is a loss for them also. Furthermore, he argues, money holdings derive partly from the need to conduct exchange on markets. Inflation will reduce money holdings partly by encouraging production to be conducted on a command basis within organisations rather than on markets, which would be detrimental to economic efficiency.

Feldstein (1979) has argued that many commentators have grossly underestimated the value of the losses involved in lower money holdings, when comparing them with losses from increased unemployment, by ignoring two major factors. Firstly, he argues, a temporary reduction in unemployment can only be gained at the expense of a *permanent* increase in inflation. Secondly, since the demand to hold money will grow with real income, the losses incurred by 'taxing' these holdings will grow year by year. Once you allow for the yearly growth in losses and their permanent nature, when discounted to the present the losses from higher inflation are enormous, one might even say fantastic. Indeed, on certain assumptions, according to Feldstein, the losses are infinite!

Finally, Minford and Hilliard have attempted to value the losses from lower money holdings for the UK. Their results are reproduced here as Table 9.2. Remarkable though it may seem, at any other than the lowest inflation rates, these losses are shown to be far greater than the losses from the various non-monetary sources. Indeed, the losses seem far greater than appears reasonable from one's own intuition and experience – they are simply not credible. Yet the difficulty of accepting the size of these estimates is mirrored by certain peculiar aspects of the theoretical analysis which are shared by other studies. Something appears to be wrong.

The first thing that is wrong is the common fault of lumping together different sorts of assets into a category called money, which is apparently sharply different from other sorts of asset. Both Feldstein and Minford and Hilliard take an M1 definition of money, which includes both notes and coin and some bank deposits. Yet interest can be paid on bank current accounts, and we can be sure that if interest rates in the UK ever reached the level of 30 per cent mentioned by Minford and Hilliard, interest *would* be paid on current accounts. Once it is accepted, moreover, that interest can and would be paid on assets with a high degree of 'moneyness', the two potential worries raised by Laidler lose nearly all significance. Furthermore, it is highly questionable whether it would be

TABLE 9.2 The monetary cost of inflation

Annual rate of expected inflation (per cent)	Welfare loss as percentage of GDP*		
	$r_0 = 1\%$	$r_0 = 3\%$	$r_0 = 5\%$
2	0.04	0.08	0.12
4	0.12	0.20	0.27
6	0.23	0.35	0.47
8	0.39	0.55	0.70
10	0.59	0.78	0.98
15	1.24	1.54	1.83
20	2.15	2.54	2.93
25	3.30	3.79	4.28
30	4.69	5.28	5.87

* Calculated on the basis of 1976 (Quarter 3) GDP figures (as per Minford and Hilliard).
r_0 = The real rate of interest.
The nominal rate of interest equals r_0 + the expected inflation rate.
Source: Minford and Hilliard (1978).

appropriate to assume with regard to notes and coin, as Feldstein does with regard to all of M1, that demand will rise with real income. On the contrary, as financial technology advances, the demand to hold real *cash* balances could fall almost to zero.

But granted that for one reason or another, interest on M1 deposits does not keep pace with inflation, so that there is some incentive to economise on M1 as a whole rather than simply on notes and coin, substitution out of M1 deposits would tend to be substitution into near monies, and in particular into other types of bank deposit. Although such substitution would undoubtedly cause wealth holders some inconvenience, it is difficult to believe that this would be consistent with the figures quoted in Table 9.2.

These results are debatable in that they derive from a particular model of money demand in the UK, and therefore from a particular assumption about interest elasticity, but this should not be the prime reason for scepticism about them. There is a much more serious theoretical problem concerning the use of the area ABCD in Figure 9.1 to measure the loss. The use of this area in analysis applying to any good, service, or asset, is strictly valid only on a number of key assumptions which will be familiar to those who make regular use of the consumer surplus concept. Most notably in this case, it must be assumed that price is equal to marginal cost in the production of the goods (in this case assets) which are close substitutes for the good in question.[13]

With regard to assets, however, there are serious problems in assessing the costs of production, but if it can be assumed (as the literature invariably does) that the marginal cost of producing current accounts is zero, then it can surely be assumed that the marginal cost of producing deposit accounts is also zero. But in this case the area BCDE does not represent a loss at all. Although this area is lost for society as a whole on the 'production' of notes and coin and M1 deposits, it is compensated by a gain of approximately equal size on the 'production' of deposit accounts. Taking the whole area ABCD as a measure of the loss represents a gross overestimate. Both Feldstein and Minford and Hilliard follow this procedure.

VII Inflation and growth in various countries

This paper has discussed the effects of inflation on the efficiency of the economic system, and by implication on the level and growth rate of the national product. Table 9.3 augments this analysis by presenting some facts on growth and inflation rates in selected countries over the ten years 1967–77. These are not intended to be in any way conclusive; even sophisticated statistical techniques could not hope satisfactorily to disentangle the web of other inter-related factors which are so important in international comparisons of this kind. Yet the figures do serve to illustrate the central thesis of this paper that, short of hyper-inflationary rates, inflation may not have major implications for economic growth. Three points stand out from this table:

(i) Although a number of countries (Belgium, Germany, Austria) have managed to combine low inflation rates with high rates of growth

TABLE 9.3 Growth rates and inflation rates in selected countries

	Average annual percentage rates 1967–77	
	Growth of GDP per capita (per cent)	Inflation* (per cent)
EEC		
Belgium	4.1	6.9
Denmark	2.7	8.9
France	3.7	7.9
Germany	3.2	5.2
Greece	5.2	9.6
Ireland	2.9	12.3
Italy	2.8	10.8
Luxembourg	2.7	6.8
Netherlands	3.2	7.8
United Kingdom	2.2	10.9
Other Europe		
Austria	4.5	5.8
Norway	3.7	7.8
Spain	4.4	11.6
Sweden	1.9	7.8
Switzerland	1.4	5.4
Other OECD		
Australia	2.8[†]	9.6
Canada	3.5	7.2
Japan	5.6	7.5
United States	1.8	5.9
Others		
Brazil	7.3	26.6
Israel	4.4	20.0

* As measured by the Implicit Price Deflator of Gross Domestic Product.
[†] To 1976.
Source: Calculated from United Nations Yearbook of National Accounts Statistics 1979, Volume II.

of per capita GDP, both the United States and Switzerland[14] achieved low inflation but also enjoyed only moderate growth.
(ii) Two countries, Brazil and Israel, which suffered the highest inflation rates, enjoyed high growth rates, Brazil being the highest of all the countries in this group.
(iii) Between these two extremes countries show a broad mix of inflation and growth performance.

It would of course be possible to argue that Brazil's very high rate of growth would have been very much higher had it not been for the debilitating effect of 26 per cent inflation, and/or that the good growth performance of Austria was substantially due to its low inflation rate, and to adduce particular explanations for countries which do not fit the pattern. A simpler explanation however, would be that except at very high rates, inflation as such does not have major implications for economic growth.

VIII Conclusions

Being against inflation is rather like being against sin – everyone agrees with you, but when you go on to define what you are talking about, and to propose action to deal with it, very real disagreement begins.

What is novel and controversial about the economic policy of the current UK Government is not its opposition to inflation, but rather the extent to which it is prepared to subordinate other objectives to the aim of defeating inflation. Although it encounters opposition on the score of the costs which this policy entails in lost output, jobs, and investment, the Government is rarely challenged on the key assumption behind this policy, namely that the defeat of inflation is a necessary condition for the achievement of prosperity and economic progress. This is, I expect, in large part due to the common tendency to associate inflation with the adverse shift of some key relative value such as wages relative to profits, or domestic costs relative to foreign costs, which in fact bear no necessary relationship to the overall rate of inflation. Indeed, it is probable that individuals' opposition to inflation is largely an opposition to *price* inflation, which erodes their real incomes, whilst companies' is largely an opposition to *pay* inflation, which erodes their profitability. There is then a real dispute about the allocation of the national cake, but while two different things are referred to by the same name, inflation, both interests seem united.

Another probable factor behind the strength of opposition to inflation is the desire for greater certainty. This is perfectly understandable but it is by no means clear that lower rates of inflation would bring greater certainty to relative values. Stability of inflation would contribute much to reducing uncertainty about relative values, and the inflation rate may be more predictable when it turns out to be 10 per cent than when it turns out to be zero. Writing in *The Times* Professor Minford (1981) recently criticised the policy of attempting to stabilise the inflation rate rather than reduce it on the grounds that recent studies have suggested very large costs for this option, 'costs which appear to be far higher than any transitional loss of output that could be involved in eliminating inflation'. He did not, however, inform the readers of *The Times* that the very large costs identified in these studies, Feldstein (1979) and Minford and Hilliard (1978) are in the latter mainly, and in the former wholly, the elusive loss from reduced money holdings whose theoretical basis and empirical measurement I have shown to rest on dubious assumptions.

Of course, there are those who see inflation as a *moral* evil and its defeat as a moral imperative. It is not difficult to understand this view; inflation may bring great unfairness and injustice. Nevertheless, as this paper has argued, it is not so much the *rate* of inflation which measures the extent of these evils, but rather the degree to which it is anticipated and embodied in money values. The evils associated with inflation may be greater when the inflation rate is 5 per cent than when it is 15 per cent. Nor should we forget that combating inflation may involve moral evils as well, not least the infliction of suffering on a section of the population, the unemployed, who are not themselves responsible for the problem. Injustice and unfairness must take their place alongside economic efficiency and welfare in a judgement on anti-inflation policy, but it is far from clear in which direction they point.

Many commentators have doubted whether the Government will be able to achieve the reduction of inflation to low single figures which it would like, and many have questioned whether, having achieved this reduction, it would be able to sustain it once the economy returned to more normal levels of demand. Others, including the present writer (Bootle, 1981c), have drawn attention to the enormous costs incurred in the attempt. These criticisms are powerful, but none of them identifies the most worrying feature of the current strategy. Its most worrying feature is the dreadful prospect that, granted success against inflation, granted even continuing success, after all we have been through, and with a now much weaker economic base, the underlying problems of the British economy would remain much as they were, almost unaffected by what the Government would regard as a tremendous achievement.

Notes

1. The author gratefully acknowledges comments on an earlier draft of the paper from the editors of this review, and also from Michael Jankowski, Stephen Lofthouse, John McGregor, Professor Brian Reddaway and Tim Sweet. The article nevertheless, expresses a personal view and neither they, nor Capel-Cure Myers, are necessarily in agreement with it. The responsibility for any errors or omissions rests with the author.
2. See Bootle (1981a).
3. See Phillips (1958).
4. There is a full analysis of the various possible theoretical underpinnings for the Phillips Curve, and the factors involved in its shift in Bootle (1975), and a summary of the Friedman–Phelps view in Newlyn and Bootle (1978).
5. Brittan (1981), p. 80.
6. CBI (1981), p. 35.
7. OECD (1978), p. 28. See also Higham (1981).
8. See Bootle (1981b) for a discussion of the relation between exchange rate policy and the counter-inflation objective.
9. Because changing prices is expensive (in the most general sense) one would not expect the frequency of price changes to increase sufficiently to keep the structure of relative values unchanged through time, but the losses thereby created should not be thought of as conceptually separate from the loss from more frequent price changes. Essentially, inflation presents economic agents with a choice – either incur the costs of changing prices more frequently or incur the costs of a distorted structure of relative values. The typical response is probably to choose a mixture of the two.
10. Hicks (1974), p. 79.
11. See Graham (1930), and Bresciani-Turroni (1937).
12. Hicks (1974), p. 77.
13. The validity of the area above the cost line and below the demand curve (the welfare triangle) as a measure of the loss from some change depends on three key assumptions:

    (i) that there are no income effects on the demand for the good in question from a change in the price of the good;
    (ii) that the prices of all other goods remain unchanged;
    (iii) that elsewhere in the economy price is equal to marginal cost.

    In this case, the assumption that the marginal cost is zero means that it is appropriate to take the area ABCD rather than the triangle ABE, but the same analysis applies. Making due allowance for the issues raised in (i) and (ii) complicates the calculation of welfare loss considerably, but in this instance these factors do not present a substantive problem. The same, however, cannot be said for (iii). As argued in the text, the reasoning which supports inclusion of BCDE in the assessment grossly violates condition (iii). See Little (1957), especially ch. 10, for an analysis of these issues.
14. Growth rates for Switzerland over this period were unusually low since the country underwent a very severe recession in 1975–76.

References

Bailey, M. J. L. (1956) 'The Welfare Cost of Inflationary Finance', *Journal of Political Economy*, April.
Bootle, R. P. (1975), 'The Role of Trade Unions in the Inflationary Process', unpublished M. Phil thesis, Nuffield College, Oxford.
Bootle, R. P. (1981a), 'So why is inflation supposed to be so harmful anyway?'. *The Guardian*, August 26.
Bootle, R. P. (1981b), 'British Government Inaction over the Exchange Rate', *The World Economy*, September.
Bootle, R. P. (1981c), 'Mrs Thatcher promised more than just monetarism', *The Daily Telegraph*, October 12.
Bresciani-Turroni, C. (1937), 'The Economics of Inflation', in *A Study of Currency Depreciation in Post-War Germany* (London: George Allen & Unwin).
Brittan, L. (1981), Speech during the Third Reading of the Finance Bill on 20 July, reported in *Hansard*, volume 9, No. 145.
CBI (1981), *Economic Situation Report*, end July.
Feldstein, M. (1979), 'The Welfare cost of Permanent Inflation and Optional Short-Run Economic Policy', *Journal of Political Economy*, August.
Friedman, M. (1969), *The Optimum Quantity of Money* (Chicago: Aldine Press).
Friedman, M. (1977), *Inflation and Unemployment: The New Dimension of Politics*, Institute of Economic Affairs Occasional Paper 51 (London: IEA).
Gordon, R. J. (1971), 'Steady Anticipated Inflation: Mirage or Oasis', *Brooking Papers on Economic Activity*, no. 2.
Graham, F. D. (1930), *Exchange, Prices and Production in Hyper-Inflation: Germany, 1920–1923* (Princeton, N: Princeton University Press).
Hicks, J. R. (1974), 'Wages and Inflation', in *The Crisis in Keynesian Economics* (Oxford: Basil Blackwell).
Higham, D. S. (1981), 'Strong currencies and economic performance: lessons from Germany, Japan and Switzerland', *The Three Banks' Review*, June.
Jaffee, D. and Kleiman, E. (1977), 'The Welfare Implications of Uneven Inflation', in E. Lundberg (ed.) *Inflation Theory and Anti-Inflation Policy* (London: Macmillan).
Laidler, D. (1977), 'The Welfare Costs of Inflation in Neo-Classical Theory', in E. Lundberg (ed.), *Inflation Theory and Anti-Inflation Policy* (London: Macmillan).
Little, I. M. D. (1957), *A Critique of Welfare Economics* (Oxford: Oxford University Press).
Logue, D. and Willett, T. (1976), 'A Note on the Relation Between the Rate and Variability of Inflation', *Economica*, May.
Minford, A. P. L. and Hilliard, G. W. (1978), 'The Costs of Variable Inflation', in M. J. Artis and A. R. Nobay (eds), *Contemporary Economic Analysis* (London: Croom Helm).
Minford, A. P. L. (1981), 'A dangerous and dishonest game', *The Times*, April 7.
Newlyn, W. T. and Bootle, R. P. (1978), *Theory of Money* (3rd edn, Oxford: Oxford University Press).
OECD (1978), *Economic Survey, Switzerland* (Paris: OECD).
Okun, A. M. (1971), 'The Mirage of Steady Inflation', *Brookings Papers on Economic Activity*, No. 2.

Okun, A. M. (1975), 'Inflation: Its Mechanics and Welfare Costs', *Brookings Papers on Economic Activity*, No. 2.

Phillips, A. W. (1958), 'The Relation Between the Rate of Change of Money Wage Rates and the Level of Unemployment in the United Kingdom, 1861–1957', *Economica*, November.

CHAPTER 10

The Role of Monetary Policy*[1]

M. FRIEDMAN[2]

There is wide agreement about the major goals of economic policy: high employment, stable prices, and rapid growth. There is less agreement that these goals are mutually compatible or, among those who regard them as incompatible, about the terms at which they can and should be substituted for one another. There is least agreement about the role that various instruments of policy can and should play in achieving the several goals.

My topic for tonight is the role of one such instrument – monetary policy. What can it contribute? And how should it be conducted to contribute the most? Opinion on these questions has fluctuated widely. In the first flush of enthusiasm about the newly created Federal Reserve System, many observers attributed the relative stability of the 1920s to the System's capacity for fine tuning – to apply an apt modern term. It came to be widely believed that a new era had arrived in which business cycles had been rendered obsolete by advances in monetary technology. This opinion was shared by economist and layman alike, though, of course, there were some dissonant voices. The Great Contraction destroyed this naive attitude. Opinion swung to the other extreme. Monetary policy was a string. You could pull on it to stop inflation but you could not push on it to halt recession. You could lead a horse to water but you could not make him drink. Such theory by aphorism was soon replaced by Keynes' rigorous and sophisticated analysis.

Keynes offered simultaneously an explanation for the presumed impotence of monetary policy to stem the depression, a nonmonetary inter-

---

American Economic Review, Vol. 58, No. 1 (March 1968), pp. 1–17.

pretation of the depression, and an alternative to monetary policy for meeting the depression and his offering was avidly accepted. If liquidity preference is absolute or nearly so – as Keynes believed likely in times of heavy unemployment – interest rates cannot be lowered by monetary measures. If investment and consumption are little affected by interest rates – as Hansen and many of Keynes' other American disciples came to believe – lower interest rates, even if they could be achieved, would do little good. Monetary policy is twice damned. The contraction, set in train, on this view, by a collapse of investment or by a shortage of investment opportunities or by stubborn thriftiness, could not, it was argued, have been stopped by monetary measures. But there was available an alternative – fiscal policy. Government spending could make up for insufficient private investment. Tax reductions could undermine stubborn thriftiness.

The wide acceptance of these views in the economics profession meant that for some two decades monetary policy was believed by all but a few reactionary souls to have been rendered obsolete by new economic knowledge. Money did not matter. Its only role was the minor one of keeping interest rates low, in order to hold down interest payments in the government budget, contribute to the "euthanasia of the rentier," and maybe, stimulate investment a bit to assist government spending in maintaining a high level of aggregate demand.

These views produced a widespread adoption of cheap money policies after the war. And they received a rude shock when these policies failed in country after country, when central bank after central bank was forced to give up the pretense that it could indefinitely keep "the" rate of interest at a low level. In this country, the public denouement came with the Federal Reserve–Treasury Accord in 1951, although the policy of pegging government bond prices was not formally abandoned until 1953. Inflation, stimulated by cheap money policies, not the widely heralded postwar depression, turned out to be the order of the day. The result was the beginning of a revival of belief in the potency of monetary policy.

This revival was strongly fostered among economists by the theoretical developments initiated by Haberler but named for Pigou that pointed out a channel – namely, changes in wealth – whereby changes in the real quantity of money can affect aggregate demand even if they do not alter interest rates. These theoretical developments did not undermine Keynes' argument against the potency of orthodox monetary measures when liquidity preference is absolute since under such circumstances the usual monetary operations involve simply substituting money for other assets without changing total wealth. But they did show how changes in the quantity of money produced in other ways could affect total spending even under such circumstances. And, more fundamentally, they did undermine Keynes' key theoretical proposition, namely, that even in a world of flexible prices, a position of equilibrium at full employment might not exist. Henceforth, unemployment had again to be explained by rigidities or imperfections, not as the natural outcome of a fully operative market process.

The revival of belief in the potency of monetary policy was fostered also by a re-evaluation of the role money played from 1929 to 1933. Keynes and most other economists of the time believed that the Great Contraction in the United States occurred despite aggressive expansionary policies by the monetary authorities – that they did their best but their best was not good enough.[3] Recent studies have demonstrated that the facts are precisely the reverse: the U.S. monetary authorities followed highly deflationary policies. The quantity of money in the United States fell by one-third in the course of the contraction. And it fell not because there were no willing borrowers – not because the horse would not drink. It fell because the Federal Reserve System forced or permitted a sharp reduction in the monetary base, because it failed to exercise the responsibilities assigned to it in the Federal Reserve Act to provide liquidity to the banking system. The Great Contraction is tragic testimony to the power of monetary policy – not, as Keynes and so many of his contemporaries believed, evidence of its impotence.

In the United States the revival of belief in the potency of monetary policy was strengthened also by increasing disillusionment with fiscal policy, not so much with its potential to affect aggregate demand as with the practical and political feasibility of so using it. Expenditures turned out to respond sluggishly and with long lags to attempts to adjust them to the course of economic activity, so emphasis shifted to taxes. But here political factors entered with a vengeance to prevent prompt adjustment to presumed need, as has been so graphically illustrated in the months since I wrote the first draft of this talk. "Fine tuning" is a marvelously evocative phrase in this electronic age, but it has little resemblance to what is possible in practice – not, I might add, an unmixed evil.

It is hard to realize how radical has been the change in professional opinion on the role of money. Hardly an economist today accepts views that were the common coin some two decades ago. Let me cite a few examples.

In a talk published in 1945, E. A. Goldenweiser, then Director of the Research Division of the Federal Reserve Board, described the primary objective of monetary policy as being to "maintain the value of Government bonds ... This country", he wrote, "will have to adjust to a $2\frac{1}{2}$ per cent interest rate as the return on safe, long-time money, because the time has come when returns on pioneering capital can no longer be unlimited as they were in the past" (p. 117).

In a book on *Financing American Prosperity*, edited by Paul Homan and Fritz Machlup and published in 1945, Alvin Hansen devotes nine pages of text to the "savings-investment problem" without finding any need to use the words "interest rate" or any close facsimile thereto (pp. 218–27). In his contribution to this volume, Fritz Machlup wrote, "Questions regarding the rate of interest, in particular regarding its variation or its stability, may not be among the most vital problems of the postwar economy, but they are certainly among the perplexing ones" (p. 466). In his contribution, John H. Williams – not only professor at Harvard but also a long-time adviser to the New York Federal Reserve Bank – wrote, "I can see no prospect of revival of a general monetary control in the postwar period" (p. 383).

Another of the volumes dealing with postwar policy that appeared at this time, *Planning and Paying for Full Employment*, was edited by Abba P. Lerner and Frank D. Graham and had contributors of all shades of professional opinion – from Henry Simons and Frank Graham to Abba Lerner and Hans Neisser. Yet Albert Halasi, in his excellent summary of the papers, was able to say, "Our contributors do not discuss the question of money supply ... The contributors make no special mention of credit policy to remedy actual depressions ... Inflation ... might be fought more effectively by raising interest rates ... But ... other anti-inflationary measures ... are preferable" (pp. 23–24). *A Survey of Contemporary Economics*, edited by Howard Ellis and published in 1948, was an "official" attempt to codify the state of economic thought of the time. In his contribution, Arthur Smithies wrote, "In the field of compensatory action, I believe fiscal policy must shoulder most of the load. Its chief rival, monetary policy, seems to be disqualified on institutional grounds. This country appears to be committed to something like the present low level of interest rates on a long-term basis" (p. 208).

These quotations suggest the flavor of professional thought some two decades ago. If you wish to go further in this humbling inquiry, I recommend that you compare the sections on money – when you can find them – in the Principles texts of the early postwar years with the lengthy sections in the current crop even, or especially, when the early and recent Principles are different editions of the same work.

The pendulum has swung far since then, if not all the way to the position of the late 1920s, at least much closer to that position than to the position of 1945. There are of course many differences between then and now, less in the potency attributed to monetary policy than in the roles assigned to it and the criteria by which the profession believes monetary policy should be guided. Then, the chief roles assigned monetary policy were to promote price stability and to preserve the gold standard; the chief criteria of monetary policy were the state of the "money market," the extent of "speculation" and the movement of gold. Today, primacy is assigned to the promotion of full employment, with the prevention of inflation a continuing but definitely secondary objective. And there is major disagreement about criteria of policy, varying from emphasis on money market conditions, interest rates, and the quantity of money to the belief that the state employment itself should be the proximate criterion of policy.

I stress nonetheless the similarity between the views that prevailed in the late twenties and those that prevail today because I fear that, now as then, the pendulum may well have swung too far, that, now as then, we are in danger of assigning to monetary policy a larger role than it can perform, in danger of asking it to accomplish tasks that it cannot achieve, and, as a result, in danger or preventing it from making the contribution that it is capable of making.

Unaccustomed as I am to denigrating the importance of money, I therefore shall, as my first task, stress what monetary policy cannot do. I shall then try to outline what it can do and how it can best make its contribution, in the present state of our knowledge – or ignorance.

I What monetary policy cannot do

From the infinite world of negation, I have selected two limitations of monetary policy to discuss: (1) It cannot peg interest rates for more than very limited periods; (2) It cannot peg the rate of unemployment for more than very limited periods. I select these because the contrary has been or is widely believed, because they correspond to the two main unattainable tasks that are at all likely to be assigned to monetary policy, and because essentially the same theoretical analysis covers both.

Pegging of interest rates

History has already persuaded many of you about the first limitation. As noted earlier, the failure of cheap money policies was a major source of the reaction against simple-minded Keynesianism. In the United States, this reaction involved widespread recognition that the wartime and postwar pegging of bond prices was a mistake, that the abandonment of this policy was a desirable and inevitable step, and that it had none of the disturbing and disastrous consequences that were so freely predicted at the time.

The limitation derives from a much misunderstood feature of the relation between money and interest rates. Let the Fed set out to keep interest rates down. How will it try to do so? By buying securities. This raises their prices and lowers their yields. In the process, it also increases the quantity of reserves available to banks, hence the amount of bank credit, and, ultimately the total quantity of money. That is why central bankers in particular, and the financial community more broadly, generally believe that an increase in the quantity of money tends to lower interest rates. Academic economists accept the same conclusion, but for different reasons. They see, in their mind's eye, a negatively sloping liquidity preference schedule. How can people be induced to hold a larger quantity of money? Only by bidding down interest rates.

Both are right, up to a point. The *initial* impact of increasing the quantity of money at a faster rate than it has been increasing is to make interest rates lower for a time than they would otherwise have been. But this is only the beginning of the process not the end. The more rapid rate of monetary growth will stimulate spending, both through the impact on investment of lower market interest rates and through the impact on other spending and thereby relative prices of higher cash balances than are desired. But one man's spending is another man's income. Rising income will raise the liquidity preference schedule and the demand for loans; it may also raise prices, which would reduce the real quantity of money. These three effects will reverse the initial downward pressure on interest rates fairly promptly, say, in something less than a year. Together they will tend, after a somewhat longer interval, say, a year or two, to return interest rates to the level they would otherwise have had. Indeed, given the tendency for the economy to overreact, they are highly likely to raise interest rates temporarily beyond that level, setting in motion a cyclical adjustment process.

A fourth effect, when and if it becomes operative, will go even farther, and definitely mean that a higher rate of monetary expansion will correspond to a higher, not lower, level of interest rates than would otherwise have prevailed. Let the higher rate of monetary growth produce rising prices, and let the public come to expect that prices will continue to rise. Borrowers will then be willing to pay and lenders will then demand higher interest rates – as Irving Fisher pointed out decades ago. This price expectation effect is slow to develop and also slow to disappear. Fisher estimated that it took several decades for a full adjustment and more recent work is consistent with his estimates.

These subsequent effects explain why every attempt to keep interest rates at a low level has forced the monetary authority to engage in successively larger and larger open market purchases. They explain why, historically, high and rising nominal interest rates have been associated with rapid growth in the quantity of money, as in Brazil or Chile or in the United States in recent years, and why low and falling interest rates have been associated with slow growth in the quantity of money, as in Switzerland now or in the United States from 1929 to 1933. As an empirical matter, low interest rates are a sign that monetary policy *has been* tight – in the sense that the quantity of money has grown slowly; high interest rates are a sign that monetary policy *has been* easy – in the sense that the quantity of money has grown rapidly. The broadest facts or experience run in precisely the opposite direction from that which the financial community and academic economists have all generally taken for granted.

Paradoxically, the monetary authority could assure low nominal rates of interest – but to do so it would have to start out in what seems like the opposite direction, by engaging in a deflationary monetary policy. Similarly, it could assure high nominal interest rates by engaging in an inflationary policy and accepting a temporary movement in interest rates in the opposite direction.

These considerations not only explain why monetary policy cannot peg interest rates; they also explain why interest rates are such a misleading indicator of whether monetary policy is "tight" or "easy." For that, it is far better to look at the rate of change of the quantity of money.[4]

Employment as a criterion of policy

The second limitation I wish to discuss goes more against the grain of current thinking. Monetary growth, it is widely held, will tend to stimulate employment; monetary contraction, to retard employment. Why, then, cannot the monetary authority adopt a target for employment or unemployment – say, 3 per cent unemployment; be tight when unemployment is less than the target; be easy when unemployment is higher than the target; and in this way peg unemployment at, say, 3 per cent? The reason it cannot is precisely the same as for interest rates – the difference between the immediate and the delayed consequences of such a policy.

Thanks to Wicksell, we are all acquainted with the concept of a "natural" rate of interest and the possibility of a discrepancy between the "natural" and the "market" rate. The preceding analysis of interest rates can be translated fairly directly into Wicksellian terms. The monetary authority can make the market rate less than the natural rate only by inflation. It can make the market rate higher than the natural rate only by deflation. We have added only one wrinkle to Wicksell – the Irving Fisher distinction between the nominal and the real rate of interest. Let the monetary authority keep the nominal market rate for a time below the natural rate by inflation. That in turn will raise the nominal natural rate itself, once anticipations of inflation become widespread, thus requiring still more rapid inflation to hold down the market rate. Similarly, because of the Fisher effect, it will require not merely deflation but more and more rapid deflation to hold the market rate above the initial "natural" rate.

This analysis has its close counterpart in the employment market. At any moment of time, there is some level of unemployment which has the property that it is consistent with equilibrium in the structure of *real* wage rates. At that level of unemployment, real wage rates are tending on the average to rise at a "normal" secular rate, i.e., at a rate that can be indefinitely maintained so long as capital formation, technological improvements, etc., remain on their long-run trends. A lower level of unemployment is an indication that there is an excess demand for labor that will produce upward pressure on real wage rates. A higher level of unemployment is an indication that there is an excess supply of labor that will produce downward pressure on real wage rates. The "natural rate of unemployment," in other words, is the level that would be ground out by the Walrasian system of general equilibrium equations, provided there is imbedded in them the actual structural characteristics of the labor and commodity markets, including market imperfections, stochastic variability in demands and supplies, the cost of gathering information about job vacancies and labor availabilities, the costs of mobility, and so on.[5]

You will recognize the close similarity between this statement and the celebrated Phillips Curve. The similarity is not coincidental. Phillips' analysis of the relation between unemployment and wage change is deservedly celebrated as an important and original contribution. But, unfortunately, it contains a basic defect – the failure to distinguish between *nominal* wages and *real* wages – just as Wicksell's analysis failed to distinguish between *nominal* interest rates and *real* interest rates. Implicitly, Phillips wrote his article for a world in which everyone anticipated that nominal prices would be stable and in which that anticipation remained unshaken and immutable whatever happened to actual prices and wages. Suppose, by contrast, that everyone anticipates that prices will rise at a rate of more than 75 per cent a year – as, for example, Brazilians did a few years ago. Then wages must rise at that rate simply to keep real wages unchanged. An excess supply of labor will be reflected in a less rapid rise in nominal wages than in anticipated prices,[6] not in an absolute decline in wages. When Brazil embarked on a policy to bring down the rate of price rise, and succeeded in bringing the price rise down to about 45 per cent a year, there was a sharp initial rise in unemployment because under the influence of earlier anticipations, wages kept rising at a pace that was higher than the new rate of price rise, though lower than earlier. This is the result experienced, and to be expected, of all attempts to reduce the rate of inflation below that widely anticipated.[7]

To avoid misunderstanding, let me emphasize that by using the term "natural" rate of unemployment, I do not mean to suggest that it is immutable and unchangeable. On the contrary, many of the market characteristics that determine its level are man-made and policy-made. In the United States, for example, legal minimum wage rates, the Walsh–Healy and Davis–Bacon Acts, and the strength of labor unions all make the natural rate of unemployment higher than it would otherwise be.

Improvements in employment exchanges, in availability of information about job vacancies and labor supply, and so on, would tend to lower the natural rate of unemployment. I use the term "natural" for the same reason Wicksell did – to try to separate the real forces from monetary forces.

Let us assume that the monetary authority tries to peg the "market" rate of unemployment at a level below the "natural" rate. For definiteness, suppose that it takes 3 per cent as the target rate and that the "natural" rate is higher than 3 per cent. Suppose also that we start out at a time when prices have been stable and when unemployment is higher than 3 per cent. Accordingly, the authority increases the rate of monetary growth. This will be expansionary. By making nominal cash balances higher than people desire, it will tend initially to lower interest rates and in this and other ways to stimulate spending. Income and spending will start to rise.

To begin with, much or most of the rise in income will take the form of an increase in output and employment rather than in prices. People have been expecting prices to be stable, and prices and wages have been set for some time in the future on that basis. It takes time for people to adjust to a new state of demand. Producers will tend to react to the initial expansion in aggregate demand by increasing output, employees by working longer hours, and the unemployed, by taking jobs now offered at former nominal wages. This much is pretty standard doctrine.

But it describes only the initial effects. Because selling prices of products typically respond to an unanticipated rise in nominal demand faster than prices of factors of production, real wages received have gone down – though real wages anticipated by employees went up, since employees implicitly evaluated the wages offered at the earlier price level. Indeed, the simultaneous fall *ex post* in real wages to employers and rise *ex ante* in real wages to employees is what enabled employment to increase. But the decline *ex post* in real wages will soon come to affect anticipations. Employees will start to reckon on rising prices of the things they buy and to demand higher nominal wages for the future. "Market" unemployment is below the "natural" level. There is an excess demand for labor so real wages will tend to rise toward their initial level.

Even though the higher rate of monetary growth continues, the rise in real wages will reverse the decline in unemployment, and then lead to a rise, which will tend to return unemployment to its former level. In order to keep unemployment at its target level of 3 per cent, the monetary authority would have to raise monetary growth still more. As in the interest rate case, the "market" rate can be kept below the "natural" rate only by inflation. And, as in the interest rate case, too, only by accelerating inflation. Conversely, let the monetary authority choose a target rate of unemployment that is above the natural rate, and they will be led to produce a deflation, and an accelerating deflation at that.

What if the monetary authority chose the "natural" rate – either of interest or unemployment – as its target? One problem is that it cannot know what the "natural" rate is. Unfortunately, we have as yet devised no method to estimate accurately and readily the natural rate of either interest or unemployment. And the "natural" rate will itself change from time to time. But the basic problem is that even if the monetary authority knew the "natural" rate, and attempted to peg the market rate at that level, it would not be led to a determinate policy. The "market" rate will vary from the natural rate for all sorts of reasons other than monetary policy. If the monetary authority responds to these variations, it will set in train longer term effects that will make any monetary growth path it follows ultimately consistent with the rule of policy. The actual course of monetary growth will be analogous to a random walk, buffeted this way and that by the forces that produce temporary departures of the market rate from the natural rate.

To state this conclusion differently, there is always a temporary trade-off between inflation and unemployment; there is no permanent trade-off. The temporary trade-off comes not from inflation per se, but from unanticipated inflation, which generally means, from a rising rate of inflation. The widespread belief that there is a permanent trade-off is a sophisticated version of the confusion between "high" and "rising" that we all recognize in simpler forms. A rising rate of inflation may reduce unemployment, a high rate will not.

But how long, you will say, is "temporary"? For interest rates, we have some systematic evidence on how long each of the several effects takes to work itself out. For unemployment, we do not. I can at most venture a personal judgment, based on some examination of the historical evidence, that the initial effects of a higher and unanticipated rate of inflation last for something like two to five years; that this initial effect then begins to be reversed; and that a full adjustment to the new rate of inflation takes about as long for employment as for interest rates, say, a couple of decades. For both interest rates and employment, let me add a qualification. These estimates are for changes in the rate of inflation of the order of magnitude that has been experienced in the United States. For much more sizable changes, such as those experienced in South American countries, the whole adjustment process is greatly speeded up.

To state the general conclusion still differently, the monetary authority controls nominal quantities – directly, the quantity of its own liabilities. In principle, it can use this control to peg a nominal quantity – an exchange rate, the price level, the nominal level of national income, the quantity of money by one or another definition – or to peg the rate of change in a nominal quantity – the rate of inflation or deflation, the rate of growth or decline in nominal national income, the rate of growth of the quantity money. It cannot use its control over nominal quantities to peg a real quantity – the real rate of interest, the rate of unemployment, the level of real national income, the real quantity of money, the rate of growth of real national income, or the rate of growth of the real quantity of money.

II What monetary policy can do

Monetary policy cannot peg these real magnitudes at predetermined levels. But monetary policy can and does have important effects on these real magnitudes. The one is in no way inconsistent with the other.

My own studies of monetary history have made me extremely sympathetic to the oft-quoted, much reviled, and as widely misunderstood, comment by John Stuart Mill. "There cannot...," he wrote, "be intrinsically a more insignificant thing, in the economy of society, than money; except in the character of a contrivance for sparing time and labour. It is a machine for doing quickly and commodiously, what would be done, though less quickly and commodiously, without it: and like many other kinds of machinery, it only exerts a distinct and independent influence of its own when it gets out of order" (p. 488).

True, money is only a machine, but it is an extraordinary efficient machine. Without it, we could not have begun to attain the astounding growth in output and level of living we have experienced in the past two centuries – any more than we could have done so without those other marvelous machines that dot our countryside and enable us, for the most part, simply to do more efficiently what could be done without them at much greater cost in labor.

But money has one feature that these other machines do not share. Because it is so pervasive, when it gets out of order, it throws a monkey wrench into the operation of all the other machines. The Great Contraction is the most dramatic example but not the only one. Every other major contraction in this country has been either produced by monetary disorder or greatly exacerbated by monetary disorder. Every major inflation has been produced by monetary expansion – mostly to meet the overriding demands of war which have forced the creation of money to supplement explicit taxation.

The first and most important lesson that history teaches about what monetary policy can do – and it is a lesson of the most profound importance – is that monetary policy can prevent money itself from being a major source of economic disturbance. This sounds like a negative proposition: avoid major mistakes. In part it is. The Great Contraction might not have occurred at all, and if it had, it would have been far less severe, if the monetary authority had avoided mistakes, or if the monetary arrangements had been those of an earlier time when there was no central authority with the power to make the kinds of mistakes that the Federal Reserve System made. The past few years, to come closer to home, would have been steadier and more productive of economic well-being if the Federal Reserve had avoided drastic and erratic changes of direction, first expanding the money supply at an unduly rapid pace, then, in early 1966, stepping on the brake too hard, then, at the end of 1966, reversing itself and resuming expansion until at least November, 1967, at a more rapid pace than can long be maintained without appreciable inflation.

Even if the proposition that monetary policy can prevent money itself from being a major source of economic disturbance were a wholly negative proposition, it would be none the less important for that. As it happens, however, it is not a wholly negative proposition. The monetary machine has gotten out of order even when there has been no central authority with anything like the power now possessed by the Fed. In the United States, the 1907 episode and earlier banking panics are examples of how the monetary machine can get out of order largely on its own. There is therefore a positive and important task for the monetary authority – to suggest improvements in the machine that will reduce the chances that it will get out of order, and to use its own powers so as to keep the machine in good working order.

A second thing monetary policy can do is provide a stable background for the economy – keep the machine well oiled, to continue Mill's analogy. Accomplishing the first task will contribute to this objective, but there is more to it than that. Our economic system will work best when producers and consumers, employers and employees, can proceed with full confidence that the average level of prices will behave in a known way in the future – preferably that it will be highly stable. Under any conceivable institutional arrangements, and certainly under those that now prevail in the United States, there is only a limited amount of flexibility in prices and wages. We need to conserve this flexibility to achieve changes in relative prices and wages that are required to adjust to dynamic changes in tastes and technology. We should not dissipate it simply to achieve changes in the absolute level of prices that serve no economic function.

In an earlier era, the gold standard was relied on to provide confidence in future monetary stability. In its heyday it served that function reasonably well. It clearly no longer does, since there is scarce a country in the world that is prepared to let the gold standard reign unchecked – and there are persuasive reasons why countries should not do so. The monetary authority could operate as a surrogate for the gold standard, if it pegged exchange rates and did so exclusively by altering the quantity of money in response to balance of payment flows without "sterilizing" surpluses or deficits and without resorting to open or concealed exchange control or to changes in tariffs and quotas. But again, though many central bankers talk this way, few are in fact willing to follow this course – and again there are persuasive reasons why they should not do so. Such a policy would submit each country to the vagaries not of an impersonal and automatic gold standard but of the policies – deliberate or accidental – of other monetary authorities.

In today's world, if monetary policy is to provide a stable background for the economy it must do so by deliberately employing its powers to that end. I shall come later to how it can do so.

Finally, monetary policy can contribute to offsetting major disturbances in the economic system arising from other sources. If there is an independent secular exhilaration – as the postwar expansion was described by the proponents of secular stagnation – monetary policy can in principle help to hold it in check by a slower rate of monetary growth than would otherwise be desirable. If, as now, an explosive federal budget threatens unprecedented deficits, monetary policy can hold any inflationary dangers in check by a slower rate of monetary growth than would otherwise be desirable. This will temporarily mean higher interest rates than would otherwise prevail – to enable the government to borrow the sums needed to finance the deficit – but by preventing the speeding up of inflation, it may well mean both lower prices and lower nominal interest rates for the long pull. If the end of a substantial war offers the country an opportunity to shift resources from wartime to peacetime production, monetary policy can ease the transition by a higher rate of monetary growth than would otherwise be desirable – though experience is not very encouraging that it can do so without going too far.

I have put this point last, and stated it in qualified terms – as referring to major disturbances – because I believe that the potentiality of monetary policy in offsetting other forces making for instability is far more limited than is commonly believed. We simply do not know enough to be able to recognize minor disturbances when they occur or to be able to predict either what their effects will be with any precision or what monetary policy is required to offset their effects. We do not know enough to be able to achieve stated objectives by delicate, or even fairly coarse, changes in the mix of monetary and fiscal policy. In this area particularly the best is likely to be the enemy of the good. Experience suggests that the path of wisdom is to use monetary policy explicitly to offset other disturbances only when they offer a "clear and present danger."

III How should monetary policy be conducted?

How should monetary policy be conducted to make the contribution to our goals that it is capable of making? This is clearly not the occasion for presenting a detailed "Program for Monetary Stability" – to use the title of a book in which I tried to do so (Friedman, 1959). I shall restrict myself here to two major requirements for monetary policy that follow fairly directly from the preceding discussion.

The first requirement is that the monetary authority should guide itself by magnitudes that it can control, not by ones that it cannot control. If, as the authority has often done, it takes interest rates or the current unemployment percentage as the immediate criterion of policy, it will be like a space vehicle that has taken a fix on the wrong star. No matter how sensitive and sophisticated its guiding apparatus, the space vehicle will go astray. And so will the monetary authority. Of the various alternative magnitudes that it can control, the most appealing guides for policy are exchange rates, the price level as defined by some index, and the quantity of a monetary total – currency plus adjusted demand deposits, or this total plus commercial bank time deposits, or a still broader total.

For the United States in particular, exchange rates are an undesirable guide. It might be worth requiring the bulk of the economy to adjust to the tiny percentage consisting of foreign trade if that would guarantee freedom from monetary irresponsibility – as it might under a real gold standard. But it is hardly worth doing so simply to adapt to the average of whatever policies monetary authorities in the rest of the world adopt. Far better to let the market, through floating exchange rates, adjust to world conditions the 5 per cent or so of our resources devoted to international trade while reserving monetary policy to promote the effective use of the 95 per cent.

Of the three guides listed, the price level is clearly the most important in its own right. Other things the same, it would be much the best of the alternatives – as so many distinguished economists have urged in the past. But other things are not the same. The link between the policy actions of the monetary authority and the price level, while unquestionably present, is more indirect than the link between the policy actions of the authority and any of the several monetary totals. Moreover, monetary action takes a longer time to affect the price level than to affect the monetary totals and both the time lag and the magnitude of effect vary with circumstances. As a result, we cannot predict at all accurately just what effect a particular monetary action will have on the price level and, equally important, just when it will have that effect. Attempting to control directly the price level is therefore likely to make monetary policy itself a source of economic disturbance because of false stops and starts. Perhaps, as our understanding of monetary phenomena advances, the situation will change. But at the present stage of our understanding, the long way around seems the surer way to our objective. Accordingly, I believe guide or criterion for monetary policy – and I believe that it matters much less which particular total is chosen than that one be chosen.

A second requirement for monetary policy is that the monetary authority avoid sharp swings in policy. In the past monetary authorities have on occasion moved in the wrong direction – as in the episode of the Great Contraction that I have stressed. More frequently, they have moved in the right direction, albeit often too late, but have erred by moving too far. Too late and too much has been the general practice. For example, in early 1966, it was the right policy for the Federal Reserve to move in a less expansionary direction – though it should have done so at least a year earlier. But when it moved, it went too far, producing the sharpest change in the rate of monetary growth of the post-war era. Again, having gone too far, it was the right policy for the Fed to reverse course at the end of 1966. But again it went too far, not only restoring but exceeding the earlier excessive rate of monetary growth. And this episode is no exception. Time and again this has been the course followed – as in 1919 and 1920, in 1937 and 1938, in 1953 and 1954, in 1959 and 1960.

The reason for the propensity to overreact seems clear: the failure of monetary authorities to allow for the delay between their actions and the subsequent effects on the economy. They tend to determine their actions by today's conditions – but their actions will affect the economy only six or nine or twelve or fifteen months later. Hence they feel impelled to step on the brake, or the accelerator, as the case may be, too hard.

My own prescription is still that the monetary authority go all the way in avoiding such swings by adopting publicly the policy of achieving a steady rate of growth in a specified monetary total. The precise rate of growth, like the precise monetary total, is less important than the adoption of some stated and known rate. I myself have argued for a rate that would on the average achieve rough stability in the level of prices of final products, which I have estimated would call for something like a 3 to 5 per cent per year rate of growth in currency plus all commercial bank deposits or a slightly lower rate of growth in currency plus demand deposits only.[8] But it would be better to have a fixed rate that would on the average produce moderate inflation or moderate deflation, provided it was steady, than to suffer the wide and erratic perturbations we have experienced.

Short of the adoption of such a publicly stated policy of a steady rate of monetary growth, it would constitute a major improvement if the monetary authority followed the self-denying ordinance of avoiding wide swings. It is a matter of record that periods of relative stability in the rate of monetary growth have also been periods of relative stability in economic activity, both in the United States and other countries. Periods of wide swings in the rate of monetary growth have also been periods of wide swings in economic activity.

By setting itself a steady course and keeping to it, the monetary authority could make a major contribution to promoting economic stability. By making that course one of steady but moderate growth in the quantity of money, it would make a major contribution to avoidance of either inflation or deflation of prices. Other forces would still affect the economy, require change and adjustment, and disturb the even tenor of our ways. But steady monetary growth would provide a monetary climate favorable to the effective operation of those basic forces of enterprise, ingenuity, invention, hard work, and thrift that are the true springs of economic growth. That is the most that we can ask from monetary policy at our present stage of knowledge. But that much – and it is a great deal – is clearly within our reach.

Notes

1. Presidential address delivered at the Eightieth Annual Meeting of the American Economic Association, Washington, DC, December 29, 1967.
2. I am indebted for helpful criticisms of earlier drafts to Armen Alchian, Gary Becker, Martin Bronfenbrenner, Arthur F. Burns, Phillip Cagan, David D. Friedman, Lawrence Harris, Harry G. Johnson, Homer Jones, Jerry Jordan, David Meiselman, Allan H. Meltzer, Theodore W. Schultz, Anna J. Schwartz, Herbert Stein, George J. Stigler, and James Tobin.
3. In Friedman (1967), I have argued that Henry Simons shared this view with Keynes, and that it accounts for the policy changes that he recommended.
4. This is partly an empirical not theoretical judgement. In principle, "tightness" or "ease" depends on the rate of change of the quantity of money supplied compared to the rate of change of the quantity demanded excluding effects on demand from monetary policy itself. However, empirically demand is highly stable, if we exclude the effect of monetary policy, so it is generally sufficient to look at supply alone.
5. It is perhaps worth noting that this "natural" rate need not correspond to equality between the number unemployed and the number of job vacancies. For any given structure of the labor market, there will be some equilibrium relation between these two magnitudes, but there is no reason why it should be one of equality.
6. Strictly speaking, the rise in nominal wages will be less rapid than the rise in anticipated nominal wages to make allowance for any secular changes in real wages.
7. Stated in terms of the rate of change of nominal wages, the Phillips Curve can be expected to be reasonably stable and well defined for any period for which the *average* rate of change of prices, and hence the anticipated rate, has been relatively stable. For such periods, nominal wages and "real" wages move together. Curves computed for different periods or different countries for each of which this condition has been satisfied will differ in level, the level of the curve depending on what the average rate of price change was. The higher the average rate of price change, the higher will tend to be the level of the curve.

For periods or countries for which the rate of change of prices varies considerably, the Phillips Curve will not be well defined. My impression is that these statements accord reasonably well with the experience of the economists who have explored empirical Phillips Curves.

Restate Phillips' analysis in terms of the rate of change of real wages – and even more precisely, anticipated real wages – and it all falls into place. That is why students of empirical Phillips Curves have found that it helps to include the rate of change of the price level as an independent variable.

8. In an as yet unpublished article on "The Optimum Quantity of Money," I conclude that a still lower rate of growth, something like 2 per cent for the broader definition, might be better yet in order to eliminate or reduce the difference between private and total costs of adding to real balances.

References

H. S. ELLIS, ed., *A Survey of Contemporary Economics*, Philadelphia 1948.
MILTON FRIEDMAN, "The Monetary Theory and Policy of Henry Simons," *Journal of Law and Economics*, Oct. 1967, *10*, 1–13.
MILTON FRIEDMAN, *A Program for Monetary Stability*, New York 1959.
E. A. GOLDENWEISER, "Postwar Problems and Policies," *Federal Research Bulletin*, Feb. 1945, *31*, 112–21.
P. T. HOMAN and FRITZ MACHLUP, eds, *Financing American Prosperity*, New York 1945.
A. P. LERNER and F. D. GRAHAM, eds, *Planning and Paying for Full Employment*, Princeton 1946.
J. S. MILL, *Principles of Political Economy*, Bk. III, Ashley ed. New York 1929.

Inflation and Unemployment*

J. TOBIN[1]

The world economy today is vastly different from the 1930s, when Seymour Harris, the chairman of this meeting, infected me with his boundless enthusiasm for economics and his steadfast confidence in its capacity for good works. Economics is very different, too. Both the science and its subject have changed, and for the better, since World War II. But there are some notable constants. Unemployment and inflation still preoccupy and perplex economists, statesmen, journalists, housewives, and everyone else. The connection between them is the principal domestic economic burden of presidents and prime ministers, and the major area of controversy and ignorance in macroeconomics. I have chosen to review economic thought on this topic on this occasion, partly because of its inevitable timeliness, partly because of a personal interest reaching back to my first published work in 1941.

I The meanings of full employment

Today, as thirty and forty years ago, economists debate how much unemployment is voluntary, how much involuntary; how much is a phenomenon of equilibrium; how much is compatible with competition, how much is to be blamed on monopolies, labor unions, and restrictive legislation; how much unemployment characterizes "full" employment.

Full employment – imagine macroeconomics deprived of the concept. But what is it? What is the proper employment goal of policies affecting aggregate demand? Zero unemployment in the monthly labor force

---

American Economic Review, Vol. 62 (March 1972) pp. 1–18.

survey? That outcome is so inconceivable outside of Switzerland that it is useless as a guide to policy. Any other numerical candidate, yes, even 4 percent, is patently arbitrary without reference to basic criteria. Unemployment equal to vacancies? Measurement problems aside, this definition has the same straightforward appeal as zero unemployment, which it simply corrects for friction.[2]

A concept of full employment more congenial to economic theory is labor market equilibrium, a volume of employment which is simultaneously the amount employers want to offer and the amount workers want to accept at prevailing wage rates and prices. Forty years ago theorists with confidence in markets could believe that full employment is whatever volume of employment the economy is moving toward, and that its achievement requires of the government nothing more than neutrality, and nothing less.

After Keynes challenged the classical notion of labor market equilibrium and the complacent view of policy to which it led, full employment came to mean maximum aggregate supply, the point at which expansion of aggregate demand could not further increase employment and output.

Full employment was also regarded as the economy's inflation threshold. With a deflationary gap, demand less than full employment supply, prices would be declining or at worst constant. Expansion of aggregate demand short of full employment would cause at most a one-shot increase of prices. For continuing inflation, the textbooks told us, a necessary and sufficient condition was an inflationary gap, real aggregate demand in excess of feasible supply. The model was tailor-made for wartime inflation.

Postwar experience destroyed the identification of full employment with the economy's inflation threshold. The profession, the press, and the public discovered the "new inflation" of the 1950s, inflation without benefit of gap, labelled but scarcely illuminated by the term "cost-push." Subsequently the view of the world suggested by the Phillips curve merged demand-pull and cost-push inflation and blurred the distinction between them. This view contained no concept of full employment. In its place came the tradeoff, along which society supposedly can choose the least undesirable feasible combination of the evils of unemployment and inflation.

Many economists deny the existence of a durable Phillips tradeoff. Their numbers and influence are increasing. Some of them contend that there is only one rate of unemployment compatible with steady inflation, a "natural rate" consistent with any steady rate of change of prices, positive, zero, or negative. The natural rate is another full employment candidate, a policy target at least in the passive sense that monetary and fiscal policy makers are advised to eschew any numerical unemployment goal and to let the economy gravitate to this equilibrium. So we have come full circle. Full employment is once again nothing but the equilibrium reached by labor markets unaided and undistorted by governmental fine tuning.

In discussing these issues, I shall make the following points. First, an observed amount of unemployment is not revealed to be voluntary simply by the fact that money wage rates are constant, or rising or even accelerating. I shall recall and extend Keynes's definition of involuntary unemployment and his explanation of why workers may accept price inflation as a method of reducing real wages while rejecting money wage cuts. The second point is related. Involuntary unemployment is a disequilibrium phenomenon; the behavior, the persistence, of excess supplies of labor depend on how and how fast markets adjust to shocks, and on how large and how frequent the shocks are. Higher prices or faster inflation can diminish involuntary, disequilibrium unemployment, even though voluntary, equilibrium labor supply is entirely free of money illusion.

Third, various criteria of full employment coincide in a theoretical full stationary equilibrium, but diverge in persistent disequilibrium. These are (1) the natural rate of unemployment, the rate compatible with zero or some other constant inflation rate, (2) zero involuntary unemployment, (3) the rate of unemployment needed for optimal job search and placement, and (4) unemployment equal to job vacancies. The first criterion dictates higher unemployment than any of the rest. Instead of commending the natural rate as a target of employment policy, the other three criteria suggest less unemployment and more inflation. Therefore, fourth, there are real gains from additional employment, which must be weighed in the social balance against the costs of inflation. I shall conclude with a few remarks on this choice, and on the possibilities of improving the terms of the tradeoff.

II Keynesian and classical interpretations of unemployment

To begin with the *General Theory* is not just the ritual piety economists of my generation owe the book that shaped their minds. Keynes's treatment of labor market equilibrium and disequilibrium in his first chapter is remarkably relevant today.

Keynes attacked what he called the classical presumption that persistent unemployment is voluntary unemployment. The presumption he challenged is that in competitive labor markets actual employment and unemployment reveal workers' true preferences between work and alternative uses of time, the presumption that no one is fully or partially unemployed whose real wage per hour exceeds his marginal valuation of an hour of free time. Orthodox economists found the observed stickiness of money wages to be persuasive evidence that unemployment, even in the Great Depression, was voluntary. Keynes found decisive evidence against this inference in the willingness of workers to accept a larger volume of employment at a lower real wage resulting from an increase of prices.

Whenever unemployment could be reduced by expansion of aggregate demand, Keynes regarded it as involuntary. He expected expansion to raise prices and lower real wages, but this expectation is not crucial to his argument. Indeed, if it is possible to raise employment without reduction in the real wage, his case for calling the unemployment involuntary is strengthened.

But why is the money wage so stubborn if more labor is willingly available at the same or lower real wage? Consider first some answers Keynes did not give. He did not appeal to trade union monopolies or minimum wage laws. He was anxious, perhaps over-anxious, to meet his putative classical opponents on their home field, the competitive economy. He did not rely on any failure of workers to perceive what a rise in prices does to real wages. The unemployed take new jobs, the employed hold old ones, with eyes open. Otherwise the new situation would be transient.

Instead, Keynes emphasized the institutional fact that wages are bargained and set in the monetary unit of account. Money wage rates are, to use an unKeynesian term, "administered prices." That is, they are not set and reset in daily auctions but posted and fixed for finite periods of time. This observation led Keynes to his central explanation: Workers, individually and in groups, are more concerned with relative than absolute real wages. They may withdraw labor if their wages fall relatively to wages elsewhere, even though they would not withdraw any if real wages fall uniformly everywhere. Labor markets are decentralized, and there is no way money wages can fall in any one market without impairing the relative status of the workers there. A general rise in prices is a neutral and universal method of reducing real wages, the only method in a decentralized and uncontrolled economy. Inflation would not be needed, we may infer, if by government compulsion, economy-wide bargaining, or social compact, all money wage rates could be scaled down together.

Keynes apparently meant that relative wages are the arguments in labor supply functions. But Alchian (pp. 27–52 in Phelps *et al.*) and other theorists of search activity have offered a somewhat different interpretation, namely that workers whose money wages are reduced will quit their jobs to seek employment in other markets where they think, perhaps mistakenly, that wages remain high.

Keynes's explanation of money wage stickiness is plausible and realistic. But two related analytical issues have obscured the message. Can there be involuntary unemployment in an equilibrium, a proper, full-fledged neoclassical equilibrium? Does the labor supply behavior described by Keynes betray "money illusion"? Keynes gave a loud yes in answer to the first question, and this seems at first glance to compel an affirmative answer to the second.

An economic theorist can, of course, commit no greater crime than to assume money illusion. Comparative statics is a nonhistorical exercise, in which different price levels are to be viewed as alternative rather than sequential. Compare two situations that differ only in the scale of exogenous monetary variables; imagine, for example, that all such magnitudes are ten times as high in one situation as in the other. All equilibrium prices, including money wage rates, should differ in the same proportion, while all real magnitudes, including employment, should be the same in the two equilibria. To assume instead that workers' supply decisions vary with the price level is to say that they would behave differently if the unit of account were, and always had been, dimes instead of dollars. Surely Keynes should not be interpreted to attribute to anyone money illusion in this sense. He was not talking about so strict and static an equilibrium.

Axel Leijonhufvud's illuminating and perceptive interpretation of Keynes argues convincingly that, in chapter 1 as throughout the *General Theory*, what Keynes calls equilibrium should be viewed as persistent disequilibrium, and what appears to be comparative statics is really shrewd and incisive, if awkward, dynamic analysis. Involuntary unemployment means that labor markets are not in equilibrium. The resistance of money wage rates to excess supply is a feature of the adjustment process rather than a symptom of irrationality.

The other side of Keynes's story is that in depressions money wage deflation, even if it occurred more speedily, or especially if it occurred more speedily, would be at best a weak equilibrator and quite possibly a source of more unemployment rather than less. In contemporary language, the perverse case would arise if a high and ever-increasing real rate of return on money inhibited real demand faster than the rising purchasing power of monetary stocks stimulated demand. To pursue this Keynesian theme further here would be a digression.

What relevance has this excursion into depression economics for contemporary problems of unemployment and wage inflation? The issues are remarkably similar, even though events and Phillips have shifted attention from levels to time rates of change of wages and prices. Phillips curve doctrine[3] is in an important sense the postwar analogue of Keynesian wage and employment theory, while natural rate doctrine is the contemporary version of the classical position Keynes was opposing.

Phillips curve doctrine implies that lower unemployment can be purchased at the cost of faster inflation. Let us adapt Keynes's test for involuntary unemployment to the dynamic terms of contemporary discussion of inflation, wages, and unemployment. Suppose that the current rate of unemployment continues. Associated with it is a path of real wages, rising at the rate of productivity growth. Consider an alternative future, with unemployment at first declining to a rate one percentage point lower and then remaining constant at the lower rate. Associated with the lower unemployment alternative will be a second path of real wages. Eventually this real wage path will show, at least to first approximation, the same rate of increase as the first one, the rate of productivity growth. But the paths may differ because of the transitional effects of increasing the rate of employment. The growth of real wages will be retarded in the short run if additional employment lowers labor's marginal productivity. In any case, the test question is whether with full information about the two alternatives labor would accept the second one – whether, in other words, the additional employment would be willingly supplied along the second real wage path. If the answer is affirmative, then that one percentage point of unemployment is involuntary.

For Keynes's reasons, a negative answer cannot necessarily be inferred from failure of money wage rates to fall or even decelerate. Actual unemployment and the real wage path associated with it are not necessarily an equilibrium. Rigidities in the path of money wage rates can be explained by workers' preoccupation with relative wages and the absence of any central economy-side mechanism for altering all money wages together.

According to the natural rate hypothesis, there is just one rate of unemployment compatible with steady wage and price inflation, and this is in the long run compatible with any constant rate of change of prices, positive, zero, or negative. Only at the natural rate of unemployment are workers content with current and prospective real wages, content to have their real wages rise at the rate of growth of productivity. Along the feasible path of real wages they would not wish to accept any larger volume of employment. Lower unemployment, therefore, can arise only from economy-wide excess demand for labor and must generate a gap between real wages desired and real wages earned. The gap evokes increases of money wages designed to raise real wages faster than productivity. But this intention is always frustrated, the gap is never closed, money wages and prices accelerate. By symmetrical argument, unemployment above the natural rate signifies excess supply in labor markets and ever-accelerating deflation. Older classical economists regarded constancy of money wage rates as indicative of full employment equilibrium, at which the allocation of time between work and other pursuits is revealed as voluntary and optimal. Their successors make the same claims for the natural rate of unemployment, except that in the equilibrium money wages are not necessarily constant but growing at the rate of productivity gain plus the experienced and expected rate of inflation of prices.

III. Is zero-inflation unemployment voluntary and optimal?

There are, then, two conflicting interpretations of the welfare value of employment in excess of the level consistent with price stability. One is that additional employment does not produce enough to compensate workers for the value of other uses of their time. The fact that it generates inflation is taken as prima facie evidence of a welfare loss. The alternative view, which I shall argue, is that the responses of money wages and prices to changes in aggregate demand reflect mechanics of adjustment, institutional constraints, and relative wage patterns and reveal nothing in particular about individual or social valuations of unemployed time vis-à-vis the wages of employment.

On this rostrum four years ago, Milton Friedman identified the noninflationary natural rate of unemployment with "equilibrium in the structure of real wage rates" (p. 8). "The 'natural rate of unemployment,'" he said, "...is the level that would be ground out by the Walrasian system of general equilibrium equations, provided that there is embedded in them the actual structural characteristics of the labor and commodity markets, including market imperfections, stochastic variability in demands and supplies, the costs of getting information about job vacancies and labor availabilities, the costs of mobility, and so on." Presumably this Walrasian equilibrium also has the usual optimal properties; at any rate, Friedman advised the monetary authorities not to seek to improve upon it. But in fact we know little about the existence of a Walrasian equilibrium that allows for all the imperfections and frictions that explain why the natural rate is bigger than zero, and even less about the optimality of such an equilibrium if it exists.

In the new microeconomics of labor markets and inflation, the principal activity whose marginal value sets the reservation price of employment is job search. It is not pure leisure, for in principle persons who choose that option are not reported as unemployed; however, there may be a leisure component in job seeking.

A crucial assumption of the theory is that search is significantly more efficient when the searcher is unemployed, but almost no evidence has been advanced on this point. Members of our own profession are adept at seeking and finding new jobs without first leaving their old ones or abandoning not-in-labor-force status. We do not know how many quits and new hires in manufacturing are similar transfers, but some of them must be; if all reported accessions were hires of unemployed workers, the mean duration of unemployment would be only about half what it is in fact. In surveys of job mobility among blue collar workers in 1946–47 (see Lloyd Reynolds, 1951, pp. 214–15, and Herbert Parnes, 1954, pp. 158–59), 25 percent of workers who quit had new jobs lined up in advance. Reynolds found that the main obstacle to mobility without unemployment was not lack of information or time, but simply "antipirating" collusion by employers.

A considerable amount of search activity by unemployed workers appears to be an unproductive consequence of dissatisfaction and frustration rather than a rational quest for improvement. This was the conclusion of Reynolds' survey twenty-five years ago (p. 215), and it has been re-emphasized for the contemporary scene by Robert Hall, and by Peter Doeringer and Michael Piore for what they term the secondary labor force. Reynolds found that quitting a job to look for a new one while unemployed actually yielded a better job in only a third of the cases. Lining up a new job in advance was a more successful strategy: two-thirds of such changes turned out to be improvements. Today, according to the dual labor market hypothesis, the basis reason for frequent and long spells of unemployment in the secondary labor force is the shortage of good jobs.

In any event, the contention of some natural rate theorists is that employment beyond the natural rate takes time that would be better spent in search activity. Why do workers accept such employment? An answer to this question is a key element in a theory that generally presumes that actual behavior reveals true preferences. The answer given is that workers accept the additional employment only because they are victims of inflation illusion. One form of inflation illusion is over-estimation of the real wages of jobs they now hold, if they are employed, or of jobs they find, if they are unemployed and searching. If they did not under-estimate price inflation, employed workers would more often quit to search, and unemployed workers would search longer.

The force of this argument seems to me diluted by the fact that price inflation illusion affects equally both sides of the job seeker's equation. He over-estimates the real value of an immediate job, but he also over-estimates the real values of jobs he might wait for. It is in the spirit of this theorizing to assume that money interest rates respond to the same correct or incorrect inflationary expectations. As a first approximation, inflation illusion has no substitution effect on the margin between working and waiting.

It does have an income effect, causing workers to exaggerate their real wealth. In which direction the income effect would work is not transparent. Does greater wealth, or the illusion of greater wealth, make people more choosy about jobs, more inclined to quit and to wait? Or less choosy, more inclined to stay in the job they have or to take the first one that comes along? I should have thought more selective rather than less. But natural rate theory must take the opposite view if it is to explain why under-estimation of price inflation bamboozles workers into holding or taking jobs that they do not really want.

Another form of alleged inflation illusion refers to wages rather than prices. Workers are myopic and do not perceive that wages elsewhere are, or soon will be, rising as fast as the money wage of the job they now hold or have just found. Consequently they under-estimate the advantages of quitting and searching. This explanation is convincing only to the extent that the payoff to search activity is determined by wage differentials. The payoff also depends on the probabilities of getting jobs at quoted wages, therefore on the balance between vacancies and job seekers. Workers know that perfectly well. Quit rates are an index of voluntary search activity. They do not diminish when unemployment is low and wage rates are rapidly rising. They increase, quite understandably. This fact contradicts the inflation illusion story, both versions. I conclude that it is not possible to regard fluctuations of unemployment on either side of the zero-inflation rate as mainly voluntary, albeit mistaken, extensions and contractions of search activity.

The new microeconomics of job search (see Edmund Phelps *et al.*), is nevertheless a valuable contribution to understanding of frictional unemployment. It provides reasons why some unemployment is voluntary, and why some unemployment is socially efficient.

Does the market produce the *optimal* amount of search unemployment? Is the natural rate optimal? I do not believe the new microeconomics has yet answered these questions.

An omniscient and beneficent economic dictator would not place every new job seeker immediately in any job at hand. Such a policy would create many mismatches, sacrificing efficiency in production or necessitating costly job-to-job shifts later on. The hypothetical planner would prefer to keep a queue of workers unemployed, so that he would have a larger choice of jobs to which to assign them. But he would not make the queue too long, because workers in the queue are not producing anything.

Of course he could shorten the queue of unemployed if he could dispose of more jobs and lengthen the queue of vacancies. With enough jobs of various kinds, he would never lack a vacancy for which any worker who happens to come along has comparative advantage. But because of limited capital stocks and interdependence among skills, jobs cannot be indefinitely multiplied without lowering their marginal productivity. Our wise and benevolent planner would not place people in jobs yielding less than the marginal value of leisure. Given this constraint on the number of jobs, he would always have to keep some workers waiting, and some jobs vacant. But he certainly would be inefficient if he had fewer jobs, filled and vacant, than this constraint. This is the common sense of Beveridge's rule – that vacancies should not be less than unemployment.

Is the natural rate a market solution of the hypothetical planner's operations research problem? According to search theory, an unemployed worker considers the probabilities that he can get a better job by searching longer and balances the expected discounted value of waiting against the loss of earnings. The employed worker makes a similar calculation when he considers quitting, also taking into account the once and for all costs of movement. These calculations are like those of the planner, but with an important difference. An individual does not internalize all the considerations the planner takes into account. The external effects are the familiar ones of congestion theory. A worker deciding to join a queue or to stay in one considers the probabilities of getting a job, but not the effects of his decision on the probabilities that others face. He lowers those probabilities for people in the queue he joins and raises them for persons waiting for the kind of job he vacates or turns down. Too many persons are unemployed waiting for good jobs, while less desirable ones go begging. However, external effects also occur in the decisions of employers whether to fill a vacancy with the applicant at hand or to wait for someone more qualified. It is not obvious, at least to me, whether the market is biased toward excessive or inadequate search. But it is doubtful that it produces the optimal amount.

Empirically the proposition that in the United States the zero-inflation rate of unemployment reflects voluntary and efficient job-seeking activity strains credulity. If there were a natural rate of unemployment in the United States, what would it be? It is hard to say because virtually all econometric Phillips curves allow for a whole menu of steady inflation rates. But estimates constrained to produce a vertical long-run Phillips curve suggest a natural rate between 5 and 6 percent of the labor force.[4]

So let us consider some of the features of an overall unemployment rate of 5 to 6 percent. First, about 40 percent of accessions in manufacturing are rehires rather than new hires. Temporarily laid off by their employers, these workers had been awaiting recall and were scarcely engaged in voluntary search activity. Their unemployment is as much a deadweight loss as the disguised unemployment of redundant workers on payrolls. This number declines to 25–30 percent when unemployment is 4 per cent or below. Likewise, a 5–6 percent unemployment rate means that voluntary quits amount only to about a third of separations, layoffs to two-thirds. The proportions are reversed at low unemployment rates.

Second, the unemployment statistic is not an exhaustive count of those with time and incentive to search. An additional 3 percent of the labor force are involuntarily confined to part-time work, and another $\frac{3}{4}$ of 1 percent are out of the labor force because they "could not find job" or "think no work available" – discouraged by market conditions rather than personal incapacities.

Third, with unemployment of 5–6 percent the number of reported vacancies is less than $\frac{1}{2}$ of 1 percent. Vacancies appear to be understated relative to unemployment, but they rise to $1\frac{1}{2}$ percent when the unemployment rate is below 4 percent. At 5–6 percent unemployment, the economy is clearly capable of generating many more jobs with marginal productivity high enough so that people prefer them to leisure. The capital stock is no limitation, since 5–6 percent unemployment has been associated with more than 20 percent excess capacity. Moreover, when more jobs are created by expansion of demand, with or without inflation, labor force participation increases; this would hardly occur if the additional jobs were low in quality and productivity. As the parable of the central employment planner indicates, there will be excessive waiting for jobs if the roster of jobs and the menu of vacancies are suboptimal.

In summary, labor markets characterized by 5–6 percent unemployment do not display the symptoms one would expect if the unemployment were voluntary search activity. Even if it were voluntary, search activity on such a large scale would surely be socially wasteful. The only reason anyone might regard so high an unemployment rate as an equilibrium and social optimum is that lower rates cause accelerating inflation. But this is almost tautological. The inferences of equilibrium and optimality would be more convincing if they were corroborated by direct evidence.

IV Why is there inflation without aggregate excess demand?

Zero-inflation unemployment is not wholly voluntary, not optimal, I might even say not natural. In other words, the economy has an inflationary bias: When labor markets provide as many jobs as there are willing workers, there is inflation, perhaps accelerating inflation. Why?

The Phillips curve has been an empirical finding in search of a theory, like Pirandello characters in search of an author. One rationalization might be termed a theory of stochastic macro-equilibrium: stochastic, because random intersectoral shocks keep individual labor markets in diverse states of disequilibrium: macro-equilibrium, because the perpetual flux of particular markets produces fairly definite aggregate outcomes of unemployment and wages. Stimulated by Phillips's 1958 findings, Richard Lipsey proposed a model of this kind in 1960, and it has since been elaborated by Archibald, pp. 212–23 and Holt, pp. 53–123 and 224–56 in Phelps et al., and others. I propose now to sketch a theory in the same spirit.

It is an essential feature of the theory that economy-wide relations among employment, wages, and prices are aggregations of diverse outcomes in heterogeneous markets. The myth of macroeconomics is that relations among aggregates are enlarged analogues of relations among corresponding variables for individual households, firms, industries, markets. The myth is a harmless and useful simplification in many contexts, but sometimes it misses the essence of the phenomenon.

Unemployment is, in this model as in Keynes reinterpreted, a disequilibrium phenomenon. Money wages do not adjust rapidly enough to clear all labor markets every day. Excess supplies in labor markets take the form of unemployment, and excess demands the form of unfilled vacancies. At any moment, markets vary widely in excess demand or supply, and the economy as a whole shows both vacancies and unemployment.

The overall balance of vacancies and unemployment is determined by aggregate demand, and is therefore in principle subject to control by overall monetary and fiscal policy. Higher aggregate demand means fewer excess supply markets and more excess demand markets, accordingly less unemployment and more vacancies.

In any particular labor market, the rate of increase of money wages is the sum of two components, an equilibrium component and a disequilibrium component. The first is the rate at which the wage would increase were the market in equilibrium, with neither vacancies nor unemployment. The other component is a function of excess demand and supply – a monotonic function, positive for positive excess demand, zero for zero excess demand, nonpositive for excess supply. I begin with the disequilibrium component.

Of course the disequilibrium components are relevant only if disequilibria persist. Why aren't they eliminated by the very adjustments they set in motion? Workers will move from excess supply markets to excess demand markets, and from low wage to high wage markets. Unless they overshoot, these movements are equilibrating. The theory therefore requires that new disequilibria are always arising. Aggregate demand may be stable, but beneath its stability is never-ending flux: new products, new processes, new tastes and fashions, new developments of land and natural resources, obsolescent industries and declining areas.

The overlap of vacancies and unemployment – say, the sum of the two for any given difference between them – is a measure of the heterogeneity or dispersion of individual markets. The amount of dispersion depends directly on the size of those shocks of demand and technology that keep markets in perpetual disequilibrium, and inversely on the responsive mobility of labor. The one increases, the other diminishes the frictional component of unemployment, that is, the number of unfilled vacancies coexisting with any given unemployment rate.

A central assumption of the theory is that the functions relating wage change to excess demand or supply are non-linear, specifically that unemployment retards money wages less than vacancies accelerate them. Nonlinearity in the response of wages to excess demand has several important implications. First, it helps to explain the characteristic observed curvature of the Phillips curve. Each successive increment of unemployment has less effect in reducing the rate of inflation. Linear wage response, on the other hand, would mean a linear Phillips relation.

Second, given the overall state of aggregate demand, economy-wide vacancies less unemployment, wage inflation will be greater the larger the variance among markets in excess demand and supply. As a number of recent empirical studies, have confirmed (see George Perry, 1970, and Charles Schultze, 1971), dispersion is inflationary. Of course, the rate of wage inflation will depend not only on the overall dispersion of excess demands and supplies across markets but also on the particular markets where the excess supplies and demands happen to fall. An unlucky random drawing might put the excess demands in highly responsive markets and the excess supplies in especially unresponsive ones.

Third, the nonlinearity is an explanation inflationary bias, in the following sense. Even when aggregate vacancies are at most equal to unemployment, the average disequilibrium component will be positive. Full employment in the sense of equality of vacancies and unemployment is not compatible with price stability. Zero inflation requires unemployment in excess of vacancies.

Criteria that coincide in full long-run equilibrium – zero inflation and zero aggregate excess demand – diverge in stochastic macro-equilibrium. Full long-run equilibrium in all markets would show no unemployment, no vacancies, no unanticipated inflation. But with unending sectoral flux, zero excess demand spells inflation and zero inflation spells net excess supply, unemployment in excess of vacancies. In these circumstances neither criterion can be justified simply because it is a property of full long-run equilibrium. Both criteria automatically allow for frictional unemployment incident to the required movements of workers between markets; the no-inflation criterion requires enough additional unemployment to wipe out inflationary bias.

I turn now to the equilibrium component, the rate of wage increase in a market with neither excess demand nor excess supply. It is reasonable to suppose that the equilibrium component depends on the trend of wages of comparable labor elsewhere. A "competitive wage," one that reflects relevant trends fully, is what employers will offer if they wish to maintain their share of the volume of employment. This will happen where the rate of growth of marginal revenue product – the compound of productivity increase and price inflation – is the same as the trend in wages. But in some markets the equilibrium wage will be rising faster, and in others slower, than the economy-wide wage trend.

A "natural rate" result follows if actual wage increases feed fully into the equilibrium components of future wage increases. There will be acceleration whenever the non-linear disequilibrium effects are on average positive, and steady inflation, that is stochastically steady inflation, only at unemployment rates high enough to make the disequilibrium effects wash out. Phillips tradeoffs exist in the short run, and the time it takes for them to evaporate depends on the lengths of the lags with which today's actual wage gains become tomorrow's standards.

A rather minor modification may preserve Phillips tradeoffs in the long run. Suppose there is a floor on wage change in excess supply markets, independent of the amount of excess supply and of the past history of wages and prices. Suppose, for example, that wage change is never negative: it is either zero or what the response functions says, whichever is algebraically larger. So long as there are markets where this floor is effective, there can be determinate rates of economy-wide wage inflation for various levels of aggregate demand. Markets at the floor do not increase their contributions to aggregate wage inflation when overall demand is raised. Nor is their contribution escalated to actual wage experience. But the frequency of such markets diminishes, it is true, both with overall demand and with inflation. The floor phenomenon can preserve a Phillips tradeoff within limits, but one that becomes ever more fragile and vanishes as greater demand pressure removes markets from contact with the zero floor. The model implies a long-run Phillips curve that is very flat for high unemployment and becomes vertical at a critically low rate of unemployment.

These implications seem plausible and even realistic. It will be objected, however, that any permanent floor independent of general wage and price history and expectation must indicate money illusion. The answer is that the floor need not be permanent in any single market. It could give way to wage reduction when enough unemployment has persisted long enough. But with stochastic intersectoral shifts of demand, markets are always exchanging roles, and there can always be some markets, not always the same ones, at the floor.

This model avoids the empirically questionable implication of the usual natural rate hypothesis that unemployment rates only slightly higher than the critical rate will trigger ever-accelerating deflation. Phillips curves seem to be pretty flat at high rates of unemployment. During the great contraction of 1930–33, wage rates were slow to give way even in the face of massive unemployment and substantial deflation in consumer prices. Finally in 1932 and 1933 money wage rates fell more sharply, in response to prolonged unemployment, layoffs, shutdowns, and to threats and fears of more of the same.

I have gone through this example to make the point that irrationality, in the sense that meaningless differences in money values *permanently* affect individual behavior, is not logically necessary for the existence of a long-run Phillips trade-off. In full long-run equilibrium in all markets, employment and unemployment would be independent of the levels and rates of change of money wage rates and prices. But this is not an equilibrium that the system ever approaches. The economy is in perpetual sectoral disequilibrium even when it has settled into a stochastic macro-equilibrium.

I suppose that one might maintain that asymmetry in wage adjustment and temporary resistance to money wage decline reflect money illusion in some sense. Such an assertion would have to be based on an extension of the domain of well-defined rational behavior to cover responses to change, adjustment speeds, costs of information, costs of organizing and operating markets, and a host of other problems in dynamic theory. These theoretical extensions are in their infancy, although much work of interest and promise is being done. Meanwhile, I doubt that significant restrictions on disequilibrium adjustment mechanisms can be deduced from first principles.

Why are the wage and salary rates of employed workers so insensitive to the availability of potential replacements? One reason is that the employer makes some explicit or implicit commitments in putting a worker on the payroll in the first place. The employee expects that his wages and terms of employment will steadily improve, certainly never retrogress. He expects that the employer will pay him the rate prevailing for persons of comparable skill, occupation, experience and seniority. He expects such commitments in return for his own investments in the job; arrangements for residence, transportation, and personal life involve set-up costs which will be wasted if the job turns sour. The market for labor services is not like a market for fresh produce where the entire current supply is auctioned daily. It is more like a rental housing market, in which most existing tenancies are the continuations of long-term relationships governed by contracts or less formal understandings.

Employers and workers alike regard the wages of comparable labor elsewhere as a standard, but what determines those reference wages? There is not even an auction where workers and employers unbound by existing relationships and commitments meet and determine a market-clearing wage. If such markets existed, they would provide competitively determined guides for negotiated and administered wages, just as stock exchange prices are reference points for stock transactions elsewhere. In labor markets the reverse is closer to the truth. Wage rates for existing employees set the standards for new employees, too.

The equilibrium components of wage increases, it has been argued, depend on past wage increases throughout the economy. In those theoretical and econometric models of inflation where labor markets are aggregated into a single market, this relationship is expressed as an autoregressive equation of fixed structure: current wage increase depends on past wage increases. The same description applies when past wage increases enter indirectly, mediated by price inflation and productivity change. The process of mutual interdependent of market wages is a good deal more complex and less mechanical than these aggregated models suggest.

Reference standards for wages differ from market to market. The equilibrium wage increase in each market will be some function of past wages in all markets, and perhaps of past prices too. But the function need not be the same in every market. Wages of workers contiguous in geography, industry, and skill will be heavily weighted. Imagine a wage pattern matrix of coefficients describing the dependence of the percentage equilibrium wage increase in each market on the past increases in all other markets. The coefficients in each row are non-negative and sum to one, but their distribution across markets and time lags will differ from row to row.

Consider the properties of such a system in the absence of disequilibrium inputs. First, the system has the "natural rate" property that its steady state is indeterminate. Any rate of wage increase that has been occurring in all markets for a long enough time will continue. Second, from irregular initial conditions the system will move toward one of these steady states, but which one depends on the specifics of the wage pattern matrix and the initial conditions. Contrary to some pessimistic warnings, there is no arithmetic compulsion that makes the whole system gravitate in the direction of its most inflationary sectors. The ultimate steady state inflation will be at most that of the market with the highest initial inflation rate, and at least that of the market with the lowest initial inflation rate. It need not be equal to the average inflation rate at the beginning, but may be either greater or smaller. Third, the adjustment paths are likely to contain cyclical components, damped or at most of constant amplitude, and during adjustments both individual and average wage movements may diverge substantially in both directions from their ultimate steady state value. Fourth, since wage decisions and negotiations occur infrequently, relative wage adjustments involve a lot of catching up and leap-frogging, and probably take a long time. I have sketched the formal properties of a disaggregated wage pattern system of this kind simply to stress again the vast simplification of the one-market myth.

A system in which only relative magnitudes matter has only a neutral equilibrium, from which it can be permanently displaced by random shocks. Even when a market is in equilibrium, it may outdo the recent wage increases in related markets. A shock of this kind, even though it is not repeated, raises permanently the steady state inflation rate. This is true cost-push – inflation generated neither by previous inflation nor by current excess demand. Shocks, of course, may be negative as well as positive. For example, upward pushes arising from adjustments in relative wage *levels* will be reversed when those adjustments are completed.

To the extent that one man's reference wages are another man's wages, there is something arbitrary and conventional, indeterminate and unstable, in the process of wage setting. In the same current market circumstances, the reference pattern might be 8 percent per year or 3 percent per year or zero, depending on the historical prelude. Market conditions, unemployment and vacancies and their distributions, shape history and alter reference patterns. But accidental circumstances affecting strategic wage settlements also cast a long shadow.

Price inflation, as previously observed, is a neutral method of making arbitrary money wage paths conform to the realities of productivity growth, neutral in preserving the structure of relative wages. If expansion of aggregate demand brings both more inflation and more employment, there need be no mystery why unemployed workers accept the new jobs, or why employed workers do not vacate theirs. They need not be victims of ignorance or inflation illusion. They genuinely want more work at feasible real wages, and they also want to maintain the relative status they regard as proper and just.

Guideposts could be in principle the functional equivalent of inflation, a neutral method of reconciling wage and productivity paths. The trick is to find a formula for mutual deescalation which does not offend conceptions of relative equity. No one has devised a way of controlling average wage rates without intervening in the competitive struggle over relative wages. Inflation lets this struggle proceed and blindly, impartially, impersonally, and nonpolitically scales down all its outcomes. There are worse methods of resolving group rivalries and social conflict.

V The role of monopoly power

Probably the most popular explanation of the inflationary bias of the economy is concentration of economic power in large corporations and unions. These powerful monopolies and oligopolies, it is argued, are immune from competition in setting wages and prices. The unions raise wages above competitive rates, with little regard for the unemployed and under-employed workers knocking at the gates. Perhaps the unions are seeking a bigger share of the revenues of the monopolies and oligopolies with whom they bargain. But they don't really succeed in that objective, because the corporations simply pass the increased labor costs, along with mark-ups, on to their helpless customers. The remedy, it is argued, is either atomization of big business and big labor or strict public control of their prices and wages.

So simple a diagnosis is vitiated by confusion between levels and rates of change. Monopoly power is no doubt responsible for the relatively high prices and wages of some sectors. But can the exercise of monopoly power generate ever-rising price and wages? Monopolists have no reason to hold reserves of unexploited power. But if they did, or if events awarded them new power, their exploitation of it would raise their real prices and wages only temporarily.

Particular episodes of inflation may be associated with accretions of monopoly power, or with changes in the strategies and preferences of those who possess it. Among the reasons that wages and prices rose in the face of mass unemployment after 1933 were NRA [editors' note:-

National Recovery Administration] codes and other early New Deal measures to suppress competition, and the growth of trade union membership and power under the protection of new federal legislation. Recently we have witnessed substantial gains in the powers of organized public employees. Unions elsewhere may not have gained power, but some of them apparently have changed their objectives in favor of wages at the expense of employment.

One reason for the popularity of the monopoly power diagnosis of inflation is the identification of administered prices and wages with concentrations of economic power. When price and wage increases are the outcomes of visible negotiations and decisions, it seems obvious that identifiable firms and unions have the power to affect the course of inflation. But the fact that monopolies, oligopolies, and large unions have discretion does not mean it is invariably to their advantage to use it to raise prices and wages. Nor are administered prices and wages found only in high concentration sectors. Very few prices and wages in a modern economy, even in the more competitive sectors, are determined in Walrasian auction markets.

No doubt there has been a secular increase in the prevalence of administered wages and prices, connected with the relative decline of agriculture and other sectors of self-employment. This development probably has contributed to the inflationary bias of the economy, by enlarging the number of labor markets where the response of money wages to excess supply is slower than their response to excess demand. The decline of agriculture as a sector of flexible prices and wages and as an elastic source of industrial labor is probably an important reason why the Phillips trade-off problem is worse now than in the 1920s. Sluggishness of response to excess supply is a feature of administered prices, whatever the market structure, but it may be accentuated by concentration of power per se. For example, powerful unions, not actually forced by competition to moderate their wage demands, may for reasons of internal politics be slow to respond to unemployment in their ranks.

VI Some reflections on policy

If the makers of macro-economic policy could be sure that the zero-inflation rate of unemployment is natural, voluntary, and optimal, their lives would be easy. Friedman told us that all macro-economic policy needs to do, all it should try to do, is to make nominal national income grow steadily at the natural rate of growth of aggregate supply. This would sooner or later result in price stability. Steady price deflation would be even better, he said, because it would eliminate the socially wasteful incentive to economize money holdings. In either case, unemployment will converge to its natural rate, and wages and prices will settle into steady trends. Under this policy, whatever unemployment the market produces is the correct result. No tradeoff, no choice, no agonizing decisions.

I have argued this evening that a substantial amount of the unemployment compatible with zero inflation is involuntary and nonoptimal. This is, in my opinion, true whether or not the inflations associated with lower rates of unemployment are steady or ever-accelerating. Neither macro-economic policy-makers, nor the elected officials and electorates to whom they are responsible, can avoid weighing the costs of unemployment against those of inflation. As Phelps has pointed out, this social choice has an intertemporal dimension. The social costs of involuntary unemployment are mostly obvious and immediate. The social costs of inflation come later.

What are they? Economists' answers have been remarkably vague, even though the prestige of the profession has reinforced the popular view that inflation leads ultimately to catastrophe. Here indeed is a case where abstract economic theory has a powerful hold on public opinion and policy. The prediction that at low unemployment rates inflation will accelerate toward ultimate disaster is a theoretical deduction with little empirical support. In fact the weight of econometric evidence has been against acceleration, let alone disaster. Yet the deduction has been convincing enough to persuade this country to give up billions of dollars of annual output and to impose sweeping legal controls on prices and wages. Seldom has a society made such large immediate and tangible sacrifices to avert an ill-defined, uncertain, eventual evil.

According to economic theory, the ultimate social cost of anticipated inflation is the wasteful use of resources to economize holdings of currency and other noninterest-bearing means of payment. I suspect that intelligent laymen would be utterly astounded if they realized that *this* is the great evil economists are talking about. They have imagined a much more devastating cataclysm, with Vesuvius vengefully punishing the sinners below. Extra trips between savings banks and commercial banks? What an anti-climax!

With means of payment – currency plus demand deposits – equal currently to 20 per cent of GNP, an extra percentage point of anticipated inflation embodied in nominal interest rates produces in principle a social cost of 2/10 of 1 per cent of GNP per year. This is an outside estimate. An unknown, but substantial, share of the stock of money belongs to holders who are not trying to economize cash balances and are not near any margin where they would be induced to spend resources for this purpose. These include hoarders of large denomination currency, about one-third of the total currency in public hands, for reasons of privacy, tax evasion, or illegal activity. They include tradesmen and consumers whose working balances turn over too rapidly or are too small to justify any effort to invest them in interest-bearing assets. They include corporations who, once they have been induced to undertake the fixed costs of a sharp-pencil money management department, are already minimizing their cash holdings. They include businessmen who are in fact being paid interest on demand deposits, although it takes the form of preferential access to credit and other bank services. But, in case anyone still regards the waste of resources in unnecessary transactions between money and interest-bearing financial assets as one of the major economic problems of the day, there is a simple and straightforward remedy, the payment of interest on demand deposits and possibly, with ingenuity, on currency too.

The ultimate disaster of inflation would be the breakdown of the monetary payments system, necessitating a currency reform. Such episodes have almost invariably resulted from real economic catastrophes – wars, defeats, revolutions, reparations – not from the mechanisms of wage-price push with which we are concerned. Acceleration is a scare word, conveying the image of a rush into hyper-inflation as relentlessly deterministic and monotonic as the motion of falling bodies. Realistic attention to the disaggregated and stochastic nature of wage and price movements suggests that they will show diverse and irregular fluctuations around trends that are difficult to discern and extrapolate. The central trends, history suggests, can accelerate for a long, long time without generating hyper-inflations destructive of the payments mechanism.

Unanticipated inflation, it is contended, leads to mistaken estimates of relative prices and consequently to misallocations of resources. An example we have already discussed is the alleged misallocation of time by workers who over-estimate their real wages. The same error would lead to a general over-supply by sellers who contract for future deliveries without taking correct account of the increasing prices of the things they must buy in order to fulfil the contract. Unanticipated deflation would cause similar miscalculations and misallocations. Indeed, people can make these same mistakes about relative prices even when the price level is stable. The mistakes are more likely, or the more costly to avoid, the greater the inflationary trend. There are costs in setting and announcing new prices. In an inflationary environment price changes must be made more frequently – a new catalog twice a year instead of one, or some formula for automatic escalation of announced prices. Otherwise, with the interval between announcements unchanged, the average misalignment of relative prices will be larger the faster the inflation. The same problem would arise with rapid deflation.

Unanticipated inflation and deflation – and unanticipated changes in relative prices – are also sources of transfers of wealth. I will not review here the rich and growing empirical literature on this subject. Facile generalizations about the progressivity or equity of inflationary transfers are hazardous; certainly inflation does not merit the cliché that it is "the cruelest tax." Let us not forget that unemployment has distributional effects as well as deadweight losses.

Some moralists take the view that the government has promised to maintain the purchasing power of its currency, but this promise is their inference rather than any pledge written on dollar bills or in the Constitution. Some believe so strongly in this implicit contract that they are willing to suspend actual contracts in the name of anti-inflation.

I have long contended that the government should make low-interest bonds of guaranteed purchasing power available for savers and pension funds who wish to avoid the risks of unforseen inflation. The common objection to escalated bonds is that they would diminish the built-in stability of the system. The stability in question refers to the effects on aggregate real demand, *ceteris paribus*, of a change in the price level. The Pigou effect tells us that government bondholders whose wealth is diminished by inflation will spend less. This brake on old-fashioned gap inflation will be thrown away if the bonds are escalated. These considerations are only remotely related to the mechanisms of wage and price inflation we have been discussing. In the 1970s we know that the government can, if it wishes, control aggregate demand – at any rate, its ability to do so is only trivially affected by the presence or absence of Pigou effects on part of the government debt.

In considering the intertemporal trade-off, we have no license to assume that the natural rate of unemployment is independent of the history of actual unemployment. Students of human capital have been arguing convincingly that earning capacity, indeed transferable earning capacity, depends on experience as well as formal education. Labor markets soggy enough to maintain price stability may increase the number of would-be workers who lack the experience to fit them for jobs that become vacant.

Macro-economic policies, monetary and fiscal, are incapable of realizing society's unemployment and inflation goals simultaneously. This dismal fact has long stimulated a search for third instruments to do the job: guideposts and incomes policies, on the one hand, labor market and manpower policies, on the other. Ten to fifteen years ago great hopes were held for both. The Commission on Money and Credit in 1961, pp. 39–40, hailed manpower policies as the new instrument that would overcome the unemployment–inflation dilemma. Such advice was taken seriously in Washington, and an unprecedented spurt in manpower programs took place in the 1960s. The Council of Economic Advisers set forth wage and price guideposts in 1961–62 in the hope of "talking down" the Phillips curve (pp. 185–90). It is discouraging to find that these efforts did not keep the problem of inflationary bias from becoming worse than ever.

So it is not with great confidence or optimism that one suggests measures to mitigate the tradeoff. But some proposals follow naturally from the analysis, and some are desirable in themselves anyway.

First, guideposts do not wholly deserve the scorn that "toothless jawboning" often attracts. There is an arbitrary, imitative component in wage settlements, and maybe it can be influenced by national standards.

Second, it is important to create jobs for those unemployed and discouraged workers who have extremely low probability of meeting normal job specifications. Their unemployment does little to discipline wage increases, but reinforces their deprivation of human capital and their other disadvantages in job markets. The National Commission on Technology, Automation and Economic Progress pointed out in 1966 the need for public service jobs tailored to disadvantaged workers. They should not be "last resort" or make-work jobs, but regular permanent jobs capable of conveying useful experience and inducing reliable work habits. Assuming that the additional services produced by the employing institutions are of social utility, it may well be preferable to employ disadvantaged workers directly rather than to pump up aggregate demand until they reach the head of the queue.

Third, a number of measures could be taken to make markets more responsive to excess supplies. This is the kernel of truth in the market-power explanation of inflationary bias. In many cases, government regulations themselves support prices and wages against competition. Agricultural prices and construction wages are well-known examples. Some trade unions follow wage policies that take little or no account of the interests of less senior members and of potential members. Since unions operate with federal sanction and protection, perhaps some means can be found to ensure that their memberships are open and that their policies are responsive to the unemployed as well as the employed.

As for macro-economic policy, I have argued that it should aim for unemployment lower than the zero-inflation rate. How much lower? Low enough to equate unemployment and vacancies? We cannot say. In the nature of the case there is no simple formula – conceptual, much less statistical – for full employment. Society cannot escape very difficult political and intertemporal choices. We economists can illuminate these choices as we learn more about labor markets, mobility, and search, and more about unemployment and inflation. Thirty-five years after Keynes, welfare macroeconomics is still a relevant and challenging subject, I dare to believe it has a bright future.

Notes

1. Presidential address delivered at the eighty-fourth meeting of the American Economic Association, New Orleans, Louisiana, December 28, 1971.

2. This concept is commonly attributed to W. H. Beveridge, but he was actually more ambitious and required a surplus of vacancies.
3. Phillips himself is not a prophet of the doctrine associated with his curve. His 1958 article was probably the most influential macro-economic paper of the last quarter century. But Phillips simply presented some striking empirical findings, which others have replicated many times for many economies. He is not responsible for the theories and policy conclusions his findings stimulated.
4. See Lucas and Rapping, pp. 257–305, in Phelps *et al.*

References

W. H. Beveridge, *Full Employment in a Free Society*, New York 1945.
Commission on Money and Credit, *Money and Credit: Their Influence on Jobs, Prices, and Growth*, Englewood Cliffs 1961.
P. Doeringer, and M. Piore, *Internal Labor Markets and Manpower Analysis*, Lexington, Mass. 1971.
Economic Report of the President, Washington 1962.
M. Friedman, "The Role of Monetary Policy," *American Economic Review* (Mar) vol. 58, pp. 1–17.
R. Hall, "Why is the Unemployment Rate so High at Full Employment?," *Brookings Papers on Economic Activity*, 3, 1970, 369–402.
J. M. Keynes, *The General Theory of Employment, Interest and Money*, New York 1936.
A. Leijonhufvud, *On Keynesian Economics and the Economics of Keynes*, New York 1968.
R. G. Lipsey, "The Relation Between Unemployment and the Rate of Change of Money Wage Rates in the United Kingdom, 1862–1957: A Further Analysis," *Economica*, vol. 27, Feb. 1960, 1–31.
H. S. Parnes, *Research on Labor Mobility*, Social Science Research Council, Bull. 65, New York 1954.
G. L. Perry, "Changing Labor Markets and Inflation," *Brookings Papers on Economic Activity*, 3, 1970, 411–41.
E. S. Phelps, "Inflation and Optimal Unemployment Over Time," *Economica*, Aug. 1967, 34, 254–81.
E. S. Phelps, *et al.*, *Micro-economic Foundations of Employment and Inflation Theory*, New York 1970.
A. W. Phillips, "The Relation Between Unemployment and the Rate of Change of Money Wage Rates in the United Kingdom, 1861–1957," *Economica*, Nov. 1958, 25, 283–99.
L. G. Reynolds, *The Structure of Labor Markets*, New York 1951.
C. L. Schultze, "Has the Phillips Curve Shifted? Some Additional Evidence," *Brookings Papers on Economic Activity*, 2, 1971, 452–67.
J. Tobin, "A Note on the Money Wage Problem," *Quarterly Journal of Economics*, May 1941, 55, 508–16.
US National Commission on Technology, Automation, and Economic Progress, *Technology and the American Economy*, Washington 1966.

PART VI

THE NATURE OF UNEMPLOYMENT

CHAPTER 12

Unemployment Policy*

R. E. LUCAS, JR.[1]

The U.S. unemployment rate was certainly too high in 1975, and most economists would agree that it is too high today. It will also be agreed that this observation poses a problem for public policy (in a sense that the observation that winters in Chicago are "too cold" does not). But what exactly is meant by the statement that unemployment is "too high," and what is the nature of the policy problem it poses? This question can be answered in more than one way, and the answer one chooses matters great deal.

One common answer to this question is that there exists a rate of unemployment – call it "full employment" – which can and should serve as a "target" for economic policy. Unemployment above this rate is regarded as being of a different character from the "frictional" unemployment required to match workers and jobs efficiently, and is treated from a welfare point of view as waste, or deadweight loss. Elimination of this waste is an objective of monetary, fiscal, and perhaps other policies. In the first part of this paper, I will argue that this way of posing the issue does not lead to an operational basis for unemployment policy, mainly on the ground that economists have no coherent idea as to that full employment means or how it can be measured.

An alternative view, prevalent prior to the Great Depression and enjoying something of a revival today, treats *fluctuations* in unemployment and other variables as posing a policy problem. On this view, the average (or natural, or equilibrium) rate of unemployment is viewed as raising policy issues only insofar as it can be shown to be "distorted" in an undesirable way by taxes, external effects, and so on. Nine percent unemployment is then viewed as too high in the same sense that 2 percent is viewed as "too low": both are symptoms of costly and preventable

---

*American Economic Review, Vol. 68, No. 2 (May 1978), pp. 353–70.

instability in general economic activity. In the concluding part of this paper, I will sketch the approaches to unemployment policy which are suggested by this alternative view and some which are not.

I Full employment: definition and measurement

The idea that policy can and should be directed at the attainment of a particular, specifiable *level* of the measured rate of unemployment (as opposed to mitigating *fluctuations* in unemployment) owes its wide acceptance to John Maynard Keynes' *General Theory*. It is there derived from the prior hypothesis that measured unemployment can be decomposed into two distinct components: "voluntary" (or frictional) and "involuntary," with full employment then identified as the level prevailing when involuntary unemployment equals zero. It seems appropriate, then, to begin by reviewing Keynes' reasons for introducing this distinction in the first place.

Keynes (ch. 2, p. 7) classifies the factors affecting equilibrium employment in a real general equilibrium theory: the mechanics of matching workers to jobs, household labor–leisure preferences, technology, and the composition of product demand. Is it the case, he asks, that spontaneous shifts in any of these four real factors can account for employment fluctuations of the magnitude we observe? Evidently, the answer is negative. It follows that two kinds of theory must be needed to account for observed unemployment movements: granted that real general equilibrium theory may account for a relatively constant, positive component, *some other theory* is needed for the rest.

Accepting the necessity of a distinction between explanations for normal and cyclical unemployment does not, however, compel one to identify the first as voluntary and the second as involuntary, as Keynes goes on to do. This terminology suggests that the key to the distinction lies in some difference in the way two different types of unemployment are *perceived by workers*. Now in the first place, the distinction we are after concerns *sources* of unemployment, not differentiated types. One may, for example, seek very different theoretical explanations for the average price of a commodity and for its day-to-day fluctuations, without postulating two types of price for the same good. Similarly, one may classify motives for holding money without imagining that anyone can subdivide his own cash holdings into "transactions balances," "precautionary balances," and so forth. The recognition that one needs to distinguish among sources of unemployment does not in any way imply that one needs to distinguish among types.

Nor is there any evident reason why one would *want* to draw this distinction. Certainly the more one thinks about the decision problem facing individual workers and firms the less sense this distinction makes. The worker who loses a good job in prosperous times does not *volunteer* to be in this situation: he has suffered a capital loss.[2] Similarly, the firm which loses an experienced employee in depressed times suffers an undesired capital loss. Nevertheless the unemployed worker at any time can always find *some* job at once, and a firm can always fill a vacancy instantaneously. That neither typically does so *by choice* is not difficult to understand given the quality of the jobs and the employees which are easiest to find. Thus there is an involuntary element in *all* unemployment, in the sense that no one chooses bad luck over good: there is also a voluntary element in all unemployment, in the sense that however miserable one's current work options, one can always choose to accept them.[3]

Keynes, in chapter 2, deals with the situation facing an *individual* unemployed worker by evasion and wordplay only. Sentences like "more labor would, as a rule, be forthcoming at the existing money wage if it were demanded" are used again and again as though, from the point of view of a jobless worker, it is unambiguous what is meant by "*the* existing money wage." Unless we define an individual's wage rate as the price someone else is willing to pay him for his labor (in which case Keynes' assertion above is *defined* to be false), what *is* it? The wage at which he would *like* to work more hours? Then it is *true* by definition and equally empty. The fact is, I think, that Keynes wanted to get labor markets out of the way in chapter 2 so that he could get on to the demand theory which really interested him. This is surely understandable, but what is the excuse for letting his carelessly drawn distinction between voluntary and involuntary unemployment dominate aggregative thinking on labor markets for the forty years following?

It is, to be sure, possible to write down theoretical models in which households are faced with an "hours constraint" limiting the hours they can supply at "the" prevailing wage, and in which, therefore, there is a clear distinction between the hours one can supply and the hours one would like to supply. Such an exercise is frequently motivated as an attempt to "explain involuntary (or Keynesian) unemployment." This misses the point: involuntary unemployment is not a fact or a phenomenon which it is the task of theorists to explain. It is, on the contrary, a theoretical construct which Keynes introduced in the hope that it would be helpful in discovering a correct explanation for a genuine phenomenon: large-scale fluctuations in measured, total unemployment. Is it the task of modern theoretical economics to "explain" the theoretical constructs of our predecessors, whether or not they have proved fruitful? I hope not, for a surer route to sterility could scarcely be imagined.

In summary, it does not appear possible, even in principle, to classify individual unemployed people as either voluntarily or involuntarily unemployed depending on the characteristics of the decision problems they face. One cannot, even conceptually arrive at a usable definition of full employment as a state in which no involuntary unemployment exists.

In practice, I think this fact has been recognized for some time. Estimates of full employment actually in use have been obtained using aggregate information rather than data on individuals. As recently as the 1960s it was widely believed that there was some level of aggregate unemployment with the property that when unemployment exceeded this rate, expansionary monetary and fiscal measures would be noninflationary, while at rates below this critical level they would lead to inflation. One could then identify unemployment rates at or below this full-employment level as frictional or voluntary, and unemployment in excess of this level as involuntary. It was understood that only unemployment of the latter type posed a problem curable by monetary or fiscal policy. As Walter Heller wrote, "Gone is the countercyclical syndrome of the 1950's. Policy now centers on gap closing and growth, on realizing and enlarging the economy's non-inflationary potential" (Preface). Later, Heller refers "to the operational concepts of the 'production gap,' 'full-employment surplus,' the 'fiscal drag,' and 'fiscal dividends'" (p. 18).

For the purpose of calculating the production gap to which Heller referred, the voluntary-involuntary terminology accurately reflects differences in the way unemployed people view their situations. The issue here is rather whether there exists an aggregate rate of unemployment (on the order of 4 or 5 percent) which is of use in measuring an economy's noninflationary potential. If there were, then objections of the sort I have raised above could be dismissed as merely terminological: if one objected to calling unemployment above the designated full-employment level involuntary, one could call it something else, perhaps wasteful or unnecessary.

The last ten years have taught us a great deal about this operational concept of a production gap. In 1975, the U.S. economy attained the combination of 9 percent inflation and an unemployment rate of 9 percent. Applying the concept of a production gap to these numbers, does one conclude that the noninflationary potential of the U.S. economy is associated with unemployment rates in excess of 9 percent? Does one redefine 9 percent inflation to be noninflationary? Or can the entire episode be somehow pinned on oil prices?

I have reviewed two possible routes by which one might hope to give the term full employment some operational significance. One was to begin at the individual worker level, classifying unemployment into two types, voluntary and involuntary, count up the number classed as voluntary, and define the total to be the unemployment level associated with full employment. A second was to determine the operating characteristics of the economy at different rates of unemployment, and then to define rates of unemployment, and then to define full employment to be the rate at which inflation rates are acceptable. Neither of these approaches leads to an operational definition of full employment. Neither yields a coherent view as to why unemployment is a problem, or as to the costs and benefits involved in economic policies which affect unemployment rates. The difficulties are not the measurement error problems which necessarily arise in applied economics. They arise because the "thing" to be measured does not exist.

II Beyond full employment policy

Abandoning the constraint that any discussion of unemployment must begin first by drawing the voluntary-involuntary distinction and then thinking in separate ways about these two types of unemployment will, I think, benefit both positive and normative analysis. Practicing social science is hard enough without crippling oneself with dogmatic constraints. A terminology which precludes asking the question: "Why do people choose to take the actions we see them taking, instead of other actions they might take instead?" precludes any serious thinking about behavior at all.

Whether or not the body of work stemming from the Edmund Phelps *et al.* volume, and earlier work of George Stigler, John McCall and others, has produced all the right answers about the determinants of employment and unemployment, it has at least begun to pose some of the right questions. By treating all unemployment as voluntary, this work has led to the examination of alternative arrangements which firms and employees might choose to adopt for dealing with fluctuations in product demand, and their reasons for choosing to react to such fluctuations in the way we observe them doing. Pursuit of this question has indicated both how very difficult it is, and even more so how much economics was swept under the rug by "explaining involuntary unemployment" by incompetent auctioneers or purely mechanical wage and price equations.

Practicing normative macroeconomics without the construct of full employment does take some getting used to. One finds oneself slipping into such sentences as: "There is no such thing as full employment, but I can tell you how it can be attained." But there are some immediate benefits. First, one dispenses with that entire meaningless vocabulary associated with full employment; phrases like potential output, full capacity, slack, and so on, which suggested that there was some *technical* reason why we couldn't all return to the 1890 workweek and produce half again the GNP we now produce. Second, one finds to one's relief that treating unemployment as a voluntary response to an unwelcome situation does not commit oneself to normative nonsense like blaming depressions on lazy workers.

The effect it does have on normative discussion is twofold. First, it focuses discussion of monetary and fiscal policy on *stabilization*, on the pursuit of price stability and on minimizing the disruptive effects of erratic policy changes. Some average unemployment rate would, of course, emerge from such a policy but as a by-product, not as a preselected target. Second, by thinking of this natural rate as an equilibrium emerging from voluntary exchange in the usual sense, one can subject it to the scrutiny of modern methods of public finance.

To take one example, as the level of unemployment compensation is varied, an entire range of average unemployment rates, all equally "natural," is available to society. At one extreme, severe penalties to declaring oneself unemployed could reduce unemployment rates to any desired level. Such a policy would result in serious real output losses, as workers retain poor jobs too long and accept poor jobs too readily. An output-maximizing unemployment compensation scheme would, with risk-averse workers, involve a subsidy to being unemployed, else workers retain a poor but relatively sure current wage in preference to the riskier but, on average, more productive return to seeking a new job. In view of the private market's inability to provide sufficient insurance against unemployment risk, still further gains in expected utility could be expected by still higher unemployment compensation, resulting in a deliberate sacrifice in real output in exchange for a preferred arrangement for allocating risk.[4] Notice that as one traces out tradeoffs of this sort, the issue of slack or waste does not arise. Different policies result in different levels of real output, but output increases are necessarily obtained at the expense of something else. Whether any particular level of unemployment compensation is too high or too low is a difficult issue in practice, but it is one that cannot be resolved simply by observing that other, unemployment-reducing, compensation levels are *feasible*.

The policy problem of reducing business cycle risk is a very real and important one, and one which I believe monetary and fiscal policies directed at price stability would go a long way toward achieving. The problem of finding arrangements for allocating unemployment risks over individuals in a satisfactory way is also important, and can be analyzed by the methods of modern welfare economics. The pursuit of a full-employment target which none can measure or even define conceptually cannot be expected to contribute to the solution of either problem.

Notes

1. University of Chicago. I am very grateful for criticism of an earlier draft by Jacob Frenkel, Sherwin Rusen, and Jose Scheinkman.

2. Given the time-consuming nature of job search and the element of luck involved in finding a good "match," there is a capital-like element in most jobs. With job-specific human capital, the capital loss involved in job (or employee) loss is increased.
3. These observations refer to easily verified features of any sizable labor market. Aggregate statistics on unemployment or on listed vacancies do not bear on their accuracy, since listing oneself as unemployed does not imply that one would accept *any* employment, nor is an advertised vacancy available to *any* job applicant.
4. See Kenneth Arrow's analysis of medical insurance.

References

K. J. Arrow, "Welfare Analysis of Changes in Health Coinsurance Rates," in Richard N. Rosett, ed., *The Role of Health Insurance in the Health Services Sector*, New York 1976.
W. W. Heller, *New Dimensions of Political Economy*, Cambridge, Mass. 1966.
John M. Keynes, *The General Theory of Employment, Interest and Money*, London 1936.
J. McCall, "The Economics of Information and Optimal Stopping Rules," *Journal of Business*, July 1965, *38*, 300–17.
Edmund S. Phelps, *et al.*, *Microeconomic Foundations of Employment and Inflation Theory*, New York 1966.
G. J. Stigler, "The Economics of Information," *Journal of Political Economy*, June 1961, *69*, 213–35.

CHAPTER 13

On Theories of Unemployment*

R. M. SOLOW[1]

There is a long-standing tension in economics between belief in the advantages of the market mechanism and awareness of its imperfections. Ever since Adam Smith, economists have been distinguished from lesser mortals by their understanding of and – I think one has to say – their admiration for the efficiency, anonymity, and subtlety of decentralized competitive markets as an instrument for the allocation of resources and the imputation of incomes. I think we all know this; for confirmation one can look at the results of a paper (James Kearl *et al.*) presented at the last annual meeting, reporting the responses of professional economists to a sort of survey of technical opinion. The propositions which generated the greatest degree of consensus were those asserting the advantages of free trade and flexible exchange rates, favoring cash transfers over those in kind, and noting the disadvantages of rent controls, interest rate ceilings, and minimum wage laws.

Views on these policy issues did not seem to represent mere conservative ideology: half of the respondents agreed and another 30 percent agreed "with provisions" that redistribution of income (presumably toward the poorest) is a legitimate function of government policy. The profession's reservations about rent control, interest rate ceilings, and minimum wage laws do not appear to reflect a rejection of the goals of those measures, but rather a feeling that nonprofessionals simply do not understand fully the consequences, often unexpected and undesired, of messing around with the market mechanism. Most of us are conscious of a conflict that arises in our minds and consciences because, while we

---

*American Economic Review, Vol. 70, No. 1 (March 1980), pp. 1–11.

think it is usually a mistake to fiddle the price system to achieve distributional goals, we realize that the public and the political process are perversely more willing to do that than to make the direct transfers we would prefer. If we oppose all distorting transfers, we end up opposing transfers altogether. Some of us seem to welcome the excuse, but most of us feel uncomfortable. I don't think there is any very good way to resolve that conflict in practice.

Simultaneously, however, there is an important current in economics that focuses on the flaws in the price system, the ways that real markets fail because they lack some of the characteristics that make idealized markets so attractive. I think that outsiders, who tend to see economists as simple-minded marketeers, would be astonished to learn how much of the history of modern economic analysis can be written in terms of the study of the sources of market failure. The catalog runs from natural and artificial monopoly, to monopolistic competition, to the importance of public goods and externalities of many other kinds, to – most recently – a variety of problems connected with the inadequate, imperfect, or asymmetric transmission of information and with the likelihood that there will simply be no markets for some of the relevant goods and services.

Even the vocabulary can be revealing. Market "imperfection" suggests a minor blemish of the sort that can make the purchase of "irregular" socks a bargain. Market "failure" sounds like something more serious. To take a more subtle example, I mentioned that one kind of flaw in the system can be the absence of certain markets. The common generic term for the reason why markets are missing is "transaction costs." That sounds rather minor, the sort of thing that might go away in due course as accounting and information processing get cheaper. But some of the cases of missing markets really go much deeper. The fact that distant future generations can not participate directly in the markets for nonrenewable resources will not be remedied by improvements in communication. Nor are the residents of densely populated areas ever likely to be able to dicker effectively with the dozens or hundreds of sources of barely traceable pollutants whose health effects, if any, cumulate over many years.

There is a large element of Rorschach test in the way each of us responds to this tension. Some of us see the Smithian virtues as a needle in a haystack, as an island of measure zero in a sea of imperfections. Others see all the potential sources of market failure as so many fleas on the thick hide of an ox, requiring only an occasional flick of the tail to be brushed away. A hopeless eclectic without any strength of character, like me, has a terrible time of it. If I may invoke the names of two of my most awesome predecessors as President of this Association, I need only listen to Milton Friedman talk for a minute and my mind floods with thoughts of increasing returns to scale, oligopolistic interdependence, consumer ignorance, environmental pollution, intergenerational inequity, and on and on. There is almost no cure for it, except to listen for a minute to John Kenneth Galbraith, in which case all I can think of are the discipline of competition, the large number of substitutes for any commodity, the stupidities of regulation, the Pareto optimality of Walrasian equilibrium, the importance of decentralizing decision-making to where the knowledge is, and on and on. Sometimes I think it is only my weakness of character that keeps me from making obvious errors.

The critics of the mainstream tradition are mistaken when they attribute to it a built-in Panglossian attitude toward the capitalist economy. The tradition has provided both the foundations for a belief in the efficiency of market allocations and the tools for a powerful critique. Economic analysis by itself has no way of choosing between them; and the immediate prospects for an empirically based model of a whole economy, capable of measuring our actual "distance" from the contract curve, are mighty slim. The missing link has to be a matter of judgment – the Rorschach test, I spoke of a minute ago. For every Dr Pangloss who makes the ink blot out to be of surpassing beauty, give or take a few minor deviations – the second-best of all possible worlds, you might say – there is Candide to whom it looks a lot like an ink blot. Maybe there are more Panglosses than Candides. But that was true in Voltaire's time too – just before the French Revolution, by the way – and has more to do with the state of society than with the nature of economics.

The tension between market efficiency and market failure is especially pointed in discussions of the working of the labor market, for obvious reasons. The labor market connects quickly with everything else in the economy and its performance matters more directly for most people than that of any other market. Moreover, the labor market's own special pathology, unemployment, is particularly visible, particularly unsettling, and particularly frustrating. The fuse leading from theory to policy in this field is short, and has been known to produce both heat and light throughout much of the history of economics.

Contemporary macro-economic theory though apparently full of technical novelties, has revived many of the old questions in only slightly different form. One of the points I want to make is that underneath the theoretical innovations – some of which are interesting and important – the basic controversial issues that come to the surface are the same ones that occupied earlier literature. The most important among them is really the old tension between market efficiency and market failure. Should one think of the the labor market as mostly clearing or at worst in the process of quick return to market-clearing equilibrium? Or should one think of it as mostly in disequilibrium, with transactions habitually taking place at nonmarket-clearing wages? In that case presumably the wage structure is either not receiving any strong signals to make it change in the right direction or is not responding to the signals it receives. My own belief in this case lies with the market-failure side. That is to say, I believe that what looks like involuntary unemployment is involuntary unemployment.

Of course that conclusion only leads to another question. If the labor market often fails to clear, we had better figure out why. There is no shortage of candidate hypotheses. Here I think it is worthwhile to insist on a commonplace: although it is natural for academic people to seek a single weighty Answer to a weighty Question, if only because it is so satisfying to find one, it is quite likely that many of the candidate hypotheses are true, each contributing a little to the explanation of labor-market failure. Now the second general point I want to make is one that I am surprised to hear myself making. While I find several of the candidate hypotheses entirely believable, I am inclined to emphasize some that might be described as noneconomic. More precisely, I suspect that the labor market is a little different from other markets, in the sense that the objectives of the participants are not always the ones we normally impute to economic agents, and some of the constraints by which they feel themselves bound are not always the conventional constraints. In other words, I think that among the reasons why market-clearing wage rates do not establish themselves easily and adjust quickly to changing conditions are some that could be described as social conventions, or principles of appropriate behavior, whose source is not entirely individualistic.

I said that I am a little surprised at myself. That is because I am generally stodgy about assumptions, and like to stay as close to the mainstream framework as the problem at hand will allow. In any case, I think that the unconventional elements in what I have to say are only part of the story. And I assure you that I am not about to peddle amateur sociology to a captive audience. All I do mean to suggest is that we may predispose ourselves to misunderstand important aspects of unemployment if we insist on modelling the buying and selling of labor within a set of background assumptions whose main merit is that they are very well adapted to models of the buying and selling of cloth. Far from advocating that we all practice sociology, I am pleasantly impressed at how much mileage you can get from the methods of conventional economic analysis if only you are willing to broaden the assumptions a little.

I

It might be interesting to have a history of the evolution of economic ideas about unemployment, and their relation both to the internal logic of the subject and to the parallel evolution of the institutions of the labor market. I am not sufficiently well read to provide that kind of survey. To make my point about the persistence of the market-efficiency market-failure tension, I took a short cut. I went back to reread Pigou's *Lapses from Full Employment*, a little book I remember having been assigned to read as a student just after the war. And that in turn sent me back to its parent book, Pigou's *Theory of Unemployment*. The Preface to The *Theory of Unemployment* is dated April 1933, after a decade of poor performance and relatively high unemployment in Great Britain, well into the Great Depression, and before the publication of the *General Theory*. The Preface to *Lapses from Full Employment* (another example of a revealing vocabulary) is dated November 1944, after five years of the war that put an end to the depression, and well after the appearance of the *General Theory*. That seemed like an interesting approach to the historical question, because current controversies in macro-economic theory are often described as a debate between "Keynesians" and others – "monetarists," "Classicals" or "equilibrium theorists" – and because Pigou, besides being a great economist, was in particular the embodiment of the Marshallian tradition, the leading figure in the "classical economics" that the Keynesian revolution was explicitly intended to overthrow.

Lapses makes interesting rereading. It emphasizes the money wage, whereas its predecessor was written almost entirely in terms of the real wage. The general macro-theoretic framework, in which the discussion of the labor market is embedded, clearly has an eye on Keynes. The underlying model could be *IS-LM* without doing much violence to the argument. There are little anachronisms: Pigou tends to think of the interest rate as being determined in the goods market (by Savings = Investment) and nominal income as being determined by the demand for money. Today we take simultaneity seriously, but the *General Theory* more or less speaks as if real output is determined in the goods market and the interest rate by liquidity preference. After what is to me a confusing description of a Keynesian low-level liquidity-trap equilibrium, Pigou invokes the Pigou effect to explain why the low level might not be as low as all that and then, characteristically, remarks that none of it is very important in practice anyway. All this is relevant here only as background for the treatment of the labor market.

Pigou says the obvious thing first, and I agree that it is the first thing to say: if there is "thorough-going competition" among workers, then the only possible equilibrium position is at full employment. That is little more than a definition of equilibrium. He is aware that he is taking a lot of dynamics for granted. Expectations of falling wages could perversely reduce the demand for labor; and he discusses the possibility that under some conditions, with the interest rate at its practical floor, nominal wage rates and prices may chase each other down and thus prevent the real-wage adjustment needed for an increase in employment. (This is where the Pigou effect makes its appearance, of course.)

It is what comes next that interests me. It is obvious to Pigou, writing in 1944, that the labor market does not behave as if workers were engaged in thorough-going competition for jobs. With the common sense that seems somehow to have escaped his modern day successors, he wonders why it does not. And he discusses three or four of the institutional factors that a reasonable person would mention even now as obstacles to the classical functioning of the labor market.

First of all, he realizes that the labor market is segmented. Not everyone in it is in competition with everyone else. I am not referring here to the obvious fact that abilities, experience, and skills differ, so that unemployed laborers can not compete for the jobs held by craftsmen. That fact of life merely reminds us that "labor" is not a well-defined homogeneous factor of production. Even within skill categories or occupational groups, however, workers have ties to localities, to industries, to special job classifications, even to individual employers. These ties can be broken, but not easily. It is interesting to me that even the *Theory of Unemployment* of 1933 devotes a lot of space to the analysis of a labor market in which there are many "centers of employment" – to use the neutral term chosen by Pigou to describe segmentation of the labor market – between which mobility is absent or slow. Of course he observes that even in a completely segmented labor market, if there is thorough-going competition within segments, full employment will be the rule, although there may be wage differentials between centers of employment for otherwise identical workers. I think that the fact of segmentation is very important, not only because it limits the scope of competition but because its pervasiveness suggests – though it can not prove – that habit and custom play a large role in labor market behavior. From the prominence that he gives it, I gather that Pigou might have agreed.

A second factor, which has been more often discussed, is trade unionism. Pigou does not have very much to say about collective bargaining, but what he says makes sense.

> Of course, these agencies in their decisions have regard to the general state of the demand for labour; they will have no wish to set wage rates so high that half the people of the country are thrown out of work. Nevertheless, there is reason to believe that they do not have regard to demand conditions in such degree as would be necessary to secure, as thorough-going competition would do, the establishment of full employment. (1945, p. 26)

Later on in this book, Pigou makes an observation that is not explicitly connected with collective bargaining. He does connect it with "actual life" however, and it fits organized workers very well, and perhaps others besides:

> In periods of expansion employers might be willing to agree to substantial advances in wage rates if they were confident that, when prosperity ended, they would be able to cancel them. They know, however, that in fact this will not be easy, that elaborate processes will have to be gone through, and that their work-people will put up a strong rear-guard action ... In periods of depression wage-earners, for precisely similar reasons, hold out against wage reductions, which they might be ready to concede if it were not for the difficulty that they foresee in getting them cancelled when times improve ... A widespread desire for 'safety first' helps to make wage-rates sticky (1945, p. 48)

These casual remarks raise more questions than they answer about the determination of nominal wages by collective bargaining. The first excerpt can be taken as a redefinition of full employment when the labor market is not competitive; the second, however, advances an account of wage stickiness and is therefore on a different footing. It would help to explain the failure of the labor market to clear on any reasonable definition, and thus provide a connection between nominal demand and real output.

The third institutional factor mentioned by Pigou has also been the subject of much analysis, past and present: the provision of unemployment insurance. There are several channels by which the availability of unemployment compensation can add to the recorded amount of unemployment. The prolongation of search is only the most obvious. My own impression is that this is currently a significant factor. As an indication of the complexity of the issues, let me just mention here that some recent research by my colleagues Peter Diamond and Eric Maskin suggests the possibility that in some environments search activity conveys a positive externality. So the optimal search strategy for the individual might provide less than the socially optimal amount of search, and unemployment compensation could be regarded as a corrective subsidy. This is a neat twist on the theme of the counterpoint between market efficiency and market failure. In any case, it can hardly be doubted that the unemployment compensation system is an important determinant of behavior on both sides of the labor market, and complicates even the definition of full employment.

The last comment of Pigou's that I want to cite is especially intriguing because it is so unlike the sort of thing that his present day successors keep saying. Already in the 1933 *Theory of Unemployment* he wrote: "...public opinion in a modern civilized State builds up for itself a rough estimate of what constitutes a reasonable living wage. This is derived half-consciously from a knowledge of the actual standards enjoyed by more or less 'average' workers ... Public opinion then enforces its view, failing success through social pressure, by the machinery of ... legislation" (p. 255). A similar remark appears in *Lapses*. Such feelings about equity and fairness are obviously relevant to the setting of statutory minimum wages and Pigou uses them that way. I think they also come into play as a deterrent to wage cutting in a slack labor market. Unemployed workers rarely try to displace their employed counterparts by offering to work for less; and it is even more surprising, as I have had occasion to point out in the past, that employers so rarely try to elicit wage cutting on the part of their laid-off employees, even in a buyer's market for labor. Several forces can be at work, but I think Occam's razor and common observation both suggest that a code of good behavior enforced by social pressure is one of them. Wouldn't you be surprised if you learned that someone of roughly your status in the profession, but teaching in a less desirable department, had written to your department chairman offering to teach your courses for less money? The fact that nominal wage rates did fall sharply during the early stages of the depression of the 1930s, and the fact that the Chrysler Corporation has been able to negotiate concessions from the UAW certainly show that wage rates are not completely rigid. But those very instances seem to me only to confirm the importance of social convention in less extreme circumstances. After all, people have been known to try to claw their way into a lifeboat who would never dream of cheating on a lift-line.

I think I have made the case that the most eminent representative of orthodox economics in the 1940s was fully aware of the many obstacles to "thorough-going competition" among workers, that is, of the many ways in which the labor market may "fail." In particular, one cannot under those circumstances expect the labor market always to clear. Pigou certainly drew that conclusion. He says, in the Preface to *Lapses*: "Professor Dennis Robertson ... has warned me that the form of the book may suggest that I am in favour of attacking the problem of unemployment by manipulating wages rather than by manipulating demand. I wish, therefore, to say clearly that this is not so" (p. v).

Pigou clearly felt the tension between market efficiency and market failure. Nevertheless, he did not come down on the side of market failure, even after the 1930s. The very title of *Lapses from Full Employment* tells us that much. Evidently he concluded that the tendency of the capitalist economy to seek (and find) its full-employment equilibrium was strong enough so that departures from full employment could be regarded as mere episodes. Is that surprising? Well, to begin with, there is no accounting for Rorschach tests. One person's ink blot is another person's work of art. But I think there is also something more systematic to be said.

In the *Theory of Unemployment*, Pigou gives an elaborate analysis of the short-run elasticity of demand for labor. He is very careful: he allows for the elasticity of supply of complementary raw materials; he allows for the (presumably very high) price elasticity of demand for exports; he discusses the effects of discounting future returns to labor. It is a masterly attempt to get a grip on orders of magnitude. It is all based on the presumption that the only possible starting point is the elasticity of the marginal-product-of-labor curve. Let me remind you that in the old standby, two-factor Cobb–Douglas case, the elasticity of demand for labor with respect to the real wage is the reciprocal of the share of capital. Everybody's back-of-the-envelope puts the capital share at $\frac{1}{4}$ and the elasticity of demand for labor at 4. This is not exactly the way Pigou proceeds, but he reaches the same conclusion: the initial estimate of the elasticity is "certain to be (numerically) much larger than −1 and may well amount to −5 or more." There follow some modifications, but the conclusion remains that in times of depression, the aggregate elasticity of demand for labor with respect to the real wage "cannot, on the least favourable assumption here suggested, be numerically less than −3 and may well be larger than −4" except perhaps in the very shortest run.

For practical purposes, one would want to know the elasticity of demand with respect to the nominal wage, taking account of the likelihood that prices will follow wages down, at least partially. (Obviously if product prices fall equiproportionally with wage rates, as Keynes though might happen in unlucky circumstances, the real wage doesn't move at all and employment will not improve.)[2] The details of Pigou's calculations do not concern us, but his conclusion does: "we may ... not unreasonably put the elasticity of the money demand for labour in times of deep depression at not less numerically than −1.5."

If I could believe that, I too could believe that the labor market generally clears. To reduce the unemployment rate by 6 percentage points is to increase employment by about 6 percent, if we ignore for this purpose the side effects that go to make up Okun's Law. If that could be accomplished by a real-wage reduction of 2 percent, or even less, that is, by foregoing one year's normal productivity increase, then I could imagine that the labor market might easily learn to adjust smoothly to fluctuations in aggregate demand. I could even imagine that workers might accept the necessary 4 percent reduction in nominal wages, in the expectation that half of it would be offset by lower prices. The trouble is that Pigou's demand elasticities are way too high. A recent econometric study by Kim Clark and Richard Freeman, based on quarterly data for U.S. manufacturing in 1950–76, puts the real-wage elasticity of demand for labor at about one-half, a whole order of magnitude smaller than Pigou's guess.[3] And the Clark–Freeman work is presented as revisionist, a counterweight to other estimates that are typically *lower*, averaging out at about 0.15 according to a survey by Daniel

Hamermesh. To my mind, smooth wage adjustment seems intrinsically unlikely in a world with such a small demand elasticity and institutions like those sketched earlier. Nothing I read in the newspapers suggests to me that 6 percent of nonfrictional unemployment produces a threat adequate to set off a quick 12–15 percent fall in the real wage, or a drop in nominal wage rates twice as large. Sellers facing inelastic demands usually try to discourage price cutting; why should workers be different?

The modern classical school seems curiously remote from all this. When they try to explain how the equilibrium volume of employment can fluctuate as widely as actual employment does in business cycles, their only substitute for Pigou's high elasticity of demand is a high elasticity of supply (of labor) in the face of a perceived temporary opportunity for unusual gains, which in this case reflects wages that differ from average expected (discounted) future wages. In other words, people who give the vague impression of being unemployed are actually engaged in voluntary leisure. They are taking it now, planning to substitute extra work later, because they think, rightly or wrongly, that current real wages are unusually low compared with the present value of what the labor market will offer in the future. They may be responding to changes in real wages or to changes in the real interest rate.

It is astonishing that believers have made essentially no effort to verify this central hypothesis. I know of no convincing evidence in its favor,[4] and I am not sure why it has any claim to be taken seriously. It is hardly plausible on its face. Even if the workers in question have misread the future, they are merely mistaken, not confused or mystified about their own motives. It is thus legitimate to wonder why the unemployed do not feel themselves to be engaged in voluntary intertemporal substitution, and why they queue up in such numbers when legitimate jobs of their usual kind are offered during a recession.[5]

When they face the market-clearing issue at all, Pigou's successors take a rather abstract line. They regard it as inherently incredible that unexploited opportunities for beneficial trade should be anything but ephemeral – which means merely that they ignore all those human and institutional facts of which Pigou was aware. Or else they argue that one cannot believe in the failure of markets to clear without having an acceptable theory to explain why that happens. That is a remarkable precept when you think about it. I remember reading once that it is still not understood how the giraffe manages to pump an adequate blood supply all the way up to its head; but it is hard to imagine that anyone would therefore conclude that giraffes do not have long necks. At least not anyone who had ever been to a zoo. Besides, I think perfectly acceptable theories can indeed be constructed, as soon as one gets away from foolishly restrictive and inappropriate assumptions.

II

That brings me to the second and last general points I had hoped to make. Suppose one chooses to accept the apparent evidence of one's senses and takes it for granted that the wage does not move flexibly to clear the labor market. By the way, my own inclination is to go further and claim that commodity prices are sticky too, at least downward. But it is the persistence of disequilibrium in the labor market that I want to emphasize. How can we account for it?

There is, as I mentioned at the beginning, a whole catalog of possible models of the labor market that will produce the right qualitative properties. Since I have surveyed this literature elsewhere, I will just list a half-dozen possibilities now, with the reminder that they are not mutually exclusive alternatives.

(1) There is Keynes's idea that case-by-case resistance to wage reductions is the only way that workers can defend traditional wage differentials in decentralized labor market. The net result is to preserve the general wage level or its trend, but that is an unintended artifact.

(2) There is a complementary hypothesis about the behavior of employers that I have proposed myself: if employers know that aggressive wage cutting in a buyer's market may antagonize the remaining work force, hurt current productivity, and make it harder to recruit high-quality workers when the labor market tightens, they will be less inclined to push their short-run advantage.

(3) Pigou realized that widely held notions of fairness, enforced by social pressure or by legislation, might have to be part of any serious account of wage determination. George Akerlof has pursued this trail further, documented the prescription of codes of good behavior in manuals of personnel practice, and showed formally that such codes of behavior can be self-enforcing if people value their reputations in the community. Obviously there are no Emily Post manuals to consult as regards the behavior of laid-off workers, but you would certainly not be astonished to learn that self-esteem and the folkways discourage laid-off workers from undercutting the wages of their still-employed colleagues in an effort to displace them from jobs. Reservation wages presumably fall as the duration of unemployment lengthens; but my casual reading suggests that this pattern shows up more in a willingness to accept lower-paid sorts of jobs than in 'thorough-going competition' for the standard job. The cost to the worker of this sort of behavior is diminished by the availability of unemployment insurance. It is worth remembering that the acceptance of lower-grade jobs is itself a form of unemployment.

(4) I need only touch on the Azariadis–Baily–Gordon implicit-contract theory, because it has been much discussed in the literature. Here wage

stability is a vehicle by which less-risk-averse firms provide income insurance for more-risk-averse workers, presumably in exchange for a lower average wages.[6] It is now understood that the theory works well only when workers have some source of income other than wages; unemployment compensation for instance. This is not really a disadvantage in a world with well-developed unemployment insurance systems. In any case such implicit contracts do not themselves account for unemployment. Their effect is to reduce the average amount of unemployment below the level that would occur in a simple spot market. The theory belongs in my list because I suspect it does help to account for the habit of wage inertia and therefore the vulnerability of employment to unexpected fluctuations in aggregate demand.

(5) Wherever there is collective bargaining in our economy, the standard pattern with few exceptions, is that wage rates are specified in the contract, and the employer chooses the amount of employment. This is not exactly simple monopoly, because the union cannot set the wage schedule unilaterally. To the extent that it can, another source of wage stickiness can be identified. Under a reasonable assumption about what the union maximizes, it turns out that the only aspect of the demand for labor that has any effect on the monopoly wage is its elasticity. So if the demand curve for labor shifts down nearly isoelastically in a recession, the contractual wage will change little or not at all, and the full effect of the fall in demand will bear on employment. The amount of unemployment compensation available plays a role here too. (There is much more to be said along these lines, and Ian McDonald of the University of Melbourne and I hope to say it on another occasion.)

(6) As a last example, I recall Pigou's observation that wage changes may be seen by the parties as hard to reverse without a struggle whose duration and outcome cannot be foreseen. The resulting uncertainty causes employers to drag their feet when demand increases temporarily and workers to reciprocate when demand falls. The result is wage stickiness in the face of fluctuating employment.

Only what Veblen called 'trained incapacity' could prevent anyone from seeing that some or all of these mechanisms do indeed capture real aspects of the modern capitalist economy. Assessing their combined significance quantitatively would be a very difficult task, and I do not pretend to be able to do that. We are all interpreting this ink blot together. Obviously I would not be giving this particular talk if I did not think that wage stickiness is a first-order factor in a reasonable theory of unemployment.

To make my position plausible, I want to try to summarize the sort of general characteristics that the labor market should have if the particular mechanisms that I have enumerated are to be important. By the way, I have no reason to believe that my list is anything like exhaustive; you may think of others. Simply to narrow the field, I have deliberately left out of account factors relating specifically to age, sex, race, and other characteristics that normally form the basis for discussions of structural unemployment as distinct from cyclical unemployment.

The sort of labor market I have in mind is segmented. It often makes sense to think of an employer or definable group of employers as facing its own labor pool. Some members of the labor pool may be unemployed, but still belong to it. Although transportation, information, and transaction costs are possible sources of segmentation, they need not be among the most important. The buildup of firm-specific or industry-specific human capital may be more fundamental, and equally a kind of mutual knowing-what-to-expect that gives both parties in the labor market a stake, a rent, in the durability of the relationship. This point is close to the distinction between auction markets and customer markets made by Arthur Okun, in a different context. The labor market, at least the "primary" labor market, is a customer market; this may be one of the important facts that differentiates the primary from the secondary labor market.

A second general characteristic is the availability of some nontrivial source of nonemployment income. The obvious one is unemployment compensation, but I imagine that fringe activity ranging from hustling to home maintenance can function in much the same way. I suppose in some societies the possibility of returning temporarily to farming is now as important as it once was here. The presence of a second earner in the family can make an obvious difference. One consequence is that it becomes easier to maintain a labor pool in the presence of fluctuating employment. In addition, as I mentioned a few moments ago, several of the specific sticky-wage mechanisms in my catalog depend for their operation on this characteristic.

Third, the stability of the labor pool makes it possible for social conventions to assume some importance. There is a difference between a long-term relationship and a one-night stand, and acceptable behavior in one context may be unacceptable in the other. Presumably most conventions are adaptive, not arbitrary, but adaptiveness may have to be interpreted broadly, so as to include pecuniary advantage but not be limited by it. Critics who deride the notion of "economic man" have a point, but usually the wrong point. Economic man is a social, not a psychological, category. There are activities in our culture in which it is socially acceptable and expected that individual pecuniary self-interest will be the overriding decision criterion: choosing a portfolio of securities, for example.[7] There are others in which it is not: choosing a mate, for example.[8] The labor market is more complicated than either, of course, and contains elements of both. Perhaps in nineteenth-century Manchester labor was bought and sold by "thorough-going competition" but I think that is unlikely to be a good approximation to contemporary wage setting. In particular, as I have emphasized, there is nothing in the data or in common observation to make you believe that moderate excess supply will evoke aggressive wage cutting on either side of the labor market.

III

I draw two conclusions from this whole train of thought, one about economics and the other about the economy.

About economics: it need not follow that we old dogs have to learn a lot of new tricks. It still seems reasonable to presume that agents do the best they can, subject to whatever constraints they perceive. But in some contexts the traditional formulations of the objective function and constraints may be inappropriate. In the labor market, the participants are firms and groups of firms on one side, and individual workers, organized trade unions, and informally organized labor pools on the other. Grant me that all feel constrained, to some nontrivial degree, by social customs that have to do with the wage and wage-setting procedures. The result is that factor prices turn up in our equations in unfamiliar ways. Let me just mention a few examples from my earlier list of hypotheses. If Keynes was right about the the conventional significance of relative wages, then ratios of wage rates appear in the objective functions on the labor side. If the current or future performance of workers depends on their feelings that wage levels are fair, then wage rates appear in the production functions constraining firms. If the individual worker's utility function depends quite conventionally on current income, then the collective objective function of a labor pool of identical workers might reasonably be a weighted average of the utility of the wage and the utility achievable when unemployed, with weights equal to the employment and unemployment fractions. This objective function contains both wage and volume of employment as arguments; and it has the interesting property that the marginal rate of substitution between wage rate and employment can depend very sensitively on the size of the unemployment insurance benefit. Constrained maximization and partial or complete reconciliation in the market can still be the bread and butter of the macrotheorist. Spread with more palatable behavior assumptions, they may make a tastier sandwich, and stick to the ribs.

About the economy: if the labor market is often not in equilibrium, if wages are often sticky, if they respond to nontraditional signals, then there is a role for macropolicy and a good chance that it will be effective. Equilibrium theories that conclude the opposite may conceivably turn out to have the right answer, but they simply assume what they purport to prove. It is not my argument that standard textbook policy prescriptions are bound to be right. That has to be worked out case by case. All I do claim is that a reasonable theory of economic policy ought to be based on a reasonable theory of economic life.

Notes

1. Presidential address delivered at the ninety-second meeting of the American Economic Association December 29, 1979, Atlanta, Georgia. Like most people, I get by with a little help from my friends, in this case especially Paul Samuelson, George Akerlof, Arnold Kling, and James Tobin.
2. Neither Pigou nor Keynes invoked Kaldor's notion that prices can be expected to fall faster than wages in a recession with the resulting rise in real wages providing the force for recovery from the demand side, through a distributional shift toward wage incomes which generate more spending per dollar than other incomes do.
3. The Clark–Freeman estimates are based on quarterly data for aggregate U.S. manufacturing. Their difference from other work appears to rest on allowing wage changes to operate with a lag different from other factor prices. According to their results the lag of employment behind wage changes is quite short; it is complete in about two quarters.
4. Just after writing those words, I received a working paper by Robert Hall which (a) concludes that the elasticity of supply of labor required to make the intertemporal-substitution hypothesis work is actually in the ballpark suggested by other facts, but (b) rejects the whole theory on other empirical grounds. I have done some further experimentation on Hall's data (with the help of Mr. Sunil Sanghvi) with results that cast doubt on the reliability of even the first conclusion. On reflection, I stand by the words in the text.
5. I have tried to phrase that carefully. For some direct evidence, see "Jobs and Want Ads: A Look Behind the Evidence," *Fortune*, Nov. 20, 1978.
6. Unemployment generated by this mechanism is in a sense, voluntary. Workers reveal a preference for steady wages over steady employment. But the aggregate welfare cost of the system can still be reduced by stabilization policies. This comment applies equally to the social customs described in the preceeding paragraph of the text. One can ask why workers cling to such costly conventions. It is the job of sociology to answer that question. But it is the job of economics to point out that, whatever the reason, the narrowly economic cost of such conventions can be reduced by the stabilization of aggregate demand.
7. The emotion aroused by the case of South Africa strikes me as one of those extreme exceptions that proves the rule.
8. In Gary Becker's defense, I should point out that he does not assume cash income to be the decisive motive in courtship.

References

G. Akerlof, "The Case Against Conservative Macroeconomics: An Inaugural Lecture," *Economica*, Aug. 1979, *46*, 219–37.

C. Azariadis, "Implicit Contracts and Unemployment Equilibria," *J. Polit. Econ.*, Dec. 1975, *83*, 1183–202.

M. N. Baily, "Wages and Employment under Uncertain Demand," *Rev. Econ. Stud.*, Jan. 1974, *41*, 37–50.

K. Clark and R. Freeman, "How Elastic is the Demand for Labour," Nat. Bur. Econ. Res. work. Paper no. 309, Cambridge, Mass., Jan. 1979.

P. Diamond and E. Maskin, "Externalities and Efficiency in a Model of Stochastic Job Matching," working paper, Mass. Inst. Technology, forthcoming.

D. F. Gordon, "A Neo-Classical Theory of Keynesian Unemployment," *Econ. Inquiry*, Dec. 1974, *12*, 431–59.

R. Hall, "Labour Supply and Aggregate Fluctuations," Nat. Bur. Econ. Res. working paper no. 385, Stanford, Aug. 1979.

D. Hamermesh, "Econometric Studies of Labour Demand and their Applications to Policy Analysis," *J. Hum. Resouces*, Fall 1976, *11*, 507–25.

J. Kearl, C. Pope, G. Whiting and L. Wimmer, "A Confusion of Economists?," *Amer. Econ. Rev. Proc.*, May 1979, *69*, 28–37.

A. Okun, "Inflation: Its Mechanics and Welfare Costs," *Brookings Papers*, Washington 1975, *2*, 351–90.

A. C. Pigou, *The Theory of Unemployment*, London 1933.

A. C. Pigou, *Lapses from Full Employment*, London 1945.

R. Solow, "Alternative Approaches to Macroeconomic Theory: A Partial View," *Canadian Journal of Economics*, Aug. 1979, *12*, 339–54.

CHAPTER 14

Efficiency Wage Models of Unemployment*

J. YELLEN[1]

Keynesian economists hold it to be self-evident that business cycles are characterized by involuntary unemployment. But construction of a model of the cycle with involuntary unemployment faces the obvious difficulty of explaining why the labor market does not clear. Involuntarily unemployed people, by definition, want to work at less than the going wage rate. Why don't firms cut wages, thereby increasing profits?

This paper surveys a recent literature which offers a convincing and coherent explanation why firms may find it unprofitable to cut wages in the presence of involuntary unemployment. The models surveyed are variants of the efficiency wage hypothesis, according to which, labor productivity depends on the real wage paid by the firm. If wage cuts harm productivity, then cutting wages may end up raising labor costs. Section I describes some of the general implications of the efficiency-wage hypothesis in its simplest form. Section II describes four distinct microeconomic approaches which justify the relation between wages and productivity. These approaches identify four benefits of higher wage payments: reduced shirking by employees due to a higher cost of job loss; lower turnover; an improvement in the average quality of job applicants; and improved morale.[2] Section III explains how the efficiency-wage hypothesis, with near rational behavior, can explain cyclical fluctuations in unemployment.

---

*American Economic Review, Vol. 74, No. 2 (May 1984), pp. 200–50.

I The efficiency wage hypothesis

The potential relevance of the efficiency-wage hypothesis in explaining involuntary unemployment and other stylized labor market facts can be seen in a rudimentary model.

Consider an economy with identical, perfectly competitive firms, each firm having a production function of the form $Q = F(e(\omega)N)$, where N is the number of employees, e is effort per worker, and ω is the real wage. A profit-maximizing firm which can hire all the labor it wants at the wage it chooses to offer (see Joseph Stiglitz, 1976a; Robert Solow, 1979), will offer a real wage, ω^*, which satisfies the condition that the elasticity of effort with respect to the wage is unity. The wage ω^* is known as the efficiency wage and this wage choice minimizes labor cost per efficiency unit. Each firm should then optimally hire labor up to the point where its marginal product, $e(\omega^*)F'(e(\omega^*)N^*)$, is equal to the real wage, ω^*. As long as the aggregate demand for labor falls short of aggregate labor supply and ω^* exceeds labor's reservation wage, the firm will be unconstrained by labor market conditions in pursuing its optimal policy so that equilibrium will be characterized by involuntary unemployment. Unemployed workers would strictly prefer to work at the real wage ω^* than to be unemployed, but firms will not hire them at that wage or at a lower wage. Why? For the simple reason that any reduction in the wage paid would lower the productivity of all employees already on the job. Thus the efficiency-wage hypothesis explains involuntary unemployment.

Extended in simple ways this hypothesis also explains four other labor market phenomena: real wage rigidity; the dual labor market; the existence of wage distributions for workers of identical characteristics; and discrimination among observationally distinct groups. Concerning real wage rigidity, in the simple model just described, real shocks which shift the marginal product of labor alter employment, but not the real wage. In more elaborate versions of the model discussed below, such shocks will change the real wage, but not sufficiently to leave unemployment unaltered.

Dual labor markets can be explained by the assumption that the wage–productivity nexus is important in some sectors of the economy, but not in others. For the primary sector, where the efficiency–wage hypothesis is relevant, we find job rationing and voluntary payment by firms of wages in excess of market clearing; in the secondary sector, where the wage–productivity relationship is weak or nonexistent, we should observe fully neoclassical behavior. The market for secondary-sector jobs clears, and anyone can obtain a job in this sector, albeit at lower pay. The existence of the secondary sector does not, however, eliminate involuntary unemployment (see Robert Hall, 1975), because the wage differential between primary- and secondary-sector jobs will induce unemployment among job seekers who choose to wait for primary-sector job openings.

Theorists who emphasize the importance of unemployment due to the frictions of the search process have frequently found it difficult to explain the reasons for a distribution of wage offers in the market. The efficiency-wage hypothesis also offers a simple explanation for the existence of wage differentials which might motivate the search process emphasized by Edmund Phelps and others. If the relationship between wages and effort differs among firms, each firm's efficiency wage will differ, and, in equilibrium, there will emerge a distribution of wage offers for workers of identical characteristics.

The efficiency-wage hypothesis also explains discrimination among workers with different observable characteristics. This occurs if employers simply prefer, say, men to women. With job rationing, the employer can indulge his taste for discrimination at zero cost. As another possibility, employers may know that the functions relating effort to wages differ across groups. Then each group has its own efficiency wage and corresponding "efficiency labor cost." If these labor costs differ, it will pay firms to hire first only employees from the lowest cost group. Any unemployment that exists will be confined to labor force groups with higher costs per efficiency unit. With fluctuations in demand, these groups will bear a disproportionate burden of layoffs.

II Microfoundations of the efficiency-wage model

Why should labor productivity depend on the real wage paid by firms? In the LDC context, for which the hypothesis was first advanced, the link between wages, nutrition, and illness was emphasized. Recent theoretical work has advanced a convincing case for the relevance of this hypothesis to developed economies. In this section, four different microeconomic foundations for the efficiency-wage model are described and evaluated.

The shirking model

In most jobs, workers have some discretion concerning their performance. Rarely can employment contracts rigidly specify all aspects of a worker's performance. Piece rates are often impracticable because monitoring is too costly or too inaccurate. Piece rates may also be nonviable because the measurements on which they are based are unverifiable by workers, creating a moral hazard problem. Under these circumstances, the payment of a wage in excess of market clearing may be an effective way for firms to provide workers with the incentive to work rather than shirk. (See Samuel Bowles, 1981, 1983; Guillermo Calvo, 1979; B. Curtis Eaton and William White, 1982; Herbert Gintis and Tsuneo Ishikawa,

1983; Hajime Miyazaki, forthcoming; Carl Shapiro and Stiglitz, 1982; and Steven Stoft, 1982.) The details of the models differ somewhat, depending on what is assumed measurable, at what cost, and the feasible payment schedules.

Bowles, Calvo, Eaton–White, Shapiro–Stiglitz, and Stoft assume that it is possible to monitor individual performance on the job, albeit imperfectly. In the simplest model, due to Shapiro–Stiglitz, workers can decide whether to work or to shirk. Workers who shirk have some chance of getting caught, with the penalty of being fired. This has been termed "cheat–threat" theory by Stoft because, if there is a cost to being fired, the threat of being sacked if caught cheating creates an incentive not to shirk. Equilibrium then entails unemployment. If all firms pay an identical wage, and if there is full employment, there would be no cost to shirking and it would pay all workers, assumed to get pleasure from loafing on the job, to shirk. In these circumstances, it pays each firm to raise its wage to eliminate shirking. When all firms do this, average wages rise and employment falls. In equilibrium, all firms pay the same wage above market clearing, and unemployment, which makes job loss costly, serves as a worker-discipline device. Unemployed workers cannot bid for jobs by offering to work at lower wages. If the firm were to hire a worker at a lower wage, it would be in the worker's interest to shirk on the job. The firm knows this and the worker has no credible way of promising to work if he is hired.

The shirking model does *not* predict, counterfactually, that the bulk of those unemployed at any time are those who were fired for shirking. If the threat associated with being fired is effective, little or no shirking and sacking will actually occur. Instead, the unemployed are a rotating pool of individuals who have quit jobs for personal reasons, who are new entrants to the labor market, or who have been laid off by firms with declines in demand. Pareto optimality, with costly monitoring, will entail some unemployment, since unemployment plays a socially valuable role in creating work incentives. But the equilibrium unemployment rate will not be Pareto optimal (see Shapiro–Stiglitz).

In contrast to the simple efficiency-wage model, the shirking model adds new arguments to the firm's effort function – the average wage, aggregate unemployment, and the unemployment benefit. The presence of the unemployment rate in the effort function yields a mechanism whereby changes in labor supply affect equilibrium wages and employment. New workers increase unemployment, raising the penalty associated with being fired and inducing higher effort at any given wage. Firms accordingly lower wages and hire more labor as a result. In a provocative recent paper, Thomas Weisskopf, Bowles, and David Gordon (1984) have used the presence of the unemployment benefit in the effort function to explain the secular decline in productivity in the

United States; they argue that a major part of the productivity slowdown is attributable to loss of employer control due to a reduction in the cost of job loss. The shirking model also offers an interpretation of hierarchical wage differentials, in excess of productivity differences (Calvo and Stanislaw Wellisz, 1979).

All these models suffer from a similar theoretical difficulty – that employment contracts more ingenious than the simple wage schemes considered, can reduce or eliminate involuntary unemployment. In the cheat-threat model, the introduction of employment fees allows the market to clear efficiently as long as workers have sufficient capital to pay them (see Eaton–White and Stoft). Unemployed workers would be willing to pay a fee to gain employment. Fees lower labor costs, giving firms an incentive to hire more workers. If all firms charge fees, any worker who shirks and is caught knows that he will have to pay another fee to regain employment. This possibility substitutes for the threat of unemployment in creating work incentives. Devices which function similarly are bonds posted by workers when initially hired and forfeited if found cheating, and fines levied on workers caught shirking. The threat of forfeiting the bond or paying the fine substitutes for the threat of being fired. Edward Lazear (1981) has demonstrated the use of seniority wages to solve the incentive problem. Workers can be paid a wage less than their marginal productivity when they are first hired with a promise that their earnings will later exceed their marginal productivity. The upward tilt in the age–earnings profile provides a penalty for shirking; the present value of the wage paid can fall to the market-clearing level, eliminating involuntary unemployment.

As a theoretical objection to these schemes, employers would be subject to moral hazard in evaluating workers' effort. Firms would have an obvious incentive to declare workers shirking and appropriate their bonds, collect fines, or replace them with new fee-paying workers. In Lazear's model, in which the firm pays a wage in excess of marginal product to senior workers, there is an incentive for the firm to fire such workers, replacing them with young workers, paid less than their productivity. The seriousness of this moral hazard problem depends on the ability of workers to enforce honesty on the firm's part. If effort is observable both by the firm and by the worker, and if it can be verified by outside auditors, the firm will be unable to cheat workers. Even without outside verification, Lazear has shown how the firm's concern for its reputation can overcome the moral hazard problem. Sudipto Bhattacharya (1983) has suggested tournament contracts that also overcome the moral hazard problem. The firm can commit itself to a fixed wage plan in which a high wage is paid to a fraction of workers and a low wage to the remaining fraction according to an *ex post*, possibly random, ranking of their effort levels. By precommitting itself to such a plan with a fixed wage bill, any moral hazard problem on the firm's part disappears.

The labor turnover model

Firms may also offer wages in excess of market clearing to reduce costly labor turnover. (See Steven Salop, 1979; Ekkehart Schlicht, 1978; and Stiglitz, 1974.) The formal structure of the labor turnover model is identical to that of the shirking model. Workers will be more reluctant to quit the higher the relative wage paid by the current firm, and the higher the aggregate unemployment rate. If all firms are identical, one possible equilibrium has all firms paying a common wage above market clearing with involuntary unemployment serving to diminish turnover.

The theoretical objection to the prediction of involuntary unemployment in this model again concerns the potential for more sophisticated employment contracts to provide Pareto-superior solutions. As Salop explains, the market for new hires fails to clear because an identical wage is paid to both trained and untrained workers. Instead, new workers could be paid a wage equal to the difference between their marginal product and their training cost. A seniority wage scheme might accomplish this, although, if training costs are large and occur quickly it might prove necessary to charge a fee to new workers. In contrast to the shirking model, an employment or training fee scheme could be employed without the problem of moral hazard. It is no longer in any firm's interest to dismiss trained workers; explicit contracts could probably be written to insure that training is actually provided to fee paying workers. Although moral hazard thus appears to be a less formidable barrier to achieving neo-classical outcomes via fees or bonds than in the shirking model, capital market imperfections or institutional or sociological constraints may in fact make them impractical.

Adverse selection

Adverse selection yields further reason for a relation between productivity and wages. Suppose that performance on the job depends on "ability" and that workers are heterogeneous in ability. If ability and workers' reservation wages are positively correlated, firms with higher wages will attract more able job candidates. (See James Malcolmson, 1981; Stiglitz, 1976b; Andrew Weiss, 1980.) In such a model, each firm pays an efficiency wage and optimally turns away applicants offering to work for less than that wage. The willingness of an individual to work for less than the going wage places an upper bound on his ability, raising the firm's estimate that he is a lemon. The model provides an explanation of wage differentials and different layoff probabilities for observationally distinct groups due to statistical discrimination if it is known that different groups have even slight differences in the joint distributions of ability and acceptance wages. However, for the adverse-selection model to provide a convincing account of involuntary unemployment, firms must be unable to measure effort and pay piece rates after workers are hired, or to fire workers whose output is too low. Clever firms may also be able to mitigate adverse selection in hiring by designing self-selection or screening devices which induce workers to reveal their true characteristics.

Sociological models

The theories reviewed above are neoclassical in their assumption of individualistic maximization by all agents. Solow (1980) has argued, however, that wage rigidity may more plausibly be due to social conventions and principles of appropriate behavior that are not entirely individualistic in origin. George Akerlof (1982) has provided the first explicitly sociological model leading to the efficiency-wage hypothesis. He uses a variety of interesting evidence from sociological studies to argue that each worker's effort depends on the work norms of his group. In Akerlof's partial gift exchange model, the firm can succeed in raising group work norms and average effort by paying workers a gift of wages in excess of the minimum required, in return for their gift of effort above the minimum required. The sociological model can explain phenomena which seem inexplicable in neoclassical terms – why firms don't fire workers who turn out to be less productive, why piece rates are avoided even when feasible, and why firms set work standards exceeded by most workers. Akerlof's paper in this issue explores alternative sociological foundations for the efficiency wage hypothesis. Sociological considerations governing the effort decisions of workers are also emphasized in Marxian discussions of the extraction of labor from labor power (see, for example, Bowles, 1983).

III Explaining the busines cycle

Any model of the business cycle must explain why changes in aggregate demand cause changes in aggregate employment and output. A potential problem of the efficiency-wage hypothesis in this regard is the absence of a link between aggregate demand and economic activity. In an economy with efficiency-wage setting, there is a positive natural rate of unemployment and real wage rigidity. But the economy's aggregate output is independent of price at this natural rate. These models have no wage or price stickiness to cause real consequences from aggregate demand shocks. However, for a natural but subtle reason, the efficiency-wage model is consistent with nominal wage rigidity and cyclical unemployment. This reason (suggested by Stoft), is explored in depth by Akerlof and myself (1983), where we argue that sticky wage and price behavior, that will cause significant business cycle fluctuations, is consistent with near rationality in an economy with efficiency wage setting. Any firm that normally chooses its wage as part of an optimizing decision will incur losses that are only second-order if it follows a rule of thumb in adjusting nominal wages which leads to a real wage error. At the point of maximum profits, the profit function relating wages to profits is flat. Thus, in the neighborhood of the optimum wage, the loss from wage errors is second-order small. This implies that firms with sticky wages have profits that are insignificantly different from firms with maximizing behavior. Furthermore, if firms have price-setting power because of downward-sloping demand curves, for similar reasons, price-setting errors also lead to insignificant losses.

In the Akerlof–Yellen model, firms are efficiency-wage setters and monopolistic competitors. In the long run, wages and prices are set by all firms in an optimal way. In the short run, in response to aggregate demand shocks, some firms keep nominal wages and prices constant, while other firms choose these variables optimally. In this model, a cut in the money supply causes a first-order change in employment, output, and profits. But the behavior of nonmaximizers is near rational in the sense that the potential gain any individual firm could experience by abandoning rule of thumb behavior is second-order small. And thus the efficiency-wage hypothesis can be extended into a full-fledged Keynesian model of the business cycle generated by sticky prices and wages.

IV Concluding remarks

It has been widely observed that the existence of excess labor supply does not lead to aggressive wage cutting by workers and firms. Firms appear content to pay workers more than the wages required by their potential replacements. The models surveyed here offer several different and plausible explanations of this seemingly paradoxical fact. In addition to accounting for the persistence of involuntary unemployment in competitive markets, these efficiency wage models can explain why unemployment varies in response to aggregate demand shocks. In sum, these models provide a new, consistent, and plausible microfoundation for a Keynesian model of the cycle.

Notes

1. University of California, Berkeley, CA 94720. I am indebted to George Akerlof, David Estenson, Michael Reich and James Wilcox for invaluable discussion and comments.
2. For a previous survey of portions of this literature, see Guillermo Calvo (1979).

References

Akerlof, George, "Labor Contracts as Partial Gift Exchange," *Quarterly Journal of Economics*, November 1982, 97, pp. 543–69.
Akerlof, G., "Gift Exchange and Efficiency Wage Theory: Four Views," *American Economic Review Proceedings*, May 1984, 74, pp. 79–83.
Akerlof, G. and Yellen, Janet, "The Macroeconomic Consequences of Near Rational, Rule of Thumb Behavior," mimeo., University of California-Berkeley, September 1983.
Bhattacharya, Sudipto, "Tournaments and Incentives: Heterogeneity and Essentiality," mimeo., Stanford University, March 1983.
Bowles, Samuel, "Competitive Wage Determination and Involuntary Unemployment: A Conflict Model," mimeo., University of Massachusetts, May 1981.
Bowles, Samuel, "The Production Process in a Competitive Economy: Walrasian, Neo-Hobbesian and Marxian Models," mimeo., University of Massachusetts, May 1983.
Calvo, Guillermo, "Quasi-Walrasian Theories of Unemployment," *American Economic Review Proceedings*, May 1979, 69, 102–7.
Calvo, Guillermo and Wellisz Stanislaw, (1979), "Hierarchy, Ability and Income Distribution," *Journal of Political Economy*, October 1979, 87, 991–1010.
Eaton, B. Curtis and White William, "Agent Compensation and the Limits of Bonding," *Economic Inquiry*, July 1982, 20, 330–43.
Gintis, Herbert and Ishikawa, Tsuneo, "Wages, Work Discipline and Macroeconomic Equilibrium," mimeo., 1983.
Hall, Robert "The Rigidity of Wages and the Persistence of Unemployment," *Brookings Papers on Economic Activity*, 2: 1975, 301–35.
Lazear, Edward, "Agency, Earnings Profiles, Productivity, and Hours Restrictions," *American Economic Review*, September 1981, 71, 606–20.
Malcolmson, James, "Unemployment and the Efficiency Wage Hypothesis," *Economic Journal*; December 1980, 91, 848–66.
Miyazaki, Hajime, "Work Norms and Involuntary Unemployment," *Quarterly Journal of Economics*, forthcoming.
Salop, Steven, "A Model of the Natural Rate of Unemployment," *American Economic Review*, March 1979, 69, 117–25.
Schlicht, Ekkehart, "Labour Turnover, Wage Structure and Natural Unemployment," *Zeitschrift für die Gesamte Staatswissenschaft*, June 1978, 134, 337–46.
Shapiro, Carl and Stiglitz, Joseph, "Equilibrium Unemployment as a Worker Discipline Device," mimeo., Princeton University, April 1982.
Solow, R., "Another Possible Source of Wage Stickiness," *Journal of Macroeconomics*, Winter 1979, 1, 79–82.
Solow, R., "On Theories of Unemployment," *American Economic Review*, March 1980, 70, 1–11.
Stiglitz, J., "Wage Determination and Unemployment in L.D.C.'s: The Labor Turnover Model," *Quarterly Journal of Economics*, May 1974, 88, 194–227.

Stiglitz, J., "The Efficiency Wage Hypothesis, Surplus Labour, and the Distribution of Income in L.D.C.s," *Oxford Economic Papers*, July 1976a, *28*, 185–207.

Stiglitz, J., "Prices and Queues as Screening Devices in Competitive Markets," IMSSS Technical Report No. 212, Stanford University, August 1976b.

Stoft, Steven, "Cheat-Threat Theory: An Explanation of Involuntary Unemployment," mimeo., Boston University, May 1982.

Weiss, Andrew, "Job Queues and Layoffs in Labor Markets with Flexible Wages," *Journal of Political Economy*, June 1980, *88*, 526–38.

Weisskopf, Thomas, Bowles, Samuel and Gordon, David, "Hearts and Minds: A Social Model of Aggregate Productivity Growth in the U.S. 1948–1979," *Brookings Papers on Economic Activity* 1984.

PART VII

THE BUSINESS CYCLE

CHAPTER 15

*The State of Long-Term Expectation**

J. M. KEYNES

I

We have seen in the previous chapter that the scale of investment depends on the relation between the rate of interest and the schedule of the marginal efficiency of capital corresponding to different scales of current investment, whilst the marginal efficiency of capital depends on the relation between the supply price of a capital-asset and its prospective yield. In this chapter we shall consider in more detail some of the factors which determine the prospective yield of an asset.

The considerations upon which expectations of prospective yields are based are partly existing facts which we can assume to be known more or less for certain, and partly future events which can only be forecasted with more or less confidence. Amongst the first may be mentioned the existing stock of various types of capital-assets and of capital-assets in general and the strength of the existing consumers' demand for goods which require for their efficient production a relatively larger assistance from capital. Amongst the latter are future changes in the type and quantity of the stock of capital-assets and in the tastes of the consumer, the strength of effective demand from time to time during the life of the investment under consideration, and the changes in the wage-unit in terms of money which may occur during its life. We may sum up the state of psychological expectation which covers the latter as being the *state of long-term expectation* – as distinguished from the short-term

---

*Chapter 12 in *The General Theory of Employment, Interest and Money* (1936), pp. 147–64.

expectation upon the basis of which a producer estimates what he will get for a product when it is finished if he decides to begin producing it today with the existing plant, which we examined in Chapter 5 [of *The General Theory* (eds)].

II

It would be foolish, in forming our expectations, to attach great weight to matters which are very uncertain.[1] It is reasonable, therefore, to be guided to a considerable degree by the facts about which we feel somewhat confident, even though they may be less decisively relevant to the issue than other facts about which our knowledge is vague and scanty. For this reason the facts of the existing situation enter, in a sense disproportionately, into the formation of our long-term expectations; our usual practice being to take the existing situation and to project it into the future, modified only to the extent that we have more or less definite reasons for expecting a change.

The state of long-term expectation, upon which our decisions are based, does not solely depend, therefore, on the most probable forecast we can make. It also depends on the *confidence* with which we make this forecast – on how highly we rate the likelihood of our best forecast turning out quite wrong. If we expect large changes but are very uncertain as to what precise form these changes will take, then our confidence will be weak.

The *state of confidence*, as they term it, is a matter to which practical men always pay the closest and most anxious attention. But economists have not analysed it carefully and have been content, as a rule, to discuss it in general terms. In particular it has not been made clear that its relevance to economic problems comes in through its important influence on the schedule of the marginal efficiency of capital. There are not two separate factors affecting the rate of investment, namely, the schedule of the marginal efficiency of capital and the state of confidence. The state of confidence is relevant because it is one of the major factors determining the former, which is the same thing as the investment demand-schedule.

There is, however, not much to be said about the state of confidence *a priori*. Our conclusions must mainly depend upon the actual observation of markets and business psychology. This is the reason why the ensuing digression on a different level of abstraction from most of this book.

For convenience of exposition we shall assume in the following discussion of the state of confidence that there are no changes in the rate of interest; and we shall write, throughout the following sections, as if changes in the values of investments were solely due to changes in the expectation of their prospective yields and not at all to changes in the rate of interest at which these prospective yields are capitalized. The effect of changes in the rate of interest is, however, easily superimposed on the effect of changes in the state of confidence.

III

The outstanding fact is the extreme precariousness of the basis of knowledge on which our estimates of prospective yield have to be made. Our knowledge of the factors which will govern the yield of an investment some years hence is usually very slight and often negligible. If we speak frankly, we have to admit that our basis of knowledge for estimating the yield ten years hence of a railway, a copper mine, a textile factory, the goodwill of a patent medicine, an Atlantic liner, a building in the City of London amounts to little and sometimes to nothing; or even five years hence. In fact, those who seriously attempt to make any such estimate are often so much in the minority that their behaviour does not govern the market.

In former times, when enterprises were mainly owned by those who undertook them or by their friends and associates, investment depended on a sufficient supply of individuals of sanguine temperament and constructive impulses who embarked on business as a way of life, not really relying on a precise calculation of prospective profit. The affair was partly a lottery, though with the ultimate result largely governed by whether the abilities and character of the managers were above or below the average. Some would fail and some would succeed. But even after the event no one would know whether the average results in terms of the sums invested had exceeded, equalled or fallen short of the prevailing rate of interest; though, if we exclude the exploitation of natural resources and monopolies, it is probable that the actual average results of investments, even during periods of progress and prosperity, have disappointed the hopes which prompted them. Business men play a mixed game of skill and chance, the average results of which to the players are not known by those who take a hand. If human nature felt no temptation to take a chance, no satisfaction (profit apart) in constructing a factory, a railway, a mine or a farm, there might not be much investment merely as a result of cold calculation.

Decisions to invest in private business of the old-fashioned type were, however, decisions largely irrevocable, not only for the community as a whole, but also for the individual. With the separation between ownership and management which prevails to-day and with the development of organised investment markets, a new factor of great importance has entered in, which sometimes facilitates investment but sometimes adds greatly to the instability of the system. In the absence of security markets, there is no object in frequently attempting to revalue an investment to which we are committed. But the Stock Exchange revalues many investments every day and the revaluations give a frequent opportunity to the individual (though not to the community as a whole) to revise his commitments. It is as though a farmer, having tapped his barometer after breakfast, could decide to remove his capital from the farming business between 10 and 11 in the morning and reconsider whether he should return to it later in the week. But the daily revaluations of the Stock Exchange, though they are primarily made to facilitate transfers of old investments between one individual and another, inevitably exert a decisive influence on the rate of current investment. For there is no sense in building up a new enterprise at a cost greater than that at which a similar existing enterprise can be purchased; whilst there is an inducement to spend on a new project what may seem an extravagant sum, if it can be floated off on the Stock Exchange at an immediate profit.[2] Thus certain classes of investment are governed by the average expectation of those who deal on the Stock Exchange as revealed in the price of shares, rather than by the genuine expectations of the professional entrepreneur.[3] How then are these highly significant daily, even hourly, revaluations of existing investments carried out in practice?

IV

In practice we have tacitly agreed, as a rule, to fall back on what is, in truth, a *convention*. The essence of this convention – though it does not, of course, work out quite so simply – lies in assuming that the existing state of affairs will continue indefinitely, except in so far as we have specific reasons to expect a change. This does not mean that we really believe that the existing state of affairs will continue indefinitely. We know from extensive experience that this is most unlikely. The actual results of an investment over a long term of years very seldom agree with the initial expectation. Nor can we rationalise our behaviour by arguing that to a man in a state of ignorance errors in either direction are equally probable, so that there remains a mean actuarial expectation based on equi-probabilities. For it can easily be shown that the assumption of arithmetically equal probabilities based on a state of ignorance leads to absurdities. We are assuming, in effect, that the existing market valuation, however arrived at, is uniquely *correct* in relation to our existing knowledge of the facts which will influence the yield of the investment, and that it will only change in proportion to changes in this knowledge; though, philosophically speaking, it cannot be uniquely correct, since our existing knowledge does not provide a sufficient basis for a calculated mathematical expectation. In point of fact, all sorts of considerations enter into the market valuation which are in no way relevant to the prospective yield.

Nevertheless the above conventional method of calculation will be compatible with a considerable measure of continuity and stability in our affairs, *so long as we can rely on the maintenance of the convention.*

For if there exist organised investment markets and if we can rely on the maintenance of the convention, an investor can legitimately encourage himself with the idea that the only risk he runs is that of a genuine change in the news *over the near future,* as to the likelihood of which he can attempt to form his own judgement, and which is unlikely to be very large. For, assuming that the convention holds good, it is only these changes which can affect the value of his investment, and he need not lose his sleep merely because he has not any notion what his investment will be worth ten years hence. Thus investment becomes reasonably "safe"; for the individual investor over short periods, and hence over a succession of short periods however many, if he can fairly rely on there being no breakdown in the convention and on his therefore having an opportunity to revise his judgment and change his investment, before there has been time for much to happen. Investments which are "fixed" for the community are thus made "liquid" for the individual.

It has been, I am sure, on the basis of some such procedure as this that our leading investment markets have been developed. But it is not surprising that a convention, in an absolute view of things so arbitrary, should have its weak points. It is its precariousness which creates no small part of our contemporary problem of securing sufficient investment.

V

Some of the factors which accentuate this precariousness may be briefly mentioned.

(1) As a result of the gradual increase in the proportion of the equity in the community's aggregate capital investment which is owned by persons who do not manage and have no special knowledge of the circumstances, either actual or prospective, of the business in question, the element of real knowledge in the valuation of investments by those who own them or contemplate purchasing them has seriously declined.

(2) Day-to-day fluctuations in the profits of existing investments, which are obviously of an ephemeral and non-significant character, tend to have an altogether excessive, and even an absurd, influence on the market. It is said, for example, that the shares of American companies which manufacture ice tend to sell at a higher price in summer when

their profits are seasonally high than in winter when no one wants ice. The recurrence of a bank-holiday may raise the market valuation of the British railway system by several million pounds.

(3) A conventional valuation which is established as the outcome of the mass psychology of a large number of ignorant individuals is liable to change violently as the result of a sudden fluctuation of opinion due to factors which do not really make much difference to the prospective yield; since there will be no strong roots of conviction to hold it steady. In abnormal times in particular, when the hypothesis of an indefinite continuance of the existing state of affairs is less plausible than usual even though there are no express grounds to anticipate a definite change, the market will be subject to waves of optimistic and pessimistic sentiment, which are unreasoning and yet in a sense legitimate where no solid basis exists for a reasonable calculation.

(4) But there is one feature in particular which deserves our attention. It might have been supposed that competition between expert professionals, possessing judgment and knowledge beyond that of the average private investor, would correct the vagaries of the ignorant individual left to himself. It happens, however, that the energies and skill of the professional investor and speculator are mainly occupied otherwise. For most of these persons are, in fact, largely concerned, not with making superior long-term forecasts of the probable yield of an investment over its whole life, but with foreseeing changes in the conventional basis of valuation a short time ahead of the general public. They are concerned, not with what an investment is really worth to a man who buys it "for keeps", but with what the market will value it at, under the influence of mass psychology, three months or a year hence. Moreover, this behaviour is not the outcome of a wrong-headed propensity. It is an inevitable result of an investment market organised along the lines described. For it is not sensible to pay 25 for an investment of which you believe the prospective yield to justify a value of 30, if you also believe that the market will value it at 20 three months hence.

Thus the professional investor is forced to concern himself with the anticipation of impending changes, in the news or in the atmosphere, of the kind by which experience shows that the mass psychology of the market is most influenced. This is the inevitable result of investment markets organised with a view to so-called "liquidity". Of the maxims of orthodox finance none, surely, is more anti-social than the fetish of liquidity, the doctrine that it is a positive virtue on the part of investment institutions to concentrate their resources upon the holding of "liquid" securities. It forgets that there is no such thing as liquidity of investment for the community as a whole. The social object of skilled investment should be to defeat the dark forces of time and ignorance which envelop our future. The actual, private object of the most skilled investment today is "to beat the gun", as the Americans so well express it, to outwit the crowd, and to pass the bad, or depreciating, half-crown to the other fellow.

This battle of wits to anticipate the basis of conventional valuation a few months hence, rather than the prospective yield of an investment over a long term of years, does not even require gulls amongst the public to feed the maws of the professional – it can be played by professionals amongst themselves. Nor is it necessary that anyone should keep his simple faith in the conventional basis of valuation having any genuine long-term validity. For it is, so to speak, a game of Snap, of Old Maid, of Musical Chairs – a pastime in which he is victor who says *Snap* neither too soon nor too late, who passes the Old Maid to his neighbour before the game is over, who secures a chair for himself when the music stops. These games can be played with zest and enjoyment,, though all the players know that it is the Old Maid which is circulating, or that when the music stops some of the players will find themselves unseated.

Or, to change the metaphor slightly, professional investment may be likened to those newspaper competitions in which the competitors have to pick out the six prettiest faces from a hundred photographs, the prize being awarded to the competitor whose choice most nearly corresponds to the average preferences of the competitors as whole; so that each competitor has to pick, not those faces which he himself finds prettiest, but those which he thinks likeliest to catch the fancy of the other competitors, all of whom are looking at the problem from the same point of view. It is not a case of choosing those which, to the best of one's judgment, are really the prettiest, nor even those which average opinion genuinely thinks the prettiest. We have reached the third degree where we devote our intelligences to anticipating what average opinion expects the average opinion to be. And there are some, I believe, who practise the fourth, fifth and higher degrees.

If the reader interjects that there must surely be large profits to be gained from the other players in the long run by a skilled individual who, unperturbed by the prevailing pastime, continues to purchase investments on the best genuine long-term expectations he can frame, he must be answered, first of all, that there are, indeed, such serious-minded individuals and that it makes a vast difference to an investment market whether or not they predominate in their influence over the game-players. But we must also add that there are several factors which jeopardise the predominance of such individuals in modern investment markets. Investment based on genuine long-term expectation is so difficult to-day as to be scarcely practicable. He who attempts it must surely lead much more laborious days and run greater risks than he who tries to guess better than the crowd how the crowd will behave; and, given equal intelligence, he may make more disastrous mistakes.

There is no clear evidence from experience that the investment policy which is socially advantageous coincides with that which is most profitable. It needs *more* intelligence to defeat the forces of time and our ignorance of the future than to beat the gun. Moreover, life is not long enough – human nature desires quick results, there is a peculiar zest in making money quickly, and remoter gains are discounted by the average man at a very high rate. The game of professional investment is intolerably boring and overexacting to anyone who is entirely exempt from the gambling instinct; whilst he who has it must pay to this propensity the appropriate toll. Furthermore, an investor who proposes to ignore near-term market fluctuations needs greater resources for safety and must not operate on so large a scale, if at all, with borrowed money – a further reason for the higher return from the pastime to a given stock of intelligence and resources. Finally it is the long-term investor, he who most promotes the public interest, who will in practice come in for most criticism, wherever investment funds are managed by committees or boards or banks.[4] For it is in the essence of his behaviour that he should be eccentric, unconventional and rash in the eyes of average opinion. If he is successful, that will only confirm the general belief in his rashness; and if in the short run he is unsuccessful, which is very likely, he will not receive much mercy. Worldly wisdom teaches that it is better for reputation to fail conventionally than to succeed unconventionally.

(5) So far we have had chiefly in mind the state of confidence of the speculator or speculative investor himself and may have seemed to be tacitly assuming that, if he himself is satisfied with the prospects, he has unlimited command over money at the market rate of interest. This is, of course, not the case. Thus we must also take account of the other facet of the state of confidence, namely, the confidence of the lending institutions towards those who seek to borrow from them, sometimes described as the state of credit. A collapse in the price of equities, which has had disastrous reactions on the marginal efficiency of capital, may have been due to the weakening either of speculative confidence or of the state of credit. But whereas the weakening of either is enough to cause a collapse, recovery requires the revival of *both*. For whilst the weakening of credit is sufficient to bring about a collapse, its strengthening, though a necessary condition of recovering, is not a sufficient condition.

VI

These considerations should not lie beyond the purview of the economist. But they must be relegated to their right perspective. If I may be allowed to appropriate the term *speculation* for the activity of forecasting the psychology of the market, and the term *enterprise* for the activity of forecasting the prospective yield of assets over their whole life, it is by no means always the case that speculation predominates over enterprise. As the organisation of investment markets improves, the risk of the predominance of speculation does, however, increase. In one of the greatest investment markets in the world, namely, New York, the influence of speculation (in the above sense) is enormous. Even outside the field of finance, Americans are apt to be unduly interested in discovering what average opinion believes average opinion to be; and this national weakness finds its nemesis in the stock market. It is rare, one is told, for an American to invest, as many Englishmen still do, "for income"; and he will not readily purchase an investment except in the hope of capital appreciation. This is only another way of saying that, when he purchases an investment, the American is attaching his hopes, not so much to its prospective yield, as to a favourable change in the conventional basis of valuation, i.e., that he is, in the above sense, a speculator. Speculators may do no harm as bubbles on a steady stream of enterprise. But the position is serious when enterprise becomes the bubble on a whirlpool of speculation. When the capital development of a country becomes a by-product of the activities of a casino, the job is likely to be ill-done. The measure of success attained by Wall Street, regarded as an institution of which the proper social purpose is to direct new investment into the most profitable channels in terms of future yield, cannot be claimed as one of the outstanding triumphs of *laissez-faire* capitalism – which is not surprising, if I am right in thinking that the best brains of Wall Street have been in fact directed towards a different object.

These tendencies are scarcely avoidable outcome of our having successfully organised "liquid" investment markets. It is usually agreed that casinos should, in the public interest, be inaccessible and expensive. And perhaps the same is true of Stock Exchanges. That the sins of the London Stock Exchange are less than those of Wall Street may be due, not so much to differences in national character, as to the fact that to the average Englishman Throgmorton Street is, compared with Wall Street to the average American, inaccessible and very expensive. The jobber's "turn", the high brokerage charges and the heavy transfer tax payable to the Exchequer, which attend dealings on the London Stock Exchange, sufficiently diminish the liquidity of the market (although the practice of fortnightly accounts operates the other way) to rule out a large proportion of the transactions characteristic of Wall Street.[5] The introduction of a substantial Government transfer tax on all transactions might prove the most serviceable reform available, with a view to mitigating the predominance of speculation over enterprise in the United States.

The spectacle of modern investment markets has sometimes moved me towards the conclusion that to make the purchase of an investment permanent and indissoluble, like marriage, except by reason of death or other grave cause, might be a useful remedy for our contemporary evils. For this would force the investor to direct his mind to the long-term prospects and to those only. But a little consideration of this expedient bring us up against a dilemma, and shows us how the liquidity of investment markets often facilitates, though it sometimes impedes, the course of new investment. For the fact that each individual investor flatters himself that his commitment is "liquid" (though this cannot be true for all investors collectively) calms his nerves and makes him much more willing to run a risk. If individual purchases of investments were rendered illiquid, this might seriously impede new investment, so long as *alternative ways* in which to hold his savings are available to the individual. This is the dilemma. So long as it is open to the individual to employ his wealth in hoarding or lending *money*, the alternative of purchasing actual capital assets cannot be rendered sufficiently attractive (especially to the man who does not manage the capital assets and knows very little about them), except by organising markets wherein these assets can be easily realized for money.

The only radical cure for the crises of confidence which afflict the economic life of the modern world would be allow the individual no choice between consuming his income and ordering the production of the specific capital-asset which, even though it be on precarious evidence, impresses him as the most promising investment available to him. It might be that, at times when he was more than usually assailed by doubts concerning the future, he would turn in his perplexity towards more consumption and less new investment. But that would avoid the disastrous, cumulative and far-reaching repercussions of its being open to him, when thus assailed by doubts, to spend his income neither on the one nor on the other.

Those who have emphasised the social dangers of the hoarding of money have, of course, had something similar to the above in mind. But they have overlooked the possibility that the phenomenon can occur without any change, or at least any commensurate change, in the hoarding of money.

VII

Even apart from the instability due to speculation, there is the instability due to the characteristic of human nature that a large proportion of our positive activities depend on spontaneous optimism rather than on a mathematical expectation, whether moral or hedonistic or economic. Most, probably, of our decisions to do something positive, the full consequences of which will be drawn out over many days to come, can only be taken as a result of animal spirits – of a spontaneous urge to action rather than inaction, and not as the outcome of a weighted average of quantitative benefits multiplied by quantitative probabilities. Enterprise only pretends to itself to be mainly actuated by the statements in it own prospectus, however candid and sincere. Only a little more than an expedition to the South Pole, is it based on an exact calculation of benefit to come. Thus if the animal spirits are dimmed and the spontaneous optimism falters, leaving us to depend on nothing but a mathematical expectation, enterprise will fade and die – though fears of loss may have a basis no more reasonable than hope of profit had before.

It is safe to say that enterprise which depends on hopes stretching into the future benefits the community as a whole. But individual initiative will only be adequate when reasonable calculation supplemented and supported by animal spirits, so that the thought of ultimate loss which often overtakes pioneers, as experience undoubtedly tells us and them, is put aside as a healthy man puts aside the expectation of death.

This means, unfortunately, not only that slumps and depressions are exaggerated in degree, but that economic prosperity is excessively dependent on a political and social atmosphere which is congenial to the average business man. If the fear of a Labour Government or a New Deal depresses enterprise, this need not be the result either of a reasonable calculation or of a plot with political intent – it is the mere consequence of upsetting the delicate balance of spontaneous optimism. In estimating the prospects of investment, we must have regard, therefore, to the nerves and hysteria and even the digestion and reactions to the weather of those upon whose spontaneous activity it largely depends.

We should not conclude from this that everything depends on waves of irrational psychology. On the contrary, the state of long-term expectation is often steady, and, even when it is not, the other factors exert their compensating effects We are merely remaining ourselves that human decisions affecting the future whether personal or political or economic, cannot depend on strict mathematical expectation, since the basis for making such calculations does not exist; and that it is our innate urge to activity which makes the wheels go round, our rational selves choosing between the alternative as best we are able, calculating where we can, but often failing back for our motive on whim or sentiment or chance.

VIII

There are, moreover, certain important factors which somewhat mitigate in practice the effects of our ignorance of the future. Owing to the operation of compound interest combined with the likelihood of obsolescence with the passage of time, there are many individual investments of which the prospective yield is legitimately dominated by the returns of the comparatively near future. In the case of the most important class of very long-term investments, namely buildings, the risk can be frequently transferred from the investor to the occupier, or at least shared between them, by means of long-term contracts, the risk being outweighed in the mind of the occupier by the advantages of continuity and security of tenure. In the case of another important class of long-term investments, namely public utilities, a substantial proportion of the prospective yield is practically guaranteed by monopoly privileges coupled with the right to charge such rates as will provide a certain stipulated margin. Finally there is a growing class of investment entered upon by, or at the risk of, public authorities, which are frankly influenced in making the investment by a general presumption of there being prospective social advantages from the investment, whatever its commercial yield may prove to be within a wide range, and without seeking to be satisfied that the mathematical expectation of the yield is at least equal to the current rate of interest – though the rate which the public authority has to pay may still play a decisive part in determining the scale of investment operations which it can afford.

Thus after giving full weight to the importance of the influence of short-period changes in the state of long-term expectation as distinct from changes in the rate of interest, we are still entitled to return to the latter as exercising, at any rate, in normal circumstances, a great, though not a decisive, influence on the rate of investment. Only experience, however, can show how far management of the rate of interest is capable of continuously stimulating the appropriate volume of investment.

For my own part I am now somewhat sceptical of the success of a merely monetary policy directed towards influencing the rate of interest. I expect to see the State, which is in a position to calculate the marginal efficiency of capital-goods on long views and on the basis of the general social advantage, taking an ever greater responsibility for directly organising investment; since it seems likely that the fluctuations in the market estimation of the marginal efficiency of different types of capital, calculated on the principles I have described above, will be too great to be offset by any practicable changes in the rate of interest.

Notes

1. By "very uncertain" I do not mean the same thing as "very improbable". *Cf.* my *Treatise on Probability*, chap. 6, on "The Weight of Arguments".
2. In my *Treatise on Money* (vol. ii, p. 195) I pointed out the when a company's shares are quoted very high so that it can raise more capital by issuing more shares on favourable terms, this has the same effect as if it could borrow at a low rate of interest. I should now describe this by saying that a high quotation

for existing equities involves an increase in the marginal efficiency of the corresponding type of capital and therefore has the same effect (since investment depends on a comparison between the marginal efficiency of capital and the rate of interest) as a fall in the rate of interest.
3. This does not apply, of course, to classes of enterprise which are not readily marketable or to which no negotiable instrument closely corresponds. The categories falling within this exception were formerly extensive. But measured as a proportion of the total value of new investment they are rapidly declining in importance.
4. The practice, usually considered prudent, by which an investment trust or an insurance office frequently calculates not only the income from its investment portfolio but also its capital valuation in the market, may also tend to direct too much attention to short-term fluctuations in the latter.
5. It is said that, when Wall Street is active, at least a half of the purchases or sales of investments are entered upon with an intention on the part of the speculator to reverse them *the same day*. This is often true of the commodity exchanges also.

CHAPTER 16

*Understanding Business Cycles**[1]

R. E. LUCAS, JR.

I

Why is it that, in capitalist economies, aggregate variables undergo repeated fluctuations about trend, all of essentially the same character? Prior to Keynes' *General Theory*, the resolution of this question was regarded as one of the main outstanding challenges to economic research, and attempts to meet this challenge were called *business cycle theory*. Moreover, among the interwar business cycle theorists, there was wide agreement as to what it would mean to solve this problem. To cite Hayek, as a leading example:

> [T]he incorporation of cyclical phenomena into the system of economic equilibrium theory, with which they are in apparent contradiction, remains the crucial problem of Trade Cycle Theory;[2]
>
> By 'equilibrium theory' we here primarily understand the modern theory of the general interdependence of all economic quantities, which has been most perfectly expressed by the Lausanne School of theoretical economics.[3]

A primary consequence of the Keynesian Revolution was the redirection of research effort away from this question onto the apparently simpler question of the determination of output at a point in time, taking history as given.[4] A secondary consequence of this Revolution, due more to Tinbergen than to Keynes, was a rapid increase in the level of precision and explicitness with which aggregate economic theories were formulated. As a result, Keynesian macro-economics has benefited from

---

*In K. Brunner and A. Meltzer (eds), *Stabilization of The Domestic International Economy*, Vol. 5 (1977), pp. 7–29.

several decades of methodological improvement whereas, from this technical point of view, the efforts of the business cycle theorists appear hopelessly outdated.

Yet from another point of view, they seem quite modern. The observation that macroeconomics is in need of a microeconomic foundation has become commonplace, and though there is much confusion about the nature of this need and about what it would mean to satisfy it, it is likely that many modern economists would have no difficulty accepting Hayek's statement of the problem as roughly equivalent to their own. Whether or not this is so, I wish in this essay to argue that it *should* be so, or that the most rapid progress toward a coherent and useful aggregate economic theory will result from the acceptance of the problem statement as advanced by the business cycle theorists, and not from further attempts to refine the jerry-built structures to which Keynesian macroeconomics has led us.

Honoring one's intellectual ancestors is a worthwhile aim in itself, but there is a more immediate reason for interpreting the contemporary search for a theoretically sound aggregative economics as a resumption of the work of pre-Keynesian theorists. Accompanying the redirection of scientific interest occasioned by the Keynesian Revolution was a sharp change in the nature of the contribution to policy which economists hoped to offer and which the public has come largely to accept. The effort to "explain business cycles" had been directed at identifying institutional sources of instability, with the hope that, once understood, these sources could be removed or their influence mitigated by appropriate institutional changes. The process envisaged was the painfully slow one of public discussion and legislative reform; on the other side, there was the hope of long-term or "permanent" institutional improvement. The abandonment of the effort to explain business cycles accompanied a belief that policy could effect immediate, or very short-term, movement of the economy from an undesirable current state, *however arrived at*, to a better state.

The belief that this latter objective is attainable, and that the attempt to come closer to achieving it is the only legitimate task of research in aggregate economics is so widespread that argument to the contrary is viewed as "destructive," a willful attempt to make life more difficult for one's colleagues who are only trying to improve the lot of mankind. Yet the situation is symmetric. If the business cycle theorists were correct, the short-term manipulation on which much of aggregative economics is now focused only diverts attention from discussion of stabilization policies which might actually be effective; such postponement is, moreover, accompanied by the steady and entirely understandable erosion in the belief on the part of noneconomists that aggregative economics has anything useful to say.

In the next section, I will review some of the main qualitative features of the events we call business cycles, and then turn to the Keynesian response to these facts, to the progress made along the line Keynes and Tinbergen initiated, and finally to the severe limits to this progress which have now become apparent. The remainder of the essay will consider the prospects of accounting for cyclical phenomena by an *economic* theory, in the narrow sense in which Hayek and other business cycle theorists have used that term.

II

Let me begin to sharpen the discussion by reviewing the main qualitative features of economic time series which we call "the business cycle." Technically, movements about trend in gross national product in any country can be well described by a stochastically disturbed difference equation of very low order. These movements do not exhibit uniformity of either period or amplitude, which is to say, they do not resemble the deterministic wave motions which sometimes arise in the natural sciences. Those regularities which are observed are in the *co-movements* among different aggregative time series.

The principal among these are the following.[5] (i) Output movements across broadly defined sectors move together. (In Mitchell's terminology, they exhibit high *conformity*: in modern time series language, they have high *coherence*.) (ii) Production of producer and consumer durables exhibits much greater amplitude than does the production of nondurables. (iii) Production and prices of agricultural goods and natural resources have lower than average conformity. (iv) Business profits show high conformity and much greater amplitude than other series. (v) Prices generally are procyclical. (vi) Short-term interest rates are procyclical; long-term rates slightly so. (vii) Monetary aggregates and velocity measures are procyclical.

There is, as far as I know, no need to qualify these observations by restricting them to particular countries or time periods: they appear to be regularities common to all decentralized market economies. Though there is absolutely no theoretical reason to anticipate it, one is led by the facts to conclude that, with respect to the qualitative behavior of co-movements among series, *business cycles are all alike*. To theoretically inclined economists, this conclusion should be attractive and challenging, for it suggests the possibility of a unified explanation of business cycles, grounded in the *general* laws governing market economies, rather than in political or institutional characteristics specific to particular countries or periods.

I have omitted the behavior of foreign trade statistics from the above catalogue of phenomena-to-be-explained, in part because, for a large economy like the U.S. trade statistics do not exhibit high enough conformity to be cyclically interesting. For a smaller country, to be sure, export movements would do much to "explain" cycles, but to focus on open-economy explanations would, I think, beg the more difficult and crucial question of the ultimate origins of cyclical movements.

Also omitted, but too striking a phenomenon to pass over without comment, is the general reduction in amplitude of *all* series in the twenty-five years following World War II. At this purely descriptive level, it is impossible to distinguish good luck from good policy. Nevertheless, so long a period of relative stability strongly suggests that there is nothing inherent in the workings of market economies which requires living with the level of instability we are now experiencing, or to which we were subject in the pre-World War II years. That is, attempts to document and account for regular cyclical movements need not be connected in any way to a presumption that such movements are an *inevitable* feature of capitalist economies.

III

The implications of Keynesian macroeconomic models conform well to the time series features reviewed above. Early versions (for example, by Hicks, 1937, and Modigliani, 1944) fit well qualitatively: the econometric models which developed from this theory and from Tinbergen's largely independent early work[6] conform well quantitatively. These models located the primary disturbances in investment behavior, linked via lags (in Tinbergen's U.S. model) to the highly volatile profit series. Movements in these high-amplitude series then induce general movements in output and employment. Since these disturbances were, in Hicks' terms, "IS shifts," they were consistent with procyclically moving interest rates and velocity. The assumption of rigid wages and prices was a good empirical first approximation. Later on, a wage-price sector (still later called a Phillips curve) was added to fit observed procyclical wage and price movement.[7]

In this description, movements in money play no important role in accounting for cycles. This feature certainly did not result directly from the theoretical models: Keynes, Hicks, and Modigliani all gave great emphasis to monetary forces. The de-emphasis on money was on empirical grounds: econometricians from Tinbergen on discovered that monetary factors did not seem very important empirically.[8]

The empirical success of these developments was measured in an original and historically apt way by Adelman and Adelman (1959) in their simulation of the Klein–Goldberger model of the U.S. economy. The Adelmans posed, in a precise way, the question of whether an observer armed with the methods of Burns and Mitchell (1946) could distinguish between a collection of economic series generated artificially by a computer programmed to follow the Klein–Goldberger equations and the analogous series generated by an actual economy. The answer, to the evident surprise of the Adelmans (and, one suspects, of Klein and Goldberger, who had in no way directed their efforts to meeting this criterion) was *no*.[9]

This achievement signaled a new standard for what it means to understand business cycles. One exhibits understanding of business cycles by constructing a *model* in the most literal sense: a fully articulated artificial economy which behaves through time so as to imitate closely the time series behavior of actual economics. The Keynesian macroeconomic models were the first to attain this level of explicitness and empirical accuracy: by doing so, they altered the meaning of the term "theory" to such an extent that the older business cycle theories could not really be viewed as "theories" at all.

These models are not, however, "equilibrium theories" in Hayek's sense. Indeed, Keynes chose to begin the *General Theory* with the declaration (for Chapter II is no more than this) that an equilibrium theory was unattainable: that unemployment was not explainable as a consequence of individual choices and that the failure of wages to move as predicted by the classical theory was to be treated as due to forces beyond the power of economic theory to illuminate.

Keynes wrote as though the "involuntary" nature of unemployment were verifiable by direct observation, as though one could somehow look at a market and verify directly whether it is in equilibrium or not. Nevertheless, there were serious empirical reasons behind this choice, for nowhere is the "apparent contradiction" between "cyclical phenomena" and "economic equilibrium" theory sharper than in labor market behavior. Why, in the face of moderately fluctuating nominal wages and prices, should households *choose* to supply labor at sharply irregular rates through time? Most business cycle theorists had avoided this crucial problem, and those who addressed it had not resolved it. Keynes saw that by simply sidestepping this problem with the unexplained postulate of rigid nominal prices, an otherwise classical model could be transformed into a model which did a fair job of accounting for observed time series.

This decision on the part of the most prestigious theorist of his day freed a generation of economists from the discipline imposed by equilibrium theory, and, as I have described, this freedom was rapidly and fruitfully exploited by macroeconometricians. Now in possession of detailed, quantitatively accurate replicas of the actual economy, economists appeared to have an inexpensive means to evaluate various proposed economic policy measures. It seemed legitimate to treat policy recommendations which emerged from this procedure as though they had been experimentally tested, even if such policies had never been attempted in any actual economy.

Yet the ability of a model to imitate actual behavior in the way tested by the Adelmans (1959) has almost nothing to do with its ability to make accurate *conditional* forecasts, to answer questions of the form: how *would* behavior have differed had certain policies been different in specified ways? This ability requires *invariance* of the structure of the model under policy variations of the type being studied. Invariance of parameters in an economic model is not, of course, a property which can be assured in advance, but it seems reasonable to hope that neither tastes nor technology vary systematically with variations in countercyclical policies. In contrast, agents' *decision rules will* in general change with changes in the environment. An equilibrium model is, by definition, constructed so as to predict how agents with stable tastes and technology will *choose* to respond to a new situation. Any disequilibrium model, constructed by simply codifying the decision rules which agents have found it useful to use over some previous sample period, without explaining *why* these rules were used, will be of no use in predicting the consequences of nontrivial policy changes.

The quantitative importance of this problem is, of course, a matter to be settled by examination of specific relationships in specific models. I have argued elsewhere[10] that it is of fatal importance in virtually all sectors of modern macroeconomic models, primarily because of the faulty treatment of expectations in these models. Rather than review these arguments in detail, let me cite the most graphic illustration: our experience during the recent "stagflation."

As recently as 1970, the major U.S. econometric models implied that expansionary monetary and fiscal policies leading to a sustained inflation of about 4 percent per annum would lead also to sustained unemployment rates of less than 4 percent, or about a full percentage point lower than unemployment has averaged during any long period of U.S. history.[11] These forecasts were widely endorsed by many economists not themselves closely involved in econometric forecasting. Earlier, Friedman (1968) and Phelps (1968) had argued, purely on the basis of the observation that *equilibrium*, behavior is invariant under the units change represented by sustained inflation, that *no* sustained decrease in unemployment would result from sustained inflation. In this instance, the policy experiment in question was most unfortunately, carried out, and its outcome is now too clear to require detailed review.

It is important that the lesson of this episode not be lost. The issue is much deeper than the addition of a few new variables to econometric Phillips curves (though this is the only revision in macroeconomic models which has followed from it), as Friedman made clear in his

Presidential Address. Friedman's argument did not proceed on the basis of a specific aggregative model, with a better "wage-price sector" than the standard models. On the contrary, it was based on a *general* characteristic of economic equilibrium: the zero-degree homogeneity of demand and supply functions. Thus, without using any very specific model, and without claiming the ability to forecast in any detail the initial response of the economy to an inflation, one can, in the case of sustained inflation, reason that, if the unemployment rate prior to the inflation were an equilibrium (or "natural") rate, then the *same* rate will be an equilibrium once the inflation is underway.

The case of sustained inflation is a relatively simple one (though apparently not *too* simple, as it is still highly controversial). For other kinds of policy questions, one would need a more explicit model. How would the variance, and other moments, of real output change if a policy of 4 percent monetary growth were adopted? Under a balanced budget fiscal rule? Under flexible rather than fixed exchange rates? One can generate numerical answers to questions of this sort from current macroeconomic models, but there is no reason for anyone to take these numbers seriously. On the other hand, neither can quantitative answers be obtained by purely theoretical reasoning. To obtain them, one needs an explicit, equilibrium account of the business cycle.

IV

I have summarized, in section II, the main features of the cyclical behavior in quantities and prices. In section III, I have argued the practical necessity of accounting for these facts in equilibrium (that is, non-Keynesian) terms. That is, one would like a theory which accounts for the observed movements in *quantities* (employment, consumption, investment) as an optimizing response to observed movements in *prices*.

In the next section, I will describe the general point of view toward individual decision making to be taken in the remainder of the paper, and will explain, in particular, why the *recurrent* character of business cycles is of central importance. Given this general view, I shall consider in sections VI and VII the way in which *relative* price movements induce fluctuations in employment and investment. Sections VIII, IX, and X examine the conditions under which these same quantity responses may be triggered by movements in general, or nominal, prices. Not surprisingly, the source of general price movements is located, in section XI, in monetary changes.

V

The view of the protoypical individual decision problem taken by modern capital theory is a useful point of departure for considering behavior over the cycle, though it is in some respects highly misleading. An agent begins a period with stocks of various kinds of capital accumulated in the past. He faces *time paths* of prices at which he can trade in the present and future. Based on his preferences over time path of labor supplied and goods consumed, he formulates a plan. Under certainty, he is viewed as simply executing a single plan without revision: with uncertainty, he must draw up a contingency plan, saying how he will react to unforeseeable events.

Even to begin to think about decision problems of this general form, one needs to imagine a fairly precise view of the future in the mind of this agent. Where does he get this view, and how can an observer infer what it is? This aspect of the problem has received rather offhand treatment in traditional capital theory, and no treatment at all in traditional macroeconomics. Since it is absolutely crucial for understanding business cycles, we must pursue it here in some detail.

At a purely formal level, we know that a rational agent must formulate a subjective joint probability distribution over all unknown random variables which impinge on his present and future market opportunities. The link between this subjective view of the future and "reality" is a most complex philosophical question, but the way it is solved has little effect on the structure of the decision problem as seen by an individual agent. In particular, any distinction between *types* of randomness (such as Knight's (1921) distinction between "risk" and "uncertainty") is, at this level, meaningless.

Unfortunately, the general hypothesis that economic agents are Bayesian decision-makers has, in many applications, little empirical content: without some way of inferring what an agent's subjective view of the future is, this hypothesis is of no help in understanding his behavior. Even psychotic behavior can be (and today, is) understood as "rational," given a sufficiently abnormal view of relevant probabilities. To practice economics, we need *some* way (short of psychoanalysis, one hopes) of understanding *which* decision problem agents are solving.

John Muth (1961) proposed to resolve this problem by identifying agents' subjective probabilities with observed frequencies of the events to be forecast, or with "true" probabilities, calling the assumed coincidence of subjective and "true" probabilities *rational expectations*. Evidently, this hypothesis will not be of value in understanding psychotic behavior. Neither will it be applicable in situations in which one cannot guess which, if any, observable frequencies are relevant: situations which Knight[12] called "uncertainty." It will *most* likely be useful in situations in which the probabilities of interest concern a fairly well defined recurrent event, situations of "risk" in Knight's terminology. In situations of risk, the hypothesis of rational behavior on the part of agents will have usable content, so that behavior may be explainable in terms of economic theory. In such situations, expectations are rational in Muth's sense. In cases of uncertainty, economic reasoning will be of no value.

These considerations explain why business cycle theorists emphasized the *recurrent* character of the cycle, and why we must hope they were right in doing so. Insofar as business cycles can be viewed as repeated instances of essentially similar events, it will be reasonable to treat agents as reacting to cyclical changes as "risk," or to assume their expectations are *rational*, that they have fairly stable arrangements for collecting and processing information, and that they utilize this information in forecasting the future in a stable way, free of systematic and easily correctable biases.

VI

In moving from these general considerations to more specific theory, it will be helpful to consider as an example a "representative" agent.[13] Imagine a single worker-producer, confronted each period with a given market price for a good which he then makes to order, at a fixed rate of output per hour. That is, he comes to his place of work, observes his current selling price, determines how many hours to work that day, sells his produce, then goes home to relax.

The good he receives in exchange for the effort is "money"; I shall not be concerned with the historical reasons for this arrangement, but simply take it for granted. This money, in turn, is spent on a wide variety of goods, different from day to day. Some purchases he makes on his way home, in an hour's break from work, or several days later. I assume for now that he holds no other securities. I assume also that this agent lives in a cycle-free world, in which the general or average level of prices does not change, though individual prices fluctuate from day to day.

Now let us postulate an increase of 10 percent in today's selling price, as compared to the average of past prices. How will this hypothetical producer respond? The answer given by economic theory must be: who knows? At this point, I have said nothing which would enable one to imagine what the producer thinks this price movement *means*. If he believes the price change signals a permanent change in his selling price, we know from much evidence that he will work no harder, and probably a little less hard. That is, we know that "long run" (very unfortunate terminology, since the "long-run" response to a permanent price change will be *immediate*) labor supply elasticities are zero or negative.

What if, at the opposite extreme, the price change is transitory (as would be the case if each period's price were an independent drawing from a fixed distribution)? The answer in this case amounts to knowing the rate at which the producer is willing to substitute labor today for labor tomorrow. If 'leisure' is highly substitutable over time, he will work longer on high price days and close early on low price days. Less is known about actual labor supply responses to transitory price movements than about the "long-run" response, but what we do know indicates that leisure in one period is an excellent substitute for leisure in other, nearby periods. Systematic evidence at the aggregate level was obtained by Rapping and myself (1970); Ghez and Becker (1975) reached the same conclusion at a disaggregative level. The small premiums required to induce workers to shift holidays and vacations (take Monday off instead of Saturday, two weeks in March rather than in August) point to the same conclusion, and this "casual" evidence is somewhat more impressive because of its probabilistic simplicity: holidays are *known* to be transitory. On the basis of this evidence, one would predict a *highly elastic* response to transitory price changes.

Before dealing with complications to this example, let us note its promise for business cycle theory, I have described a producer who responds to small price fluctuations with large fluctuations in output and employment: exactly what we observe over the cycle. The description rests on economically intelligible substitution effects, not on unintelligible "disequilibria." Yet let us go slowly: our aggregative observations refer to co-movements of output and prices *generally*: the example refers to *relative* price movements in a stationary environment.

Before facing this difficult issue, let us consider some variations on the example just considered. First, from a descriptive point of view, it often seems more realistic to think of demand information being conveyed to producers by *quantity* changes: new orders, inventory rundowns, and the like. There seems to be no compelling substantive reason to focus exclusively on *prices* as signals of current and future demand. At this verbal level, it seems to me harmless and accurate to use the terms price increase and sales increase interchangeably. Somewhat surprisingly, however, rigorous analysis of equilibrium determination when producers set prices is extremely difficult, and no examples relevant to business cycle behavior exist.

A second variation is easy to carry out. Rather than consider a worker-entrepreneur, one could separate these functions, introduce firms, and consider labor and product markets separately. In the present context, this would introduce a distinction between wages and prices, and raise the issue of risk-allocating arrangements between employers and workers.[14] It would also permit the study of possibly different information sets for firms and workers. None of these questions is without interest, but all are, in my opinion, peripheral for business cycle theory. Observed real wages are not constant over the cycle, but neither do they exhibit consistent pro- or countercyclical tendencies. This suggests that any attempt to assign systematic real wage movements a central role in an explanation of business cycles is doomed to failure. Accordingly, I will proceed as though the real wage were fixed, using the terms "wages" and "prices" interchangeably.

Additional variations can be obtained by distinguishing among various uses of the worker-producer's time when he is not working. Many writers have attempted, for example, to interpret measured unemployment as time engaged in job search. Certainly, if one substitutes away from work one substitutes *into* some other activity, and experience shows that one's belief in the importance of substitution is bolstered by some plausible illustrations. Nevertheless, there is little evidence that much time is spent in job search, that search is less costly when unemployed than when employed, or, for that matter, that measured unemployment measures any *activity* at all. Economically, the important issue is the magnitude of the elasticity of employment with respect to transitory wage and price movements, not the reasons why that elasticity is what it is.

Indeed, I suspect that the unwillingness to speak of workers in recession as enjoying "leisure" is more a testimony to the force of Keynes' insistence that unemployment is "involuntary" than a response to observed phenomena. One doesn't want to suggest that people *like* depressions! Of course, the hypothesis of a cleared labor market carries with it no such suggestion, any more than the observation that people go hungry in cleared food markets suggests that people enjoy hunger.

VII

More complex variations on this example arise when *capital* of various kinds is introduced. Let us do this, retaining still the assumption of stability over time in the general level of prices.

Three possibilities of interest arise. First, suppose that current production can be stored as finished goods inventory. This possibility seems to work *against* the account of price-output co-movements sketched above. The producer will surely produce in low price periods for sale later when price is high, smoothing labor supply relative to the case where storage is precluded. On the industry level, however, this behavior also dampens price movements. The net result is likely to be a reduction in the elasticity of employment-production with respect to price, and an increase in the real sales-price elasticity.

As a second possibility, suppose the producer can use a part of his current production to acquire a machine which will raise his output-per-hour in all future periods. As a third, suppose he can take a course in school which will have the same effect. Since these two possibilities do not differ economically, they may be considered as one. In the example of purely transitory price movements, discussed earlier, it is clear that neither of these options will ever be exercised – provided the producer was satisfied with his original stock of capital. By the time the new capital can be applied to production, the price movement which made it appear profitable will have vanished.

Current relative price movements will have their maximal effect on capital accumulation when, at the opposite extreme, they are regarded as permanent. In this case, however, as I have noted, employment will be insensitive to price movements. Thus, to observe investment and employment moving systematically in the direction of relative price movements, it must be the case that such movements are a *mix* of transitory and permanent elements. In such a situation, the producer will find himself obliged to engage in what engineers call "signal processing": he observes a single variable (price) changing through time: these movements arise from movements in more fundamental variables (the transitory and permanent components of price) which cannot be observed directly: from these observed price movements, together with his knowledge of the relative importance of the two unobserved sources of price change, he imperfectly infers the movement in the two components. Based on his solution to this implied conditional probability calculation, he takes a decision. Not surprisingly, the decision turns out to be an average of the decisions appropriate to the two extremes.

To recapitulate, our hypothetical producer is taken to face stochastic price variability, which is describable as a mix of transitory and permanent components, both unobserved. His optimal response to price movements depends on two factors: the way he interprets the information contained in these changes, and his preferences concerning intertemporal substitution of leisure and consumption. Under assumptions consistent with rational behavior and available evidence, his response to an unforeseen price increase is a sizable increase in labor supplied, a decline in finished goods inventory, and an expansion in productive capital accumulation of all kinds. This behavior is symmetric; the responses to price decreases are the opposite.[15]

VIII

It is time to think of situating this representative producer in an economy comprised of similar agents, though of course producing different goods and subject to different individual price movements. To do this, one must go behind price movements to the changes in technology and taste which underlie them. These changes are occurring all the time and indeed, their importance to individual agents dominates by far the relatively minor movements which constitute the business cycle. Yet these movements should, in general, lead to relative, not general price movements. A new technology, reducing costs of producing an old good or making possible the production of a new one, will draw resources into the good which benefits, and *away from* the production of other goods. Taste shifts in favor of the purchase of one good involve reduced expenditures on others. Moreover, in a complex modern economy, there will be a large number of such shifts in any given period, each small in importance relative to total output. There will be much "averaging out" of such effects across markets.

Cancellation of this sort is, I think, the most important reason why one cannot seek an explanation of the *general* movements we call business cycles is the mere presence, per se, of unpredictability of conditions in individual markets. Yet this argument is not entirely tight. It is surely *possible* for a large number of agents spontaneously to feel an urge to increase their work weeks and expand investments. More seriously, there have been many instances of shocks to supply which affect all, or many, sectors of the economy simultaneously. Such shocks will not cancel in the way I have described, and they will induce output fluctuations in the aggregate. They will not, however, lead to movements which fit the description sketched in section II: all supply shifts will lead to countercyclical price movements (other things being equal) in contrast to the procyclical movements we observe.

It is, then, possible to situate our hypothetical producer in a general equilibrium setting, in which his price and output fluctuate, yet aggregate levels do not. His responses to these *relative* prices movements will mimic the aggregate responses to general price movements which constitute the business cycle. We have then a coherent model, but not one which as yet accounts for the general phenomena to be explained. This model can, without difficulty, be modified to permit general, supply-induced output fluctuations, but these bear no resemblance to the modern business cycle.

Before leaving this world of stable aggregates, it is worth stressing that most of the risk which troubles and challenges economic agents would be present in such a setting. Will consumers take to a novel automobile design, or will it become a national joke? Will a dozen years of training in piano lead to the concert stage, or just a pleasurable hobby? Will this week's overtime wages help finance a child's education, or tide the family over next month's strike? By the time one has acquired the information necessary to resolve questions like these, it is too late: one way or the other, one is committed.

Compared to risks of this nature and magnitude, the question of whether the hours actually worked in the year ahead will be 1.03 times what one plans for now, or .97, seems a minor one, and seems so because it is. In aggregative economic theory, we are accustomed to think of business cycles as a kind of risk imposed on an otherwise stable environment. Such habits of thought reflect the transfer of abstractions useful for some purposes into contexts where they involve fatal distortions of reality.

IX

Let us now drop the assumption of stability in average prices. From the point of view of the individual producer, this involves only a slight change in the nature of the signal processing problem which must be solved. Before, a given movement in his "own price" could mean a permanent relative price change or a transitory one. Now, it can also mean that *all* prices are changing, a situation which, if correctly diagnosed, would lead to no real response on the producer's part. Yet, for the same reason that permanent and transitory relative price movements cannot be sorted out with certainty at the time, neither can relative and general movements be distinguished. General price increases, exactly as with relative price increases, will induce movements in the same direction in employment and investment.

Unlike the responses to taste and technology changes described earlier, these responses to general price increases will not tend to cancel over markets. To be sure, some producers will observe declines in demand even during price expansions, but more will observe increases (this is what a *general* price increase means), and therefore more will be expanding in real terms than will be contracting. The net effect will be co-movements in prices, output, and investment at the aggregate level, just as is observed over the actual cycle.

It is *essential* to this argument that general price movements not be perceived as such as they are occurring. Within the context of the aggregative models ordinarily used, this assumption may seem implausible: how could traders not know *the* price of goods? In the reality of a multi-commodity world, however, no one would want to observe all prices every day, nor would many traders find published price indices particularly useful. An optimizing trader will process those prices of most importance to his decision problem most frequently and carefully, those of less importance less so, and most prices not at all. Of the many sources of risk of importance to him, the business cycle and aggregate behavior generally is, for most agents, of no special importance, and there is no reason for traders to specialize their own information systems for diagnosing general movements correctly.

By the same reasoning, one can see that *sustained* inflation will not affect agents' real decisions in the way that transitory price movements do. Nothing is easier than to spot and correct systematic *bias* in forecasts. Such corrections involve no changes in agents' information systems, or in the costs of processing information. There may, of course, be some lag in diagnosing sustained inflation for what it is; about as often, agents will incorrectly perceive a transitory inflation as though it were sustained.

Changes in the degree of price variability will have more fundamental effects on agents' information processing behavior, because they affect the "weights" placed on price information in forecasting future prices. The general idea is that one trusts "noisy" price signals less.

X

The aggregate or average response to general price movements becomes more complex as one considers investment as well as employment responses. Investment decisions will be distorted by general price movements, for the same reasons as will employment, and in the same direction as the responses induced by relative price movements.

Further complications follow, however, from the observation that current investment affects future *capacity*, and hence future prices. This effect can be seen to extend in time, perhaps even to amplify, the initial effects of general price movements.

To spell this out in more detail, imagine that some event occurs which would, if correctly perceived by all, induce an increase in prices generally. Sooner or later, then, this adjustment will occur. Initially, however, more traders than not perceive a relative price movement, possibly permanent, in their favor. As a result, employment and investment both increase. Through time, as price information diffuses through the economy, these traders will see they have been mistaken. In the meantime, however, the added capacity *retards* price increases generally, postponing the recognition of the initial shock. In this way, unsystematic or short-term shocks to prices can lead to much longer swings in prices.

In addition, there is a downturn automatically built in to this expansion of capacity. When recognition of general inflation does occur, investment will have to become less than normal for a time while capacity readjusts downward. There is no reason to expect this readjustment to come rapidly, or to be describable as a "crash," or "bust."

This scenario, like the earlier description of the employment response, depends crucially on the confusion on the part of agents between relative and general price movements. This is especially clear in the case of investment, since optimal investment policy has a great deal of "smoothing" built into it: since investment is a long-term commitment, it will respond only to what seem to be relatively permanent relative price shifts.

This observation has led, on serious grounds, to skepticism as to the importance of accelerator effects in the business cycle. How can moderate cyclical movements in prices lead to the high-amplitude movements in durable goods purchases which are observed? Here again, one must insist on the minor contribution of economy-wide risk to the general risk situation faced by agents. For individual investment projects, rates of return are highly variable, often negative, and often measured in hundreds of percent. A quick, current response to what seems to others a weak "signal" is often the key to a successful investment. The agent who waits until the situation is clear to everyone is too late: someone else has already added the capacity to meet the high demand. What appears, at the aggregate level, to be a high-amplitude response pattern to low-amplitude shocks is, at the level at which decisions are made, a high-amplitude response to still higher amplitude movements in returns to individual investments.[16]

XI

I began section II with a definition of business cycles as repeated fluctuations in employment, output, and the composition of output, associated with a certain typical pattern of co-movements in prices and other variables. Since in a competitive economy, employment and output of various kinds are chosen by agents in response to price movements, it seemed appropriate to begin by rationalizing the observed quantity movements as rational or optimal responses to observed price movements. This has been accomplished in the preceding five sections. I turn next to the *sources* of price movements.

For explaining *secular* movements in prices generally, secular movements in the quantity of money do extremely well. This fact is as well established as any we know in aggregative economics, and is not sensitive to how one measures either prices or the quantity of money.[17] There is no serious doubt as to the direction of effect in this relationship: no one argues that the anticipation of sixteenth-century inflation sent Columbus to the New World to locate the gold to finance it. This evidence has no direct connection to business cycles, since it refers to averages over much longer periods, but the indirect connections are too strong to be ignored: we have accounted for the pattern of co-movements among real variables over the cycle as responses to general price movements: we know that, in the "long run," general price movements arise primarily from changes in the quantity of money. Moreover, cyclical movements in money are large enough to be quantitatively interesting. All these arguments point to a monetary shock as the force triggering the real business cycle.

The direct evidence on short-term correlations between money, output, and price is much more difficult to read. Certain extreme episodes appear to indicate that depressions and recoveries are money-induced.[18] In general, however, the link between money and these and other variables is agreed to be subject, in Friedman's terms, to "long and variable lags."

Paradoxically, this weakness in the short-term evidence linking money to economic activity, and in particular to prices, is *encouraging* from the point of view of monetary business cycle theory. To see why, recall the theoretical link between general price movements and economic activity as sketched above. This connection rested on the hypothesis that the signal processing problem of identifying general price movements from observations of a few individual prices was *too difficult* to be solved perfectly by agents. Now suppose it were true that one could describe short-term general price movements by a simple, fixed function of lagged movements in some published monetary aggregate. Then, far from being difficult, the signal processing problem to be solved by agents would be *trivial*: they could simply observe current monetary aggregates, calculate the predicted current and future price movements they imply, and correct their behaviour for these units changes perfectly. The result would be a very tight relationship between money and prices, over even very short periods, and no relationship at all between these movements and changes in real variables.

These remarks do not, of course, explain *why* monetary effects work with long and variable lags. On this question little is known. It seems likely that the answer lies in the observation that a monetary expansion can occur in a variety of ways, depending on the way the money is "injected" into the system, with different price response implications depending on which way is selected. This would suggest that one should describe the monetary "state" of the economy as being determined by some *unobservable* monetary aggregate, loosely related to observed aggregates over short periods but closely related secularly.

Let me recapitulate the main features of the business cycle theory sketched in the preceding sections. We began by imagining an economy with fluctuating tastes and technology, implying continually changing *relative* prices, and studied the co-movements in quantities and prices which would emerge if agents behaved in their own interest and utilized their incomplete information effectively. We then superimposed on this economy sizable, unsystematic movements in a monetary aggregate, adding an additional source of "noise" to individual price movements. The result is to generate a pattern of co-movements among aggregate series which appears to match the observations summarized in section II.

In retrospect, this account seems rather embarrassingly simple: one wonders why it seems to be necessary to undo a Revolution to arrive at it. Yet one must be careful not to overstate what has, in fact, been arrived at. I think it is fairly clear that there is nothing in the behavior of observed economic time series which precludes ordering them in equilibrium terms, and enough theoretical examples exist to lend confidence to the hope that this can be done in an explicit and rigorous way. To date, however, no equilibrium model has been developed which meets these standards and which, at the same time, could pass the test posed by the Adelmans (1959). My own guess would be that success in this sense is five, but not twenty-five years off.[19]

The implications for economic policy of a successful business cycle theory of the sort outlined here are, I think, easy to guess at even when the theory itself is in a preliminary state. Indeed, much of the above is simply an attempt to understand and make more explicit the implicit model underlying the policy proposals of Henry Simons, Milton Friedman, and other critics of activist aggregative policy. By seeking an equilibrium account of account cycles, one accepts *in advance* rather severe limitations on the scope of governmental countercyclical policy which might be rationalized by the theory. Insofar as fluctuations are induced by gratuitous monetary instability, serving no social purpose, then increased monetary stability promises to reduce aggregate, real variability and increase welfare. There is no doubt, however, that *some* real variability would remain even under the smoothest monetary and fiscal policies. There is no *prima facie* case that this residual variability would be better dealt with by centralized, governmental policies than by individual, decentralized responses.[20]

In view of this lack of novelty in the realm of policy, it seems a fair question to ask: why do we need the theory? The general answer, I think, is that in a democratic society it is not enough to believe oneself to be right; one must be able to explain *why* one is right. We live in a society in which the unemployment rate fluctuates between, say, 3 and 10 percent. It follows that both situations are attainable, and it is clear that most people are happier at three than at ten. It is also clear that government policies have much to do with which of these situations prevails at any particular time. What could be more natural, then, than to view the task of aggregative economics as that of discovering which policies will lead to the more desirable situation, and then advocating their adoption? This was the promise of Keynesian economics, and even now, when the scientific emptiness of this promise is most evident, its appeal is understandable to all who share the hope that social science offers more than elegant rationalization of the existing state of affairs.

The economically literate public has had some forty years to become comfortable with two related ideas: that market economies are inherently subject to violent fluctuations which can only be eliminated by flexible and forceful governmental responses; and that economists are in possession of a body of scientifically tested knowledge enabling them to determine, at any time, what these responses should be. It is doubtful if many who are not professionally committed hold, today, to the latter of these beliefs. This in itself settles little in the dispute as to whether the role of government in stabilization policy should be to reduce its own disruptive part or actively to offset private sector instability. As long as the business cycle remains "in apparent contradiction" to economic theory, both positions appear tenable. There seems to be no way to determine how business cycles are to be dealt with short of understanding what they are and how they occur.

Notes

1. Paper prepared for the Kiel Conference on Growth without Inflation, June 22–23, 1976: revised, August 1976. I would like to thank Gary Becker, Jacob Frenkel, Don Patinkin, Thomas Sargent, and Jose Scheinkman for their comments and suggestions.
2. Hayek (1933), p. 33n.
3. Hayek (1933), p. 42n.
4. This redirection was conscious and explicit on Keynes' part. See, for example, the first sentence of his chapter on the trade cycle: "Since we claim to have shown in the preceding chapters what determines the volume of employment at any time, it follows, if we are right that our theory must be capable of explaining the phenomena of the trade cycle" (1936), p. 313.
5. The features of economic time series listed here are, curiously, both "well known" and expensive to document in any careful and comprehensive way. A useful, substantively oriented introduction is given by Mitchell (1951), who summarizes mainly interwar, U.S. experience. The basic technical reference for these methods is Burns and Mitchell (1946), U.S. monetary experience is best displayed in Friedman and Schwartz (1963). An invaluable source for earlier British series is Gayer, Rostow, and Schwartz (1953), esp. Vol. II. The phenomena documented in these sources are, of course, much more widely observed. Most can be inferred, though with some difficulty, from the estimated structure of modern econometric models.

An important recent contribution is Sargent and Sims (1976), which summarizes postwar U.S. quarterly series in several suggestive ways, leading to a qualitative picture very close to that provided by Mitchell, but within an

explicit stochastic framework, so that their results are replicatable and criticizable at a level at which Mitchell's are not.
6. For example, see Tinbergen (1939). This work was not explicitly Keynesian: indeed, it was conceived as an empirical complement to Haberler's review and synthesis of theoretical work on business cycles (1936). Keynes, on his part, was actively hostile towards Tinbergen's work. See Moggridge (1973), pp. 285–320. In referring to those who built in part on Tinbergen's work as "Keynesian" I am, then, contributing to the continuation of an historical injustice.
7. Klein and Goldberger (1955).
8. Tinbergen (1939), pp. 183–185. Tinbergen, as did most subsequent macroeconometricians, used the significance of interest rates to test the importance of money.
9. It is not correct that a search for "good fits" could have led to a model satisfying the Adelmans' criteria: think of fitting polynomials in time to "explain" each series over the sample period.
10. Lucas (1976).
11. Hirsch (1972), de Menil and Enzler (1972).
12. Knight (1921). I am interpreting the risk-uncertainty distinction as referring *not* to a classification of different types of individual decisions problems but to the *relationship* between decision maker and observer.
13. Many of the arguments in this and subsequent sections have been developed more explicitly elsewhere. The closest single parallel treatment is in Lucas (1975). See also Phelps *et al.* (1970), Barro (1976), Sargent and Wallace (1975), Sargent (1976), in what follows. I will not document particular arguments, nor will I attempt to apportion credit (or blame) for ideas discussed.
14. One such arrangement is the practice of "laying off" workers. See Azariadis (1975).
15. What is happening to consumption expenditures as these employment and investment responses take place? In his critique of equilibrium business cycle models, Grossman (1973) argues that consumption must *necessarily* move in the *opposite* direction from labour supplied. Since this is not what is in fact observed over the cycle, it would indeed by a serious paradox if a negative correlation were a consequence of utility theory. One *can* derive it for special cases (see Lucas, 1972, Fig. 1) but this implication is certainly *not* a general fact for optimizing households; it does *not*, for example, follow from Rapping's and my (1970) theory or from that of Ghez and Becker (1975, ch. 4).
16. "Austrian" or "monetary-over-investment" business cycle theory (see Haberler, 1936, or Hayek, 1933) was based on this same idea of mistaken investment decisions triggered by spurious price signals. However, the price which this theory emphasized was the rate of interest, rather than product prices as stressed here. Given the cyclical amplitude of interest rate, the investment-interest elasticity needed to account for the observed amplitude in investment is *much* too high to be consistent with other evidence.
17. Friedman and Schwartz (1963).
18. Again, see Friedman and Schwartz (1963).
19. Proceeding further out on this limb, it is likely that such a "successful" model will be a close descendant of Sargent's (1976).

20. That is to say, active countercyclical policy would require the same kind of cost–benefit defense used in evaluating other types of government policies. See Phelps (1972), and also Prescott's review (1975).

References

Adelman, I. and Adelman, F. L., "The Dynamic Properties of the Klein–Goldberger Model," *Econometrica*, 27, No. 4 (October 1959), 596–625.
Azariadis, C., "Implicit Contracts and Underemployment Equilibria," *Journal of Political Economy*, 83, No. 6 (December 1975), 1183–202.
Barro, R. J., "Rational Expectations and the Role of Monetary Policy," *Journal of Monetary Economics*, 2, No. 1 (January 1976), 1–32.
Burns, A. F. and Mitchell, W. C., *Measuring Business Cycle*, New York: National Bureau of Economic Research, 1946.
Friedman, M., "The Role of Monetary Policy," Presidential Address to the American Economic Association, *American Economic Review*, 58, No. 1 (March 1968), 1–17.
Friedman, M. and Schwartz, A. J., *A Monetary History of the United States, 1867–1960*, Princeton: Princeton University Press for the National Bureau of Economic Research, 1963.
Gayer, A. D., Rostow, W. W. and Schwartz, A. J., *The Growth and Fluctuation of the British Economy, 1790–1850*, Oxford: The Clarendon Press 1953.
Ghez, G. R. and Becker, G. S., *The Allocation of Time and Goods Over the Life Cycle*, New York: National Bureau of Economic Research, 1975.
Grossman, H. I., "Aggregate Demand, Job Search, and Employment," *Journal of Political Economy*, 81, No. 6 (November/December 1973), 1353–69.
Haberler, G., *Prosperity and Depression*, Geneva: League of Nations 1936.
Hayek, F. A. von, *Monetary Theory and the Trade Cycle*, London: Jonathan Cape, 1933.
Hicks, J. R., "Mr. Keynes and the 'Classics': A Suggested Interpretation," *Econometrica*, 5 (1937), 147–59.
Hirsch, A. A., "Price Simulations with the OBE Econometric Model," in *The Econometrics of Price Determination Conference* (ed. O. Eckstein), Washington, DC: Board of Governors of the Federal Reserve System and Social Science Council, 1972.
Keynes, J. M., *The General Theory of Employment, Interest and Money*, London: Macmillan, 1936.
Klein, L. A. and Goldberger, A. S., *An Econometric Model of the United States, 1929–52*, Amsterdam: North-Holland, 1955.
Knight, F. H., *Risk, Uncertainty and Profit*, Boston: Houghton Mifflin, 1921.
Lucas, R. E., Jr., "Expectations and the Neutrality of Money," *Journal of Economic Theory*, 4, No. 2 (April 1972), 103–23.
Lucas, R. E., Jr., "An Equilibrium Model of the Business Cycle," *Journal of Political Economy*, 83, No. 6 (December 1975), 1113–44.
Lucas, R. E., Jr., "Econometric Policy Evaluations: A Critique," in *The Phillips Curve and Labour Markets*, eds. K. Brunner and A. H. Meltzer, Carnegie-Rochester Conference Series on Public Policy, 1, Amsterdam: North-Holland 1976, 19–46.

Lucas, R. E., Jr. and Rapping, L. A., "Real Wages, Employment, and Inflation," in *Microeconomic Foundations of Employment and Inflation Theory*, (eds. E. S. Phelps, et al.), New York: Norton, 1970.

de Menil, G. and Enzler, J. J., "Price and Wages in the FR-MIT Econometric Model," in *The Econometrics of Price Determination Conference* (ed. O. Eckstein), Washington, D.C.: Board of Governors of the Federal Reserve System and Social Science Council, 1972.

Mitchell, W. C., *What Happens During Business Cycles*, New York: National Bureau of Economic Research, 1951.

Modigliani, F., "Liquidity Preference and the Theory of Interest and Money," *Econometrica*, 12, No. 1 (January 1944), 45–88.

Moggridge, D. (ed.), *The Collected Writings of John Maynard Keynes*, Vol. XIV, London: Macmillan, 1973.

Muth, J., "Rational Expectations and the Theory of Price Movements," *Econometrica*, 29, No. 3 (July 1961), 315–35.

Phelps, E. S., "Money Wage Dynamics and Labour Market Equilibrium," *Journal of Political Economy*, 76, No. 4, II (July/August 1968), 687–711.

Phelps, E. S., *Inflation Policy and Unemployment Theory: The Cost-Benefit Approach to Monetary Planning*, London: Macmillan, 1972.

Phelps, E. S. et al., *Microeconomic Foundations of Employment and Inflation Theory*, New York: Norton, 1970.

Prescott, E. C., "Efficiency of the Natural Rate," *Journal of Political Economy*, 83, No. 6 (December 1975), 1229–36.

Sargent, T. J., "A Classical Macroeconometric Model for the United States," *Journal of Political Economy*, 84, No. 2 (April 1976), 207–37.

Sargent, T. J. and Sims, C. A., "Business Cycle Modeling Without Pretending to Have Too Much A Priori Economic Theory," University of Michigan working paper, March 1976.

Sargent, T. J. and Wallace, N., "'Rational' Expectations, the Optimal Monetary Instrument, and the Optimal Money Supply Rule," *Journal of Political Economy*, 83, No. 2 (April 1975), 241–54.

Tinbergen, J., *Business Cycles in the United States of America, 1919–32*, Geneva: League of Nations, 1939.

Real Business Cycles: A New Keynesian Perspective*

N. G. MANKIW

The debate over the source and propagation of economic fluctuations rages as fiercely today as it did 50 years ago in the aftermath of Keynes's *The General Theory* and in the midst of the Great Depression. Today, as then, there are two schools of thought. The classical school emphasizes the optimization of private economic actors, the adjustment of relative prices to equate supply and demand, and the efficiency of unfettered markets. The Keynesian school believes that understanding economic fluctuations requires not just studying the intricacies of general equilibrium, but also appreciating the possibility of market failure on a grand scale.

Real business cycle theory is the latest incarnation of the classical view of economic fluctuations. It assumes that there are large random fluctuations in the rate of technological change. In response to these fluctuations, individuals rationally alter their levels of labor supply and consumption. The business cycle is, according to this theory, the natural and efficient response of the economy to changes in the available production technology.

My goal in this essay is to appraise this newly revived approach to the business cycle. I should admit in advance that I am not an advocate. In my view, real business cycle theory does not provide an empirically plausible explanation of economic fluctuations. Both its reliance on large technological disturbances as the primary source of economic fluctu-

---

Journal of Economic Perspectives, Vol. 3, No. 3 (Summer 1989), pp. 79–89.

ations and its reliance on the intertemporal substitution of leisure to explain changes in employment are fundamental weaknesses. Moreover, to the extent that it trivializes the social cost of observed fluctuations, real business cycle theory is potentially dangerous. The danger is that those who advise policy-makers might attempt to use it to evaluate the effects of alternative macroeconomic policies or to conclude that macroeconomic policies are unnecessary.

Walrasian equilibrium and the classical dichotomy

The typical undergraduate course in microeconomics begins with partial equilibrium analysis of individual markets. A market for a good is characterized by a downward sloping demand curve and an upward sloping supply curve. The price of the good is assumed to adjust until the quantity supplied equals the quantity demanded.

The course then builds up to Walrasian general equilibrium. In this Walrasian equilibrium, prices adjust to equate supply and demand in every market simultaneously. The general equilibrium system determines the quantities of all goods and services sold and their relative prices. The most important theoretical result, after the existence of such a Walrasian equilibrium, is the "invisible hand" theorem: the equilibrium is Pareto efficient.

Courses in microeconomics thus show how employment, production, and relative prices are determined without any mention of the existence of money, the medium of exchange. The simplest way to append money to the model is to specify a money demand function and an exogenous money supply. Money demand depends on the level of output and the price level. The level of output is already determined in the Walrasian system. The price level, however, can adjust to equate supply and demand in the money market.

Introducing money in this way leads to the classical dichotomy (Patinkin, 1956). Real variables, such as employment, output, and relative prices, including the real interest rate, are determined by the Walrasian system. Nominal variables, such as the price level, the nominal wage, and the nominal interest rate, are then determined by the equilibrium in the money market. Of course, since nominal variables do not affect real variables, the money market is not very important. This classical view of the economy suggests that, for most policy discussions, the money market can be ignored.

The professor of macroeconomics must in some way deal with the classical dichotomy. Given the assumptions of Walrasian equilibrium, money is largely irrelevant. The macroeconomist must either destroy this classical dichotomy or learn to live with it.

Keynesian macroeconomics destroys the classical dichotomy by abandoning the assumption that wages and prices adjust instantly to clear markets. This approach is motivated by the observation that many nominal wages are fixed by long-term labor contracts and many product prices remain unchanged for long periods of time. Once the inflexibility of wages and prices is admitted into a macroeconomic model, the classical dichotomy and the irrelevance of money quickly disappear.

Much of the early work in the new classical revolution of the 1970s attempted to destroy the classical dichotomy without abandoning the fundamental axiom of continuous market clearing (Lucas, 1972; 1973). These models were based on the assumption that individuals have imperfect information regarding prices. These individuals therefore confuse movements in the overall price level (which under the classical dichotomy should not matter) with movements in relative prices (which should matter). An unanticipated decrease in the money supply leads individuals to infer that the relative prices of the goods they produce are temporarily low, which induces them to reduce the quantity supplied. While the fascination with this sort of story was substantial in the 1970s, it has attracted relatively few adherents in the 1980s. It is hard to believe that confusion about the price level is sufficiently great to generate the large changes in quantities observed over the business cycle.

In contrast to both the Keynesian and the early new classical approaches to the business cycle, real business cycle theory embraces the classical dichotomy. It accepts the complete irrelevance of monetary policy, thereby denying a tenet accepted by almost all macroeconomists a decade ago. Nominal variables, such as the money supply and the price level, are assumed to have no role in explaining fluctuations in real variables, such as output and employment.

Real business cycle theory thus pushes the Walrasian model farther than it has been pushed before. In evaluating whether it provides a successful explanation of recessions and booms, two questions naturally arise. First, why are there such large fluctuations in output and employment? And second, why do movements in nominal variables, such as the money supply, appear related to movements in real variables, such as output?

Classical and Keynesian views of economic fluctuations

The only forces that can cause economic fluctuations, according to real business cycle theory, are those forces that change the Walrasian equilibrium. The Walrasian equilibrium is simply the set of quantities and relative prices that simultaneously equate supply and demand in all markets in the economy. To understand how real business cycle theory explains the business cycle, it is necessary to look into the fundamental forces that change the supplies and demands for various goods and services.

Many sorts of macroeconomic disturbances can in principle generate fluctuations in real business cycle models. For example, changes in the level of government purchases or in the investment tax credit alter the demand for goods and therefore affect the Walrasian equilibrium. Changes in the relative price of oil alter the equilibrium allocation of labor among alternative uses. Many of the macroeconomic disturbances that receive much attention among Keynesian macroeconomists will also have important effects in real business cycle models. There is, however, substantial disagreement between the two schools regarding the mechanisms through which these disturbances work.

Consider the case of a temporary increase in government purchases. Almost all macroeconomists agree that such a change causes an increase in output and employment, and the evidence, mainly from wartime experience, supports this prediction. Yet the explanations of this effect of government purchases differ greatly.

Real business cycle theory emphasizes the intertemporal substitution of goods and leisure (Barro, 1987). It begins by pointing out that an increase in government purchases increases the demand for goods. To achieve equilibrium in the goods market, the real interest rate must rise, which reduces consumption and investment. The increase in the real interest rate also causes individuals to reallocate leisure across time. In particular, at a higher real interest rate, working today becomes relatively more attractive than working in the future; today's labor supply therefore increases. This increase in labor supply causes equilibrium employment and output to rise.

While Keynesian theory also predicts an increase in the real interest rate in response to a temporary increase in government purchases, the effect of the real interest rate on labor supply does not play a crucial role. Instead, the increase in employment and output is due to a reduction in the amount of labor unemployed or underutilized. In most Keynesian theory, the labor market is characterized as often in a state of excess supply. In contrast, the Walrasian approach of real business cycle theory does not allow for the possibility of involuntary unemployment.

Both real business cycle theory and Keynesian theory thus conclude that increases in government purchases increase output and employment. This example shows that some of the prominent implications of Keynesian models also come out of intertemporal Walrasian models. Macroeconomists face a problem of approximate observational equivalence: many observed phenomena are consistent with both the classical and Keynesian paradigms.

The central role of technological disturbances

While many sorts of macroeconomic disturbances can in principle cause economic fluctuations in real business cycle models, most attention has focused on technological disturbances. The reason is that other sorts of disturbances are unlikely to generate fluctuations in real business cycle models that resemble actual economic fluctuations.

An obvious but important fact is that over the typical business cycle, consumption and leisure move in opposite directions. When the economy goes into a recession, consumption falls and leisure rises. When the economy goes into a boom, consumption rises and leisure falls. Explaining this phenomenon is potentially problematic for real business cycle theory: consumption and leisure would often be expected to move together, since both are normal goods. In the example of a temporary increase in government purchases, both consumption and leisure should fall. Many other changes in the demand for goods, such as a change due to a temporary investment tax credit, also should cause consumption and leisure to move together.

Real business cycle theory must explain why individuals in a recession find it rational to increase the quantity of leisure they demand at the same time they decrease the quantity of goods they demand. The answer must be that the price of leisure relative to goods, the real wage, falls in a recession. Hence, a crucial implication of real business cycle theory is that the real wage is procyclical.[1]

If the production function were unchanging and demand shocks were the source of fluctuations, real business cycle theory would have trouble generating a procyclical real wage. Since labor input is low in a recession, one would expect that the marginal product of labor and thus the real wage should be high. With an unchanging production function, diminishing marginal returns to labor would produce a countercyclical real wage, not the procyclical real wage necessary to explain the fluctuations in consumption and leisure.

Real business cycle theorists therefore assume that there are substantial fluctuations in the rate of technological change. In a recession, the available production technology is relatively unfavorable. The marginal product of labor and thus the real wage are low. In response to the low return to working, individuals reduce consumption and increase leisure.

Since real business cycle theory describes economic fluctuations as a changing Walrasian equilibrium, it implies that these fluctuations are efficient. Given the tastes of individuals and the technological possibilities facing society, the levels of employment, output, and consumption cannot be improved. Attempts by the government to alter the allocations of the private market, such as policies to stabilize employment, at best are ineffective and at worst can do harm by impeding the "invisible hand."

Of all the implications of real business cycle theory, the optimality of economic fluctuations is perhaps the most shocking. It seems undeniable that the level of welfare is lower in a recession than in the boom that preceded it. Keynesian theory explains the reduction in welfare by a failure in economic coordination: because wages and prices do not adjust instantaneously to equate supply and demand in all markets, some gains from trade go unrealized in a recession. In contrast, real business cycle theory allows no unrealized gains from trade. The reason welfare is lower in a recession is, according to these theories, that the technological capabilities of society have declined.

The evidence on technological disturbances

Advocates of real business cycle theories have trouble convincing skeptics that the economy is subject to such large and sudden changes in technology. It is a more standard presumption that the accumulation of knowledge and the concurrent increase in the economy's technological opportunities take place gradually over time. Yet to mimic observed fluctuations, real business cycle theorists must maintain that there are substantial short-run fluctuations in the production function.

Edward Prescott (1986) has offered some direct evidence on the importance of technological disturbances. He examines changes in total factor productivity for the United States economy – the percent change in output less the percent change in inputs, where the different inputs are weighted by their factor shares. This "Solow residual" should measure the rate of technological progress. Prescott points out that there are substantial fluctuations in the Solow residual, a finding which suggests a potentially important role for technological disturbances as a source of business cycle fluctuations.

Figure 17.1 presents my calculation of the Solow residual and the percent change in output yearly since 1948. (Both variables are for the private economy less agriculture and housing services.) Like Prescott, I find substantial fluctuations in measured total factor productivity. For example, in 1982 total factor productivity fell by 3.5 percent, while in 1984 it rose by 3.4 percent. One might interpret these numbers as showing that the economy's ability to convert inputs into outputs – the aggregate production function – varies substantially from year to year.

Figure 17.1 also shows that measured productivity is highly cyclical. In every year in which output fell, total factor productivity also fell. If the

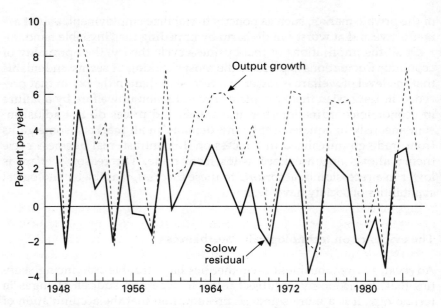

FIGURE 17.1 Solow residuals and output growth

Solow residual is a valid measure of the change in the available production technology, then recessions are periods of technological regress.

The Solow residual need not be interpreted as evidence regarding exogenous technological disturbances, however. The standard explanation of cyclical productivity is that it reflects labor hoarding and other "off the production function" behavior. Productivity appears to fall in a recession because firms keep unnecessary and underutilized labor. In a boom the hoarded laborers begin to put out greater effort; output increases without a large increase in measured labor input.[2]

An examination of the data from the early 1940s appears to support this standard explanation of the cyclical behavior of productivity. The increase in output associated with the World War II build-up is most plausibly a demand-driven phenomenon. Yet from 1939 to 1944 measured total factor productivity grew an average of 7.6 percent per year. (By contrast, the most productivity has grown in any year since then is 5.2 percent in 1950.) One might interpret this finding as showing that the economic boom of the 1940s was in fact driven by supply shocks rather than demand shocks. A more appealing interpretation is that the Solow residual is not a good measure over short horizons of changes in the economy's technological abilities.

Once the Solow residual is rejected as a measure of year-to-year changes in the available production technology, there is no longer any direct evidence for substantial technological disturbances. Yet to generate fluctuations that mimic observed fluctuations, real business cycle models require such disturbances. The existence of large fluctuations in the available technology is a crucial but unjustified assumption of real business cycle theory.

An advocate of real business cycle theory might respond that economic models often rely on assumptions for which there is no formal evidence. Yet more casual evidence also does not give plausibility to the assumption of substantial technological disturbances. Recessions are important events; they receive widespread attention from policy-makers and the media. There is, however, no discussion of declines in the available technology. If society suffered some important adverse technological shock, we would be aware of it. My own reading of the newspaper, however, does not lead me to associate most recessions with some exogenous deterioration in the economy's productive capabilities.

The OPEC energy price changes of the 1970s illustrate that when the economy experiences large real shocks, these shocks are easily identifiable and much discussed. Figure 17.1 indeed shows that the economy experienced large negative Solow residuals in 1974 and 1979, as one might have expected.[3] Yet the five other recessions in the postwar period also exhibit large negative Solow residuals. To explain these Solow residuals as adverse changes in the aggregate production function, one would need to find events with the economic significance of the OPEC price increases. The apparent absence of such events is evidence that these recessions cannot be easily attributed to exogenous real shocks.[4]

Labor supply and intertemporal substitution

Real business cycle theorists assume that fluctuations in employment are fully voluntary. In other words, they assume the economy always finds itself on the labor supply curve. Yet over the typical business cycle, employment varies substantially while the determinants of labor supply – the real wage and the real interest rate – vary only slightly. To mimic this observed pattern, real business cycle models require that individuals be very willing to reallocate leisure over time. Individuals must significantly reduce the quantity of labor they supply in response to small temporary reductions in the real wage or in response to small decreases in the real interest rate.

It is unlikely, however, that individuals are so responsive to intertemporal relative prices. Econometric evidence on labor supply typically finds that the willingness of individuals to substitute leisure over time is slight. If leisure were highly intertemporally substitutable, as real business cycle theorists assume, then individuals facing expected increases in their real wage should work little today and much in the future. Individuals facing expected decreases in their real wage should work hard today and enjoy leisure in the future. Yet studies of individual labor supply over time find that expected changes in the real wage lead to only small changes in hours worked (Altonji, 1986; Ball, 1985). Individuals do not respond to expected real wage changes by substantially reallocating leisure over time.

Personal experience and introspection provide another way to judge the behavioral responses on which real business cycle models rely. One key behavioral response is that quantity of labor supplied reacts substantially to the real interest rate. Without such intertemporal substitution, real business cycle models are unable to explain how a temporary increase in government purchases increases output and employment. Yet such a behavioral response does not seem plausible. The real interest rate is simply not a significant consideration when individuals decide to leave their jobs or to accept new employment. While economists can easily convince laymen and students that the quantity of apples demanded depends on the price of apples, it is much harder to convince them that labor supply depends on the real interest rate. The implication I draw from this observation is that the intertemporal substitutability of leisure is very likely far too weak to get real business cycle models to work.

Real business cycle theories with multiple sectors

The real business cycle theories I have been discussing so far treat production as if it takes place in a single industry. This abstraction, however, is not characteristic of all real business cycle theories.

Some real business cycle theories emphasize changes in the technologies of different sectors, rather than economy-wide changes in technology (Long and Plosser, 1983). These models highlight the interactions among the sectors. Even if the shocks to the different sectors are independent, the outputs of the different sectors move together. For example, an adverse shock to one sector reduces the wealth of the individuals in the economy; these individuals respond by reducing their demand for all goods. An observer would see an aggregate business cycle, even without a single aggregate shock.

To get these real business cycle models to work, however, the number of independent sectoral shocks cannot be too great. If there were many independent sectoral shocks and labor were mobile between sectors, then the law of large numbers would guarantee that these shocks and their effect on the aggregate economy would average out to zero. To get an aggregate business cycle, these models therefore require that there be only a few sectors and that these sectors be subject to large technological disturbances. These models are therefore similar to the single-sector theories and suffer form the same weaknesses: the absence of any direct evidence for such large technological disturbances and the implausibility of strong intertemporal substitutability of leisure.

A second type of sectoral shock theory emphasizes the costly adjustment of labor among sectors (Lilien, 1982). These models, which depart more from the Walrasian paradigm, assume that when a worker moves from one sector to another, a period of unemployment is required, perhaps for job search. In this case, independent shocks across many sectors do not offset each other. Recessions are, according to these theories, periods of more sectoral shocks and thus greater intersectoral adjustment.

This type of real business cycle theory may appear more plausible than those relying on substantial aggregate productivity shocks and intertemporal substitution. It is perhaps easier to imagine that recessions are characterized by an unusually great need for intersectoral reallocation than by some sort of major technological regress that makes leisure unusually attractive. Yet the available evidence appears not to support this intersectoral story. If workers were unemployed voluntarily in recessions because they were moving to new jobs in other sectors, we would expect to find high unemployment coinciding with high job vacancy. Yet observed fluctuations have just the opposite pattern: high unemployment rates coincide with low levels of help wanted advertising (Abraham and Katz, 1986). Moreover, in contrast to the prediction of this theory, the measured mobility of workers between sectors is strongly procyclical (Murphy and Topel, 1987). This real business cycle theory is also unable to be plausibly reconciled with observed economic fluctuations.

Money and prices over the business cycle

Before real business cycle theory entered the macroeconomic debate in the early 1980s, almost all macroeconomics seemed to agree on one conclusion: money matters. Both historical discussions of business cycles (Friedman and Schwartz, 1963) and more formal econometric work (Barro, 1977) pointed to the Federal Reserve as an importance source of macroeconomic disturbances. While there was controversy as to whether systematic monetary policy could stabilize the economy, it was universally accepted that bad monetary policy could be destabilizing.

It is ironic that real business cycle theory arose in the wake of Paul Volcker's disinflation. Many economists view this recent experience as clear confirmation of the potency of monetary policy. Volcker announced he was going to slow the rate of money growth to achieve a lower rate of inflation; the rate of money growth in fact slowed down; and one of the deepest postwar recessions followed, as did an eventual reduction in the rate of inflation. This set of events is easy to explain within the context of Keynesian theory with its emphasis on the gradual adjustment of wages and prices. It is less easy to explain within the context of real business cycle theory.[5]

Robert King and Charles Plosser (1984) explain the historical association between money and output by arguing that the money supply endogenously responds to fluctuations in output. Standard measures of the money supply such as M1 are mostly inside money: that is, money created by the banking system. King and Plosser suggest that the transactions services of inside money should be viewed as simply the "output" of one sector of the economy, the banking sector. Just as one should expect the outputs of different sectors to move together within a multi-sector real business cycle model, one should expect the output of the banking sector to move with the outputs of other sectors. An increase in productivity in any sector will tend to increase the demand for transactions services; the banking system responds by creating more inside money. Hence, the procyclical behavior of standard monetary aggregates cannot necessarily be interpreted as evidence that changes in outside money caused by the monetary authority have real effects.

While the story of King and Plosser can explain the procyclical behavior of money, it cannot explain the procyclical behavior of prices. It is a well-documented fact that, in the absence of identifiable real shocks such as the OPEC oil price changes, inflation tends to rise in booms and fall in recessions. This famous Phillips curve correlation played a central role in the macroeconomic debate of the 1960s, and it was the primary empirical motivation for the early new classical theories in the 1970s (Friedman, 1968; Lucas, 1972). Yet since the model of King and Plosser generates procyclical money through the demand for transactions services, these fluctuations in money will be associated with fluctuations in real balances not with fluctuations in prices. The short-run Phillips curve has thus been left without an explanation by real business cycle theorists.[6]

The trade-off between internal and external consistency

A good theory has two characteristics : internal consistency and external consistency. An internally consistent theory is one that is parsimonious; it invokes no *ad hoc* or peculiar axioms. An externally consistent theory is one that fits the facts; it makes empirically refutable predictions that are not refuted. All scientists, including economists, strive for theories that are both internally and externally consistent. Yet like all optimizing agents, scientists face tradeoffs. One theory may be more "beautiful," while another may be easier to reconcile with observation.

The choice between alternative theories of the business cycle – in particular, between real business cycle theory and new Keynesian theory – is partly a choice between internal and external consistency. Real business cycle theory extends the Walrasian paradigm, the most widely understood and taught model in economics, and provides a unified explanation for economic growth and economic fluctuations. New Keynesian theory, in its attempt to mimic the world more accurately, relies on nominal rigidities that are observed but only little understood. Indeed, new Keynesians sometimes suggest that to understand the business cycle, it may be necessary to reject the axiom of rational, optimizing individuals, an act that for economists would be the ultimate abandonment of internal consistency.

The tension between these two goals of science will undoubtedly continue. Each school of macroeconomic thought will highlight its strength while trying to improve on its weaknesses. My own forecast is that real business cycle advocates will not manage to produce convincing evidence that there are substantial shocks to technology and that leisure is highly substitutable over time. Without such evidence, their theories will be judged as not persuasive. New Keynesians, however, have made substantial progress in recent years toward providing rigorous microeconomic foundations, the absence of which was the fatal flaw of the Keynesian consensus of the 1960s. While real business cycle theory has served the important function of stimulating and provoking the scientific debate, it will, I predict, ultimately be discarded as an explanation of observed fluctuations.

Notes

I am grateful to Lawrence Ball, Susanto Basu, Marianne Baxter, Mark Bils, Lawrence Katz, Deborah Mankiw, David Romer, Joseph Stiglitz, Lawrence Summers, Timothy Taylor, David Weil and Michael Woodford for helpful discussions and comments, and to the National Science Foundation for financial support.

1. Alternatively, one could explain the observed pattern without a procyclical real wage by positing that tastes for consumption relative to leisure vary over time. Recessions are then periods of "chronic laziness." As far as I know, no one has seriously proposed this explanation of the business cycle.
2. A related explanation of the procyclical behavior of the Solow residual has recently been proposed by Hall (1987). Hall points out that if price exceeds marginal cost because of imperfect competition, then the measured Solow

residual will appear procyclical even if the true production technology is unchanging. Alternatively, the Solow residual could reflect endogenous changes in technology due to demand shocks; such endogeneity might arise if, for example, learning-by-doing is important.
3. Whether changes in energy prices affect the Solow residual computed from GNP depends on a variety of issues involving the construction of index numbers like GNP. See Bruno and Sachs (1985, pp. 43) for a discussion.
4. Hamilton (1983) finds oil price changes are also associated with the pre-OPEC recession. Yet these price changes are much too small to explain plausibly such large declines in productivity.
5. The recent disinflation is not unusual. Romer and Romer (1989) show that output typically falls after the Fed makes an explicit decision to reduce inflation, which they interpret as evidence against real business cycle theory.
6. Indeed, as King and Plosser point out, their model makes the counterfactual prediction that the price level should be countercyclical: since the demand for real outside money probably rises in a boom, and it is the outside money stock that pins down the price level, equilibrium in the market for outside money requires that the price level fall in a boom.

References

Abraham, Katharine G. and Lawrence F. Katz, "Cyclical Unemployment Sectoral Shifts or Aggregate Disturbances," *Journal of Political Economy*, June 1986, 94, 507–22.

Altonji, Joseph G., "Intertemporal Substitution in Labour Supply: Evidence from Micro Data," *Journal of Political Economy*, June 1986, Part 2, 94, S176–S215.

Ball, Laurence, "Intertemporal Substitution and Constraints on Labour Supply: Evidence from Panel Data," manuscript, M.I.T., 1985.

Barro, Robert J., "Unanticipated Money Growth and Unemployment in the United States," *American Economic Review*, 1977, 67, 101–15.

Barro, Robert J., *Macroeconomics*, New York: Wiley, 1987.

Bruno, Michael and Jeffrey Sachs, *Economics of Worldwide Stagflation*, Cambridge, MA: Harvard University Press, 1985.

Friedman, Milton, "The Role of Monetary Policy," *American Economic Review*, 1968, 58, 1–17.

Friedman, Milton and Anna Schwartz, *A Monetary History of the United States*, Princeton, NJ: Princeton University Press, 1963.

Hall, Robert E., "Market Structure and Macroeconomic Fluctuations," *Brookings Papers on Economic Activity*, 1987, 1, 285–322.

Hamilton, James D., "Oil and the Macroeconomy since World War II," *Journal of Political Economy*, April 1983, 91, 228–48.

King, Robert G. and Charles I. Plosser, "Money, Credit, and Prices in a Real Business Cycle," *American Economic Review*, June 1984, 74, 363–80.

Lilien, David M., "Sectoral Shifts and Cyclical Unemployment," *Journal of Political Economy*, August 1982, 90, 777–93.

Long, John B., Jr. and Charles I. Plosser, "Real Business Cycles," *Journal of Political Economy*, February 1983, 91, 39–69.

Lucas, Robert E. Jr., "Expectations and the Neutrality of Money," *Journal of Economic Theory*, 1972, 4, pp. 103–24.

Lucas, Robert E. Jr., "International Evidence on Output-Inflation Tradeoffs," *American Economic Review*, 1973, 63, pp. 326–34.

Murphy, Kevin M. and Robert H. Topel, "The Evolution of Unemployment in the United States: 1968–1985," *NBER Macroeconomics Annual*, 1987.

Patinkin, Don, *Money, Interest, and Prices: An Integration of Monetary and Value Theory*, Evanston, Il: Row, Peterson, 1956.

Prescott, Edward, "Theory Ahead of Business Cycle Measurement," *Carnegie-Rochester Conference on Public Policy*, Autumn 1986, 25, pp. 11–44.

Romer, Christina and David Romer, "Does Monetary Policy Matter: A New Test in the Spirit of Friedman and Schwartz," *NBER Macroeconomics Annual*, 1989.

PART VIII

CONTROL OF MACROECONOMIC FLUCTUATIONS

CHAPTER 18

*A Monetary and Fiscal Framework for Economic Stability**

M. FRIEDMAN[1]

During the late 19th and early 20th centuries, the problems of the day were of a kind that led economists to concentrate on the allocation of resources and, to a lesser extent, economic growth, and to pay little attention to short-run fluctuations of a cyclical character. Since the Great Depression of the 1930s, this emphasis has been reversed. Economists now tend to concentrate on cyclical movements, to act and talk as if any improvement, however slight, in control of the cycle justified any sacrifice, however large, in the long-run efficiency, or prospects for growth, of the economic system. Proposals for the control of the cycle thus tend to be developed almost as if there were no other objectives and as if it made no difference within what general framework cyclical fluctuations take place. A consequence of this attitude is that inadequate attention is given to the possibility of satisfying both sets of objectives simultaneously.

In constructing the monetary and fiscal framework proposed in this paper, I deliberately gave primary consideration to long-run objectives. That is, I tried to design a framework that would be appropriate for a world in which cyclical movements, other than those introduced by "bad" monetary and fiscal arrangements, were of no consequence. I then

---

American Economic Review, Vol. 38, No. 3 (June 1948), pp. 245–64.

examined the resulting proposal to see how it would behave in respect of cyclical fluctuations. It behaves surprisingly well; not only might it be expected not to contribute to cyclical fluctuations, it tends to offset them and therefore seems to offer considerable promise of providing a tolerable degree of short-run economic stability.

This paper is devoted to presenting the part of the analysis dealing with the implications of the proposal for cyclical stability. Nonetheless, in view of the motivation of the proposal it seems well to begin by indicating the long-run objectives adopted as a guide, even though a reasonably full discussion of these long-run objectives would not be appropriate here.

The basic long-run objective, shared I am sure by most economists, are political freedom, economic efficiency, and substantial equality of economic power. These objectives are not, of course, entirely consistent and some compromise among them may be required. Moreover, objectives stated on this level of generality can hardly guide proximate policy choices. We must take the next step and specify the general institutional arrangements we regard best suited for the attainment of these objectives. I believe – and at this stage agreement will be far less widespread – that all three objectives can best be realized by relying, as far as possible, on a market mechanism within a "competitive order" to organize the utilization of economic resources. Among the specific propositions that follow from this general position, three are particularly relevant: (1) Government must provide a monetary framework for a competitive order since the competitive order cannot provide one for itself; (2) This monetary framework should operate under the "rule of law" rather than the discretionary authority of administrators; (3) While a truly free market in a "competitive order" would yield far less inequality than current exists, I should hope that the community would desire to reduce inequality even further. Moreover, measures to supplement the market would need to be taken in the interim. For both purposes, general fiscal measures (as contrasted with specific intervention) are the most desirable non-free-market means of decreasing inequality.

The extremely simple proposal which these long-run objectives lead me to advance contains no new elements. Indeed, in view of the number of proposals that have been made for altering one or another part of the present monetary or fiscal framework, it is hard to believe that anything completely new remains to be added. The combination of elements that emerges is somewhat less hackneyed; yet no claim of originality can be made even for this. As is perhaps not surprising from what has already been said, the proposal is something like the greatest common denominator of many different proposals. This is perhaps the chief justification for presenting it and urging that it receive full professional discussion. Perhaps it, or some variant, can approach a minimum program for which economists of the less extreme shades of opinion can make common cause.

This paper deals only with the broad outlines of the monetary and fiscal framework and neglects, or deals superficially with, many difficult, important, and closely related problems. In particular, it neglects almost entirely the transition from the present framework to that outlined here; the implications of the adoption of the recommended framework for international monetary arrangements; and the special requirements of war finance. These associated problems are numerous and serious and are likely to justify compromise at some points. It seems well, however, to set forth the ultimate ideal as clearly as possible before beginning to compromise.

I The proposal

The particular proposal outlined below involves four main elements: the first relates to the monetary system; the second, to government expenditures on goods and services; the third, to government transfer payments; and the fourth, to the tax structure. Throughout, it pertains entirely to the federal government and all references to "government" should be so interpreted.[2]

1. A reform of the monetary and banking system to eliminate both the private creation or destruction of money and discretionary control of the quantity of money by central bank authority. The private creation of money can perhaps best be eliminated by adopting the 100 per cent reserve proposal, thereby separating the depositary from the lending function of the banking system.[3] The adoption of 100 per cent reserves would also reduce the discretionary powers of the reserve system by eliminating rediscounting and existing powers over reserve requirements. To complete the elimination of the major weapons of discretionary authority, the existing powers to engage in open market operations and the existing direct controls over stock market and consumer credit should be abolished.

These modifications would leave as the chief monetary functions of the banking system the provision of depositary facilities, the facilitation of check clearance, and the like; and as the chief function of the monetary authorities, the creation of money to meet government deficits or the retirement of money when the government has a surplus.[4]

2. A policy of determining the volume of government expenditures on goods and services – defined to exclude transfer expenditures of all kinds – entirely on the basis of the community's desire, need, and willingness to pay for public services. Changes in the level of expenditure should be made solely in response to alterations in the relative value

attached by the community to public services and private consumption. No attempt should be made to vary expenditures, either directly or inversely, in response to cyclical fluctuations in business activity. Since the community's basic objectives would presumably change only slowly – except in time of war or immediate threat of war – this policy would, with the same exception, lead to a relatively stable volume of expenditures on goods and services.[5]

3. A predetermined program of transfer expenditures, consisting of a statement of the conditions and terms under which relief and assistance and other transfer payments will be granted.[6] Such a program is exemplified by the present system of social security under which rules exist for the payment of old-age and unemployment insurance. The program should be changed only in response to alterations in the kind and level of transfer payments the community feels it should and can afford to make. The program should not be changed in response to cyclical fluctuations in business activity. Absolute outlays, however, will vary automatically over the cycle. They will tend to be high when unemployment is high and low when unemployment is low.[7]

4. A progressive tax system which places primary reliance on the personal income tax. Every effort should be made to collect as much of the tax bill as possible at source and to minimize the delay between the accrual of the tax liability and the actual collection of the tax. Rates, exemptions, etc., should be set in light of the expected yield at a level of income corresponding to reasonably full employment at a predetermined price level. The budget principle might be either that the hypothetical yield should balance government expenditure, including transfer payments (at the same hypothetical level of income) or that it should lead to a deficit sufficient to provide some specified secular increase in the quantity of money.[8] The tax structure should not be varied in response to cyclical fluctuations in business activity, though actual receipts will, of course, vary automatically.[9] Changes in the tax structure should reflect changes in the level of public services or transfer payments the community chooses to have. A decision to undertake additional public expenditures should be accompanied by a revenue measure increasing taxes. Calculations of both the cost of additional public services or transfer payments and the yield of additional taxes should be made at the hypothetical level of income suggested above rather than at the actual level of income. The government would thus keep two budgets: the stable budget, in which all figures refer to the hypothetical income, and the actual budget. The principle of balancing outlays and receipts at a hypothetical income level would be substituted for the principle of balancing actual outlays and receipts.

II Operation of the proposal

The essence of this fourfold proposal is that it uses automatic adaptations in the government contribution to the current income stream to offset, at least in part, changes in other segments of aggregate demand and to change appropriately the supply of money. It eliminates discretionary action in response to cyclical movements as well as some extraneous or perverse reactions of our present monetary and fiscal structure.[10] Discretionary action is limited to the determination of the hypothetical level of income underlying the stable budget; that is, essentially to the determination of a reasonably attainable objective. Some decision of this kind is unavoidable in drawing up the government's budget; the proposal involves a particular decision and makes it explicit. The determination of the income goal admittedly cannot be made entirely objective or mechanical. At the same time, this determination would need to be made only at rather long intervals – perhaps every five or ten years – and involves a minimum of forecasting. Further, as will be indicated later, errors in the income goal tend to be automatically neutralized and do not require a redetermination of the goal.

Under the proposal, government expenditures would be financed entirely by either tax revenues or the creation of money, that is, the issue of non-interest-bearing securities. Government would not issue interest-bearing securities to the public; the Federal Reserve System would not operate in the open market. This restriction of the sources of government funds seems reasonable for peacetime. The chief valid ground for paying interest to the public on government debt is to offset the inflationary pressure of abnormally high government expenditures when, for one reason or another, it is not feasible or desirable to levy sufficient taxes to do so. This was the justification for wartime issuance of interest-bearing securities, though, perversely, the rate of interest on these securities was pegged at a low level. It seems inapplicable in peacetime, especially if, as suggested, the volume of government expenditures on goods and services is kept relatively stable. Another reason sometimes given for issuing interest-bearing securities is that in a period of unemployment it is less deflationary to issue securities than to levy taxes. This is true. But it is still less deflationary to issue money.[11]

Deficits or surpluses in the government budget would be reflected dollar for dollar in changes in the quantity of money; and, conversely, the quantity of money would change only as a consequence of deficits or surpluses. A deficit means an increase in the quantity of money; a surplus, a decrease.[12]

Deficits or surpluses themselves become automatic consequences of changes in the level of business activity. When national money income is high, tax receipts will be large and transfer payments small; so a surplus will tend to be created, and the higher the level of income, the larger the surplus. This extraction of funds from the current income stream makes aggregate demand lower than it otherwise would be and reduces the volume of money, thereby tending to offset the factors making for a further increase in income. When national money income is low, tax receipts will be small and transfer payments large, so a deficit will tend to be created, and the lower the level of income, the larger the deficit. This addition of funds to the current income stream makes aggregate demand higher than it otherwise would be and increases the quantity of money, thereby tending to offset the factors making for a further decline in income.

The size of the effects automatically produced by changes in national income obviously depends on the range of activities government undertakes, since this will in turn determine the general order of magnitude of the government budget. Nonetheless, an essential element of the proposal is that the activities to be undertaken by government be determined entirely on other grounds. In part, this element is an immediate consequence of the motivation of the proposal. The motivation aside, however, it seems a desirable element of any proposal to promote stability. First, there is and can be no simple, reasonably objective, rule to determine the optimum share of activity that should be assigned to government – short of complete socialization – even if stability were the only objective. Changes in circumstances are likely to produce rapid and erratic variations in the share that seems desirable. But changes in the share assigned to government are themselves likely to be destabilizing, both directly and through their adverse effects on anticipations. The attempt to adapt the magnitude of government operations to the requirements of stability may therefore easily introduce more instability than it corrects. Second, the share of activity assigned to government is likely to have far more important consequences for other objectives – particularly political freedom and economic efficiency – than for stability.[13] Third, means other than changes in the share of activity assigned to government are readily available for changing the size of the reaction to changes in income, if experience under the proposal should prove this desirable. And some of these means need not have anything like the same consequences for other objectives.

Under the proposal, the aggregate quantity of money is automatically determined by the requirements of domestic stability. It follows that changes in the quantity of money cannot also be used – as they are in a fully operative gold standard – to achieve equilibrium in international trade. The two criteria will by no means always require the same changes in the quantity of money; when they conflict, one or the other must dominate. The decision, implicit in the framework recommended, to select domestic stability means that some other technique must be used to bring about adjustments to changes in the conditions of international trade. The international arrangement that seems the logical counterpart of the proposed framework is flexible exchange rates, freely determined in foreign exchange markets, preferably entirely by private dealings.[14]

III   Effect of proposal under present institutional conditions

The fluctuations in the government contribution to the income stream under the proposed monetary and fiscal framework are clearly in the 'right' direction. Nonetheless, it is not at all clear that they would, without additional institutional modifications, necessarily lead either to reasonably full employment or to a reasonable degree of stability. Rigidities in prices are likely to make this proposal, and indeed most if not all other proposals for attaining cyclical stability, inconsistent with reasonably full employment; and, when combined with lags in other types of response, to render extremely uncertain their effectiveness in stabilizing economic activity.

Price rigidities

Under existing circumstances, when many prices are moderately rigid, at least against declines, the monetary and fiscal framework described above cannot be expected to lead to reasonably full employment of resources, even though lags in other kinds of response are minor. The most that can be expected under such circumstances is a reasonably stable or moderately rising level of money income. As an extreme example, suppose that the economy is in a relatively stable position at reasonably full employment and with a roughly balanced actual government budget and that the great bulk of wage rates are rigid against downward pressure. Now, let there be a substantial rise in the wage rates of a particular group of workers as a consequence either of trade union action or of a sharp but temporary increase in the demand for that type of labor or decrease in its supply, and let this higher wage rate be rigid against downward pressure. Employment of resources as full as previously would imply a higher aggregate money income since, under the assumed conditions of rigidity, other resources would receive the same amount as previously whereas the workers whose wage rates rose would receive a larger aggregate amount if fully employed. But if this higher money income, which also of course would imply a higher price structure, were attained, the government would tend to have a surplus since receipts would rise by more than expenditures. There is nothing that has occurred that would, in the absence of other independent changes, offset the deflationary effect of the surplus. The assumed full employment position would not therefore be an equilibrium position. If attained by accident, the resultant budgetary surplus would reduce effective demand and, since prices are assumed rigid, the outcome could only be unemployment. The equilibrium level of income will be somewhat higher than before, primarily because transfer payments to the unemployed will be larger, so that some of the unemployment will be offset. But there is no mechanism for offsetting the rest. The only escape from this situation is a permit inflation.

As is widely recognized, the difficulty just described is present also in most other monetary and fiscal proposals; they, too, can produce full employment under such circumstances only by inflation. This dilemma often tends, however, to be concealed in their formulation, and, in practice, it seems fairly likely that inflation would result. The brute fact is that a rational economic program for a free enterprise system (and perhaps even for a collectivist system) must have flexibility of prices (including wages) as one of its cornerstones. This need is made clear by a proposal like the present. Moreover, the adoption of such a proposal would provide some assurance against cumulative deflation and thereby tend to make flexibility of prices a good deal easier to achieve since government support for monopolistic practices of special occupational and industrial groups derives in large measure from the obvious waste of general deflation and the need for protection against it.

Lags in response

Our economy is characterized not only by price rigidities but also by significant lags in other types of response. These lags make impossible any definitive statement about the actual degree of stability likely to result from the operation of the monetary and fiscal framework described above. One could reasonably expect smaller fluctuations than currently exist; though our ignorance about lags and about the fundamental causes of business fluctuations prevents complete confidence even in this outcome. The lag between the creation of a government deficit and its effects on the behavior of consumers and producers could conceivably be so long and variable that the stimulating effects of the deficit were often operative only after other factors had already brought about a recovery rather than when the initial decline was in progress. Despite intuitive feelings to the contrary, I do not believe we know enough to rule out completely this possibility. If it were realized, the proposed framework could intensify rather than mitigate cyclical fluctuations; that is, long and variable lags could convert the fluctuations in the government contribution to the income stream into the equivalent of an additional random disturbance.[15]

About all one can say about this possibility is that the completely automatic proposal outlined above seems likely to do less harm under the circumstances envisaged than alternative proposals which provide for discretionary action in addition to automatic reactions. There is a strong presumption that these discretionary actions will in general be subject to longer lags than the automatic reactions and hence will be destabilizing even more frequently.

The basis for this presumption can best be seen by subdividing into three parts of the total lag involved in any action to offset a disturbance: (1) the lag between the need for action and the recognition of this need; (2) the lag between recognition of the need for action and the taking of action; and (3) the lag between the action and its effects.

The first lag, which is nonexistent for automatic reactions of the kind here proposed, could be negative for discretionary proposals if it were possible to forecast accurately the economic changes that would occur in the absence of government action. In view of the record of forecasters, it hardly needs to be argued that it would be better to shun forecasting and rely instead on as prompt an evaluation of the current situation as possible. The lag between the need for action and the recognition of that need then becomes positive. Its exact magnitude depends on the particular discretionary proposal, though the past record of contemporary interpreters of business conditions indicates that it is not likely to be negligible.[16]

The second lag is present even for automatic reactions because all taxes will not or cannot be collected at source simultaneously with the associated payments, and transfer payments will not or cannot be made immediately without some kind of a waiting period or processing period. It is clear, however, that this lag can be reduced to a negligible time by appropriate construction and administration of the system of taxes and transfer payments. For discretionary action, the length of the lag between the recognition of the need for action and the taking of action depends very much on the kind of action taken. Action can be taken very promptly to change the form or amount of the community's holdings of assets by open market purchases or sales of securities or by changes in rediscount rates or reserve requirements. A considerably longer time is required to change the net contribution of the government to the income stream by changing the tax structure. Even though advance prescription for alternative possibilities eliminates any delay in deciding what changes to make in tax rates, exemptions, kinds of taxes levied, or the like, administrative considerations will enforce a substantial delay before the change becomes effective. Taxpayers, businesses or individuals acting as intermediaries in collecting the taxes, and tax administrators must all be informed of the change and be given an opportunity to make the appropriate adjustments in their procedures; new forms must be printed or at least circulated; and so on.

The longest delay of all is likely to be involved in changing the net contribution of government to the income stream by changing government expenditure policy, particularly for goods and services. No matter how much advance planning may have been done, the rate of expenditure cannot be stepped up or curtailed overnight unless the number of names on the payroll is to be the only basis in terms of which the expenditure is to be controlled or judged. Time is involved in getting projects under way with any degree of efficiency; and considerable waste in ceasing work on projects abruptly.

The third lag, that between the action and its effects, is present and significant both for automatic reactions and discretionary actions, and little if anything can be done about it by either legal or administrative reform of the fiscal and monetary structure.[17] We have no trustworthy empirical evidence on the length of this lag for various kinds of action, and much further study of this problem is clearly called for. Some clues about the direction such study should take are furnished by *a priori* considerations which suggest, as a first approximation, that the order of the various policies with respect to the length of this lag is the reverse of their order with respect to the length of the lag between the recognition of the need for action and the taking of action. Changes in government expenditures on goods and services lead to almost immediate changes in the employment of the resources used to produce those goods and services. They have secondary effects through the changes thereby induced in the expenditures of the individuals owing the resources so employed.

The lag in these induced changes might be expected to be less than the lag in the adjustment of expenditures to changed taxes or to a change amount or form of asset holdings. Changes in taxes make the disposable incomes of individuals larger or smaller than they would otherwise be. Individuals might be expected to react to a change in disposable income as a result of a tax change only slightly less rapidly than to a change in disposable income as a result of a change in aggregate income.

These indications are, however, none too trustworthy. There are likely to be important indirect effects that depend on such things as the kinds of goods and services directly affected by changed government expenditures, the incidence of the changes in disposable income that result from changed expenditures or taxes, and the means employed to finance government deficits. For example, if deficits are financed through increases in the quantity of money and surpluses are used to reduce the quantity of money, part of the effect of changes in government expenditures or taxes will be produced by changes in interest rates and the kind and volume of assets held by the community. The entire effect of open-market operations, changes in rediscount rates and reserve requirements, and the like will be produced in this way, and it seems likely that these effects would take the longest to make themselves felt.

The automatic reactions embodied in the proposal here advanced operate in part like tax changes – in so far as tax receipts vary – and in part like expenditure changes – in so far as transfer payments vary; and like both of these, some part of their effect is through changes in the quantity of money. One might expect, therefore, that the lag between action and its effects would be roughly the same for automatic reactions as for discretionary tax changes, a good deal shorter for automatic reactions than for discretionary monetary changes, and somewhat longer for automatic reactions than for discretionary changes in government expenditures on goods and services.

This analysis, much of which is admittedly highly conjectural, suggests that the total lag is definitely longer for discretionary monetary or tax changes than for automatic reactions, since each of the three parts into which the total lag has been subdivided is longer. There is doubt about the relative length of the total lag only for discretionary expenditure changes. Even for these, however, it seems doubtful that the shorter lag between action and its effects can more than offset the longer lag between the need for action and the taking of action.

Given less extreme conditions than those required to convert the present proposal into a destabilizing influence, the reduction achieved in the severity of fluctuations would depend on the extent and rapidity of price adjustments, the nature of the responses of individuals to these price changes and to the changes in their incomes and asset holdings resulting from the induced surpluses or deficits, and the lags in such responses. If these were such as to make the system operate reasonably well, the improvement would tend to be cumulative, since the experience of damped fluctuations would lead to patterns of expectations on the part of both businessmen and consumers that would make it rational for them to take action that would damp fluctuations still more. This favourable result would occur, however, only if the proposed system operated reasonably well without such aid; hence, in my view, this proposal, and all others as well, should be judged primarily on their direct effects, not on their indirect effects in stimulating a psychological climate favorable to stability. It must be granted, however, that the present proposal is less likely to stimulate such a favorable psychological climate than a proposal which has a simpler and more easily understood goal, for example, a proposal which sets a stable price level as its announced goal. *If the business world were sufficiently confident of the ability of the government to achieve the goal*, it would have a strong incentive to behave in such a way as greatly to simplify the government's task.

IV Implications of the proposal if prices are flexible and lags in response minor

The ideal possibilities of the monetary and fiscal framework proposed in this paper, and the stabilizing economic forces on which these possibilities depend, can be seen best if we put aside the difficulties that have been detaining us and examine the implications of the proposal in an economy in which prices of both products and factors of production are flexible[18] and lags in other types of response are minor. In such an economy, the monetary and fiscal system described above would tend toward an equilibrium characterized by reasonably full employment.

To describe the forces at work, let us suppose that the economy is initially in a position of reasonably full employment with a balanced actual budget and is subjected to a disturbance producing a decline in aggregate money demand that would be permanent if no other changes occurred.[19] The initial effect of the decline in aggregate demand will be a decline in sales and the piling up of inventories in at least some parts of the economy, followed shortly by unemployment and price declines caused by the attempt to reduce inventories to the desired level. The lengthening of the list of unemployed will increase government transfer payments; the loss of income by the unemployed will reduce government tax receipts. The deficit created in this way is a net contribution by the government to the income stream which indirectly offsets some of the decline in aggregate demand, thereby preventing unemployment from becoming as large as it otherwise would and serving as a shock absorber while more fundamental correctives come into play.

These more fundamental correctives, aside from changes in relative prices and interest rates, are (1) a decline in the general level of prices which affects (a) the real value of the community's assets and (b) the government contribution to the income stream, and (2) an increase in the stock of money.

The decline in the general level of prices that follows the initial decline in aggregate demand will clearly raise the real value of the community's stock of money and government bonds since the nominal value of these assets will not decrease. The real value of the remainder of the community's assets may be expected to remain roughly the same, so the real value of the total stock of assets will rise.[20] The rise in the real value of assets will lessen the need for additional saving and hence increase the fraction of any given level of real income that the community will wish to consume. This force, in principle, would alone be sufficient to assure full employment even if the government maintained a rigidly balanced actual budget and kept the quantity of money constant, since there would presumably always be some price level at which the community could be made to feel rich enough to spend on consumption whatever fraction or multiple of its current income is required to yield an aggregate demand sufficient to permit full employment.

This effect of a lower price level in increasing the fraction of current private (disposable) income devoted to consumption is reinforced by its effect on the government's contribution to the income stream. So long as the price level and with it money income, is below its initial level, the government will continue to run a deficit. This will be true even if employment is restored to its initial level, so that transfer payments and loss in tax receipts on account of unemployment are eliminated. The tax structure is progressive, and exemptions, rates, etc., are expressed in absolute dollar amounts. Receipts will therefore fall more than in proportion to the fall in the price level; expenditures, at most, proportionately.[21] Because of the emergence of such a deficit, the price decline required to restore employment will be smaller than if the government were to maintain a rigidly balanced actual budget, and this will be true even aside from the influence of the deficit on the stock of money. The reason is that the price level will have to fall only to the point at which the amount the community desires to add to its hoards equals the government deficit, rather than to the point at which the community desires to add nothing to its hoards.[22]

The decline in the price level may restore the initial level of employment through the combined effects of the increased average propensity to consume and the government deficit. But so long as a deficit exists, the position attained is not an equilibrium position. The deficit is financed by the issue of money. The resultant increase in the aggregate stock of money must further raise the real value of the community's stock of assets and hence the average propensity to consume. This is the same effect as that discussed above except that it is brought about by an increase in the absolute stock of money rather than by a decline in prices. Like the corresponding effect produced by a decline in prices, the magnitude of this effect is, in principle, unlimited. The rise in the stock of money and hence in the average propensity to consume will tend to raise prices and reduce the deficit. If we suppose no change to occur other than the one introduced to start the analysis going, the final adjustment would be attained when prices had arisen sufficiently to yield a roughly balanced actual budget.

A disturbance increasing aggregate money demand would bring into play the same forces operating in the reverse direction: the increase in employment would reduce transfer payments and raise tax receipts, thus creating a surplus to offset part of the increase in aggregate demand; the rise in prices would decrease the real value of the community's stock of money and hence the fraction of current income spent on consumption; the rise in prices would also mean that even after 'overemployment' was eliminated, the government would run a surplus that would tend to offset further the initial increase in aggregate demand;[23] and, finally, the surplus would reduce the stock of money.

As this analysis indicates, the proposed fiscal and monetary framework provides defense in depth against changes in aggregate demand. The first line of defense is the adjustment of transfer payments and tax receipts to changes in employment.[24] This eases the shock while the defense is taken over by changes in prices. These raise or lower the real value of the community's assets and thereby raise or lower the fraction of income consumed. They also produce a government deficit or surplus in addition to the initial deficit or surplus resulting from the effect of changes in employment on transfer payments and tax receipts. The final line of defense is the cumulative effect of the deficits or surpluses on the stock of money. These changes in the stock of money tend to restore prices to their initial level. In some measure, of course, these defenses all operate simultaneously; yet their main effects are likely to occur in the temporal order suggested in the preceding discussion.

Even given flexible prices, the existence of the equilibrating mechanism described does not of course mean that the economy will in fact achieve relative stability. This depends in addition on the number and magnitude of the disturbances to which the economy is subject, the speed with which the equilibrating forces operate, and the importance of such disequilibrating forces as adverse price expectations. If the lags of response are minor, and initial perverse reactions unimportant, adjustments would be completed rapidly and there would be no opportunity for disequilibria to cumulate, so that relative stability would be attained. Even in this most favorable case, however, the equilibrating mechanism does not prevent disturbances from arising and does not counteract their effects instantaneously – as, indeed, no system can in the absence of ability to predict everything in advance with perfect accuracy. What the equilibrating mechanism does accomplish is, first, to keep governmental monetary and fiscal operations from themselves contributing disturbances and, second, to provide an automatic mechanism for adapting the system to the disturbances that occur.

Given flexible prices, there would be a tendency for automatic neutralization of any errors in the hypothetical income level assumed or in the calculations of the volume of expenditures and revenues at the hypothetical income level. Further, it would ultimately be of no great importance exactly what decision was reached about the relation to establish between expenditures and revenue at the hypothetical income level (i.e., whether exactly to balance, to strive for a deficit sufficient to provide a predetermined secular increase in the quantity of money, etc.). Suppose, for example, that errors in the assumed income level, the calculated volume of expenditures and receipts, and the relation established between expenditures and receipts combined to produce a deficit larger than was consistent with stable prices. The resulting inflationary pressure would be analogous to that produced by an external disturbance and the same forces would come into play to counteract it. The result would be that prices would rise and the level of income tend to stabilize at a higher level than the hypothetical level initially assumed.

Similarly, the monetary and fiscal framework described above provides for adjustment not only to cyclical changes but also to secular changes. I do not put much credence in the doctrine of secular stagnation or economic maturity that is now so widely held. But let us assume for the sake of argument that this doctrine is correct, that there has been such a sharp secular decline in the demand for capital that, at the minimum rate of interest technically feasible, the volume of investment at a full-employment level of income would be very much less than the volume of savings that would be forthcoming at this level of income and at the current price level.[25] The result would simply be that the equilibrium position would involve a recurrent deficit sufficient to provide the hoards being demanded by savers. Of course, this would not really be a long-run equilibrium position, since the gradual increase in the quantity of money would increase the aggregate real value of the community's stock of money and thereby of assets, and this would tend to increase the fraction of any given level of real income consumed. As a result, there would tend to be a gradual rise in prices and the level of money income and a gradual reduction in the deficit.[26]

V Conclusion

In conclusion, I should like to emphasize the modest aim of the proposal. It does not claim to provide full employment in the absence of successful measures to make prices of final goods and of factors of production flexible. It does not claim to eliminate entirely cyclical fluctuations in output and employment. Its claim to serious consideration is that it provides a stable framework of fiscal and monetary action, that it largely eliminates the uncertainty and undesirable political implications of discretionary action by governmental authorities, that it provides for adaptation of the governmental sector to changes occurring in other sectors of the economy of a kind designed to offset the effects of these changes, and that the proposed fiscal and monetary framework is consistent with the long-run considerations stated at the outset of this paper. It is not perhaps a proposal that one would consider at all optimum if our knowledge of the fundamental causes of cyclical fluctuations were considerably greater than I, for one, think it to be; it is a proposal that involves minimum reliance on uncertain and untested knowledge.

The proposal has of course its dangers. Explicit control of the quantity of money by government and explicit creation of money to meet actual government deficits may establish a climate favorable to irresponsible government action and to inflation. The principle of a balanced stable budget may not be strong enough to offset these tendencies. This danger may well be greater for this proposal than for some others, yet in some measure it is common to most proposals to mitigate cyclical fluctuations. It can probably be avoided only by moving in a completely different direction, namely, toward an entirely metallic currency, elimination of any governmental control of the quantity of money, and the re-enthronement of the principle of a balanced actual budget.

The proposal may not succeed in reducing cyclical fluctuations to tolerable proportions. The forces making for cyclical fluctuations may be so stubborn and strong that the kind of automatic adaptations contained in the proposal are insufficient to offset them to a tolerable degree. I do not see how it is possible to know now whether this is the case. But even if it should prove to be, the changes suggested are almost certain to be in the right direction and, in addition, to provide a more satisfactory framework on which to build further action.

A proposal like the present one, which is concerned not with short-run policy but with structural reform, should not be urged on the public unless and until it has withstood the test of professional criticism. It is in this spirit that the present paper is published.

Notes

1. An earlier version of this paper was presented before the Econometric Society on September 17, 1947, at a meeting held in conjunction with the International Statistical Conferences in Washington, DC. I am deeply indebted for helpful criticisms and constructive suggestions to Arthur F. Burns, Aaron Director, Albert G. Hart, H. Gregg Lewis, Lloyd W. Mints, Don Patinkin and George J. Stigler.
2. The reason for restricting the discussion to the federal government is simply that it alone has ultimate monetary powers, not any desire to minimize the role of smaller governmental units. Indeed, for the achievement of the long-run objectives stated above it is highly desirable that the maximum amount of government activity be in the hands of the smaller governmental units to achieve as much decentralization of political power as possible.
3. This proposal was advanced by Henry C. Simons. See his *A Positive Program for Laissez-Faire: Some Proposals for a Liberal Economic Policy*, Public Policy Pamphlet No. 15 (Univ. of Chicago Press, 1934); 'Rules *vs.* Authorities in Monetary Policy', *Jour. Pol. Econ.*, Vol. XLIV (Feb., 1936), pp. 1–30. Both of these are reprinted in Henry C. Simons, *Economic Policy for a Free Society* (Chicago, Univ. of Chicago Press, 1948).

4. The adoption of 100 per cent reserves is essential if the proposed framework is to be entirely automatic. It should be noted, however, that the same results could, in principle, be achieved in a fractional reserve system through discretionary authority. In order to accomplish this, the monetary authorities would have to adopt the rule that the quantity of money should be increased only when the government has a deficit, and then by the amount of the deficit, and should be decreased only when the government has a surplus, and then by the amount of the surplus.
5. The volume of expenditures might remain stable either in money or real terms. The principle of determining the volume of expenditures by the community's objectives would lead to a stable real volume of expenditures on current goods and services. On the other hand, the usual legislative procedure in budget making is to grant fixed sums of money, which would lead to stability of money expenditures and provides a slight automatic contracyclical flexibility. If the volume of real expenditures were stabilized, money expenditures would vary directly with prices.
6. These transfer payments might perhaps more appropriately be regarded as negative revenue.
7. It may be hoped that the present complex structure of transfer payments will be integrated into a single scheme co-ordinated with the income tax and designed to provide a universal floor to personal incomes. But this is a separate issue.
8. These specifications about the hypothetical level of income to be used and the budget principle to be followed are more definite and dogmatic than is justified. In principle, the economic system could ultimately adjust to any tax structure and expenditure policy, no matter what level of income or what budget principle they were initially based on, provided that the tax structure and expenditure policy remained stable. That is, there corresponds some secular position appropriate to each possible tax structure and expenditure policy. The best level of income and the best budget principle to choose depend therefore on short-run adjustment considerations: what choice would require the least difficult adjustment? Moreover, the level of income and budget principle must be chosen jointly: the same final result can obviously be obtained by combining a high hypothetical income with a surplus budget principle or a low hypothetical income with a deficit budget principle or by any number of intermediate combinations. My own conjecture is that the particular level of income and budget principles suggested above are unlikely to lead to results that would require radical short-run adjustments to attain the corresponding secular position. Unfortunately, our knowledge about the relevant economic interrelationships is too meager to permit more than reasonably informed conjecture. See Section IV below, especially footnote 23.
9. The principle of setting taxes so as to balance the budget at a high level of employment was suggested by Beardsley Ruml and H. Chr. Sonne, *Fiscal and Monetary Policy*, National Planning Pamphlet no. 35 (July, 1944).

Since the present paper was written, the Committee for Economic Development has issued a policy statement in which it makes essentially the same tax and expenditure recommendations – that is, it calls for adoption of a stable tax structure capable of balancing the budget at a high level of employment, a stable expenditure policy, and primary reliance on automatic adjustments of absolute revenue and expenditures to provide cyclical stability. They call this policy the "stabilizing budget policy." The chief difference between the present proposal and the C.E.D proposal is that the C.E.D is silent on the monetary framework and almost silent on public debt policy, whereas the present proposal covers both. Presumably the C.E.D plans to cover monetary and debt policy in separate statements still to be issued. See *Taxes and the Budget: A Program for Prosperity in a Free Economy*, a statement on national policy by the Research and Policy Committee of the Committee for Economic Development (Nov., 1947).

10. For example, the tendency under the existing system of fractional reserve banking for the total volume of money to change when there is a change in the proportion of its total stock of money the community wishes to hold in the form of deposits; the tendency to reduce tax rates and increase government expenditures in booms and to do the reverse in depressions; and the tendency for the government to borrow from individuals at the same time as the Federal Reserve System is buying government bonds on the open market.

11. See Henry C. Simons, "On Debt Policy," *Journal of Political Economy*, Vol. LII (Dec., 1944), pp. 356–61.

   This paragraph deliberately avoids the question of the payment of interest to banks on special issues of government bonds, as has been proposed in some versions of the 100 per cent reserve proposal. The fundamental issue involved in judging such proposals is whether government should subsidize the use of deposit money and a system of check clearance and if so, what form the subsidy should take.

   The large volume of government bonds now outstanding raises one of the most serious problems in accomplishing the transition from the present framework. This problem would be eased somewhat by the monetization of bonds that would occur in the process of going over to 100 per cent reserves. But there would still remain a substantial volume. Two alternatives suggest themselves : (1) freeze the volume of debt at some figure, preferably by converting it into perpetuities ("consols"); (2) use the monetization of the debt as a means of providing a secular increase in the quantity of money. Under the second plan, which, on a first view, seems more attractive, the principle of balancing the stable budget would be adopted and the government would commit itself to retiring, through the issuance of new money, a predetermined amount of the public debt annually. The amount to be retired would be determined so as to achieve whatever secular increase in the quantity of money seemed desirable. This problem, however, requires much additional study.

12. These statements refer, of course, to the ultimate operation of the proposal. Under the second of the alternatives suggested in the preceding footnote, the change in the quantity of money during the transitional period would equal the excess of government expenditures over receipts plus the predetermined amount of money issued to retire debt.

13. An example of the relevance of these two points is provided by the tendency during the thirties to recommend an increase in the progressiveness of the tax structure as a means of increasing the propensity to consume and hence, it was argued, employment. Applied to the postwar period, the same argument would call for a shift to regressive taxes, yet I wonder if many economists would wish to recommend regressive taxes on these grounds.
14. Though here presented as a byproduct of the proposed domestic framework, flexible exchange rates can be defended directly. Indeed, it would be equally appropriate to present the proposed domestic framework as a means of implementing flexible exchange rates. The heart of the matter is that domestic and international monetary and trade arrangements are part of one whole.
15. See Milton Friedman, "Lerner on the Economics of Control," *Journal of Political Economy*, Vol. LV, No. 5 (Oct., 1947), p. 414, especially footnote 12.
16. *Ibid*, p. 414, especially footnote 11.
17. Reforms of other types, for example, reforms increasing the flexibility of prices, might affect this lag.
18. The concept of flexible prices, though one we use continually and can hardly avoid using, is extremely difficult to define precisely. Fortunately, a precise definition is not required for the argument that follows. All that is necessary for the argument is that there be a "substantial" range of prices that are not "rigid" because of long-term contracts or organized noncontractual agreements to maintain price and that these prices should react reasonably quickly to changes in long-run conditions of demand or supply. It is not necessary that there be "perfect" flexibility of prices, however that might be defined, or that contracts involving prices be subject to change at will, or that every change in long-run conditions of demand or supply be reflected instantaneously in market price.
19. The same analysis would apply to disturbances producing only a temporary decline. The reason for assuming a permanent decline is to trace through the entire process of adjustment to a new equilibrium position.
20. If the real value of other assets and the community should fall, this would simply mean that the price level would have to fall farther in order to raise the real value of the community's total stock of assets. Note that under the proposed framework, all money in the community is either a direct government obligation (nondeposit currency) or is backed one hundred per cent by a direct government obligation (deposits in the central bank). If this analysis were to be applied to a fractional reserve system, the assets whose aggregate real value could be guaranteed to rise with no directly offsetting fall in the real value of private assets would be the total amount of government obligations (currency and bonds) held outside the treasury and central bank. On this and what follows, see A. C. Pigou, "The Classical Stationary State," *Economics Journal*, Vol. LIII (Dec., 1943), pp. 342–51, and "Economic Progress in a Stable Environment," *Economica*, n.s. XIV (Aug., 1974), pp. 180–90; and Don Patinkin, "Price Flexibility and Full Employment," in the *American Economic Review*, September, 1948 number of this *Review*.
21. The effect of the lower price level on expenditures depends somewhat on the precise expenditure and transfer policy adopted. If, as is called for by the

principle of determining the expenditure program, by the community's objectives, the real volume of government expenditures on goods and services is kept cyclically stable and if the program of transfer payments is also stated in real terms, expenditures will decline proportionately. If government expenditures on goods and services are kept cyclically stable in dollar terms, or the program of transfer expenditures is stated in dollar terms, expenditures will decline less than proportionately.

22. If the real volume of government expenditures on goods and services is kept cyclically stable and the transfer program is also stated in real terms, the aggregate expenditures of government under fixed expenditure and transfer programs would tend to be the same fraction of the full-employment income of society no matter what the price level. This fraction would be the maximum net contribution the government could make to the income stream no matter how low prices, and with them money income and government receipts, fell. Consequently, this force alone would be limited in magnitude and might not, even in principle, be able to offset every disturbance. If either program is in absolute terms, there would be no limit to the fraction that the government contribution could constitute of the total income stream.

An alternative way to describe this effect is in terms of the relation between the expected expenditures and receipts of consumers, business, and government. It is a condition of equilibrium that the sum of the desired expenditures of these groups equal the sum of their receipts. If the government maintains a rigidly balanced budget, equilibrium requires that consumers and business together plan to spend what they receive, i.e., not seek to add to their money hoards. If the government runs a deficit, consumers and business together need not plan to spend all they receive; equilibrium requires that their planned expenditures fall short of their receipts by the amount of the deficit i.e., that they seek to add to their hoards per period the amount of the deficit.

23. The limit to the possible effect of the surplus on the current income stream would be set by the character of the tax structure, since there would probably be some maximum percentage of the aggregate income that could be taken by taxes no matter how high the price level and the aggregate income.

24. It should be noted that this is the only effect taken into account by Musgrave and Miller in their calculations of the possible magnitude of the effect of automatic variations in government receipts and expenditures. (R. A. Musgrave and M. H. Miller, "Built-in Flexibility," this *Review*, March, 1948, pp. 122–28.) They conclude that "the analysis here provided lends no justification to the view now growing in popularity that 'built-in flexibility' can do the job alone and that deliberate countercyclical fiscal policy can be dispensed with." While this is a valid conclusion, it does not justify rejecting the view that "built-in flexibility" can do the job alone, since the "analysis here provided" takes no account of what have been termed above the "more fundamental correctives."

25. Because of the effect discussed above of price changes on the real value of assets, and in this way on the average propensity to consume, it seems to me that such a state of affairs would not lead to secular unemployment even if

the quantity of money were kept constant, provided that prices are flexible (which is the reason for including the qualification "at the current price level" in the sentence to which this footnote is attached). But I am for the moment accepting the point of view of those who deny the existence or importance of this equilibrating force. Moreover, if the quantity of money were constant, the adjustment would be made entirely through a secular decline in prices, admittedly a difficult adjustment. Once again changes in the government contribution to the income stream and through this in the quantity of money can reduce the extent of the required price change.

26. This and the preceding paragraph, in particular, and this entire section, in general suggest a problem that deserves investigation and to which I have no satisfactory answer, namely, the characteristics of the system of equations implicit in the proposal and of their equilibrium solution. It is obvious that under strictly stationary conditions, including a stationary population, the equilibrium solution would involve constancy of prices, income per head, etc., and a balanced actual budget. The interesting question is whether there is any simple description of the equilibrium solution under specified dynamic situations. For example, are there circumstances, and if so what are they, under which the equilibrium solution will tend to involve constant money income per head with declining prices, or constant prices with rising money income per head, etc? It is obvious that no such simple description will suffice in general, but there may well be broad classes of circumstances under which one or another will.

Rational Expectations and the Theory of Economic Policy*[1]

T. J. SARGENT AND N. WALLACE

There is no longer any serious debate about whether monetary policy should be conducted according to rules or discretion. Quite appropriately, it is widely agreed that monetary policy should obey a rule, that is, a schedule expressing the setting of the monetary authority's instrument (e.g., the money supply) as a function of all the information it has received up through the current moment. Such a rule has the happy characteristic that in any given set of circumstances, the optimal setting for policy is unique. If by remote chance, the same circumstances should prevail at two different dates, the appropriate settings for monetary policy would be identical.

The central practical issue separating monetarists from Keynesians is the appropriate form of the monetary policy rule. Milton Friedman has long advocated that the monetary authority adopt a simple rule having no feedback from current and past variables to the money supply. He recommends that the authority cause the money supply to grow at some rate of x percent per year without exception. In particular, the Fed ought not to try to 'lean against the wind' in an effort to attenuate the business cycle.

---

*This paper is intended as a popular summary of some recent work on rational expectations and macroeconometric policy and was originally prepared for a conference on that topic at the Federal Reserve Bank of Minneapolis in October 1974. The paper was first published as Paper 2 of the *Studies in Monetary Economics* series of the Federal Reserve Bank of Minneapolis, and later in *Journal of Monetary Economics* (July 1976), pp. 199–214.

Within the context of macroeconometric models as they are usually manipulated, Friedman's advocacy of a rule without feedback seems indefensible. For example, suppose that a variable y_t, which the authority is interested in controlling, is described by the stochastic difference equation,

$$y_t = \alpha + \lambda y_{t-1} + \beta m_t + u_t, \tag{19.1}$$

where u_t is a serially independent, identically distributed random variable with variance σ_u^2 and mean zero; m_t is the rate of growth of the money supply; and α, λ and β are parameters. The variable y_t can be thought of as the unemployment rate or the deviation of real GNP from 'potential' GNP. This equation should be thought of as the reduced form of a simple econometric model.

Suppose that the monetary authority desires to set m_t in order to minimize the variance over time of y_t around some desired level y^*. It accomplishes this by appropriately choosing the parameters g_0 and g_1 in the feedback rule,

$$m_t = g_0 + g_1 y_{t-1}. \tag{19.2}$$

Substituting for m_t from (19.2) into (19.1) gives

$$y_t = (\alpha + \beta g_0) + (\lambda + \beta g_1) y_{t-1} + u_t. \tag{19.3}$$

From this equation the steady-state mean of y is given by

$$E(y) = (\alpha + \beta g_0)/[1 - (\lambda + \beta g_1)], \tag{19.4}$$

which should be equated to y^* in order to minimize the variance of y around y^*. From (19.3) the steady-state variance of y around its mean (and hence around y^*) is given by

$$\text{var } y = (\lambda + \beta g_1)^2 \text{ var } y + \sigma_u^2$$

or

$$\text{var } y = \sigma_u^2/[1 - (\lambda + \beta g_1)^2] \tag{19.5}$$

The monetary authority chooses g_1 to minimize the variance of y, then chooses g_0 from eq. (19.4) to equate $E(y)$ to y^*. From eq. (19.5), the variance of y is minimized by setting $\lambda + \beta g_1 = 0$, so that g_1 equals $-\lambda/\beta$. Then from eq. (19.4) it follows that the optimal setting of g_0 is $g_0 = (y^* - \alpha)/\beta$. So the optimal feedback rule for m_t is

$$m_t = (y^* - \alpha)/\beta - (\lambda/\beta)y_{t-1}, \tag{19.6}$$

Substituting this control rule into (19.1) gives

$$y_t = y^* + u_t,$$

which shows that application of the rule sets y_t equal to y^* plus an irreducible noise. Notice the application of the rule eliminates all serial correlation in y, since this is the way to minimize the variance of y. Use of rule (19.6) means that the authority always expects to be on target, since its forecast of y, at time $t - 1$ is

$$\hat{y}_t = \alpha + \lambda y_{t-1} + \beta m_t$$

which under rule (19.6) equals y^*.

Friedman's x-percent growth rule in effect sets g_1 equal to zero. So long as λ is not zero, that rule is inferior to the feedback rule (19.6).

This example illustrates all of the elements of the usual proof that Friedman's simple x-per cent growth rule is suboptimal. Its logic carries over to larger stochastic difference equation models, ones with many more equations and with many more lags. It also applies where criterion functions have more variables. The basic idea is that where the effects of shocks to a goal variable (like GNP) display a stable pattern of persistence (serial correlation), and hence are predictable, the authority can improve the behavior of the goal variable by inducing offsetting movements in its instruments.

The notion that the economy can be described by presumably a large system of stochastic difference equations with fixed parameters underlies the standard Keynesian objections to the monism of monetarists who argue that the monetary authority should ignore other variables such as interest rates and concentrate on keeping the money supply on a steady growth path. The view that, on the contrary, the monetary authority should 'look at (and respond to) everything,' including interest rates, rests on the following propositions:[2] (a) the economic structure is characterized by extensive simultaneity, so that shocks that impinge on one variable, e.g. an interest rate, impinge also on most others; (b) due to lags in the system, the effects of shocks on the endogenous variables are distributed over time, and so are serially correlated and therefore somewhat predictable; and (c) the 'structure' of these lags is constant over time and does not depend on how the monetary authority is behaving. These propositions imply that variables that the authority observes very frequently, e.g. daily, such as interest rates, carry information useful for revising its forecasts of future value of variables that it can't observe as often, such as GNP and unemployment. This follows because the same shocks are affecting both the observed and the unobserved variables, and because those shocks have effects that persist. It follows then from (c) that the monetary authority should in general revise its planned setting for its policy instruments each time it receives some new and surprising reading on a variable that is determined simultaneously with a variable, like GNP or unemployment, that it is interested in controlling. Such an argument eschewing a simple x-percent growth rate rule in favor of 'looking at everything' has been made by Samuelson (1970):

> when I learned that I ha[d] been wrong in my beliefs about how fast M was growing from December, 1968 to April, 1969, this news was just one of twenty interesting items that had come to my knowledge that week. And it only slightly increased my forecast for the strength of aggregate demand at the present time. That was because my forecasts, so to speak, do not involve 'action at a distance' but are loose Markov processes in which a broad vector of current variables specify the 'phase space' out of which tomorrow's vector develops. (In short, I knowingly commit that most atrocious of sins in the penal code of the monetarists – I pay a great deal of attention to all dimensions of 'credit conditions' rather than keeping my eye on the solely important variable M/M.)
>
> ... often, I believe, the prudent man or prudent committee can look ahead six months to a year and with some confidence predict that the economy will be in other than an average or 'ergodic' state. Unless this assertion of mine can be demolished, the case for a fixed growth rate for M, or for confining M to narrow channels around such a rate, melts away.
>
> These general presumptions arise out of what we know about plausible models of economics and about the findings of historical experience.[3]

There can be little doubt about the inferiority of an x-percent growth rule for the money supply in a system satisfying proportions (a), (b), and (c) above. A reasonable disagreement with the 'look at everything, respond to everything' view would seemingly have to stem from a disbelief of one of those three premises. In particular, proposition (c) asserting the invariance of lag structures with respect to changes in the way policy is conducted would probably not be believed by an advocate of a rule without feedback.

Thus, returning to our simple example, a critical aspect of the proof of the suboptimality of Friedman's rule is clearly the assumption that the parameters x, λ, and β of the reduced form (19.1) are independent of the settings for g_0 and g_1 in the feedback rule. Macroeconometric models are almost always manipulated under such an assumption. However, Lucas (forthcoming) has forcefully argued that the assumption is inappropriate, and that the parameters of estimated reduced forms like (19.1) in part reflect the policy responses in operation during the periods over which they are estimated. This happens because in the reduced forms are embedded the responses of expectations to the way policy is formed. Changes in the way policy is made then ought not to leave the parameters of estimated reduced forms unchanged.

To illustrate this point while continuing with our example, suppose that our reduced form (19.1) has been estimated during some sample period and suppose that it comes from the 'structure':

$$y_t = \xi_0 + \xi_1(m_t - E_{t-1}m_t) + \xi_2 y_{t-1} + u_t, \tag{19.7}$$

$$m_t = g_0 + g_1 y_{t-1} + \epsilon_t, \tag{19.8}$$

$$E_{t-1}m_t = g_0 + g_1 y_{t-1}. \tag{19.9}$$

Here ξ_0, ξ_1 and ξ_2 are fixed parameters; ϵ_t is a serially independent random term with mean zero. We assume that it is statistically independent of u_t. Eq. (19.8) governed the money supply during the estimation period. The variable $E_{t-1}m_t$ is the public's expectation of m_t as of time $t-1$. According to eq. (19.9), the public knows the monetary authority's feedback rule and takes this into account in forming its expectations. According to (19.7), unanticipated movements in the money supply cause movements in y, but anticipated movements do not. The above structure can be written in the reduced form

$$y_t = (\xi_0 - \xi_1 g_0) + (\xi_2 - \xi_1 g_1) y_{t-1} + \xi_1 m_t + u_t, \tag{19.10}$$

which is in the form of (19.1) with $\alpha = (\xi_0 - \xi_1 g_0)$, $\lambda = (\xi_2 - \xi_1 g_1)$ and $\beta = \xi_1$. While the form of (19.10) is identical with that of (19.1), the coefficients of (19.10) are clearly functions of the control parameters, the gs, that were in effect during the estimation period.

Suppose now that the monetary authority desires to design a feedback rule to minimize the variance of y around y^* under the assumption that the public will know the rule it is using and so use the currently prevailing gs in (19.8) in forming its expectations, rather than the old gs that held during the estimation period. The public would presumably know the gs if the monetary authority were to announce them. Failing that, the public might be able to infer the gs from the observed behavior of the money supply and other variables. In any case, on the assumption that the public knows what gs the authority is using, α and λ of eq. (19.1) come to depend on the authority's choice of gs. This fundamentally alters the preceding analysis, as can be seen by substituting $g_0 + g_1 y_{t-1}$ for m_t in (19.10) to arrive at

$$y_t = (\xi_0 - \xi_1 g_0) + (\xi_2 - \xi_1 g_1) y_{t-1} + \xi_1(g_0 + g_1 y_{t-1}) + u_t$$

or

$$y_t = \xi_0 + \xi_2 y_{t-1} + u_t + \xi_1 \epsilon_t. \tag{19.11}$$

According to (19.1), the stochastic process for y_t does not even involve the parameters g_0 and g_1. Under different values of g_0 and g_1, the public's method of forming its expectations is also different, implying differences in the values of α and λ in (19.1) under different policy regimes. In our hypothetical model, the resulting differences in α and λ just offset the differences in g_0 and g_1, leaving the behavior of y identical as a result. Put somewhat differently, our old rule 'set $g_1 = -\lambda/\beta$' can no longer be fulfilled. For on the assumption that the public uses the correct gs in forming its expectations, it implies

$$g_1 = -\lambda/\beta = (\xi_1 g_1 - \xi_2)/\xi_1 = g_1 - \xi_2/\xi_1$$

or

$$0 = -\xi_2/\xi_1,$$

which is an equality not involving the gs, and one that the monetary authority is powerless to achieve. The rule '$g_1 = -\lambda/\beta$' in no way restricts g_1.

The point is that estimated reduced forms like (19.1) or (19.10) often have parameters that depend partly on the way unobservable expectations of the public are correlated with the variables on the right side of the equation, which in turn depends on the public's perception of how policymakers are behaving. If the public's perceptions are accurate, then the way in which its expectations are formed will change whenever policy changes, which will lead to changes in the parameters α and λ of the reduced-form equation. It is consequently improper to manipulate that reduced form as if its parameters were invariant with respect to changes in g_0 and g_1. According to this argument, then, the above 'proof' of the inferiority of a rule without feedback is fallacious. The argument for the 'look at everything, respond to everything' view is correspondingly vitiated.

The simple model above is one in which there is no scope for the authority to conduct countercyclical policy by suitably choosing g_0 and g_1 so as to minimize the variance of y. Indeed, one choice of the gs is as good as another, so far as concerns the variance of y, so that the authority might as well set g_1 equal to zero, thereby following a rule without feedback. It seems, then, that our example contains the ingredients for constructing a more general defense of rules without feedback. These ingredients are two: first, the authority's instrument appears in the reduced form for the real variable y only as the discrepancy of the instrument's setting from the public's prior expectation of that setting; and second, the public's psychological expectation of the setting for the instrument equals the objective mathematical expectation conditioned on data available when the expectation was formed. The first property in part reflects a homogeneity of degree zero of supply with respect to prices and expected prices, the natural unemployment rate hypothesis. But it also derives partly from the second property, which is the specification that the public's expectations are 'rational,' that is, are formed using the appropriate data and objective probability distributions.

The natural rate hypothesis posits that fully anticipated increases in prices have no effects on the rate of real economic activity, as indexed for example by the unemployment rate. A Phillips Curve that obeys the natural rate hypothesis can be written as

$$p_t - p_{t-1} = \phi_0 + \phi_1 U_t + {}_{t-1}p^*_t - p_{t-1} + \epsilon_t, \qquad \phi_1 < 0, \qquad (19.12)$$

or

$$p_t - {}_{t-1}p^*_t = \phi_0 + \phi_1 U_t + \epsilon_t, \qquad (19.13)$$

where U_t is the unemployment rate, p_t is the log of the price level, ${}_{t-1}p^*_t$ is the log of the price level that the public expects to prevail at time t as of time $t-1$, and ϵ_t is a random term. According to (19.12), the Phillips Curve shifts up by the full amount of any increase in expected inflation. That implies, as indicated by eq. (19.13), that if inflation is fully anticipated, so that $p_t = {}_{t-1}p^*_t$, then the unemployment rate is unaffected by the rate of inflation, since (19.13) becomes one equation,

$$0 = \phi_0 + \phi_1 U_t + \epsilon_t,$$

that is capable of determining the unemployment rate independently of the rate of inflation.

As Phelps (1972) and Hall (forthcoming) have pointed out, in and of itself, the natural rate hypothesis does not weaken the logical foundations for 'activist' Keynesian macroeconometric policy, i.e., rules with feedback. This fact has prompted some to view the natural rate hypothesis as an intellectual curiosity, having but remote policy implications.[4] To illustrate, we complete the model by adding to (19.13) a reduced form aggregate demand schedule and an hypothesis about the formation of expectations. We subsume 'Okun's Law' in the former and assume it takes the form

$$p_t = am_t + bx_t + cU_t, \qquad c > 0, \qquad (19.14)$$

where m_t is the log of the money supply, the authority's instrument; and x_t is a vector of exogenous variables that follows the Markov scheme

$x_t = \delta x_{t-1} + u_t$, u_t being a vector of random variables. For price expectations, we posit the ad hoc, in general 'irrational' scheme,

$$_{t-1}p^*_t = \lambda p_{t-1}, \tag{19.15}$$

where λ is a parameter. Using (19.3) – (19.5), we can easily solve for unemployment as a function of m_t and x_t,

$$U_t = [\phi_0 - a(m_t - \lambda m_{t-1}) - b(x_t - \lambda x_{t-1}) + c\lambda U_{t-1} + \epsilon_t]/(c - \phi_1). \tag{19.16}$$

It follows that the current setting for m_t affects both current and future values of unemployment and inflation. Given that the authority wishes to minimize a loss function that depends on current and future unemployment and perhaps inflation, the choice of m_t is a nontrivial dynamic optimization problem, the solution to which can often be characterized as a control rule with feedback. The optimal policy rule will depend on all of the parameters of the model and on the parameters of the authority's loss function. The policy problem in this context has been studied by Hall and Phelps. The authority can improve the characteristics of the fluctuations in unemployment and inflation by setting m so as to offset disturbances to the x's.

In this system, if the authority has a 'humane' loss function that assigns regret to unemployment and that discounts the future somewhat, the authority should to some extent exploit the tradeoff between inflation and unemployment implied by (19.14) and (19.16). As Hall (forthcoming) has emphasized, the authority is able to do this by fooling people:

> ... the benefits of inflation derive from the use of expansionary policy to trick economic agents into behaving in socially preferable ways even though their behavior is not in their own interests. ... The gap between actual and expected inflation measures the extent of the trickery. ... The optimal policy is not nearly as expansionary when expectations adjust rapidly, and most of the effect of an inflationary policy is dissipated in costly anticipated inflation.

Hall has pinpointed the source of the authority's power to manipulate the economy. This can be seen by noting that removing the assumption that the authority can systematically trick the public eliminates the implication that there is an exploitable tradeoff between inflation and unemployment in any sense pertinent for making policy. The assumption that the public's expectations are 'rational' and so equal to objective mathematical expectations accomplishes precisely this. Imposing rationality amounts to discarding (19.15) and replacing it with

$$_{t-1}p^*_t = E_{t-1}p_t, \tag{19.17}$$

where E_{t-1} is the mathematical expectation operator conditional on information known at the end of period $t-1$. If (19.17) is used in place of (19.15), (19.16) must be replaced with[5]

$$U_t = [a(m_t - E_{t-1}m_t) + b(x_t - E_{t-1}x_t) - \epsilon_t]/(\phi_1 - c) - \phi_0/\phi_1. \tag{19.18}$$

To solve the model for U_t, it is necessary to specify how the authority is behaving. Suppose we assume that the authority uses the feedback rule,

$$m_t = G\theta_{t-1} + \eta_t, \tag{19.19}$$

where θ_{t-1} is a set of observations on variables dated $t-1$ and earlier, and η_t is a serially uncorrelated error term obeying $E[\eta_t \mid \theta_{t-1}] = 0$; G is a vector conformable with θ_{t-1}.

If the rule is (19.19) and expectations about m are rational, then

$$E_{t-1}m_t \equiv Em_t \mid \theta_{t-1} = G\theta_{t-1}, \tag{19.20}$$

since $E[\eta_t \mid \theta_{t-1}] = 0$. So we have

$$m_t - E_{t-1}m_t = \eta_t. \tag{19.21}$$

Substituting from (19.21) into (19.18) we have

$$U_t = [a\eta_t + b(x_t - E_{t-1}x_t) - \epsilon_t]/(\phi_1 - c) - \phi_0/\phi_1. \tag{19.22}$$

Since the parameters G of the feedback rule don't appear in (19.22), we can conclude that the probability distribution of unemployment is independent of the values chosen for G. The distribution of the random, unpredictable component of m, which is η, influences the distribution of unemployment but there is no way in which this fact provides any logical basis for employing a rule with feedback. The ηs have a place in (19.22) only because they are unpredictable noise. On the basis of the information in θ_{t-1}, there is no way that the ηs can be predicted, either by the authority or the public.

In this system, there is no sense in which the authority has the option to conduct countercyclical policy. To exploit the Phillips Curve, it must somehow trick the public. But by virtue of the assumption that expectations are rational, there is no feedback rule that the authority can employ and expect to be able systematically to fool the public. This means that the authority cannot expect to exploit the Phillips Curve even for one period. Thus, combining the natural rate hypothesis with the assumption that expectations are rational transforms the former from a curiosity with perhaps remote policy implications into an hypothesis with immediate and drastic implications about the feasibility of pursuing countercyclical policy.[6]

As indicated above, by a countercyclical policy we mean a rule with feedback from current and past economic variables to the authority's instrument, as in a regime in which the authority 'leans against the wind.' While the present model suggests reasons for questioning even the possibility of a successful counter-cyclical policy aimed at improving the behavior of the unemployment rate or some closely related index of aggregate activity, the model is compatible with the view that there is an optimal rule for the monetary authority, albeit one that need incorporate no feedback. Such an optimal rule could be determined by an analysis that determines the optimal rate of expected inflation, along the lines of Bailey (1956) or Tobin (1967). If there is an optimal expected rate of inflation, it seems to imply restrictions on the constant and trend terms (and maybe the coefficients on some slow moving exogenous variables like the labor force) of a rule for the money supply, but is not a cause for arguing for a feedback rule from endogenous variables to the money supply. The optimal rate of inflation, if there is one, thus has virtually no implications for the question of countercyclical policy. Furthermore, there is hardly any theoretical agreement about what the optimal rate of expected inflation is, so that it seems to be a weak need for a control rule to lean on.

The simple models utilized above illustrate the implications of imposing the natural rate and rational expectations hypotheses in interpreting the statistical correlations summarized by the reduced forms of macroeconometric models, reduced forms that capture the correlations between monetary and fiscal variables on the one hand, and various real variables on the other hand. What is there to recommend these two hypotheses? Ordinarily, we impose two requirements on an economic model: first that it be consistent with the theoretical core of economics-optimizing behavior within a coherent general equilibrium framework; and second, that it not be refuted by observations. Empirical studies have not turned up much evidence that would cause rejection at high confidence levels of models incorporating our two hypotheses.[7] Furthermore, models along these lines seem to be the only existing ones consistent with individuals' maximizing behavior that are capable of rationalizing certain important correlations, such as the Phillips Curve, that exist in the data and are summarized by the reduced forms of macroeconometric models. The key feature of models that imply our hypotheses has been described by Lucas (1973): 'All formulations of the natural rate theory postulate rational agents, whose decisions depend on relative prices only, placed in an economic setting in which they cannot distinguish relative from general price movements.' Their inability separately to identify relative and overall nominal price changes is what gives rise to reduced forms like (19.1). But their rationality implies that only the surprise components of the aggregate demand variables enter. And this has the far-reaching policy implications described above.

Several reasons can be given for using the hypotheses of rational expectations. An important one is that it is consistent with the findings that large parts of macroeconometric models typically fail tests for structural change (essentially versions of Chow tests).[8] As eq. (19.10) illustrates, if expectations are rational and properly take into account the way policy instruments and other exogenous variables evolve, the coefficients in certain representations of the model (e.g., reduced forms) will change whenever the processes governing those policy instruments and exogenous variables change. A major impetus to work on rational expectations is thus that it offers one reason, but probably not the only reason, that macroeconometric models fail tests for structural change. Indeed, the hypothesis of rational expectations even offers some hope for explaining how certain representations of the model change out of the sample.

A second reason for employing the hypothesis of rational expectations is that in estimating econometric models it is a source of identifying restrictions. The usual method of modelling expectations in macroeconometric models – via a distributed lag on the own variable – leaves it impossible to sort out the scalar multiplying the public's expectations from the magnitude of the weights in the distributed lag on own lags by which expectations are assumed to be formed. Therefore, the coefficients on expectations are generally underidentified econometrically. The way out of this has usually been to impose a unit sum on the distributed lag whereby expectations are formed. The problem is that this is an ad hoc identifying restriction with no economic reason to recommend it. It is generally incompatible with the hypothesis of rational expectations, which can be used to supply an alternative identifying restriction.[9]

A third reason for using the rational expectations hypothesis is that it accords with the economist's usual practice of assuming that people behave in their own best interests. This is not to deny that some people are irrational and neurotic. But we have no reason to believe that those irrationalities cause *systematic and predictable* deviations from rational behavior that a macroeconomist can model and tell the monetary authority how to compensate for. In this regard, it should be noted that the rational expectations hypothesis does not require that people's expectations equal conditional mathematical expectations, only that they equal conditional mathematical expectations plus what may be a very large random term (random with respect to the conditioning information). Thus we need only assume, for example, that

$$_{t-1}p^*_t = E_{t-1}p_t + \phi_t, \tag{19.18a}$$

where $E_{t-1}\phi_t = 0$, and ϕ_t is a random 'mother-in-law' term allowing for what may be very large random deviations from rationality. It is easy to verify that all of our results about countercyclical policy go through when (19.18a) is assumed. Therefore, in the context of the natural rate hypothesis, random deviations from perfectly rational expectations buy the monetary authority no leverage in making countercyclical policy. To be able to conduct a countercyclical policy, there must be systematic deviations from rational expectations which the monetary authority somehow knows about and can predict.

A fourth reason for adopting the hypothesis of rational expectations is the value of the questions it forces us to face. We must specify exactly the horizon over which the expectations are cast and what variables people are assumed to see and when, things that most macroeconometric models are silent on. In doing policy analysis under rational expectations, we must specify whether a given movement in a policy variable was foreseen beforehand or unforseen, an old and important distinction in economics, but one that makes no difference in the usual evaluations of policy made with macroeconometric models.

Although the imposition of the natural rate and rational expectations hypotheses on reduced-form equations like (19.1) has allowed us to state some important results, such reasoning is no substitute for analysis of the underlying microeconomic models. Manipulation of such reduced forms even under the interpretation given by eqs. (19.7)–(19.9), which imposes the natural rate and rational expectations hypotheses, can be misleading because it leaves implicit some of the dependencies between parameters and rules. (For example, the 'structure' consisting of (19.7)–(19.9) is itself a reduced form suggested by Lucas (1973), some of whose parameters depend on the variance of ϵ_t in (19.8). Also, a welfare analysis using such a model can be misleading because it requires adoption of an ad hoc welfare criterion, like the 'humane' loss function described above. In general, such a loss function is inconsistent with the usual welfare criterion employed in models with optimizing agents – Pareto optimality.

Finally, we want to take note of a very general implication of rationality that seems to present a dilemma. Dynamic models that invoke rational expectations can be solved only by attributing to the agents whose behavior is being described a way of forming views about the dynamic processes governing the policy variables. Might it not be reasonable at times to attribute to them a systematically incorrect view? Thus suppose an economy has been operating under one rule for a long time when secretly a new rule is adopted. It would seem that people would learn the new rule only gradually as they acquired data and that they would for some time make what from the viewpoint of the policymaker are forecastable predictable errors. During this time, a new rule could be affecting real variables.

A telling objection to this line of argument is that new rules are not adopted in a vacuum. Something would cause the change – a change in administrations, new appointments, and so on. Moreover, if rational agents live in a world in which rules can be and are changed, their behavior should take into account such possibilities and should depend on the process generating the rule changes. But invoking this kind of complete rationality seems to rule out normative economics completely by, in effect, ruling out freedom for the policymaker. For in a model with completely rational expectations, including a rich enough description of policy, it seems impossible to define a sense in which there is any scope for discussing the optimal design of policy rules. That is because the equilibrium values of the endogenous variables already reflect, in the proper way, the parameters describing the authorities' prospective subsequent behavior, including the probability that this or that proposal for reforming policy will be adopted.

Thus, suppose that a policy variable x_t is described by the objective probability distribution function,

$$\text{Prob}[x_{t+1} < F \mid Y_t, Z_t] = G[F, Y_t, Z_t; g_1, \ldots, g_p], \tag{19.23}$$

where $Y_t = [y_t, y_{t-1}, \ldots]$ is a set of observations on current and past values of an endogenous variable, or vector of endogenous variables y; and where $Z_t = [z_t, z_{t-1}, \ldots]$ is a set of observations on current and past values of a list of n exogenous variables and disturbances z_t^i, $i = 1, \ldots, n$. The probability distribution has p parameters $g_1, \ldots, g_p$.

The probability distribution in (19.23) represents a very general description of the prospects about policy. It obviously can describe a situation in which policy is governed by a deterministic feedback rule, in which case the probability distribution collapses to a trivial one. The probability distribution in (19.23) can also model the case in which the monetary authority follows a feedback rule with random coefficients, coefficients that themselves obey some probability law. This situation is relevant where the monetary authority might consider changing the feedback rule from time to time for one reason or another. The probability distribution (19.23) can also model the case in which policy is in part simply random. The parameters $[g_1, \ldots, g_p]$ determine the probability function (19.23) and summarize all of the factors making up the objective prospects for policy. Policy settings appear to be random drawings from the distribution given in (19.23).

Now consider a rational expectations, structural model for y_t leading to a reduced form,

$$y_t = h(x_t, x_{t-1}, \ldots, Z_t, E_t y_{t+1}), \tag{19.24}$$

where $E_t y_{t+1}$ is the objective expectation of y_{t+1} conditioned on information observed up through time t. The Z_ts are assumed to obey some probability distribution functions,

$$\text{Prob}[z^1_{t+1} < H^1, z^2_{t+1} < H^2, \ldots, z^n_{t+1} < H^n \mid Z_t]$$

$$= F[H^1, H^2, \ldots, H^n, Z_t].$$

A final form solution for the model is represented by an equation of the form

$$y_t = \phi(x_t, x_{t-1}, \ldots, Z_t; \bar{g}), \tag{19.25}$$

with the property that

$$E_t y_{t+1} = \iint \phi(x_{t+1}, x_t, \ldots, Z_{t+1}; \bar{g}) \, dG \, dF,$$

so that the expectation of y_{t+1} equals the prediction from the final form. The parameters $\bar{g} = [g_1, \ldots, g_p]$ turn out to be parameters of the final form (19.25), which our notation is intended to emphasize. Those parameters make their appearance in (19.25) via the process of eliminating $E_t y_{t+1}$ from (19.24) by expressing it in terms of the xs and Zs. The parameters of F also are embedded in ϕ for the same reason. That is, the function ϕ must satisfy the equation

$$\phi(x_t, x_{t-1}, \ldots, Z_t; \bar{g})$$

$$= h[x_t, x_{t-1}, \ldots, Z_t, \iint \phi(x_{t+1}, x_t, \ldots, Z_{t+1}; \bar{g}) \, dG \, dF]$$

in which the parameters of F and G make their appearance by virtue of the integration with respect to G and F.

The final form (19.25) formally resembles the final forms of the usual macroeconometric models without rational expectations. But there is a crucial difference, for in (19.25) there are no parameters that the authority is free to choose. The parameters in the vector $\bar{g}$ describe the objective characteristics of the policymaking process and cannot be changed. They capture all of the factors that determine the prospects for policy. The authority in effect makes a random drawing of x from the distribution described by (19.23). The persons on the committee and staffs that constitute the authority 'matter' in the sense that they influence the prospects about policy and so are represented by elements of $\bar{g}$. But the authority has no freedom to influence the parameters of the final form (19.23), since the objective prospects that it will act wisely or foolishly are known to the public and are properly embedded in the final form (19.25).

The conundrum facing the economist can be put as follows. In order for a model to have normative implications, it must contain some parameters whose values can be chosen by the policymaker. But if these can be chosen, rational agents will not view them as fixed and will make use of schemes for predicting their values. If the economist models the economy taking these schemes into account, then those parameters become endogenous variables and no longer appear in the reduced-form equations for the other endogenous variables. If he models the economy without taking the schemes into account, he is not imposing rationality.

Notes

1. To make the main points simple, the paper illustrates things by using simple ad hoc linear models. However, the ideas cannot really be captured fully within this restricted framework. The main ideas we are summarizing are due to Robert E. Lucas, Jr., and were advanced by him most elegantly in the context of a stochastic general equilibrium model (see Lucas (1972a)). Lucas's paper analyzes policy questions in what we regard to be the proper way, namely, in the context of a consistent general equilibrium model. The present paper is a popularization that fails to indicate how Lucas's neutrality proposition are derived from a consistent general equilibrium model with optimizing agents. It is easy to overturn the 'neutrality' results that we derive below from an ad hoc structure by making ad hoc changes in that structure. The advantage of Lucas's model is that ad hockeries are given much less of a role and, consequently, the neutrality proposition he obtains is seen to be a consequence of individual agents' optimizing behavior. In summary, this paper is not intended to be a substitute for reading the primary sources, mainly Lucas (1972a, 1972b, 1973, forthcoming).
2. See Kareken, Muench, and Wallace (1973) for a detailed presentation of this view.
3. Perhaps the 'look at everything' view goes some way toward rationalizing the common view that policy ought not to be made by following a feedback rule derived from an explicit, empirically estimated macroeconometric model. It might be argued that the models that have been estimated omit some of the endogenous variables that carry information about the shocks impinging on the system as a whole. If the authority has in mind an a priori model that assigns those variables an important role, it is appropriate for it to alter its policy settings in response to new information about those variables. Perhaps this is what some people mean by 'discretion,' although we aren't sure.
4. For example, see the remarks attributed to Franco Modigliani in *Brookings Papers on Economic Activity* 2 (1973, p. 480).
5. Using (19.17), compute E_{t-1} of both sides of (19.13) and subtract the result from (19.13) to get

$$p_t - {}_{t-1}p^*{}_t = \phi_1(U_t - E_{t-1}U_t) + \epsilon_t. \tag{19.i}$$

Perform the same operation on (19.14) to get

$$p_t - {}_{t-1}p^*{}_t = a(m_t - E_{t-1}m_t) + b(x_t - E_{t-1}x_t) + c(U_t - E_{t-1}U_t). \tag{19.ii}$$

Solve (19.i) for $(U_t - E_{t-1}U_t)$ and substitute the result into (19.ii) to get

$$(1 - c/\phi_1)(p_t - {}_{t-1}p^*_t) = a(m_t - E_{t-1}m_t) - (c/\phi_1)\epsilon_t + b(x_t - E_{t-1}x_t). \quad (19.\text{iii})$$

Upon substituting the implied expression for $(p_t - {}_{t-1}p^*_t)$ into (19.13), we get (19.18).

6. The original version of such a 'neutrality' result is due to Lucas (1972a). His formulation is much deeper and more elegant than the one here, since his procedure is to start from individual agents' objectives and their information and then to investigate the characteristics and of general equilibria. Less elegant formulations of neutrality results are in Sargent (1973) and Sargent and Wallace (1975).
7. See Lucas (1973) and Sargent (1976) for empirical tests of the natural rate hypothesis.
8. For example, see Muench et al. (1974).
9. See Lucas (1972b, 1973) and Sargent (1971).

References

Bailey, M. (1956), The welfare cost of inflationary finance, *Journal of Political Economy*, vol. 64 (April).
Hall, R. G. (1976), The Phillips Curve and macroeconometric policy, in K. Brunner (ed.), The Phillips Curve and labor markets, *Journal of Monetary Economics*, supplement.
Kareken, J. H., T. Muench and N. Wallace (1973), Optimal open market strategy: The use of information variables, *American Economic Review*, March.
Lucas, R. E., Jr. (1972a), Expectations and the neutrality of money, *Journal of Economic Theory*, vol. 4 (April), p. 103–24.
Lucas, R. E., Jr. (1972b), Econometric testing of the natural rate hypothesis, in O. Eckstein (ed.), *The Econometrics of Price Determination Conference*, sponsored by the Board of Governors of the Federal Reserve System and Social Science Research Council.
Lucas, R. E., Jr. (1973), Some international evidence on output–inflation trade-offs, *American Economic Review*, vol. 63 (June).
Lucas, R. E., Jr. (1976), Econometric policy evaluation: A critique, in K. Brunner (ed.), The Phillips Curve and labour markets, *Journal of Monetary Economics*, supplement.
Muench, T., A. Rolnick, N. Wallace and W. Weiler (1974) Tests for structural change and prediction intervals for the reduced forms of two structural models of the U.S.: The FRB–MIT and Michigan quarterly models, *Annals of Economic and Social Measurement*, vol. 3, no. 3.
Phelps, E. S. (1972), *Inflation policy and unemployment theory* (New York: Norton).
Samuelson, P. A. (1970), Reflections on recent federal reserve policy, *Journal of Money, Credit, and Banking*, February.
Sargent, T. J. (1971), A note on the accelerationist controversy, *Journal of Money, Credit, and Banking*, August.

Sargent, T. J. (1973), Rational expectations, the real rate of interest, and the natural rate of unemployment, *Brookings Papers on Economic Activity*, 2.
Sargent, T. J. (1976), A classical macroeconometric model for the United States, *Journal of Political Economy*.
Sargent, T. J. and N. Wallace (1975), Rational expectations, the optimal monetary instrument, and the optimal money supply rule, *Journal of Political Economy*, March–April.
Tobin, J. (1967), Notes on optimal monetary growth, *Journal of Political Economy*, supplement.

CHAPTER 20

The Monetarist Controversy, or, Should we Forsake Stabilization Policies?

F. MODIGLIANI[1]

In recent years and especially since the onset of the current depression, the economics profession and the lay public have heard a great deal about the sharp conflict between "monetarists and Keynesians" or between "monetarists and fiscalists." The difference between the two "schools" is generally held to center on whether the money supply or fiscal variables are the major determinants of aggregate economic activity, and hence the most appropriate tool of stabilization policies.

My central theme is that this view is quite far from the truth, and that the issues involved are of far greater practical import. There are in reality no serious analytical disagreements between leading monetarists and leading nonmonetarists. Milton Friedman was once quoted as saying, 'We are all Keynesians, now', and I am quite prepared to reciprocate that 'we are all monetarists' – if by monetarism is meant assigning to the stock of money a major role in determining output and prices. Indeed, the list of those who have long been monetarists in this sense is quite extensive, including among other[s] John Maynard Keynes as well as myself, as is attested by my 1944 and 1963 articles.

American Economic Review, Vol. 67, No. 2 (March 1977), pp. 1–17.

In reality the distinguishing feature of the monetarist school and the real issues of disagreement with nonmonetarists is not monetarism, but rather the role that should probably be assigned to stabilization policies. Nonmonetarists accept what I regard to be the fundamental practical message of *The General Theory*: that a private enterprise economy using an intangible money *needs* to be stabilized, *can* be stabilized, and therefore *should* be stabilized by appropriate monetary and fiscal policies. Monetarists by contrast take the view that there is no serious need to stabilize the economy; that even if there were a need, it could not be done, for stabilization policies would be more likely to increase than to decrease instability; and, at least some monetarists would, I believe, go so far as to hold that, even in the unlikely event that stabilization policies could on balance prove beneficial, the government should not be trusted with the necessary power.

What has led me to address this controversy is the recent spread of monetarism, both in a simplistic, superficial form and in the form of growing influence on the practical conduct of economic policy, which influence, I shall argue presently, has played at least some role in the economic upheavals of the last three years.

In what follows then, I propose first to review the main arguments bearing on the *need* for stabilization policies, that is, on the likely extent of instability in the absence of such policies, and then to examine the issue of the supposed destabilizing effect of pursuing stabilization policies. My main concern will be with instability generated by the traditional type of disturbances – demand shocks. But before I am through, I will give some consideration to the difficult problems raised by the newer type of disturbance – supply shocks.

I The Keynesian case for stabilization policies

The General Theory

Keynes' novel conclusion about the need for stabilization policies, as was brought out by the early interpreters of *The General Theory* (for example, John Hicks, the author, 1944), resulted from the interaction of a basic contribution to traditional monetary theory – liquidity preference – and an unorthodox hypothesis about the working of the labor market – complete downward rigidity of wages.

Because of liquidity preference, a change in aggregate demand, which may be broadly defined as any event that results in a change in the market clearing or equilibrium rate of interest, will produce a corresponding change in the real demand for money or velocity of circulation, and hence in the real stock of money needed at full employment. As long as wages are perfectly flexible, even with a constant nominal supply, full employment could and would be maintained by a change of wages and prices as needed to produce the required change in the real money supply – though even in this case, stability of the price level would require a countercyclical monetary policy. But, under the Keynesian wage assumption the classical adjustment through prices can occur only in the case of an increased demand. In the case of a decline, instead, wage rigidity prevents the necessary increase in the real money supply and the concomitant required fall in interest rates. Hence, if the nominal money supply is constant, the initial equilibrium must give way to a new stable one, characterized by lower output and by an involuntary reduction in employment, so labeled because it does not result from a shift in notional demand and supply schedules in terms of real wages, but only from an insufficient real money supply. The nature of this equilibrium is elegantly captured by the Hicksian *IS-LM* paradigm, which to our generation of economists has become almost as familiar as the demand–supply paradigm was to earlier ones.

This analysis implied that a fixed money supply far from insuring approximate stability of prices and output, as held by the traditional view, would result in a rather unstable economy, alternating between periods of protracted unemployment and stagnation, and bursts of inflation. The extent of downward instability would depend in part on the size of the exogenous shocks to demand and in part on the strength of what may be called the Hicksian mechanism. By this I mean the extent to which a shift in *IS*, through its interaction with *LM*, results in some decline in interest rates and thus in a change in income which is smaller than the original shift. The stabilizing power of this mechanism is controlled by various parameters of the system. In particular, the economy will be more unstable the greater the interest elasticity of demand for money, and the smaller the interest responsiveness of aggregate demand. Finally, a large multiplier is also destabilizing in that it implies a larger shift in *IS* for a given shock.

However, the instability could be readily counteracted by appropriate stabilization policies. Monetary policy could change the nominal supply of money so as to *accommodate* the change in real demand resulting from shocks in aggregate demand. Fiscal policy, through expenditure and taxes, could *offset* these shocks, making full employment consistent with the initial nominal money stock. In general, both monetary and fiscal policies could be used in combination. But because of a perceived uncertainty in the response of demand to changes in interest rates, and because changes in interest rates through monetary policy could meet difficulties and substantial delays related to expectations (so-called liquidity traps), fiscal policy was regarded as having some advantages.

The early Keynesians

The early disciples of the new Keynesian gospel, still haunted by memories of the Great Depression, frequently tended to outdo Keynes' pessimism about potential instability. Concern with liquidity traps fostered the view that the demand for money was highly interest elastic; failure to distinguish between the short- and long-run marginal propensity to save led to overestimating the long-run saving rate, thereby fostering concern with stagnation, and to underestimating the short-run propensity, thereby exaggerating the short-run multiplier. Interest rates were supposed to affect, at best, the demand for long-lived fixed investments, and the interest elasticity was deemed to be low. Thus, shocks were believed to produce a large response. Finally, investment demand was seen as capriciously controlled by "animal spirits," thus providing an important source of shocks. All this justified calling for very active stabilization policies. Furthermore, since the very circumstances which produce a large response to demand shocks also produce a large response to *fiscal* and a small response to *monetary* actions, there was a tendency to focus on fiscal policy as the main tool to keep the economy at near full employment.

The Phillips Curve

In the two decades following *The General Theory*, there were a number of developments of the Keynesian system including dynamization of the model, the stress on taxes versus expenditures and the balanced budget multiplier, and the first attempts at estimating the critical parameters through econometric techniques and models. But for present purposes, the most important one was the uncovering of a "stable" statistical relation between the rate of change of wages and the rate of unemployment, which has since come to be known as the Phillips curve. This relation, and its generalization by Richard Lipsey to allow for the effect of recent inflation, won wide acceptance even before an analytical underpinning could be provided for it, in part because it could account for the "puzzling" experience of 1954 and 1958, when wages kept rising despite the substantial rise in unemployment. It also served to dispose of the rather sterile "cost push"–"demand pull" controversy.

In the following years, a good deal of attention went into developing theoretical foundations for the Phillips curve, in particular along the lines of search models (for example, Edmund Phelps et al., 1970). This approach served to shed a new light on the nature of unemployment by tracing it in the first place to labor turnover and search time rather than to lack of jobs as such: in a sense unemployment is all frictional – at least in developed countries. At the same time it clarified how the availability of more jobs tends to reduce unemployment by increasing vacancies and thus reducing search time.

Acceptance of the Phillips curve relation implied some significant changes in the Keynesian framework which partly escaped notice until the subsequent monetarists' attacks. Since the rate of change of wages decreased smoothly with the rate of unemployment, there was no longer a unique Full Employment but rather a whole family of possible equilibrium rates, each associated with a different rate of inflation (and requiring, presumably, a different long-run growth of money). It also impaired the notion of a stable underemployment equilibrium. A fall in demand could still cause an initial rise in unemployment but this rise, by reducing the growth of wages, would eventually raise the real money supply, tending to return unemployment to the equilibrium rate consistent with the given long-run growth of money.

But at the practical level it did not lessen the case for counteracting lasting demand disturbances through stabilization policies rather than by relying on the slow process of wage adjustment to do the job, at the cost of protracted unemployment and instability of prices. Indeed, the realm of stabilization policies appeared to expand in the sense that the stabilization authority had the power of choosing the unemployment rate around which employment was to be stabilized, though it then had to accept the associated inflation. Finally, the dependence of wage changes also on past inflation forced recognition of a distinction between the short- and the long-run Phillips curve, the latter exhibiting the long-run equilibrium rate of inflation implied by a *maintained* unemployment rate. The fact that the long-run tradeoff between unemployment and inflation was necessarily less favorable than the short-run one, opened up new vistas of "enjoy-it-now, pay-later" policies, and even resulted in an entertaining literature on the political business cycle and how to stay in the saddle by riding the Phillips curve (see for example, Ray Fair, and William Nordhaus).

II The monetarists' attack

The stabilizing power of the Hicksian mechanism

The monetarists' attack on Keynesianism was directed from the very beginning not at the Keynesian framework as such, but at whether it really implied a need for stabilization. It rested on a radically different empirical assessment of the value of the parameters controlling the stabilizing power of the Hicksian mechanism and of the magnitude and duration of response to shocks, given a stable money supply. And this different assessment in turn was felt to justify a radical downgrading of the *practical relevance* of the Keynesian framework as distinguished from its *analytical validity*.

Liquidity preference was a fine contribution to monetary theory but in practice the responsiveness of the demand for money, and hence of velocity, to interest rates, far from being unmanageably large, was so small that according to a well-known paper by Milton Friedman (1969), it could not even be detected empirically. On the other hand, the effect of interest rates on aggregate demand was large and by no means limited to the traditional fixed investments but quite pervasive. The difficulty of detecting it empirically resulted from focusing on a narrow range of measured market rates and from the fact that while the aggregate could be counted on to respond, the response of individual components might not be stable. Finally, Friedman's celebrated contribution to the theory of the consumption function (1957) (and my own work on the life cycle hypothesis with Richard Brumberg and others, reviewed by the author, 1975) implied a very high short-run marginal propensity to save in response to transient disturbances to income and hence a small short-run multiplier.

All this justified the conclusion that (i) though demand shocks might qualitatively work along the lines described by Keynes, quantitatively the Hicks mechanism is so strong that their impact would be *small* and *transient*, provided the stock of money was kept on a steady growth path; (ii) fiscal policy actions, like other demand shocks, would have *minor* and *transitory* effects on demand, while changes in money would produce *large* and *permanent* effects on money income; and, therefore, (iii) the observed instability of the economy, which was anyway proving moderate as the postwar period unfolded, was most likely the result of the unstable growth of money, be it due to misguided endeavors to stabilize income or to the pursuit of other targets, which were either irrelevant or, in the case of balance of payments goals, should have been made irrelevant by abandoning fixed exchanges.

The demise of wage rigidity and the vertical Phillips curve

But the most serious challenge came in Friedman's 1968 Presidential Address, building on ideas independently put forth also by Phelps (1968). Its basic message was that, despite appearances, wages were in reality perfectly flexible and there was accordingly *no* involuntary unemployment. The evidence to the contrary, including the Phillips curve, was but a statistical illusion resulting from failure to differentiate between price changes and *unexpected* price changes.

Friedman starts out by reviving the Keynesian notion that, at any point of time, there exists a unique full-employment rate which he labels the "natural rate." An unanticipated fall in demand in Friedman's competitive world leads firms to reduce prices and also output and employment along the short-run marginal cost curve – unless the nominal wage declines together with prices. But workers, failing to judge correctly the current and prospective fall in prices, misinterpret the reduction of nominal wages as a cut in *real* wages. Hence, assuming a positively sloped supply function, they reduce the supply of labor. As a result, the effective real wage rises to the point where the resulting decline in the demand for labor matches the reduced supply. Thus, output falls not because of the decline in demand, but because of the entirely voluntary reduction in the supply of labor, in response to erroneous perceptions. Furthermore, the fall in employment can only be temporary, as expectations must soon catch up with the facts, at least in the absence of new shocks. The very same mechanism works in the case of an increase in demand, so that the responsiveness of wages and prices is the same on either side of the natural rate.

The upshot is that Friedman's model also implies a Phillips-type relation between inflation, employment or unemployment, and past inflation, provided the latter variable is interpreted as a reasonable proxy for expected inflation. But it turns the standard explanation on its head: instead of (excess) employment causing inflation, it is (the unexpected component of) the rate of inflation that causes excess employment.

One very basic implication of Friedman's model is that the coefficient of price expectations should be precisely unity. This specification implies that whatever the shape of the short-run Phillips curve – a shape determined by the relation between expected and actual price changes, and by the elasticity of labor supply with respect to the perceived real wage – the long-run curve *must be vertical*.

Friedman's novel twist provided a fresh prop for the claim that stabilization policies are not really needed, for, with wages flexible, except possibly for transient distortions, the Hicksian mechanism receives powerful reinforcement from changes in the real money supply. Similarly, the fact that full employment was a razor edge provided new support for the claim that stabilization policies were bound to prove destabilizing.

The macro rational expectations revolution

But the death blow to the already badly battered Keynesian position was to come only shortly thereafter by incorporating into Friedman's model the so-called rational expectation hypothesis, or *REH*. Put very roughly, this hypothesis, originally due to John Muth, states that rational economic agents will endeavor to form expectations of relevant future variables by making the most efficient use of all information provided by past history. It is a fundamental and fruitful contribution that has already found many important applications, for example, in connection with speculative markets, and as a basis for some thoughtful criticism by Robert Lucas (1976) of certain features of econometric models. What I am concerned with here is only its application to macro-economics, or *MREH*, associated with such authors as Lucas (1972), Thomas Sargent (1976), and Sargent and Neil Wallace (1975).

The basic ingredient of *MREH* is the postulate that the workers of Friedman's model hold rational expectations, which turns out to have a number of remarkable implications: (i) errors of price expectations, which are the only source of departure from the natural state, cannot be avoided but they can only be short-lived and random. In particular, there cannot be persistent unemployment above the natural rate for this would imply high serial correlation between the successive errors of expectation, which is inconsistent with rational expectations; (ii) any attempts to stabilize the economy by means of stated monetary or fiscal rules are bound to be totally ineffective because their effect will be fully discounted in rational expectations; (iii) nor can the government successfully pursue *ad hoc* measures to offset shocks. The private sector is already taking care of any anticipated shock; therefore government policy could conceivably help only if the government information was better than that of the public, which is impossible, by the very definition of rational expectations. Under these conditions, *ad hoc* stabilization policies are most likely to produce instead further destabilizing shocks.

These are clearly remarkable conclusions, and a major *rediscovery* – for it had all been said 40 years ago by Keynes in a well-known passage of *The General Theory*:

> If, indeed, labour were always in a position to take action (and were to do so), whenever there was less than full employment, to reduce its money demands by concerted action to whatever point was required to make money so abundant relatively to the wage-unit that the rate of interest would fall to a level compatible with full employment, we should, in effect, have monetary management by the Trade Unions, aimed at full employment, instead of by the banking systems. (p. 267)

The only novelty is that *MREH* replaces Keynes' opening "if" with a "since."

If one accepts this little amendment, the case against stabilization policies is complete. The economy is inherently pretty stable – except possibly for the effect of government messing around. And to the extent that there is a small residual instability, it is beyond the power of human beings, let alone the government, to alleviate it.

III How valid is the monetarist case?

The monetarist model of wage price behavior

In setting out the counterattack it is convenient to start with the monetarists' model of price and wage behavior. Here one must distinguish between the model as such and a specific implication of that model, namely that the long-run Phillips curve is vertical, or, in substance, that, in the long run, money is neutral. That conclusion, by now, does not meet serious objection from nonmonetarists, at least as a first approximation.

But the proposition that other things equal, and given time enough, the economy will eventually adjust to any indefinitely maintained stock of money, or nth derivative thereof, can be derived from a variety of models and, in any event, is of very little practical relevance, as I will argue below. What is unacceptable, because inconsistent with both micro and macro evidence, is the specific monetarist model set out above and its implication that all unemployment is a voluntary, fleeting response to transitory misperceptions.

One may usefully begin with a criticism of the Macro Rational Expectations model and why Keynes' "if" should not be replaced by "since." At the logical level, Benjamin Friedman has called attention to the omission from *MREH* of an explicit learning model, and has suggested that, as a result, it can only be interpreted as a description not of short-run but of long-run equilibrium in which no agent would wish to recontract. But then the implications of *MREH* are clearly far from startling, and their policy relevance is almost nil. At the institutional level, Stanley Fischer has shown that the mere recognition of long-term contracts is sufficient to generate wage rigidity and a substantial scope for stabilization policies. But the most glaring flaw of *MREH* is its inconsistency with the evidence: if it were valid, deviations of unemployment from the natural rate would be small and transitory – in which case *The General Theory* would not have been written and neither would this paper. Sargent (1976) has attempted to remedy this fatal flaw by hypothesizing that the persistent and large fluctuations in unemployment reflect merely corresponding swings in the natural rate itself. In other words, what happened to the United States in the 1930s was a severe attack of contagious laziness! I can only say that, despite Sargent's ingenuity, neither I nor, I expect, most others at least of the nonmonetarists' persuasion are quite ready yet to turn over the field of economic fluctuations to the social psychologist!

Equally serious objections apply to Friedman's modeling of the commodity market as a perfectly competitive one – so that the real wage rate is continuously equated to the *short-run* marginal product of labor –

and to his treatment of labor as a homogenous commodity traded in an auction market, so that, at the going wage, there never is any excess demand by firms or excess supply by workers. The inadequacies of this model as a useful formalization of present day Western economies are so numerous that only a few of the major ones can be mentioned here.

Friedman's view of unemployment as a voluntary reduction in labor supply could at best provide an explanation of variations in labor force – and then only under the questionable assumption that the supply function has a significantly positive slope – but cannot readily account for changes in unemployment. Furthermore, it cannot be reconciled with the well-known fact that *rising* unemployment is accompanied by a fall, not by a *rise* in quits, nor with the role played by temporary layoffs to which Martin Feldstein has recently called attention. Again, his competitive model of the commodity market, accepted also in *The General Theory*, implies that changes in real wages, adjusted for long-run productivity trend, should be significantly negatively correlated with cyclical changes in employment and output and with changes in money wages. But as early as 1938, John Dunlop showed that this conclusion was rejected by some eighty years of British experience and his results have received some support in more recent tests of Ronald Bodkin (1969) for the United States and Canada. Similar tests of my own, using quarterly data, provide striking confirmation that for the last two decades from the end of the Korean War until 1973, the association of trend adjusted real compensations of the private nonfarm sector with either employment or the change in nominal compensation is prevailingly positive and very significantly so.[2]

This evidence can, instead, be accounted for by the oligopolistic pricing model – according to which price is determined by *long-run* minimum average cost up to a mark-up reflecting entry-preventing considerations (see the author, 1958) – coupled with some lags in the adjustment of prices to costs. This model implies that firms respond to a change in demand by endeavoring to adjust output and employment, without significant changes in prices relative to wages; and the resulting changes in available jobs have their initial impact not on wages but rather on unemployment by way of layoffs and recalls and through changes in the level of vacancies, and hence on the length of average search time.

If, in the process, vacancies rise above a critical level, or "natural rate," firms will endeavour to reduce them by outbidding each other, thereby raising the rate of change of wages. Thus, as long as jobs and vacancies remain above, and unemployment remains below, some critical level which might be labeled the "noninflationary rate" (see the author and Lucas Papademos, 1975), wages and prices will tend to accelerate. If, on the other hand, jobs fall below, and unemployment rises above, the noninflationary rate, firms finding that vacancies are less than optimal – in the limit the unemployed queuing outside the gate will fill them instantly – will have an incentive to reduce their relative wage offer. But in this case, in which too much labor is looking for too few jobs, the trend toward a sustained decline in the rate of growth of wages is likely to be even weaker than the corresponding acceleration when too many jobs are bidding for too few people. The main reason is the nonhomogeneity of labor. By far the largest and more valuable source of labor supply to a firm consists of those already employed who are not readily interchangeable with the unemployed and, in contrast with them, are concerned with protecting their earnings and not with reestablishing full employment. For these reasons, and because the first to quit are likely to be the best workers, a reduction of the labor force can, within limits, be accomplished more economically, not by reducing wages to generate enough quits, but by firing or, when possible, by layoffs which ensure access to a trained labor force when demand recovers. More generally, the inducement to reduce relative wages to eliminate the excess supply is moderated by the effect that such a reduction would have on quits and costly turnover, even when the resulting vacancies can be readily filled from the ranks of the unemployed. Equally relevant are the consequences in terms of loss of morale and good will, in part for reasons which have been elaborated by the literature on implicit contracts (see Robert Gordon, 1976). Thus, while there will be some tendency for the rate of change of wages to fall, the more so the larger the unemployment – at least in an economy like the United States where there are no overpowering centralized unions – that tendency is severely damped.

And whether, given an unemployment rate significantly and persistently above the noninflationary level, the rate of change of wages would, eventually, tend to turn negative and decline without bound or whether it would tend to an asymptote is a question that I doubt the empirical evidence will ever answer. The one experiment we have had – the Great Depression – suggests the answer is negative, and while I admit that, for a variety of reasons, that evidence is muddied, I hope that we will never have the opportunity for a second, clean experiment.

In any event, what is really important for practical purposes is not the long-run equilibrium relation as such, but the speed with which it is approached. Both the model sketched out and the empirical evidence suggest that the process of acceleration or deceleration of wages when unemployment differs from the noninflationary rate will have more nearly the character of a crawl than of a gallop. It will suffice to recall in this connection that there was excess demand pressure in the United States at least from 1965 to mid-1970, and during that period the growth of inflation was from some 1.5 to only about 5.5 percent per year. And the response to the excess supply pressure from mid-1970 to early 1973, and from late 1974 to date was equally sluggish.

The power of self-stabilizing mechanisms: the evidence from econometric models

There remains to consider the monetarists' initial criticism of Keynesianism, to wit, that even without high wage flexibility, the system's response to demand shocks is small and short-lived, thanks to the power of the Hicksian mechanism. Here it must be acknowledged that every one of the monetarists' criticisms of early, simple minded Keynesianism has proved in considerable measure correct.

With regard to the interest elasticity of demand for money, post-Keynesian developments in the theory of money, and in particular, the theoretical contributions of William Baumol, James Tobin, Merton Miller, and Daniel Orr (1966), point to a modest value of around one-half to one-third, and empirical studies (see for example, Stephen Goldfeld) are largely consistent with this prediction (at least until 1975!). Similarly, the dependence of consumption on long-run, or life cycle, income and on wealth, together with the high marginal tax rates of the postwar period, especially the corporate tax, and leakages through imports, lead to a rather low estimate of the multiplier.

Last but not least, both theoretical and empirical work, reflected in part in econometric models, have largely vindicated the monetarist contention that interest effects on demand are pervasive and substantial. Thus, in the construction and estimation of the MIT–Penn–Social Science Research Council *(MPS)* econometric model of the United States, we found evidence of effects, at least modest, on nearly every component of aggregate demand. One response to money supply changes that is especially important in the *MPS*, if somewhat controversial, is via interest rates on the market value of all assets and thus on consumption.

There is, therefore, substantial agreement that in the United States the Hicksian mechanism is fairly effective in limiting the effect of shocks, and that the response of wages and prices to excess demand or supply will also work *gradually* toward eliminating largely, if not totally, any effect on employment. But in the view of nonmonetarists, the evidence overwhelmingly supports the conclusion that the *interim* response is still of significant magnitude and of considerable duration, basically because the wheels of the offsetting mechanism grind slowly. To be sure, the first link of the mechanism, the rise in short-term rates, gets promptly into play and heftily, given the low money demand elasticity; but most expenditures depend on long-term rates, which generally respond but gradually, and the demand response is generally also gradual. Furthermore, while this response is building up, multiplier and accelerator mechanisms work toward amplifying the shock. Finally, the classical mechanism – the change in real money supply through prices – has an even longer lag because of the sluggish response of wages to excess demand.

These interferences are supported by simulations with econometric models like the *MPS*. Isolating, first, the working of the Hicksian mechanism by holding prices constant, we find that a 1 per cent demand shock, say a rise in real exports, produces an impact effect on aggregate output which is barely more than 1 per cent, rises to a peak of only about 2 per cent a year later, and then declines slowly toward a level somewhat over 1.5 per cent.

Taking into account the wage–price mechanism hardly changes the picture for the first year because of its inertia. Thereafter, however, it becomes increasingly effective so that a year later the real response is back at the impact level, and by the end of the third year the shock has been fully offset (thereafter output oscillates around zero in a damped fashion). Money income, on the other hand, reaches a peak of over 2.5, and then only by the middle of the second year. It declines thereafter, and tends eventually to oscillate around a *positive* value because normally, a demand shock requires eventually a change in interest rates and hence in velocity and money income.

These results, which are broadly confirmed by other econometric models, certainly do not support the view of a highly unstable economy in which fiscal policy has powerful and everlasting effects. But neither do they support the monetarist view of a highly stable economy in which shocks hardly make a ripple and the effects of fiscal policy are puny and fast vanishing... [a discussion of U.S. econometric studies has been omitted here (eds).]

From the theory and evidence reviewed, we must then conclude that opting for a constant of growth of the nominal money supply can result in a stable economy only in the absence of significant exogenous shocks. But obviously the economy has been and will continue to be exposed to many significant shocks, coming from such things as war and peace, and other large changes in government expenditure, foreign trade, agriculture, technological progress, population shifts, and what not. The clearest evidence on the importance of such shocks is provided by our postwar record with its six recessions.

IV The record of stabilization policies: stabilizing or destabilizing

Was postwar instability due to unstable money growth?

At this point, of course, monetarists will object that, over the postwar period, we have *not* had a constant money growth policy and will hint that the observed instability can largely be traced to the instability of money. The only way of meeting this objection squarely would be, of course, to rerun history with a good computer capable of calculating 3 percent at the helm of the Fed.

A more feasible, if less conclusive approach might be to look for some extended periods in which the money supply grew fairly smoothly and see how the economy fared. Combing through our post-Korean War history, I have been able to find just two stretches of several years in which the growth of the money stock was relatively stable, whether one chooses to measure stability in terms of percentage deviations from a constant growth or of dispersion of four-quarter changes. It may surprise some that one such stretch occurred quite recently and consists of the period of nearly four years beginning in the first quarter of 1971 (see the author and Papademos, 1976). During this period, the average growth was quite large, some 7 percent, but it was relatively smooth, generally well within the 6 to 8 percent band. The average deviation from the mean is about 0.75 percent. The other such period lasted from the beginning of 1953 to the first half of 1957, again a stretch of roughly four years. In sharp contrast to the most recent period, the average growth here is quite modest, only about 2 percent; but again, most four-quarter changes fell well within a band of two percentage points, and the average deviation is again 0.7. By contrast, during the remaining 13-year stretch from mid-1957 to the end of 1970, the variability of money growth was roughly twice as large if measured by the average deviation of four quarter changes, and some five times larger if measured by the percentage deviation of the money stock from a constant growth trend.

How did the economy fare in the two periods of relatively stable money growth? It is common knowledge that the period from 1971 to 1974, or from 1972 to 1975 if we want to allow a one-year lag for money to do its trick, was distinctly the most unstable in our recent history, marked by sharp fluctuations in output and wild gyrations of the rate of change of prices. As a result, the average deviation of the four-quarter changes in output was 3.3 percent, more than twice as large as in the period of less stable money growth. But the first stretch was also marked by well above average instability, with the contraction of 1954, the sharp recovery of 1955, and the new contraction in 1958, the sharpest in postwar history except for the present one. The variability of output is again 50 percent larger than in the middle period.

To be sure, in the recent episode serious exogenous shocks played a major role in the development of prices and possibly output, although the same is not so readily apparent for the period 1953 to 1958. But, in any event, such extenuating circumstances are quite irrelevant to my point; for I am not suggesting that the stability of money was the major cause of economic instability – or at any rate, not yet! All I am arguing is that (i) there is no basis for the monetarists' suggestion that our postwar instability can be traced to monetary instability – our most unstable periods have coincided with periods of relative monetary stability; and (ii) stability of the money supply is not enough to give us a stable economy, precisely because there are exogenous disturbances.

Finally, let me mention that I have actually made an attempt at rerunning history to see whether a stable money supply would stabilize the economy, though in a way that I readily acknowledge is much inferior to the real thing, namely through a simulation with the *MPS*. The experiment, carried out in cooperation with Papademos, covered the relatively quiet period from the beginning of 1959 to the introduction of price-wage controls in the middle of 1971. If one eliminates all major sources of shocks, for example, by smoothing federal government expenditures, we found, as did Otto Eckstein in an earlier experiment, that a stable money growth of 3 percent per year does stabilize the economy, as expected. But when we allowed for all the historical shocks, the result was that with a constant money growth the economy was far from stable – in fact, it was distinctly less stable than actual experience, by a factor of 50 percent.

The overall effectiveness of post-war stabilization policies

But even granted that a smooth money supply will not produce a very stable world and that there is therefore room for stabilization policies, monetarists will still argue that we should nonetheless eschew such policies. They claim, first, that allowing for unpredictably variable lags and unforseeable future shocks, we do not know enough to successfully design stabilization policies, and second, that the government would surely be incapable of choosing the appropriate policies or be politically willing to provide timely enforcement. Thus, in practice, stabilization policies will result in destabilizing the economy much of the time.

This view is supported by two arguments, one logical and one empirical. The logical argument is the one developed in Friedman's Presidential Address (1968) [see chapter 10]. An attempt at stabilizing the economy at full employment is bound to be destabilizing because the full employment or natural rate is not known with certainty and is subject to shifts in time; and if we aim for the incorrect rate, the result must perforce be explosive inflation or deflation. By contrast, with a constant money supply policy, the economy will automatically hunt for, and eventually discover, that shifty natural rate, wherever it may be hiding.

This argument, I submit, is nothing but a debating ploy. It rests on the preposterous assumption that the only alternative to a constant money growth is the pursuit of a very precise unemployment target which will be adhered to indefinitely no matter what, and that if the target is off in the second decimal place, galloping inflation is around the corner. In reality, all that is necessary to pursue stabilization policies is a rough target range that includes the warranted rate, itself a range and not a razor edge; and, of course, responsible supporters of stabilization policies have long been aware of the fact that the target range needs to be adjusted in time on the basis of forseeable shifts in the warranted range, as well as in the light of emerging evidence that the current target is not consistent with price stability. It is precisely for this reason that I, as well as many other nonmonetarists, would side with monetarists in strenuous opposition to recent proposals for a target unemployment rate rigidly fixed by statute (although there is nothing wrong with Congress committing itself and the country to work toward the eventual achievement of some target unemployment rate through *structural* changes rather than aggregate demand policies).

Clearly, even the continuous updating of targets cannot guarantee that errors can be avoided altogether or even that they will be promptly recognized; and while errors persist, they will result in some inflationary (or deflationary) pressures. But the growing inflation to which Friedman refers is, to repeat, a crawl not a gallop. One may usefully recall in this connection the experience of 1965–70 referred to earlier, with the further remark that the existence of excess employment was quite generally recognized at the time, and failure to eliminate it resulted overwhelmingly from political considerations and not from a wrong diagnosis.[3]

There remains then only the empirical issue: have stabilization policies worked in the past and will they work in the future? Monetarists think the answer is negative and suggest, as we have seen, that misguided attempts at stabilization, especially through monetary policies, are responsible for much of the observed instability. The main piece of evidence in support of this contention is the Great Depression, an episode well documented through the painstaking work of Friedman and Anna Schwartz, although still the object of dispute (see, for example, Peter Temin). But in any event that episode, while it may attest to the power of money, is irrelevant for present purposes since the contraction of the money supply was certainly not part of a comprehensive stabilization program in the post-Keynesian sense.

When we come to the relevant postwar period, the problem of establishing the success or failure of stabilization policies is an extremely taxing one. Many attempts have been made at developing precise objective tests, but in my view, none of these is of much value, even though I am guilty of having contributed to them in one of my worst papers (1964). Even the most ingenious test, that suggested by Victor Argy, and relying on a comparison of the variability of income with that of the velocity of circulation, turns out to be valid only under highly unrealistic restrictive assumptions.

Dennis Starleaf and Richard Floyd (1972) have proposed testing the effectiveness of stabilization by comparing the stability of money growth with that of income growth, much as I have done above for the United States, except that they apply their test to a cross section of industrialized countries. They found that for a sample of 13 countries, the association was distinctly positive. But this test is again of little value. For while a negative association for a given country, such as suggested by my U.S. test, does provide some weak indication that monetary activism helped rather than hindered, the finding of a positive association across countries proves absolutely nothing. It can be readily shown, in fact, that, to the extent that differential variability of income reflects differences in the character of the shocks – a most likely circumstance for their sample – successful stabilization also implies a positive correlation between the variability of income and that of money.

But though the search for unambiguous quantitative tests has so far yielded a meager crop, there exists a different kind of evidence in favor of Keynesian stabilization policies which is impressive, even if hard to quantify. To quote one of the founding fathers of business cycle analysis, Arthur Burns, writing in 1959, 'Since 1937 we have had five recessions, the longest of which lasted only 13 months. There is no parallel for such a sequence of mild – or such a sequence of brief – contractions, at least during the past hundred years in our country' (p. 2). By now we can add to that list the recessions of 1961 and 1970.

There is, furthermore, evidence that very similar conclusions hold for other industrialized countries which have made use of stabilization policies; at any rate that was the prevailing view among participants to an international conference held in 1967 on the subject, "Is the business cycle obsolete?" (see Martin Bronfenbrenner, 1969). No one seemed to question the greater postwar stability of all Western economies – nor is this surprising when one recalls that around that time business cycle specialists felt so threatened by the new-found stability that they were arguing for redefining business cycles as fluctuations in the *rate of growth* rather than in the *level* of output.

It was recognized that the reduced severity of fluctuations might in part reflect structural changes in the economy and the effect of stronger built-in stabilizers, inspired, of course, by the Keynesian analysis. Furthermore, the greater stability in the United States, and in other industrialized countries, are obviously not independent events. Still, at least as of the time of that conference, there seemed to be little question and some evidence that part of the credit for the greater stability should go to the conscious and on balance, successful endeavor at stabilizing the economy.

V The case of supply shocks and the 1974–76 episode

Was the 1974 Depression due to errors of commission or omission?

In pointing out our relative postwar stability and the qualified success of stabilization policies, I have carefully defined the postwar period as ending somewhere in 1973. What has happened since that has so tarnished the reputation of economists? In facing this problem, the first question that needs to be raised is whether the recent combination of unprecedented rates of inflation as well as unemployment must be traced to crimes of commission or omission. Did our monetary and fiscal stabilization policies misfire, or did we instead fail to use them?

We may begin by establishing one point that has been blurred by monetarists' blanket indictments of recent monetary policy: the virulent explosion that raised the four-quarter rate of inflation from about 4 percent in 1972 to 6.5 percent by the third quarter of 1973, to 11.5 per cent in 1974 with a peak quarterly rate of 13.5, can in no way be traced to an excessive, or to a disorderly, growth of the money supply. As already mentioned, the average rate of money growth from the beginning of 1970 to the second half of 1974 was close to 7 percent. To be sure, this was a high rate and could be expected sooner or later to generate an undesirably high inflation – but how high? Under any reasonable assumption one cannot arrive at a figure much above 6 percent. This might explain what happened up to the fall of 1973, but not from the third quarter of 1973 to the end of 1974, which is the really troublesome period. Similarly, as was indicated above, the growth of money was reasonably smooth over this period, smoother than at any other time in the postwar period, staying within a 2 percent band. Hence, the debacle of 1974 can just not be traced to an erratic behavior of money resulting from a misguided attempt at stabilization.

Should one then conclude that the catastrophe resulted from too slavish an adherence to a stable growth rate, forsaking the opportunity to use monetary policy to stabilize the economy? In one sense, the answer to this question must in my view be in the affirmative. There is ample ground for holding that the rapid contraction that set in toward the end of 1974, on the heels of a slow decline in the previous three quarters, and which drove unemployment to its 9 percent peak, was largely the result of the astronomic rise in interest rates around the middle of the year. That rise in turn was the unavoidable result of the Fed's stubborn refusal to accommodate, to an adequate extent, the exogenous inflationary shock due to oil, by letting the money supply growth exceed the 6 percent rate announced at the beginning of the year. And this despite repeated warnings about that unavoidable result (see, for example, the author 1974).

Monetarists have suggested that the sharp recession was not the result of too slow a monetary growth throughout the year, but instead of the deceleration that took place in the last half of 1974, and early 1975. But this explanation just does not stand up to the facts. The fall in the quarterly growth of money in the third and fourth quarters was puny, especially on the basis of revised figures now available: from 5.7 percent in the second to 4.3 and 4.1 – hardly much larger than the error of estimate for quarterly rates! To be sure, in the first quarter of 1975 the growth fell to 0.6 percent. But, by then, the violent contraction was well on its way – between September 1974 and February 1975, industrial production fell at an annual rate of 25 percent. Furthermore, by the next quarter, monetary growth had resumed heftily. There is thus no way the monetarist proposition can square with these facts unless their long and variable lags are so variable that they sometimes turn into substantial leads. But even then, by anybody's model, a one-quarter dip in the growth of money could not have had a perceptible effect.

What macro stabilization policies can accomplish, and how

But recognizing that the adherence to a stable money growth path through much of 1974 bears a major responsibility for the sharp contraction does not per se establish that the policy was mistaken. The reason is that the shock that hit the system in 1973–74 was not the usual type of demand shock which we have gradually learned to cope with, more or less adequately. It was, instead, a supply or price shock, coming from a cumulation of causes, largely external. This poses an altogether different stabilization problem. In particular, in the case of demand shocks, there exists in principle an ideal policy which avoids all social costs, namely to offset completely the shock thus, at the same time, stabilizing employment and the price level. There may be disagreement as to whether this target can be achieved and how, but not about the target itself.

But in the case of supply shocks, there is no miracle cure – there is no macro policy which can both maintain a stable price level and keep employment at its natural rate. To maintain stable prices in the face of the exogenous price shock, say a rise in import prices, would require a fall in all domestic output prices; but we know of no macro policy by which domestic prices can be made to fall except by creating enough slack, thus putting downward pressure on wages. And the amount of slack would have to be substantial in view of the sluggishness of wages in the face of unemployment. If we do not offset the exogenous shock completely, then the initial burst, even if activated by an entirely transient rise in some prices, such as a once and for all deterioration in the terms of trade, will give rise to further increases, as nominal wages rise in a vain attempt at preserving real wages; this secondary reaction too can only be cut short by creating slack. In short, once a price shock hits, there is no way of returning to the initial equilibrium except after a painful period of both above equilibrium unemployment and inflation.

There are, of course, in principle, policies other than aggregate demand management to which we might turn, and which are enticing in view of the unpleasant alternatives offered by demand management. But so far such policies, at least those of the wage–price control variety, have proved disappointing. The design of better alternatives is probably the greatest challenge presently confronting those interested in stabilization. However, these policies fall outside my present concern. Within the realm of aggregate demand management, the only choice open to society is the cruel one between alternative feasible paths of inflation and associated paths of unemployment, and the best the macroeconomist can offer is policies designed to approximate the chosen path.

In light of the above, we may ask: is it conceivable that a constant rate of growth of the money supply will provide a satisfactory response to price shocks in the sense of giving rise to an unemployment–inflation path to which the country would object least?

The monetarist prescription: or, constant money growth once more

The monetarists are inclined to answer this question affirmatively, if not in terms of the country's preferences, at least in terms of the preferences they think it should have. This is evidenced by their staunch support of a continuation of the 6 percent or so rate of growth through 1974, 1975, and 1976.

Their reasoning seems to go along the following lines. The natural rate hypothesis implies that the rate of inflation can change only when employment deviates from the natural rate. Now suppose we start from the natural rate and some corresponding steady rate of inflation, which without loss of generality can be assumed as zero. Let there be an exogenous shock which initially lifts the rate of inflation, say, to 10 percent. If the Central Bank, by accommodating this price rise, keeps employment at the natural rate, the new rate of 10 percent will also be maintained and will in fact continue forever, as long as the money supply accommodates it. The only way to eliminate inflation is to increase unemployment enough, above the natural rate and for a long enough time, so that the cumulated reduction of inflation takes us back to zero. There will of course be many possible unemployment paths that will accomplish this. So the next question is: Which is the least undesirable?

The monetarist answer seems to be – and here I confess that attribution becomes difficult – that it does not make much difference because, to a first approximation, the cumulated amount of unemployment needed to unwind inflation is independent of the path. If we take more unemployment early, we need to take less later, and conversely. But then it follows immediately that the specific path of unemployment that would be generated by a constant money growth is, if not better, at least as good as any other. Corollary: a constant growth of money is a satisfactory answer to supply shocks just as it is to demand shocks – as well as, one may suspect, to any other conceivable illness, indisposition, or disorder.

Why constant money growth cannot be the answer

This reasoning is admirably simple and elegant, but it suffers from several flaws. The first one is a confusion between the price level and its rate of change. With an unchanged constant growth of the nominal money stock, the system will settle back into equilibrium not when the rate of inflation is back to zero but only when, in addition, the price level itself is back to its initial level. This means that when inflation has finally returned back to the desired original rate, unemployment cannot also be back to the original level but will instead remain above it as long as is necessary to generate enough deflation to offset the earlier cumulated inflation. I doubt that this solution would find many supporters and for a good reason; it amounts to requiring that none of the burden of the price shock should fall on the holder of long-term money fixed contracts – such as debts – and that all other sectors of society should shoulder entirely whatever cost is necessary to insure this result. But if, as seems to be fairly universally agreed, the social target is instead to return the system to the original rate of inflation – zero in our example – then the growth of the money supply cannot be kept constant. Between the time the shock hits and the time inflation has returned to the long-run level, there must be an additional increase in money supply by as much as the price level or by the cumulant of inflation over the path.

A second problem with the monetarists' argument is that it implies a rather special preference function that depends only on cumulated unemployment. And, last but not least, it requires the heroic assumption that the Phillips curve be not only vertical in the long run but also linear in the short run, an assumption that does not seem consistent with empirically estimated curves. Dropping this last assumption has the effect that, for any given social preference, there will be in general a unique optimal path. Clearly, for this path to be precisely that generated by a constant money growth, would require a miracle – or some sleight of the invisible hand!

Actually, there are grounds for holding that the unemployment path generated by a constant money growth, even if temporarily raised to take care of the first flaw, could not possibly be close to an optimal. This conclusion is based on an analysis of optimal paths, relying on the type of linear welfare function that appears to underlie the monetarists' argument, and which is also a straightforward generalization of Okun's famous "economic discomfort index." That index (which according to Michael Lovell appears to have some empirical support) is the sum of unemployment and inflation. The index used in my analysis is a weighted average of the cumulated unemployment and cumulated inflation over the path. The weights express the relative social concern for inflation versus unemployment.

Using this index, it has been shown in a forthcoming thesis of Papademos that, in general, the optimum policy calls for raising unemployment at once to a certain critical level and keeping it there until inflation has substantially abated. The critical level depends on the nature of the Phillips curve and the relative weights, but does not depend significantly on the initial shock – as long as it is appreciable. To provide an idea of the order of magnitudes involved, if one relies on the estimate of the Phillips curve reported in my joint paper with Papademos (1975), which is fairly close to vertical and uses Okun's weights, one finds that (i) at the present time, the noninflationary rate of unemployment corresponding to a 2 percent rate of inflation can be estimated at 5.6 percent, and (ii) the optimal response to a large exogenous price shock consists in increasing unemployment from 5.6 to only about 7 percent. That level is to be maintained until inflation falls somewhat below 4 percent; it should then be reduced slowly until inflation gets to 2.5 (which is estimated to take a couple of years), and rapidly thereafter. If, on the other hand, society were to rate inflation twice as costly as unemployment, the initial unemployment rate becomes just over 8 percent, though the path to final equilibrium is then shorter. These results seem intuitively sensible and quantitatively reasonable, providing further justification for the assumed welfare function, with its appealing property of summarizing preferences into a single readily understandable number.

One important implication of the nature of the optimum path described above is that a constant money growth could not be possibly be optimal while inflation is being squeezed out of the system, regardless of the relative weights attached to unemployment and inflation. It would tend to be prevailingly too small for some initial period and too large thereafter.

One must thus conclude that the case for a constant money growth is no more tenable in the case of supply shocks than it is in the case of demand shocks.

VI Conclusion

To summarize, the monetarists have made a valid and most valuable contribution in establishing that our economy is far less unstable than the early Keynesians pictured it and in rehabilitating the role of money as a determinant of aggregate demand. They are wrong, however, in going as far as asserting that the economy is sufficiently shockproof that stabilization policies are not needed. They have also made an important contribution in pointing out that such policies might in fact prove destabilizing. This criticism has had a salutary effect on reassessing what stabilization policies can and should do, and on trimming down fine-tuning ambitions. But their contention that postwar fluctuations resulted from an unstable money growth or that stabilization policies decreased rather than increased stability just does not stand up to an impartial examination of the postwar record of the United States and other industrialized countries. Up to 1974, these policies have helped to keep the economy reasonable stable by historical standards, even though one can certainly point to some occasional failures.

The serious deterioration in economic stability since 1973 must be attributed in the first place to the novel nature of the shocks that hit us, namely, supply shocks. Even the best possible aggregate demand management cannot offset such shocks without a lot of unemployment together with a lot of inflation. But, in addition, demand management was far from the best. This failure must be attributed in good measure to the fact that we had little experience or even an adequate conceptual framework to deal with such shocks; but at least from my reading of the record, it was also the result of failure to use stabilization policies, including too slavish adherence to the monetarists' constant money growth prescription.

We must, therefore, categorically reject the monetarist appeal to turn back the clock forty years by discarding the basic message of *The General Theory*. We should instead concentrate our efforts in an endeavor to make stabilization policies even more effective in the future than they have been in the past.

Notes

1. Presidential address delivered at the eighty-ninth meeting of the American Economic Association, Atlantic City, New Jersey September 17,1976. The list of those to whom I am indebted for contributing to shape the ideas expressed above is much too large to be included in this footnote. I do wish, however, to single out two lifetime collaborators to whom my debt is especially large, Albert Ando and Charles Holt. I also wish to express my thanks to Richard Cohn, Rudiger Dornbusch, and Benjamin Friedman for their valuable criticism of earlier drafts, and to David Modest for carrying out the simulations and other computations mentioned in the text.
2. Thus, in a logarithmic regression of private nonfarm hourly compensation deflated by the private nonfarm deflator on output per man-hour, time, and private nonfarm employment, after correcting for first-order serial correlation,

the latter variable has a coefficient of .17 and a *t*-ratio of 5. Similar though less significant results were found for manufacturing. If employment is replaced by the change in nominal compensation, its coefficient is .40 with a t-ratio of 6.5. Finally, if the change in compensation is replaced by the change in price, despite the negative bias from error of measurement of price, the coefficient of this variable is only − .09 with an entirely insignificant *t*-ratio of .7. The period after 1973 has been omitted from the tests as irrelevant for our purposes, since the inflation was driven primarily by an exogenous price shock rather than by excess demand. As a result of the shock, prices, and to some extent wages, rose rapidly while employment and real wages fell. Thus, the addition of the last two years tends to increase spuriously the positive association between real wages and employment, and to decrease that between real wages and the change in nominal wages or prices.

3. Friedman's logical argument against stabilization policies and in favor of a constant money growth rule is, I submit, much like arguing to a man from St. Paul wishing to go to New Orleans on important business that he would be a fool to drive and should instead get himself a tub and drift down the Mississippi: that way he can be pretty sure that the current will eventually get him to his destination; whereas, if he drives, he might make a wrong turn and, before he notices he will be going further and further away from his destination and pretty soon he may end up in Alaska, where he will surely catch pneumonia and he may never get to New Orleans!

References

L. C. Andersen and K. M. Carlson, "A Monetarist Model for Economic Stabilization," *Federal Reserve Bank St Louis Review*, April 1970, 52, 7–25.

L. C. Andersen and J. L. Jordan, "Monetary and Fiscal Action: A Test of Their Relative Importance in Economic Stabilization," *Federal Reserve Bank St Louis Review*, Nov. 1986, 50, 11–23.

V. Argy, "Rules, Discretion in Monetary Management, and Short-Term Stability," *Journal of Money, Credit, Banking*, Feb. 1971, 3, 102–22.

W. J. Baumol, "The Transactions Demand for Cash: An Inventory Theoretic Approach," *Quarterly Journal of Economy*, Nov. 1952, 66, 545–56.

R. G. Bodkin, "Real Wages and Cyclical Variations in Employment: A Reexamination of the Evidence," *Canadian Journal of Economy*, Aug. 1969, 2, 353–74.

Martin Bronfenbrenner, *Is the Business Cycle Obsolete?*, (New York 1969).

A. F. Burns, "Progress Towards Economic Stability," *American Economic Review*, Mar. 1960, 50, 1–19.

J. T. Dunlop, "The Movement of Real and Money Wage Rates," *Economic Journal*, Sept. 1938, 48, 413–34.

O. Eckstein and R. Brinner, "The Inflation Process in the United States," in Otto Eckstein, ed., *Parameters and Policies in the U.S. Economy*, Amsterdam: North-Holland, 1976.

R. C. Fair, "On Controlling the Economy to Win Elections," unpub. paper, Cowles Foundation, 1975.

M. S. Feldstein, "Temporary Layoffs in the Theory of Unemployment," *Journal of Political Economy*, Oct. 1976, 84, 937–57.

S. Fischer, "Long-term Contracts, Rational Expectations and the Optimal Money Supply Rule," *Journal of Political Economy*, 1977.

B. M. Friedman, "Rational Expectations Are Really Adaptive After All," unpub. paper, Harvard University, 1975.

Milton Friedman, *A Theory of the Consumption Function*, Princeton 1957.

Milton Friedman, "The Role of Monetary Policy," *American Economic Review*, Mar. 1968, 58, 1–17.

Milton Friedman, "The Demand for Money: Some Theoretical and Empirical Results," in his *The Optimum Quantity of Money, and Other Essays*, Chicago 1969.

Milton Friedman and A. Schwartz, *A Monetary History of the United States 1867–1960*, Princeton 1963.

S. Goldfeld, "The Demand for Money Revisited," *Brookings Papers*, Washington 1973, 3, 577–646.

R. J. Gordon, "Recent Developments in the Theory of Inflation and Unemployment," *Journal of Monetary Economics*, Apr. 1976, 2, 185–219.

J. R. Hicks, "Mr. Keynes and the 'Classics'; A Suggested Interpretation," *Econometrica*, Apr. 1937, 5, 147–59.

John Maynard Keynes, *The General Theory of Employment, Interest and Money*, New York 1936.

R. G. Lipsey, "The Relation Between Unemployment and the Rate of Change of Money Wage Rates in the United Kingdom, 1862–1957: A Further Analysis," *Economica*, Feb. 1960, 27, 1–31.

M. Lovell, "Why Was the Consumer Feeling So Sad?," *Brookings Papers*, Washington 1975, 2, 473–9.

R. E. Lucas Jr., "Econometric Policy Evaluation: A Critique," *Journal Monetary Economics*, suppl. series, 1976, 1, 19–46.

R. E. Lucas Jr., "Expectations and the Neutrality of Money," *Journal of Economic Theory*, Apr. 1972, 4, 103–24.

M. Miller and D. Orr, "A Model of the Demand for Money by Firms," *Quarterly Journal of Economy*, Aug. 1966, 80, 413–35.

F. Modigliani, "Liquidity Preference and the Theory of Interest and Money," *Econometrica*, Jan. 1944, 12, 45–88.

F. Modigliani, "New Development on the Oligopoly Front," *Journal of Political Economy*, June 1958, 66, 215–33.

F. Modigliani, "The Monetary Mechanism and Its Interaction with Real Phenomena," *Review of Economic Statistics*, Feb. 1963, 45, 79–107.

F. Modigliani, "Some Empirical Tests of Monetary Management and of Rules versus Discretion," *Journal of Political Economy*, June 1964, 72, 211–45.

F. Modigliani, "The 1974 Report of the President's Council of Economic Advisers: A Critique of Past and Prospective Policies," *American Economics Review*, Sept. 1974, 64, 544–77.

F. Modigliani, "The Life Cycle Hypothesis of Saving Twenty Years Later," in Michael Parkin, ed., *Contemporary Issues in Economics*, Manchester 1975.

F. Modigliani and A. Ando, "The Relative Stability of Monetary Velocity and the Investment Multiplier," *American Economics Review*, Sept. 1965, 55, 693–728.

F. Modigliani and A. Ando, "Impacts of Fiscal Actions on Aggregate Income and the Monetarist Controversy: Theory and Evidence," in Jerome L. Stein, ed., *Monetarism*, Amsterdam 1976.

F. Modigliani and R. Brumberg, "Utility Analysis and the Consumption Function: Interpretation of Cross-Section Data," in Kenneth Kurihara, ed., *Post-Keynesian Economics*, New Brunswick 1954.

F. Modigliani and L. Papademos, "Targets for Monetary Policy in the Coming Years," *Brookings Papers*, Washington 1975, 1, 141–65.

F. Modigliani, and L. Papademos, "Monetary Policy for the Coming Quarters: The Conflicting Views," *New England Economic Review*, Mar./Apr. 1976, 2–35.

J. F. Muth, "Rational Expectations and the Theory of Price Movements," *Econometrica*, July 1961, 2, 315–35.

W. D. Nordhaus, "The Political Business Cycle," *Revised Economic Studies*, Apr. 1975, 42, 169–90.

A. M. Okun, "Inflation: Its Mechanics and Welfare Costs," *Brookings Papers*, Washington 1975, 2, 351–90.

D. O'Neill, "Directly Estimated Multipliers of Monetary and Fiscal Policy," doctoral thesis in progress, M.I.T.

L. Papademos, "Optimal Aggregate Employment Policy and Other Essays," doctoral thesis in progress, M.I.T.

Edmond S. Phelps, "Money-Wage Dynamics and Labor-Market Equilibrium," *Journal of Political Economy*, July/Aug. 1968, 16, 678–711.

Edmond Phelps et al., *Microeconomic Foundations of Employment and Inflation Theory*, New York 1970.

A. W. Phillips, "The Relation Between Unemployment and the Rate of Change of Money Wage Rates in the United Kingdom, 1861–1957," *Economica*, Nov. 1958, 25, 283–99.

T. J. Sargent, "A Classical Macroeconomic Model for the United States," *Journal of Political Economy*, Apr. 1976, 84, 207–37.

T. J. Sargent and N. Wallace, "'Rational' Expectations, the Optimal Monetary Instrument, and the Optimal Money Supply Rule," *Journal of Political Economy*, Apr. 1975, 83, 241–57.

D. Starleaf and R. Floyd, "Some Evidence with Respect to the Efficiency of Friedman's Monetary Policy Proposals," *Journal of Money, Credit, Banking*, Aug. 1972, 4, 713–22.

Peter Temin, *Did Monetary Forces Cause the Great Depression?*, New York 1976.

James Tobin, *Essays in Economics: Vol. 1, Macroeconomics*, Chicago 1971.

Index

Note: 'n.' after a page reference indicates the number of a note on that page.

Abreu, D. 103, 122n.8
absolute cost advantages 111
acquisitions 86
Adelman, F. L. 309–10
Adelman, I. 309–10
adverse selection 180–1, 186n.2
   efficiency wage hypothesis 285–6
advertising
   costs 86; *see also* marketing costs
   entry barriers 118
agricultural sector 249
Akerlof, George A. 6, 175–88, 274, 286–7
Allen, R. G. D. 75
antitrust policy 104
Arrow 186n.2
auction markets 197–8
Austria 210
automobiles market 6, 176–9
average net receipts curve 72
Azariadis–Baily–Gordon implicit-contract theory 274–5

Bailey, M. J. L. 205
Bain, Joe
   entry barriers 93, 111–12, 115, 117, 118
   structure-conduct-performance paradigm 92
Bator, Francis M. 4–5, 129–58
Batt, Professor 50, 52n.20
Baumol, W. 93, 112
Beveridge, W. H. 254n.2
Bhattacharya, Sudipto 284
Bodkin, Ronald 392
bonds, government 362n.11
Bootle, Roger 11, 191–214
Bowen, Howard R. 165–7

brand names 118, 185
Brazil 210, 222
Brittan, Leon 193
Bulow, J. 118
Burns, Arthur 399
business cycle 14–15, 306–24, 399
   efficiency wage hypothesis 286–7
   real 15, 328–9

cartels 103
chains, and quality 185
cheat–threat theory 283, 284
Clark, J. B. 38, 53n.35
Clark, Kim 272
classical dichotomy 329–30
Co-operative Movement 184
co-ordination games 96
Coase, R. H. 3, 37–54
collective bargaining 269–70, 275; *see also* trades unions
collusion 97–8
   non-cooperative 100–4
combination 45
commodities, definition 64–7
commodity tax 31–2
competition
   inflation 193–4
   labour market 269
   monopoly 59–62
   oligopoly 91–3, 99–122
concentrated industries 106, 107
conflict games 96
consumer's surplus 28–32
   inflation 205
   monopoly 57, 58
consumption
   business cycles 331, 332
   demand theory 21, 22–3, 26

consumption—*continued*
  and inflation 196
  monopoly 60–1
contestable markets 112–14
contracts
  costs 40–1
  efficiency wage hypothesis 284, 285
cost curve
  firm, nature of 48, 49
  monopoly 61–2, 78
Cournot 96
credit market
  long-term expectations 300
  in underdeveloped countries 183–5
customer markets 197–8

Darling, Sir Malcolm 184
Dasgupta, P. 105, 107
Dawes, Harry 51n.15
decision-making, interdependent 94–9
demand: elasticity: labour market 272–3; monopoly 67–9, 74–5n.3, 78, 79–82, 86; oligopoly 106
  inflation 242–8
  quality uncertainty 178, 179
  theory 3, 19–32
diminishing marginal utility
  Marshall 19, 32n.1
  Pareto 32n.4
diminishing returns to management 43, 44
discrimination 282
dishonesty, costs of 182–3
disinflation 337–8, 340n.5
Dixit, A. 115–16, 117
Dobb, Maurice 39, 45, 46, 53n.32
dominant strategies 96
dominated strategies 96
dual labour markets 281
duality theorem 130–1
Dunlop, John 392
duopoly 116
Dupuit, Jules 29, 153n.40

economies of scale 111
efficiency
  of firm, and size 42–4, 45

  of market: conditions 130–2; neo–classical external economies 135; statical 147; and unemployment 266, 271
efficiency wage models of unemployment 12–14, 280–7
employment fees 284
enforcement, failure by 131, 138, 150n.13
entrepreneurs
  firm, nature of 39, 40–2, 43, 44–5
  quality uncertainty 182–3
entry barriers 92, 93–4, 111–20
Epstein, Ralph C. 79, 82, 84–5
Estrin, Saul 1–16
exchange rates
  economic stability 351
  inflation 193–4
  monetary policy 228
existence, failure by 131, 143
expectations
  long-term 293–304
  rational 16, 313–14, 366–80, 389–90

factors of production
  demand theory 27
  firm, nature of 38, 39, 40–1, 43, 44–5
failure, market 4–5, 129–48, 265
  unemployment 266, 267, 271
Feldstein, Martin 206–8, 211, 392
firms, nature of 3, 37–51
fiscal policy
  and monetary policy 216, 217
  stabilization 385
Fischer, Stanley 391
Fisher, Irving 220, 221
Floyd, R. 399
Freeman, Richard 272
Friedman, Benjamin 391
Friedman, J. 116
Friedman, Milton 7, 9, 265–6
  business cycles 311–12
  economic stability 15, 345–65, 388–9, 397–8
  inflation 201, 206
  liquidity preference 388
  monetary policy, role of 11–12, 215–31, 366–7, 368, 369
  national income 249
  Phillips Curve 11

unemployment 238
wage price behaviour 391–2
Fudenberg, D. 118, 119
full employment 232–4, 257–61, 271
   economic stability 356, 384–5, 390, 397

Galbraith, John Kenneth 266
game theory 93, 94–9, 100–4
Germany 203, 206
gift exchange model 286
gilt-edged market 200
gold standard 226–7
Goldberger, A. S. 309–10
Goldenweiser, E. A. 217
good will 84
Green, E. 103
Gresham's law 176–7
Grossman, H. I. 325n. 15
growth, economic
   and inflation 206, 208–10
   and postwar instability 395–7
   recession 400–4
guarantees, quality 185

Halasi, Albert 218
Hall, R.
   business cycles 339–40n.2
   labour market 278n.4
   rational expectations 372, 373
Hansen, Alvin 217–18
Harberger, Arnold C. 3–4, 77–90
Hayek, F. A. von 306
Heller, Walter 260
Hicks, J. R.
   demand theory 3, 19–33
   flexprice and fixprice markets 198
   inflation 206
   monopoly 74n.4
   stabilization policy 385, 387–8, 394, 395
Hilliard, G. W. 203, 204, 207, 211
holdings of money balances 204–8
horizontally differentiated products 109
Hotelling, Harold
   consumer's surplus 33n.14
   decreasing cost 153n.40
   monopoly 65, 83, 87–8n.2
   product differentiation 108, 109

housing market 200
hyperinflation 206

implicit–contract theory 274–5
incentive, failure by 131, 140
income
   demand theory 19–24
   economic stability 349–50, 357, 361n.8
   firm, nature of 41–2
   inflation 195
   monetary policy 223; *see also* wages
income–consumption curve 21, 23
income effects
   demand theory 24, 25–6, 27;
     consumer's surplus 30–1
   inflation illusion 239
income tax
   consumer's surplus 31–2
   economic stability 348
India
   managing agencies 183–4
   quality uncertainty 182
indifference curves
   demand theory 20, 21, 23;
     consumer's surplus 29–31, 32–3n.13
   monopoly 61–3
   public goods 160–1, 163–5
indivisibility 139, 153n.38, 154n.47
inferior goods 21, 26, 27
inflation
   anticipated and unanticipated 197–201
   business cycles 320
   costs 203–8
   and economic stability 352, 389, 402–4
   effects 11, 191–2, 210–11
   and growth 208–10
   illusion 239–40
   level and variability 201–3
   monetary policy 216, 221, 224
   rational expectations 372, 373, 375
   and unemployment 8–9, 11, 192–6, 224, 232–53
information uncertainty 6, 175–85
initiative 50
innocent entry barriers 112
innovations 104–8

insurance 180–1
integration 45
interdependent decision-making 94–9
interest rates
  business cycles 331, 336
  economic stability 349, 386
  long-term expectations 295
  monetary policy 216, 219–21, 227
intermediate sector 83
investment
  business cycles 320–1
  and inflation 195–6, 202
  volatility 14, 294–304
'invisible hand'
  competitive position 60
  contestable markets 114
  neo-classical external economies 133
Iran 185
Israel 210

Jaffee, D. 198–9
job seeking 238–9, 240–1, 270
  business cycles 316

Kaldor, N. 52n.18, 278n.2
Keynes, John Maynard 6–8
  business cycles 306–7, 310
  full employment 390
  long-term expectation 14, 293–305
  monetary policy 215–17
  short-run analysis 11
  stabilization policies 384–5
  uncertainty 10
  unemployment 234–7, 258–9, 268, 274, 316
  wages 277
King, Robert 338, 340n.6
Kleiman, E. 198–9
Klein, L. A. 309–10
Klemperer, P. 104
Knight, F. H.
  firm, nature of 38, 41–3, 46–8
  risk and uncertainty 313, 314
Kreps, D. 102, 119

labour turnover model 285
labour
  division of 45
  supply 8
Laidler, D. 206
Lange–Lerner systems 131–2

lateral integration 45
Lazear, Edward 284
Leijonhufvud, Axel 236
leisure 315, 331, 332, 335–6
Lerner, Abba 3, 55–76
licensing practices 185
lighthouses 146
Lindahl, Erik 166–7
liquidity preference 298–9, 302, 384, 388
Logue, D. 202
long-term expectation 293–304
Lucas, Robert E., Jr.
  business cycles 14, 306–27
  rational expectations 369, 375, 380n.1, 381n.6
  unemployment 12, 257–63

Machlup, Fritz 218
management 50
  diminishing returns to 43, 44
managing agencies 183–4
Mankiw, N. Gregory 15, 328–41
marginal utility
  demand theory 19–20, 24;
    consumer's surplus 29, 30
  diminishing 19, 32n.1, 32n.4
  monopoly 57
marginalism 50
Marin, Alan 1–16
market structure 104–10, 120
marketing costs
  firm, nature of 41, 43, 52n.24
  monopoly 71–2, 86
Marshall
  consumer's surplus 28–31;
    monopoly 57
  firm, nature of 38
  inferior gods 26
  marginal substitution 37
  marginal utility of money 19, 20, 24, 29–30
  neo-classical external economies 132, 133, 136
Mason, Edward 92
Meade, J. E. 134, 135–6, 138, 144
medical insurance 180–1
meeting–competition clauses (MCCs) 104
mergers and acquisitions 86
Milgrom, R. 119
Mill, John Stuart 225

Miller, M. H.   364n.24
Minford, A. P. L.   203, 204, 207, 211
minorities, employment of   181–2
missing markets   265
Mitchell, W. C.   308
mixed motive games   96
Modigliani, Franco   16, 383–408
Monetarism   7–8, 10, 16, 383–405
monetary policy
  role of   11–12, 215–30
  stabilization   385
money illusion   236
monopoly
  concept   55–7, 63–4
  firm, nature of   42–3
  position   58–62
  power   3, 64–74, 85; inflation 248–9
  resource allocation   3–4, 77–87
  revenue   55, 57–8, 59–60, 67, 68–9
  'social' degree   70–1
  transitiveness   70
monopsony   63
  revenue   58, 59–60
moral hazard   186n.2
  efficiency wage model   284, 285; piece rates   282
Morgenstern   94
most-favoured nation (MFN) clauses   103–4
Musgrave, Richard A.
  economic stability   364n.24
  public expenditure   166, 170n.7
Muth, John   313–14, 389–90

Nash, John   96
Nash equilibrium   96, 98–9
  non-cooperative collusion   102
neo-classical external economies   132–7
nonappropriability
  importance   147
  neo-classical external economies   137, 152n.26
  technical externalities   141

Okun, Arthur
  auction and customer markets   197–8, 276
  economic discomfort index   404
  inflation   201–2
Okun's Law   372

oligopoly
  natural   109
  theory   4, 91–4, 120–2;
    interdependent decision-making 94–9; potential competition and strategic entry deterrence 111–20; strategic competition 99–111
OPEC price increases   335
output *see* productivity
ownership externalities   137–9

Panzar, J.   112
Paretian efficiency   129, 147–8
Pareto   32n.4
partial gift exchange model   286
patents   84, 117–18
pecuniary external economies   133–4, 136
pensions   200
Phelps, E. S.
  business cycles   311
  rational expectations   372, 373
Phillips Curve   8–9, 193
  business cycles   338
  full employment   233
  long-run   245
  monetary policy   222
  rational expectations   372, 374, 375
  stabilization policies   386–7, 403, 404
  unemployment   236, 241, 243
  vertical   388–9
piece rates   282
Pigou, A. C.
  consumer's surplus   33n.14
  elasticity of demand   68
  neo-classical external economies   133, 136, 139, 152n.28
  unemployment theory   268–72, 274, 275
planning, economic   8, 51n.14
Plosser, Charles   338, 340n.6
Porter, R.   103
predatory pricing
  entry barriers   119
  game theory   98–9, 122n.7
preferences, consumer
  business cycles   318
  market failure   149n.4
  oligopoly   106
  public goods   160

414   Index

Prescott, Edward   333
price–consumption curve   22–3
price–cost margin   106–7
prices
   business cycles   314–18, 319–23, 337–8
   costs of changing   197, 203–4, 251
   demand theory   19–20, 22–4, 25, 27; consumer's surplus   31
   economic stability   356–9, 385, 401–2, 403
   firm, nature of   39–41, 42, 44
   limit   119
   monetarist model   391–4
   monetary policy   228
   predatory: entry barriers   119; game theory   98–9
   and quality   177
   rigidities   351–2
product differentiation   108–10
   as entry barrier   111, 118
production gap   260
productivity
   business cycles   331, 333–4
   contestable markets   113
   entry barriers   115
   monopoly   58–9, 82–3
   oligopoly   110
profit
   contestable markets   113
   efficiency wage hypothesis   287
   entry barriers   114, 115
   inflation   195
   long-term expectations   297–8, 300
   market failure: neo-classical external economies   134–5; technical externalities   141
   monopoly   78–82, 84, 85–6, 89n.6
   oligopoly   105–6
public goods
   diagrammatic exposition   5, 159–69
   externalities   141–3, 145, 147
punishment strategies   103

quality of products
   oligopoly   109–10
   uncertainty   6, 175–86
quotas   42

Ramsey prices   123n.11
rational expectations
   business cycles   313–14

   and economic policy   16, 366–80
   stabilization policy   389–90
rationalization   52n.26
rationing
   firm, nature of   42
   technical externalities   141
real business cycles   15, 328–39
real wage rigidity   281
rent   57–8
repeated games   100–4
reputation
   as entry barrier   120
   non-cooperative collusion   102
research and development (R&D)   105, 106–8, 121
   strategic commitment   110–11
reservation demand   27–8
resource allocation   3–4, 77–87
retailing costs   52n.24
Reynolds, L.G.   239
risk   313–14
Robbins, L.   39
Roberts, J.   119
Robertson, D. H.   38
Robinson, E. A. G.   54n.44, 54n.45
Robinson, Joan
   firm, nature of   37, 48, 49
   monopoly   76n.10, 76n.13
   monopsony   75n.5
Rosenstein-Rodan, P. N.   156n.60

sales tax   42
Salop, S.
   efficiency wage hypothesis   285
   entry barriers   112, 114
   non-cooperative collusion   103–4
Salter, Sir Arthur   38
Samuelson, P. A   5, 159–71
   economic policy theory   369
   public good externalities   141–2, 145
Sargent, Thomas J.   15–16, 366–82, 391
savings   196
scale economies   111
Schelling, Thomas   91–2
Schmalensee, R.   118
Schultz, T. W.   68, 181
Scitovsky, Professor   144–5
self-stabilizing mechanisms   394–5
selling costs   89n.6
Selten, R.   99

seniority wages   284, 285
serfdom   53n.32
Shaked, A.   109
shirking model   282–4
Shove, G. F.   49, 52n.17
Sidgwick   146
signal, failure by   131, 140
signal processing problem   317, 319, 322
Simons, Henry C.   230n.3, 360n.3
size of firm   42–4, 45, 50
slavery, voluntary   52n.20
Smith, Adam   66
Smithies, Arthur   218
social loss   56–7
social welfare function   162–3, 164–5
sociological models, efficiency wage hypothesis   286
Solow, Robert M.
  efficiency wage hypothesis   286
  neo-classical external economies   152n.27
  unemployment theories   12–13, 264–79
Solow residual   333–5
Spence, M.   107–8
stability, economic   15, 345–60
stabilization policies   16, 383–405
stagflation   311
Starleaf, D.   399
statical externalities   137–43
Stigler, George J.   181
Stiglitz, J.   105, 107
strategic entry barriers   111, 114–20
structure, failure by   131, 140, 143, 150n.13
structure–conduct–performance paradigm   92
subsidies   108
substitution
  demand theory   24, 25–7
  intertemporal   335–6
  monopolies   65–6, 84–5
sunk costs   112, 113, 114
supply
  income and substitution effects   27–8
  labour   335–6
  quality uncertainty   178, 179
  shocks   400–4, 405
surplus, consumer's   28–32
  inflation   205

monopoly   57, 58
Sutton, J.   109
switching costs   104
Switzerland   194
Sylos-Labini, P.   115, 117

taste *see* preferences, consumer
taxation   348, 353–4, 355, 363n.13, 364n.23; *see also* commodity tax; income tax; sales tax
technical externalities   139–41
technical unit of firm   53n.30
technological external economies   133–4, 136, 152n.24
technology
  business cycles   318, 332–5, 336–7
  oligopoly   106, 109–10; entry barriers   117–18
Tinbergen, J.   309
Tirole, J.   118, 119
tit-for-tat strategies   102
Tobin, James   12, 232–54
tournament contracts   284
trades unions
  inflation   253; monopoly power   248, 249
  unemployment   269–70, 275
transaction costs   265
transfer payments   347–8, 353
trigger strategies   101, 102

uncertainty   10
  business cycles   313–14
  as entry barrier   118, 119
  and expectations   294
  firm, nature of   41, 46–8
  and inflation   195–6, 197, 203, 211
  quality   6, 175–86
unemployment
  business cycles   310, 311, 316, 331, 337
  compensation   262, 270, 275
  economic stability   348–9, 352, 356, 386–7, 397–8, 402–4
  efficiency wage models   12–14, 280–7
  and inflation   8–9, 11, 12, 192–6, 232–53
  monetarist model   391–3
  monetary policy   217, 221–5
  policy   12, 257–62

unemployment—*continued*
  rational expectation 372, 373, 374–5, 390
  theories 12–13, 264–78
Usher, Professor 4, 5, 52n.19

value added 82–3
vertical integration 45
vertically differentiated products 108–9
Vickers, John 5, 91–125
Viner 133, 134
Volcker, Paul 337–8
von Neumann 94
von Weizsäcker, C. 123n.9

wages
  business cycles 315–16, 332
  costs of changing 203–4
  economic stability 351, 385, 387
  monetarist model 391–4
  monetary policy 222, 223
  reductions 271
  rigidity 388–9
  seniority 284, 285
  trades unions 248, 253, 269–70, 275
  and unemployment 235, 236–7, 239–40, 243, 244–8; efficiency

wage models 12–14, 280–7;
  policy 259; theory 272–3, 277;
  see also income
Wallace, Neil 15–16, 366–82
Walras 28
Walrasian equilibrium 329, 330
Ward, Barbara 184
wars 227
welfare economics 4
  business cycles 333
  employment 238
  inflation 192
  market failure 129, 132
  monopoly 83–4, 85–7, 88n.2, 90n.6
  public expenditure 162–3, 164–5
  rational expectations 377
Weston, J. Fred 86
White, Horace J., Jr 54n.45
Wicksell 221
Willett, T. 202
Williams, John H. 218
Willig, R. 112
Wilson, R. 119

Yellen, Janet L. 12–14, 280–9

zero-inflation unemployment 238–42, 244